D1498343

The Passing of the Hapsburg Monarchy 1914-1918

The Passing of the Hapsburg Monarchy

1914-1918

VOLUME ONE

BY

ARTHUR J. MAY

Professor of History in the University of Rochester

Philadelphia
University of Pennsylvania Press

© 1966 by the Trustees of the University of Pennsylvania

Published in Great Britain, India, and Pakistan
by the Oxford University Press
London, Bombay, and Karachi

Library of Congress Catalogue Card Number: 64–22874

To Dexter Perkins
Inspiring Colleague
Beloved Friend

7463
Printed in the United States of America

Preface

WHEN BRITISH LORD PALMERSTON ALLUDED TO THE HAPS-
burg realm as a "fortuitous concourse of atoms," he was
not wide of the mark. He had in mind, of course, the
diversity of peoples and tongues in that strangest of
modern European states. If an American, taking into
account the disparity in size between the United States
and the Danube Monarchy, could imagine German-speaking folk predominating in the Pacific seaboard states and
eastward from California, Czechs in Montana, the
Dakotas, and Minnesota, Slovaks in Wisconsin and
Michigan, Poles and Ukrainians in New York and New
England, Slovenes in Texas, Croats and Serbs in much
of the Deep South (Florida corresponding to Bosnia-
Herzegovina), Italians in Louisiana, Magyars in the
Middle West with Chicago as their capital, Rumanians
in Pennsylvania and the border states, he would then
have a crude approximation of the variety and distribu-
tion of the national groupings embraced in the Hapsburg
Monarchy of 1914.

In many respects this multinationality realm was a clumsy anachronism, nearly every province being burdened with an "Ulster" problem, and by reason of ceaseless nationalistic wranglings in both its Austrian and Hungarian halves, the Dual Monarchy attracted the dismal designation of the Dual Anarchy. Mutual tolerance and understanding among nationalities fell below the level prerequisite for harmony, and the managers of the complicated machinery of state, altogether the most involved and paradoxical governmental institution of Europe, neglected to respond appropriately to the dynamic secular impulses of the age.

Yet in retrospect it is clear that the Danube Monarchy afforded a good deal that was admirable in terms of security, economic well-being, and cultural betterment, a prototype and forerunner of an integrated multinationality union toward which the nations of western Europe appear to be groping, slowly and hesitantly. More than that, the disparate Hapsburg peoples had for long generations contrived somehow to live with one another and to weather seemingly irreparable political disasters, and in the gruelling ordeal of the First World War almost all of them fought shoulder to shoulder virtually to the close.

A foreign minister of Germany during the war, Richard von Kühlmann, described the titanic struggle as the War of the Dissolution of the Hapsburg Monarchy. It was, of course, far more than that, but the war and the peace treaties radically altered the political configuration of central Europe. For many contemporaries the disruption of the Monarchy occasioned little or no astonishment since they shared the conviction of Leon Trotsky that the realm on the Danube "had long ago hung out a sign for an undertaker, not demanding any high qualifications of him." How often in the literature of the time one encounters the well-known aphorism of Professor Albert Sorel, "Quand la Turquie aura quitté le lit de l'homme malade, c'est l'Autriche qui viendra l'y remplacer." Other observers dissented, however, and interpreted the dissolution as an illogical and internationally perilous outcome of the war. It was the ripe opinion of the wartime British Prime Minister, David Lloyd George, for instance, who coined the epithet "the ramshackle realm" for Austria-Hungary, that into the spring of 1918 the Monarchy could have been preserved on autonomous foundations.

This book is the sequel to my *Hapsburg Monarchy, 1867–1914*, which appeared in 1951 and was reprinted in 1965. Unlike its predecessor, the present volume, confined to a short span, penetrates its somber theme—a recognized Great Power in its death throes—in depth. While the pages are weighted with diplomatic and military affairs, a studied effort has been made to allocate proper attention to the internal evolution in its more important aspects in the Siamese twinship of dualism. Because of the intricate pattern of this multinationality state a limited measure of repetition could not be avoided.

A short time ago a young scholar who is preparing a dissertation on a facet of wartime Austria-Hungary lamented to me that he was experiencing great difficulty in tying his research findings into "neat packages"; this characteristic challenge cannot be learned too early by any student contemplating the recreation of any phase of the complex of complexities known as the Hapsburg Monarchy.

In an epilogue devoid of nostalgia, the diverse and tangled elements, long-term and proximate, that carried the Danubian realm to destruction are appraised. It needs scarcely be remarked that the writer has striven conscientiously and continuously to negate the cynical aphorism that history is the propaganda of the victor and the nominalist heresy that victorious countries make their own history.

All reconstruction of the past, save for microscopic monographs, represents in greater or lesser degree a synthesis and the more imposing the edifice the more dependent is the architect upon the meticulous labors of fellow craftsmen. A main object of this book is to send the serious reader to the specialized treatises cited in the bibliography.

On aspects of the Hapsburg Monarchy at war not hitherto explored by other students—or not adequately done—the narrative is based upon original sources, particularly the vast manuscript holdings of the Haus-, Hof- und Staatsarchiv (HHSA) in Vienna; since the investigation was undertaken certain files have been reclassified, so that footnote references to collections will not be wholly accurate in every instance. No mere words can testify to my boundless gratitude to Dr. Gebhard Rath, presently the director-general of the Austrian National Archives, and to his learned colleague, Dr. Rudolf Neck, for their unsparing kindness and their invariably cheerful assistance in unearthing documentary materials that were required. Considerable study has also been made of photostated copies of captured diplomatic documents of imperial Germany now in the London Public Record Office and of unpublished American official papers to most of which access was granted by the late Dr. Carl L. Lokke of the National Archives in Washington.

Messrs. Hugh and Christopher Seton-Watson generously allowed me to examine the rich treasury of the wartime papers of their father, the late Professor Robert W. Seton-Watson; they are cited as the Seton-Watson Papers. Under his editorship very largely, *The New Europe* (1916–1920) carried instructive articles and invaluable translations of materials from the various tongues spoken in the Dual Monarchy. For the press of Austria-Hungary itself reliance has rested primarily upon the bourgeois *Neue Freie Presse* of Vienna and the Socialist *Arbeiter Zeitung*, amplified by sheaves of clippings from other papers in the war era accumulated in the Vienna Stadtbibliothek. A list of abbreviations employed in footnotes will be found on page 13.

In carrying on my studies, unrequited debts have piled up not only to many scholars, but to institutions designed to promote the cause of learning. It is a pleasure to acknowledge my profound appreciation for a Guggenheim Fellowship, two Fulbright Grants for Austria, and a grant-in-aid from the American Council of Learned Societies.

It is not possible to express adequately my sense of gratitude to my wife, Hilda Jones May, who has been a constant inspiration along the lengthy trail, and my feeling of obligation to Miss Ruth M. Harper of Rochester, New York, who expertly typed the larger part of the manuscript. Hearty thanks are due also to Mr. Thomas Yoseloff, Director of the University of Pennsylvania Press, and his editorial staff for their skill and care in steering the book through the process of production.

After more than thirty-five years of almost daily companionship with the Hapsburg Monarchy, I take leave of the fascinating theme with mixed emotions, regretful that other interests preclude an attempt, once cherished, to recreate the tortuous saga of the countries which were the heirs of the venerable Danubian institution in the "long armistice" between World Wars.

Union, Maine
September 14, 1964 Arthur J. May

Contents

VOLUME I

Abbreviations in Notes

AZ — *Arbeiter Zeitung* (Vienna)

BM — *Berliner Monatshefte* or *Die Kriegschuldfrage*

F.O. — Foreign Office Papers in Public Record Office (London)

JMH — *The Journal of Modern History*

KSF — see, *BM* above

NFP — *Neue Freie Presse* (Vienna)

Ö M — István Tisza, *Összes Munkái (Collected Works)* (6 vols., Budapest, 1924–37).

Ö R — *Österreichisches Rundschau*

P.A. — Politische Archiv in Haus-Hof-und Staatsarchiv (Vienna)

The Passing of the Hapsburg Monarchy
1914-1918

1. Tragedy at Sarajevo

IN JUNE OF 1914, THE ASSASSINATION OF THE ARCHDUKE Francis Ferdinand, heir-presumptive of the multinationality Hapsburg Monarchy, and his wife unloosed a chain of events unexampled in consequences in modern times.[1] That crime, committed in the obscure Balkan community of Sarajevo, formed the prelude to the destruction of ten millions of men and to agonies of body and mind

[1] The indispensable guide to the immense library of literature, specialist and official, on the coming of war in 1914 is George P. Gooch, *Recent Revelations of European Diplomacy* (4th ed., revised and enlarged, London, 1940). Any selection of comprehensive books on the subject must include Luigi Albertini, *Origins of the War of 1914* (translated from Italian, 3 vols., New York, 1952–1957); Erich Brandenburg, *From Bismarck to the World War* (translated from German, London, 1927); Sidney B. Fay, *Origins of the World War* (2nd edition, reprinted, 2 vols., New York, 1938); George P. Gooch, *Before the War* (2 vols., New York, 1936–1938), a biographical approach; Pierre Renouvin, *The Immediate Origins of the War* (translated from French, New Haven, 1928); Bernadotte E. Schmitt, *The Coming of the War* (2 vols., New York, 1930), and a supplementary piece, "July 1914: Thirty Years After," *Journal of Modern History*, XVI (1944), 169–204; Alan J. P. Taylor, *The Struggle for Mastery in Europe* (Oxford, 1954), pp. 511–531, readable but wrong frequently; Alfred von Wegerer, *A Refutation of the Versailles War Guilt Thesis* (translated from German, New York, 1930).

which none but a Dante could faithfully depict. And as a sequel to the tragedy at Sarajevo, the Hapsburg Monarchy passed away; yet, in the considered judgment of an archly realistic British statesman, "There is not one of the peoples or provinces that constituted the Empire of the Hapsburgs to whom gaining their independence has not brought the tortures which ancient poets and theologians had reserved for the damned." [2] More, the First World War heralded momentous political and revolutionary developments, which affected virtually all facets of human affairs, marking the close of one epoch of history and ushering in another. What happened was pithily crystallized by a sensitive, informed, and perceptive contemporary in this language:

A man and a woman were struck down in a hill town of Bosnia. It was the pistol-shot which started the race to Hell. Events tumbled one another down like ninepins, and, in the opening days of August, men by the millions were marched to slaughter. The swiftness of it was paralyzing. An avalanche starts slowly. This world destruction was an explosion. The solid earth had been mined. We had watched the sappers at work as children watch the stage, and thought they were acting.[3]

Set in a cramped valley with lofty, wooded mountains encircling, Sarajevo ranks as one of the more picturesque and charming communities of the Balkans; admirers of an uncritical turn of mind dubbed it "the Damascus of the North." Gleaming white minarets on scores of mosques and the Sheriat school to train Moslem judges testified to the long Turkish dominion; Orthodox churches and the residence of the Serbian Orthodox Metropolitan reminded the traveler of ancient ties with Constantinople, and the Catholic cathedral proclaimed a historic linkage with Rome. Quite strikingly in Sarajevo, East met West.

[2] Winston Churchill, *The Gathering Storm* (Boston, 1948), p. 10.
[3] Ellery Sedgwick, "Thoughts on the New Year," *Atlantic Monthly*, CXV (1915), 2.

HAPSBURG MONARCHY 1914
The Nationality Situation
— Boundary of Monarchy
------- Boundary between Austria and Hungary

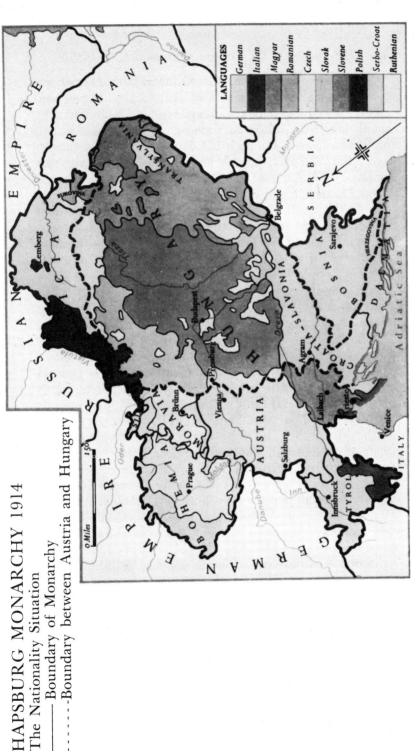

(Adapted from the *Atlas of European History*, edited by Edward W. Fox, Oxford University Press, 1957. By permission of the publishers.)

Along a tracery of lanes, dim Oriental bazaars or shops, in which skilled artisans fashioned quaint textile and metal specialties, looked out upon newly-built barracks, small factories, solid warehouses, spacious parks, and public buildings. Through the city meandered a narrow river, the Miljačka, pebbly and shallow in the summer months, and spanned by short, stone bridges, nine of them. On one side of the river ran a narrow quay, scarcely double the width of the street-car line traversing it, and toward the end stood the curious stone Town Hall (part of which served as the meeting place of the Bosnian assembly), Moorish in architecture, as a concession to the Moslem population.

After centuries of rule by the Turk, Bosnia in 1878 had been placed under the administration of the Hapsburg Monarchy by the statecraft of Europe; thirty years later, Vienna proclaimed that the province had been integrally incorporated in the Monarchy, thus precipitating a grave diplomatic crisis, which might have led into a general war if the authorities of tsarist Russia had felt equal to an armed duel with the Central Empires. By that merger about two million more South Slavs had become citizens of the Monarchy, and they were sharply divided in religious heritage and political outlook. Better than forty per cent belonged to the Orthodox Eastern communion, nearly a third venerated Mohammed, and almost a quarter worshipped in the Roman Catholic tradition. Many a politically articulate Bosnian, especially among the Orthodox, pro-Serb element, hotly resented the annexation of 1908 and the allegedly oppressive, unenlightened Austrian rule, sentiments that echoed widely and with passion in the adjoining kingdom of Serbia.

Symbolical of the partial westernization of Bosnia in the Hapsburg era, Sarajevo exhibited central European standards of municipal tidiness, orderliness, and hygiene; but the Austrian administration had not rallied all the inhabitants in loyalty to the Hapsburgs any more than British rule in Egypt, for example, had won universal acclaim there. Across the years, the vision of a united Yugoslavia, centering upon Serbia, embracing Montenegro and districts of the Ottoman and Hapsburg realms inhabited by South Slavs, had been gathering force. These last areas covered Bosnia-Herzegovina (or Bosnia for short), the Austrian region peopled by Slovenes; Dalmatia, and Istria; and in Hungary, the semi-autonomous kingdom of Croatia and a segment of the Banat of Temesvár. Concerning the future of the South Slavs— the Serbian dream—a princely pair had recently declared:

The sentiment for union and the determination to bring all Servian regions into a great State organism that shall be national in its expression, in its genius, and in its aims, embodying the will and the ideals of the race [sic], are common today to all Serbs.

It is the belief of the Servians that neither the Habsburgs [Austria-Hungary] nor other European Powers will be able in the long run to prevent unification.

Too bold is the man who presumes to forecast the course of future events, but Destiny ever endows her children with opportunity, and the Serbs believe that, matching an alert will with opportunity, the inhabitants of the various regions of the Serb block of territory will, in course of time, as by the action of natural forces, come together in one great State . . . and the dreams of all Serbs still under foreign rule, will culminate in the realization of the concept dear to them these many centuries—a great and united Servia.[4]

On the standard pattern, nationalistic attitudes of mind and emotion favorable to Yugoslav unification had been formulated by intellectuals, diffused by public officials, schoolmasters, clergy, and newspapermen and had taken lodgement among some townsmen and peasants alike.

[4] Prince and Princess Lazarovich-Hrebelianovich, *The Servian People. Their Past Glory and Their Destiny* (2 vols., New York, 1910), II, 729–730.

Far from being merely the heart's desire of a coterie of obscure fanatics, the idea of Yugoslavia (or of a Greater Serbia) had made a deep impression upon many ordinary folk and had captured many a superficially educated Serbo-Croat youth. A wandering Scotsman, whose sympathies lay with the South Slav national aspirations and who knew the population well, believed that "Whether they be Croat, Serb or Slovene, the overwhelming majority of young men . . . are overwhelmingly imbued with the idea of a common Southern Slav patriotism and eager to establish" a free and united Yugoslavia.[5] Many a young man, under the sway of radical literature, much of it from Russian anarchist pens or inspired by legends of violence and bloodshed stemming from a revolutionary outbreak against Turkish lordship in 1875, was prepared for bloody deeds to prove his patriotic zeal. Five attempts in under four years were made to assassinate important Hapsburg officials, in Croatia especially; the Sarajevo outrage of 1914 carried acts of anarchical terrorism to a climax.

Smouldering social and economic grievances of poorer Bosnian peasants played squarely into the hands of revolutionary nationalism. Whether valid or not, the feeling that the countryfolk of Serbia were better off materially than their counterparts in Bosnia, despite Austrian efforts at agrarian improvement and the conviction that schooling was insufficiently supplied, fed resentment against Hapsburg rule (or misrule). Antipathy to Austria-Hungary, in a sentence, welled up spontaneously in South Slav-peopled areas of the Monarchy and that emotion was immensely nourished by political developments in Serbia; of direct significance were the glittering achievements of Serbian arms in Balkan wars of 1912–1913. Affection and enthusiasm for Serbia were also stimulated

[5] R. W. Seton-Watson to editor, London *Times*, Sept. 16, 1914; *ibid.* to H. A. L. Fisher, Oct. 9, 1916. Seton-Watson Papers.

in Bosnia by Serbian nationalist societies, secret and open, newspapers, and political clubs, which possessed an anti-Hapsburg cutting edge.

After the Bosnian annexation excitement of 1908–09, the government of Serbia had promised to live on terms of the good neighbor with Austria-Hungary, yet that pledge had been wantonly and flagrantly transgressed. With a view to curbing the Yugoslav ferment in Bosnia, Hapsburg authorities had suspended the local diet at Sarajevo in 1913 and had imposed heavy clamps upon inflammatory newspapers and patriotic organizations. Instead of repressing, however, repression stimulated agitations for freedom and national union, carried on openly or by clandestine underground societies of Bosnian students and countryfolk of small means. It was entirely within the logic of the age that partisans of the South Slav national ambition should solicit the help of great Russia—the big Slav brother. Despite scrupulous and meticulous investigation, much mystery still surrounds the role of Russian agents in furthering the Yugoslav national interest and in preparing the way for the melancholy events of June, 1914. At the minimum, it may be asserted that cockiness among Serbian politians was quickened by their confidence of support from the managers of affairs on the Neva.

2.

For many a politically articulate South Slav, the heir-presumptive to the Hapsburg crowns of Austria and of Hungary, the Archduke Francis Ferdinand, perfectly personified the hateful and the detestable in the Danube Monarchy—its strength, its determination to live, and its obstinacy to the realization of the ideal of Yugoslavdom. Therein lay one of the multiple motives that led to his assassination. Strong-willed, the most resolute and capable Hapsburg prince since Emperor Joseph II of the late eighteenth century, Francis Ferdinand, then fifty years of age, had few well-wishers outside of a small band of cronies and his immediate family. His marriage to a beautiful Czech countess, Sophie Chotek, a love transaction, had required a special dispensation from the reluctant Emperor Francis Joseph, since she was not of royal or princely blood; it was formally prescribed that children born to the union should be excluded from the throne. A proud lady, the Countess, elevated to the rank of Duchess of Hohenberg, was nevertheless treated by the bluest of Austrian blue-bloods and by "Spanish" court protocol as an inferior; husband and wife hotly resented the slights and indignities of which she was victim. Consolation they sought—and found—in a serene, gracious, and aloof family life; four children blessed the marriage, one dying at birth.

The Archduke, full of strong likes and dislikes, haughty, autocratic, ungenerous, ambitious yet shy, never learned to control his explosive temper. He thoroughly appreciated that the disparate multinationality realm over which he presumably one day would rule and on the maintenance of which he was resolved, needed drastic constitutional reformation, and he devoted prolonged and careful study to this complicated problem. Although he had once looked sympathetically upon the creation of a south Slav state as a third partner alongside of the Empire of Austria and the Kingdom of Hungary in the Hapsburg complex, that idea had been abandoned, it is evident, in favor of some sort of a federal structure, equipped with strong central organs of government.[6] Any project of that nature, however cautiously advanced, would certainly invite the resistance of the Magyar oligarchy which formed the ruling caste of Hungary.

[6] Rudolf Kiszling, "Erzherzog Franz Ferdinands Pläne für den Umbau der Donaumonarchie," *Neues Abendland*, XI (1956), 362–369.

Yet the Archduke appears to have been prepared, if necessary, even for civil war with Hungary as in 1848–49, though more likely he thought that subtle pressure from Berlin would persuade the Hungarian Prime Minister Count Stephan Tisza and his political allies to accept constitutional revision. However that may be, Magyar politicians detested the heir-presumptive as threatening their privileges by constitutional changes, while patriotic South Slav zealots detested him because by reformation he wished to keep the Monarchy from breaking asunder. On his part, Francis Ferdinand heartily despised the "Asiatic" Magyar hierarchs, directly because of the nationalities policy they espoused, more particularly as it affected the Rumanian minority of which the Archduke was singularly fond.

Whether Francis Ferdinand, had he become head of the Monarchy, would have been able to prevent the collapse of the realm has been the subject of much popular and learned conjecture, as unfruitful as it is intriguing. His most respected biographers incline to the belief that he would have contrived somehow to preserve the realm intact.[7] Wedded firmly to the outmoded concept of the divine right of a monarch to rule, Francis Ferdinand distrusted anything savoring of government by discussion and consent; in matters of religion, he was devotedly attached to Roman Catholicism—to call him a bigot would go too far—out of personal conviction and training and in the sound belief that the Catholic Church formed an invaluable cement in this state of many nationalities. His estimate of his fellow beings, particularly

[7] Theodor von Sosnosky, *Franz Ferdinand: der Erzherzog-Thronfolger* (Munich, 1929); Leopold von Chlumecky, *Erzherzog Franz Ferdinands Wirken und Wollen* (Berlin, 1929); Victor Eisenmenger, *Erzherzog Franz Ferdinand* (Eng. ed., London, 1931); Maurice Muret, *L'Archiduc François Ferdinand* (Paris, 1932); Rudolf Kiszling. *Erzherzog Franz Ferdinand* (Graz, 1953). Useful on all aspects of the Sarajevo tragedy is *Sarajevo* (New York, 1959) by Joachim Remak.

of men prominent in public affairs, was low almost to the point of cynicism.

Although Emperor William II of Germany could hardly be called a close friend of the Archduke, the two men were certainly intimates, exchanging visits freely, and Francis Ferdinand greatly appreciated the Kaiser's treatment of his wife as a social equal; the same held true for the Hohenzollern ruler of Rumania, King Carol. Into his personal circle of advisers the Archduke drew a set of aristocratic Bohemian grandees, a few governmental experts and university professors, representatives of the national minorities, and the principal personalities of the Austrian clerical party, the Christian Socialists.[8]

Some observers, aware that Francis Ferdinand had an abnormal passion for the hunt and for killing animals wholesale, concluded that he was cruel and inhumane—certainly he had a marked strain of meanness in him. He pushed steadily for the expansion of the Hapsburg armed forces, relied upon the great German ally as the shield and buckler of the realm, wished to revive a cordial understanding with the conservative empire of the Tsar, disliked republican France, respected democratic Britain, and had only contempt and loathing for Italy and Serbia. Far from being the flaming militarist of popular imagination, Francis Ferdinand more than once had intransigently —and successfully—resisted pressure for "preventative" wars.

From the viewpoint of Pan-German extremism, the Hapsburg Crown Prince seemed bent upon building an essentially Slav state in central Europe, to the detriment of the German-speaking element in the Monarchy. Adolf Hitler set out that hypothesis in Mein Kampf. "The royal house," he wrote, "became Czech wherever possible; and

[8] High among his influential associates was the prolific publicist and one of his eventual biographers, Leopold von Chlumecky; on him, see an unpublished doctoral dissertation by Ingeborg Engerth, Vienna, 1950.

it must have been the hand of the goddess of eternal justice and inexorable retribution that caused the most deadly enemy of Germanism in Austria, the Archduke Francis Ferdinand, to fall by the very bullets he had himself helped to mold. He was the chief patron of the movement, working from above, to make Austria a Slav State." [9] Another writer, who should have known better, blandly supposed that "It was the Slavophile policy which Francis Ferdinand had advocated which brought about his death, the dissolution of the Monarchy, and the dismemberment of Hungary . . ." [10]

The enigma as to how Francis Ferdinand would actually have proceeded, had he been spared to rule, is graphically illustrated by the contrasting appraisals of the two keenest, private experts on the Dual Monarchy in Great Britain. The one-time correspondent of the London *Times* in Vienna, H. Wickham Steed, "had little faith in Francis Ferdinand." After the tragedy at Sarajevo, he wrote, "He was within reasonable distance of *folia furiosa*. His disappearance is such a godsend to the dynasty that I am tempted to believe that somebody must have jogged the elbow of Providence." But for Steed's friend, Professor R. W. Seton-Watson, the Archduke was the one man who possessed the energy, courage, and convictions necessary to achieve a reform of the Dual System, and the consequent emancipation of the subject minorities of Hungary.

I had pinned all my hopes for the future upon him . . . If Francis Ferdinand had been allowed his chance, he would have helped on this idea a further stage [i.e. a federal monarchy], by a modified form of Trialism . . . Unfortunately, the thrice-accursed young fools who planned the murder . . . mistook the foremost political opponent of the present political system in the Monarchy for that system itself . . . He [Francis

---

[9] Adolf Hitler, *Mein Kampf* (Munich, 1933), p. 13.
[10] Denis Sinor, *A History of Hungary* (London, 1959), p. 281.

Ferdinand] represented a progressive idea in the Europe of today, and all Europe is the loser by his death . . ."

3.

In the autumn of 1913, the Crown Prince accepted an invitation to visit Bosnia the following summer, partly to observe Hapsburg troops on routine field maneuvers. Certain officials both in Vienna and Sarajevo thought that the trip, if attended by regal pomp and circumstance, would raise Hapsburg prestige in the area, notably among impressionable Moslems; that had surely been the result of a Bosnian good-will tour of 1910 by Francis Joseph. And the Archduke had a special reason of his own for undertaking the journey: he would be accompanied by his wife and together they would be received with high dignity and honors such as were denied the parvenu Duchess in Vienna. Rumors of the projected mission to Bosnia penetrated as far away as Chicago, where a radical Serbian-language newspaper clamored for revenge upon and destruction of the Hapsburg dynasty; Pan-Serb zealots nearer home thought along parallel lines. It was not until June 4, 1914, that an official announcement of the impending errand appeared in the *Fremdenblatt* of Vienna.[12] At his final audience with the Emperor before setting off for Bosnia, the Archduke expressed mixed emotions about going through with the plan, for his health was none too good and the prospect was that the Balkans would be uncomfortably hot; possibly he sensed personal peril, as certainly his wife did. Told by Francis Joseph to make up his own mind, Francis Ferdinand decided affirmatively. The army Chief of Staff Conrad von

[11] H. W. Steed to Scotus, July 6, 1914, and R. W. Seton-Watson to Madame Gruić, July 21, 1914. Seton-Watson Papers; Scotus Viator to editor, *Spectator*, Aug. 15, 1914, 232–233.

[12] Consult Albertini, *op.cit.*, II, 1–18; Fay, *op.cit.*, II, 43–52, a pioneer and learned treatment.

Hötzendorf, alarmed by murderous attempts in South Slav areas upon Austrian officials, advised the Archduke against venturing into the danger zone—but to no avail.

While the Duchess made the trip into Bosnia all the way by rail, the Archduke boarded the spanking new dreadnaught "Viribus Unitis" at Trieste—pleasing to a prince who had taken a close and intelligent interest in the upbuilding of the imperial navy. Going ashore at Metković in Dalmatia, he traveled by narrow-gauge train up to Sarajevo; along the way the spirit of the heir-presumptive was cheered by hearty crowd ovations, and the local press, save for extremist Serbophile sheets, enthusiastically welcomed the archducal couple. They were quartered at a hotel in Ilidže, a favorite watering spot since the Roman era, only a half-dozen miles away from Sarajevo. As scheduled, Francis Ferdinand watched troop maneuvers and, despite excessive cold and rain, expressed pleasure over the outstanding performance. His lady, meantime, had visited churches and points of interest in and about Sarajevo and together they had made an un-heralded shopping mission to the city, mingling with crowds of natives in the narrow lanes of the bazaar area, and purchasing Bosnian curiosities. Nothing untoward happened—the higher purposes of the errand were being abundantly fulfilled.

4.

News that Francis Ferdinand intended to visit Bosnia kindled lively excitement in the breast of many a Serbian national extremist. As the determined opponent of Serbian national visions, as the known advocate of constitutional reconstruction of the Monarchy, he might as sovereign reconcile many discontented southern Slav citizens to the House of Hapsburg and thus sound the knell for the dreams and schemes of Serbian nationalists. It seemed, too, that his accession would not long be delayed, for Francis Joseph had passed his eighty-third milestone and the press recurrently reported that his health was failing rapidly.

Chauvinists in Serbia resolved to remove the Archduke forever during his visit to Sarajevo. Whether the bloody plot originated inside an extremist Serbian secret nationalist society "Union or Death" (Ujedinjenje ili Smrt), popularly referred to as the "Black Hand," or with certain Bosnian youths sojourning in Belgrade, may never be answered in a definitive manner. Founded in the spring of 1911, "Union or Death" was dedicated to the merger of the Southern Slavs, Serbia forming the nucleus as Piedmont had served in the process of Italian unity. Its chosen weapons were terrorism and revolutionary propaganda, incitement to rebellion against the alien authority of the Hapsburg. Headed by patriotic and unscrupulous Colonel Dimitri Dimitriyević leadership in the society was assumed by Serbian army officers, several of whom had taken part in the savage assassination of the King and Queen of Serbia in 1903. They wished the kingdom to be managed not by civilians but by military men, which provoked controversy with Prime Minister Nikola Pašić. Although the foreign office in Vienna started receiving detailed information on "Union or Death," its aims and techniques, within six months after the founding Viennese diplomatists inexplicably confused that organization with an older Serbian patriotic society, National Defense (Narodna Odbrana). At its establishment during the Bosnian crisis of 1908, this latter society had been militantly bellicose, but it had quickly taken on a decidedly more pacific, propagandist complexion.

Many Bosnian youths, residing in Belgrade, associated with Black Handers. Among them were Gavrilo Princip, who apparently belonged to the society, and Nedjeljko Čabrinović, sons of poor countrymen, and Trifko Grabež, child of an Orthodox priest. These were the three prin-

cipal conspirators in the Sarajevo crime. Drifting to Belgrade ostensibly to study or to work, they indulged in
an assortment of extracurricular activities congenial to
their wild anarchistic temperaments, and they were in
close touch with Black Hand fire-brands. Those contacts
have made it impossible to ascertain precisely where the
murder conpsiracy was in fact hatched, though no doubt
it was in Black Hand circles, and quite probably in the
fertile brain of Dimitriyević, called Apis, who headed
the espionage service of the Serbian general staff.[13] In
any event, the plot could not have been carried out if
Black Handers had not equipped the immature, frustrated, patriotic Bosnian teen-agers with funds and tools
with which to do the job. So far as can be learned, the
three lads in entering upon the fateful plot were animated
above all by a desire for vengeance upon the House of
Hapsburg because of alleged maltreatment of their native
Bosnia and neglect to effect betterment in the rural eco-
nomy, in schooling, and cultural facilities. Possessing the
courage of their emotions, they wished also to contribute
to the Yugoslav national cause and to achieve for themselves enduring fame as "big shots"—literally just that.
"We are not criminals," Čabrinović dramatically exclaimed at the trial of the assassins. "We are honest
people, animated by noble sentiments; we are idealists;
we wanted to do good; we have loved our people; and
we shall die for our ideals." [14]

Laden with the murder weapons furnished by Black
Handers, the three youths departed from Belgrade toward
the end of May, 1914, threaded their way across Serbia
and Bosnia and down to Sarajevo. The journey was replete with earthy thrills and high adventure; any one of
several incidents, including near arrests by Austrian
police, might have ruined the plot. By one stratagem and

[13] The evidence is carefully analyzed in Albertini op.cit., II, 72–82.
Cf. Z.A.B. Zeman, The Break-up of the Habsburg Empire (London,
1961), pp. 26–35.
[14] Remak, op.cit., p. 243.

another, the merchandise for murder was fetched to the Bosnian capital in anticipation of an official reception for the archducal couple on Sunday, June 28.

5.

Certain Black Handers kept ministers in the Serbian cabinet, presided over Pašić, reliably acquainted with the secret projects and plottings of the society. A key personality in the building of Yugoslavia, Pašić has been described by a shrewd, kindly British judge who encountered him during a wartime visit to London as a man who "might have passed for a venerable Noncomformist minister; but his disarming innocence was only the outer shell, for he could claim the title of the Fox of the Balkans with as much right as Ferdinand [of Bulgaria] himself." [15] It appears that Milan Ciganović, a Bosnian-born minor official on the Serbian state railways, joined "Union or Death" at the behest of the prime minister, so as to be able to report on the doings of the organization. Allegations that Pašić and his Minister of the Interior Stojan Protić belonged to the Black Hand have not been proved and seem unlikely. In fact, the ministry and an assertive military camarilla, composed of Black Handers, had clashed violently on public questions, forcing the dissolution of parliament; electioneering was rising to a peak when the Sarajevo tragedy intervened.

Yet it is reasonably clear that the Pašić cabinet possessed foreknowledge of a specific conspiracy to assassinate the Archduke with men of the Black Hand privy to the plot.[16] Though not known as incontestable fact,

[15] George P. Gooch, *Under Six Reigns* (London, 1958), p. 208.
[16] Hans Bauer, *Sarajewo, die Frage der Verantwortlichkeit der Serbischen Regierung an dem Attentat von 1914* (Stuttgart; 1930)—an older monograph which sweeps together much documentation, but omits to evaluate evidence controverting the central thesis of the involvement of the Belgrade cabinet.

that much was suspected in Vienna in July of 1914, and the assumption was given sensational confirmation a decade later by Ljuba Jovanović, minister of education in the Pašić cabinet. Reared under the Austrian flag, Jovanović as a youth ardently preached the idea of South Slav unity and fled into Serbia, where in time he became professor of history in the University of Belgrade. He was chosen president of the Academy of Sciences, the loftiest distinction that could be conferred upon a man of learning in Serbia, and as a political personality he was frequently referred to as the certain successor to Pášić in the office of premier. Far from being an inconsequential nobody, Jovanović was one of the most esteemed and prominent citizens of the kingdom of Serbia.

In an essay of 1924 setting out a portion of his recollections, Jovanović, at the time president of the Yugoslav *Skupština*, recalled:

I do not remember whether it was at the end of May or the beginning of June [1914], when one day M. Pašić said to us . . . that there were people who were preparing to go to Sarajevo to kill Francis Ferdinand, who was to go there to be solemnly received . . . M. Pašić, and the rest of us said, and Stojan agreed, that he [Protić] should issue instructions to the frontier authorities . . . to deny a crossing to the youths . . . But the frontier authorities themselves belonged to that organization [Union or Death] and did not carry out Stojan's instructions, but reported to him—and he afterwards reported to us—that the order had reached them too late, for the young men had already got across . . .

On the afternoon of Vidov Dan [June 28] . . . an official . . . told me what had happened at noon at Sarajevo. Even though I knew what had been prepared there, nevertheless, I felt . . . as though someone had dealt me an unexpected blow . . . Not for a moment did I doubt that Austria-Hungary would make this the occasion for declaring war upon Serbia . . .[17]

[17] W. H. Cooke and Edith P. Stickney, *Readings in European International Relations Since 1879* (New York, 1931), pp. 299 ff.

This astounding disclosure provoked profound excitement among students of the origins of the War of 1914 and created consternation among foreign friends of Serbia, which had become Yugoslavia. For instance, Professor Robert W. Seton-Watson of the University of London, properly described as a maker of Yugoslavia, begged Pašić to disprove the Jovanović allegations, if he could; for his pains the Briton was reviled in the Yugoslav press as a "Germanophile and a defender of German interests"! [18]

For nearly two years longer Pašić and his ministerial colleagues preserved an obstinate silence concerning the Jovanović revelations and then repudiated them as crude fabrications. Yet promises to release state papers to prove that Jovanović had allowed his imagination to run beserk were never fulfilled. That crass negligence has been attributed to the indifference of Pašić on what foreigners thought or to his advanced age or to exigencies of party politics, in which the Prime Minister was contesting with Jovanović, who was eager to build personal political capital. Whatever the explanation, in the absence of persuasive testimony to the contrary, it must be accepted that the Belgrade ministry possessed exact knowledge of a carefully prepared plot to murder the Archduke nearly a month before the outrage was in fact committed.

[18] Likening the Jovanović reminiscences to "a bomb that has suddenly burst under my feet," Seton-Watson wrote, ". . . I thought it over for a long time, but could see no possibility of remaining silent . . . I found keen interest in America on this question and was driven on to the defensive when Professor [Sidney B.] Fay brought up the Ljuba Jovanović revelations before an audience of 350 professors of history . . . I managed to knock him out for the time being by putting the question on a broader basis than that of Sarajevo; but this does not alter the fact that unless Belgrade can disprove his admissions, we are definitely driven back to our second line of trenches . . . I admitted that the Serbian government, unless it can refute and repudiate Jovanović's statements, stands convicted of conniving at the assassination. a crime which only differs in degree from sharing in the plot . . ." R. W. Seton-Watson to Jovan Jovanović, Dec. 4, 1924, Feb. 16, 1925; and *ibid.* to William Miller, Feb. 17, 1925. Seton-Watson Papers. Cf. Alfred von Wegerer, "Der Unglaubige Seton-Watson," *KSF,* III (1925), 287–292. Hans Uebersperger, *Österreich zwischen Russland und Serbien* (Cologne, 1958), pp. 262–266.

Early in June, indeed, the Serbian minister to Vienna, Jovan Jovanović, vaguely hinted that Francis Ferdinand would be well-advised to abandon the projected journey into Bosnia.[19] Acting almost certainly on official instructions from Belgrade, the envoy proffered this suggestion in an interview with Léon R. Biliński, the Austro-Hungarian finance minister, who was by virtue of that office the chief administrator of Bosnia. Without mentioning that a concrete conspiracy was afoot to assassinate the Archduke, the Serb minister merely warned that a traitorous incident might occur, and the language in which the remark was couched was of such gossamer quality as to make little impression upon Biliński. After all, a measure of danger lurked in the Balkans for any foreigner of distinction, and Biliński seems to have kept the conversation to himself. In retrospect, it is evident that in neglecting to pass this warning, however vague, along to the foreign office, Biliński was guilty of a grave dereliction of duty. Why the Belgrade authorities, or more exactly Pašić, failed to inform Vienna of a definite plot belongs in the realm of conjecture; perhaps the Premier reasoned that if he did so, the news might reach the ears of the Black Hand—Jovan Jovanović had friends in the society —and his own life would be in jeopardy.

6.

About ten in the morning of June 28, a sunny day after a week of miserable weather, the archducal party arrived in Sarajevo from Ilidzě.[20] Rare excitement gripped the

[19] Uebersberger, op. cit., pp. 259–261.

[20] Authoritative information from the Austrian side on the Sarajevo events is available in Ludwig Bittner and Hans Uebersperger, (eds.), Österreich-Ungarns Aussenpolitik von der Bosnischen Krise 1908 zum Kriegsausbruch 1914 (9 vols., Vienna, 1930), VIII, nos. 9947, 9949, 9975, 9981, 9992, 10023; hereafter this collection is cited as "Ö.-U.A.," and the documents by number in volume VIII. From the beginning, Austrian officials stationed in the Balkans insisted that the individuals really responsible for the crime lived in the kingdom of Serbia.

community, for not only were the future sovereigns to be formally entertained, but Serbophile families were celebrating a gladsome national holiday that recalled a crushing military defeat by Moslem Turks five and a quarter centuries before—a catastrophe spelling the obliteration of the illustrious medieval empire of the Serbs and opening the long night of subjection to Ottoman authority. The site of the battle with the Turks had been converted into the most precious parcel of ground on earth for the patriotic Serb, the inspiration of folklore and ballads. But in the Balkan wars of 1912–13, Serbian triumphs over the Turk had redeemed the ancient memory and seemed to betoken for a great few the imminent union of all South Slavs.

Therefore, it is easy to understand why ardent Serbophiles looked upon the archducal visitation on this sacred holiday as a deliberate insult and provocation. And, much more serious, the Austrian officials in charge of arrangements, especially Governor Oskar Potiorek, neglected to provide adequate security measures for the distinguished guests. When the Emperor, four years before, called in Sarajevo, a veritable forest of troops and police had furnished protection; Francis Joseph in fact reproached the local administrators for excessive precautions. It must be recalled, however, that on the shopping errand three days earlier, the Archduke and his wife had been given only slight police protection and even that had proved unnecessary. Francis Ferdinand, moreover, felt that the presence of large security forces would be displeasing to the local population—from the beginning the cultivation of goodwill in Bosnia had ranked as a prime objective of the mission. A fantastically bizarre theory insists that Hapsburg officialdom withheld proper security arrangements because it desired to be rid of the heir-presumptive.

The archducal procession of six motor cars would move

along the narrow quay bordering the Miljačka River and drive on to the Town Hall. Along this route, six assassins, the three lads who had just come over from Belgrade, and as many more native high school pupils who had been drawn into the plot by a local revolutionary nationalist, took their assigned places; in their pockets were bombs and loaded guns brought from Belgrade. When the car bearing Francis Ferdinand and his wife drew abreast of Čabrinović, he hurled his bomb, which passed wide of its intended target, exploded in the street damaging the next automobile in the procession and slightly injuring a colonel riding in it. The Archduke approved orders for the victim to be removed to a nearby garrison hospital for treatment; police at once arrested Čabrinović. So rapidly did the Archduke's motor race on to the Town Hall that the other gangsters did nothing.

The exasperated Crown Prince rudely abbreviated the short ceremonial of welcome at the Town Hall, and, being assured by local dignitaries that it would not be hazardous, indicated that he would call on the wounded colonel before leaving the city. To do so required shifts in the itinerary originally devised. Whether or not the chauffeurs were clearly instructed on the modification in route remains an unsolved riddle; if they were, in the heat of excitement they failed to take heed. Chivalrously, Count Francis Harrach posted himself on the running board of the archducal car, ready if need be, to protect the occupants, but as ill-fortune had it, he chose the wrong side. Proceeding back along the quay, the drivers turned off at a street corner as initially planned, and when told that it was not the correct route, they brought the cars to a full stop.

Right alongside of the archducal car lounged Princip, boldest of the assassins, who discharged his revolver at the passengers; one bullet penetrated the abdomen of the Duchess, a second cut through the jugular vein of her husband and lodged in his spine. Francis Ferdinand and his wife died in a matter of minutes. Thwarted in an attempt at suicide, Princip was nearly lynched by by-standers and was hauled off for a comprehensive police examination; several other Bosnians connected with the conspiracy were at once rounded up. Enflamed mobs violently assaulted the persons and sacked the properties of known Serbophiles in the city—even the residence of the Orthodox Metropolitan. Troops were rushed in to stop rioting and disorders, and martial law was soon laid upon the community.

From Sarajevo the coffins of the murdered couple were hauled by railway to the Adriatic, placed on the "Viribus Unitis," which steamed along the Dalmatian coast, thence to Trieste, and by train to Vienna, where they were placed in the chapel of the Hofburg. Out of curiosity or of a sense of bereavement, throngs lined the route of the return journey. The Court Chamberlain Prince Alfred Montenuovo, who despised the Archduke and disdained his morganatic wife as a parvenu, decreed an extremely simple funeral, at variance with customary Hapsburg pageantry. A proposal that the archducal couple should rest in separate burial places was vetoed by Emperor Francis Joseph as a monstrous affront to the dead. Un-loved though the Archduke was, after the funeral cortège passed through the streets of the imperial capital, a maddened mob tried to storm the Serb Legation and when blocked by police, broke out with the Austrian and German national anthems. There was no public mourning in Budapest and little genuine grief over the sudden passing of the prospective wearer of the crown of St. Stephen.[21]

Religious obsequies in the small Hofburg chapel, with Gustav Cardinal Piffl in charge, were hurried and shabby.

[21] George P. Gooch and H. W. V. Temperley (eds.), *British Documents on the Origins of the War* (11 vols., London, 1926–1937), Vol. XI, no. 70; hereafter this collection is cited as "B.D.," and the documents by number in volume XI.

For diplomatic reasons the foreign office desired invitations to the memorial services extended to a large array of foreign royalties, but the court guardians of etiquette restricted attendance to the imperial family and to diplomatists stationed in Vienna. Representatives of the Slovaks and of the Hungarian Rumanians laid wreaths on the catafalque of the Archduke carrying the inscription, "To our last hope, in loyal devotion." Only the diplomatic corps and the children of the deceased were permitted to place flowers on the coffin of the Duchess, which was set at a lower level than her husband's. Since the lady was of inferior birth, the couple could not be interred in the vaults of Vienna's Capuchin Church in keeping with Hapsburg usage; instead, they would be buried in a private crypt beneath the choir of the parish church at Artstetten, about sixty miles distant.

Hotly indignant over deviations from tradition for an imperial funeral, young Archduke Charles, heir-apparent now, and a host of high aristocrats and officers in uniform ostentatiously marched in the procession from the Hofburg to the West railway station, whence the bodies were transported, in the dead of night, to Artstetten. Huge crowds of ordinary Viennese flanked the streets leading to the railway depot.[22] At Pöchlarn, the coffins were transferred to hearses which were ferried across the Danube; a terrific thunderstorm, attended by lightning, so frightened the horses that it looked as though the coffins might be dumped into the river. The gruesome episode anticipated ominously the fearful storms that would presently sweep across Europe.

7.

Bosnian authorities, meanwhile, administrative and judicial, had initiated thorough inquiries into the Sarajevo crime. Information was extracted from Princip and his

[22] *B.D.*, nos. 28, 34, 37.

fellow conspirators, save one who had fled to Montenegro, from accomplices whom they named, and from suspects picked up by the police. Summaries of the findings flowed in a regular stream to Vienna, and on July 11, Friedrich von Wiesner, an experienced and competent legal specialist of the foreign office, though only casually acquainted with South Slav complexities, arrived in Sarajevo to study the facts in the case and to consult with local officials. On the basis of a quick and superficial examination of the available evidence, von Wiesner composed a preliminary memorandum in which he implicated political organizations and officials of Belgrade in the murder conspiracy, though he absolved the Serbian ministry of direct complicity in the assassination, however much it was responsible for tolerating anti-Austrian activities which encouraged outrages such as that at Sarajevo. The indications, he decided, were that it was impossible that the Belgrade cabinet had even knowledge of the plot, a judgment that later hung round his neck like an albatross.

Fuller and less hurried study, however, convinced von Weisner that certain members of the Serbian cabinet possessed knowledge of the conspiracy weeks in advance of its execution, knowledge, too, of the passing of the young criminals across the frontier into Bosnia, and that they did next to nothing to prevent the carrying out of the plans. These judgments tallied with conclusions earlier arrived at by Governor Potiorek—a man well versed in the ways of Bosnia and of Serbia—and were transmitted (July 14) to Field Marshal Conrad. That document, which pleaded for prompt punitive action against Serbia, carried greater weight in Vienna than the original dispatch of von Wiesner.[23]

[23] Edward von Steinitz (ed.), *Rings um Sasonow* (Berlin, 1928), Friedrich von Wiesner, "Meine Despeche von 13. Juli, 1914," pp. 167–186; Friedrich von Wiesner, "Österreich und der Krieg," ÖR, XLI (1914), 259–272, more a propagandistic tract than a sober historical reconstruction.

In October of 1914, the formal trial of the assassins and their alleged accomplices, twenty-five altogether, was conducted at Sarajevo.[24] Decent standards of judical procedure prevailed in the court, presided over by a veteran jurist, Alois von Curinaldi. In the course of more than a fortnight, testimony was taken from better than a hundred witnesses and defendants, which is indispensable in piecing together the elaborate conspiracy puzzle. Of the sixteen culprits convicted, three adults were hanged, ten other accomplices were given jail sentences, while Princip and his two fellow assassins were sent to jail for twenty years; since they were minors they could not under Austrian law be condemned to death. They were imprisoned in a fortress town of northern Bohemia, Theresienstadt (Terezin, the site of a notorious Nazi concentration camp in another generation), where they died during the war years. To the day of his death (1918), Princip never expressed anything akin to regret for his terrible deed. In 1920, the three corpses were transferred to Sarajevo, with deputies of the Yugoslav parliament serving as a guard of honor, and the mortal remains were laid to rest beneath stone slabs in a graveyard overlooking the murder city; the middle one, under which Princip lies, is slightly raised. Western visitors do not find the memorial especially impressive. Yet the killer has been lauded as a noble Yugoslav patriot who had sacrificed his life in a glorious national cause. Somewhat like John Brown in the history of the United States, another bloodthirsty, idealistic fanatic, Princip was bent upon righting what he conceived to be an intolerable wrong; to achieve their objectives both men had recourse to criminal violence, and legends invested them with haloes of martyrdom assuring them a lasting niche in the national pantheons of their respective countries.[25]

[24] Remak, *op.cit.*, pp. 211–246.
[25] A sheaf of legends and popular ballads on the Sarajevo crime has been published by René Pelletier, "L'Attentat de Sarajevo Chanté par les *Guslars* Yougoslaves," *Le Monde Slave*, XIII (2) (1936), 161–205.

8.

On the bridge near the scene of the Sarajevo tragedy, Austrian officials placed busts of the murdered couple with a marble plaque carrying an inscription in Latin, "On this spot, June 28, 1914, Archduke Francis Ferdinand and his wife the Duchess Sophie of Hohenberg gave their life and blood for God and Country"; close by a chaste note read, "Traveler, stop" (*Siste viator*).[26] After the war was over this expiatory memorial was crudely and provocatively torn down, and in 1930, following a solemn religious service, a fresh tablet was unveiled on a building in front of which Princip stood as he discharged his revolver. It proclaimed: "On this historic spot, Gavrilo Princip, on St. Vitus' Day, June, 1914, heralded the advent of Liberty." At the unveiling ceremony relatives of the conspirators of 1914 were honored guests and impassioned songs recalled the life and death of the gunman. While the affair was advertised as a purely local party, it frankly acclaimed Princip and his companions as national heroes; the Yugoslav government could easily have prevented this wanton glorification of murder had it chosen to do so. Righteously indignant over this "open affront to all right-thinking people," Seton-Watson, calling himself one who was "specially active in defending Serbia against the charge of precipitating the World War by her deliberate policy," protested publicly —and to no purpose. In a kindred spirit the London *Times* condemned the Sarajevo votive tablet as "public commemoration of an act which was the immediate cause of the Great War, of its attendant horrors and of the general suffering which has been the sequel." Winston Churchill remarked, "Princip died in prison, and a monu-

---

[26] Wolfgang Ackermann, *And We Are Civilized* (New York, 1936), p. 157.

ment erected . . . by his fellow countrymen records his infamy and their own." [27]

And the exaltation of the criminal revolutionary nationalists was far from being a passing aberration. After the Second World War a museum was set up in Sarajevo under the Tito Communist regime, devoted to Princip and the young Bosnia movement; and footmarks were scooped out of the pavement showing the stance of the murderer as he fired the fatal shots. On the fortieth anniversary of the tragedy and on other special occasions, wreaths of glory were ceremoniously laid on the graves of the assassins. One accomplice in the crime, mild-mannered Vaso Čubrilović, attained cabinet rank in Yugoslavia, helped to overthrow Prince Paul when he yielded to Nazi blandishments in 1941, and subsequently joined the faculty of the University of Belgrade; a second, Cvetko Popović, was appointed curator of the ethnographic division of the splendid Sarajevo Museum.

As for the Black Hand and its dominant spirit, Colonel Dimitriyević-Apis, in whose wild brain the Sarajevo crime may first have germinated, they came to an ignominious end. During the war the Serbian army and ministry, driven from the homeland, set up headquarters eventually in Greek Salonica, and there in May of 1917, a grotesque military trial of Black Handers was staged. It was asserted that these officers harbored anti-dynastic convictions and had plotted to do away with Crown Prince (Regent) Alexander of Serbia and perhaps with Premier Pašić as well; thereafter, it was charged, peace by negotiation with the Central Empires might be sought by the conspirators. The Salonica trial yielded hundreds of pages of evidence, not a little of it relevant to the Sarajevo tragedy and to the role of Serbian citizens therein. In written

[27] London *Times*, Feb. 1, 3, 1930; Winston Churchill, *The Unknown War* (New York, 1931), p. 54.

testimony, blending fact and fiction, Apis disclosed his part in the grim conspiracy.

Courts-martial condemned Dimitriyević and two colleagues to death, and failing in their efforts to secure a reprieve, they were shot with Serbian bullets; ten others were sentenced to prison for life, and scores more were banished to Egypt. Many scholars (as well as less dispassionate mortals) think that the Black Handers were in reality victims of calculated injustice; hypotheses vary on what evidently was the judicial murder of Apis. At the time of the Salonica trial, coming on the heels of the March Revolution of 1917 in Russia, it appeared highly improbable that the war could end victoriously for Serbia. Perhaps Crown Prince Alexander and the principal civilian authorities persuaded the tribunal to punish Black Handers for "reasons of state"; the removal of the leaders of the society implicated in the Sarajevo assassination might facilitate a decently favorable peace settlement with the enemy powers. As a second possibility the Serbian chiefs of state, meditating on a separate peace, may have wanted the Black Hand fanatics out of the way, lest they should try to set up a competing military regime and exact blood vengeance upon the would-be peacemakers. Or, it may be that the Pašić ministry wished to seal the lips of Dimitriyević forever; otherwise, he might make revelations on the planning of the Sarajevo conspiracy that would upset official assertions to the effect that the Belgrade cabinet was innocent of any advance knowledge of the plot.

Whatever the reason, the Black Hand was liquidated, though controversy over the Salonica verdict raged on, a Yugoslav leftist faction insisting that gross irregularities had marred the conduct of the Salonica tribunal and that a cruel wrong had been perpetrated. Matters came to a head in the spring of 1953 when Communist Yugoslavia staged a retrial, lasting two weeks; in the end, the men condemned in 1917 were exonerated, and Dimitriyević was adjudged a proper revolutionary done to death by Serbian capitalist landowners who were treasonably trafficking with enemy agents.[28]

9.

How then had the official world of Austria-Hungary and public sentiment reacted to the terrible events at Sarajevo? Knowledge of the murders reached Francis Joseph in his simple villa at Ischl, deep in the Salzkammergut. Momentarily stunned to speechlessness, he muttered something about the will of the Almighty operating in human affairs, which seemed to imply that he felt a heavy burden had been lifted from his heart. It was common knowledge that the old gentleman resented the concern of his nephew for constitutional reform and was apprehensive over the complications that would arise from renunciation of rulership by the children of the Archduke. These nagging worries had been suddenly and unexpectedly swept into the spacious waste-basket of history.

Returning to Vienna, the Emperor greeted his new heir-apparent, Archduke Charles, with an unaccustomed display of warmth; for a short time his comments on relations with Serbia were conspicuously reserved, but presently he came to think that Serbia must be taught a deserved lesson, and that if the Monarchy should go under by reason of the course it pursued, it should do so with head proudly held high. True to the mentality

---

[28] Hans Uebersperger (ed.), *Der Saloniki Prozess* (Berlin, 1933), a translation of the available records of the court martial; *ibid.*, *Österreich zwischen Russland und Serbien*, pp. 267–314; Wayne S. Vucinich, *Serbia between East and West* (Stanford, 1954), pp. 104–105, 233; Mil. Ž. Živanović, "The Salonica Trial and the Political Emigrants," *Review of International Affairs* (Belgrade), IV (1953), 12–14; Stoyan Gavrilović, "New Evidence on the Sarajevo Assassination," JMH, XXVII (1955), 410–414.

of the professional soldier of his generation, Chief of Staff Conrad would countenance nothing other than military chastisement of Serbia—nothing else, that is, if the House of Hapsburg wished to avoid collapsing into ruin. Likewise Foreign Minister Leopold Berchtold, who hitherto had guided international policy with a rather uncertain hand, reasoned that Serbia must be punished as responsible for the Sarajevo crime.

Vienna was extremely muggy and uncomfortable on June 28, 1914, and citizens in the thousands learned what had befallen at Sarajevo only upon coming home from Sunday outings. At first, popular response to the grim news was apathetic without anything suggestive of sorrow over the fate of the Archduke and his wife or of war spirit; anti-Serb passions welled up, however, when the bodies of the murdered couple were brought to the capital. Newspapers in Vienna reacted, to be sure, along divergent lines. One segment of the press, best typified by the clerical *Reichspost*, which had been close to the murdered prince, candidly called spades spades, adopted a belligerent tone and demanded that the mailed fist should be applied against Serbia. On the other side, the traditionally Serbophile *Zeit* and the Socialist organ *Arbeiter Zeitung*, deplored all thought of violent action and pilloried the archducal good-will mission to Sarajevo in shrill accents. The moderate, conformist, and internationally esteemed *Neue Freie Presse* simply asked that guilty culprits should be appropriately punished. There was no hint that what had transpired in Sarajevo might lead into a clash of arms. As late as July 12, this influential paper, although it insisted that the Monarchy must defend its integrity and well-being, painted the horrors of military conflict in colors befitting a philosophical pacifist.

Directly after the Sarajevo murders an atmosphere of calm pervaded the Vienna bourse, but on July 13, securities tumbled in the worst decline of thirty years. By then more complete information on the Sarajevo crime had come into circulation, and Austro-Hungarian tempers had been inflamed by provocative insults in Serbian newspapers and impassioned diatribes against the wicked Monarchy to the north. In response, the language of moderate journalism in Vienna turned more bellicose, feeding the slanging brawl with Belgrade by thousands of words of grief and anger, an emphasis that nourished a popular psychology receptive to armed conflict. An eminent personification of the calm and judicial temperament, Professor Josef Redlich of Vienna, believed that the murders amply demonstrated the impossibility of coexisting on good neighborly terms with the Serbian kingdom, and he came to think that the "hideous deed was the outcome of the unscrupulous campaign of direct action carried on in Belgrade in furtherance of the Greater Servia idea," backed by Russia and France. "Austria-Hungary," Redlich explained for the enlightenment of British eyes, "stands despite all its failures, and has for centuries stood, as an unshakeable focus of European civilization, the firm bulwark of Western culture . . . Servian imperialism . . . is the fruit of that diseased and bloated nationalism which . . . is characteristic of the modern Balkan races. If Europe is to judge justly she must keep these things in mind." The agitation for a Greater Serbia would have to be halted even at the cost of war, he stated.[29]

Across in Hungary, Premier Stephan Tisza, who thoroughly detested Francis Ferdinand because of his insistence that the Dual Monarchy must be remodelled and because of his friendliness toward national minorities, learned of the assassination with an unconcealed sense of relief. Piously, the Hungarian Calvinist observed that mortals must bow to the iron designs of Providence, and

[29] Josef Redlich to the editor, London *Economist*, LXXIX, July 25, Aug. 1, 1914, 179–180, 233–234.

he let it be known that a decision to punish Serbia militarily would be "a fatal mistake." Deputies in the Budapest parliament delivered glowing tributes to the late Archduke, expatiating on the text that the departed "was not always as bad as he was some times"; yet the formal resolution of condolence adopted by parliament possessed merely a conventional flavor. Moderate Hungarian papers at first seemed little disturbed by the tragedy in Bosnia, but soon they indulged in sharp invective against Serbia and the Serbs, and in a manner calculated to heighten the martial temper of readers.[30] The consul-general of the United States in Hungary reported that "the news of the death of the Crown Prince was received quietly in Budapest . . . as a whole the people seem to feel that the event has solved a very difficult problem. Some apprehension has been expressed as to the possibility of a war with Serbia as a result of the murder. Editorial comment in the newspapers has been very conservative . . . Count Tisza expressed to me an opinion that the Slav movement had latterly been exhibiting tendencies toward anarchistic affiliations."[31] Sobriety rapidly yielded, however, to militancy as Hungarian emotions and sentiments, reflected in parliament and press, passed through an evolution paralleling that in Austria. Hapsburg makers of policy could move forward with full assurance of basic popular support for any program that might be determined upon.

10.

In Belgrade, meanwhile, the ministry of Serbia adopted a formally correct posture on the Sarajevo crime, dispatching a stereotyped message of condolence to Francis

[30] B.D. no. 70.
[31] William Coffin to F. C. Penfield, June 30, 1914, American Embassy Papers, Vienna, vol., XLIII.

Joseph, and in the official paper, *Samouprava,* denouncing the assassins as irresponsible children. Yet other newspapers of Belgrade cut loose in a bitter and sustained chorus, not of regret, but of indecent jubilation over the assassination. That much might have been expected of extremist sheets like *Piémont,* mouthpiece of Union or Death, but even responsible papers charged up the tragedy to Hapsburg misrule in Bosnia, exaggerated the physical outrages against Serbophiles in Austria-Hungary, advocated a total boycott on trade with the Monarchy, and indulged in scurrilous vituperation disgusting to staunch foreign friends of the country. Serbia's historic mission to liberate South Slavs in the Hapsburg realm was the theme of much editorial commentary, and abusive epithets, such as "the worm-eaten Monarchy," provoked hot resentment in even sober sections of the press of the Dual Monarchy.[32]

Flame kindled flame. Fierce press feuding carried to crescendo a full decade of mutual snarling and quarreling. Afraid of physical assault, Hapsburg citizens residing in Serbia secluded themselves in their homes, and the Austrian minister in Belgrade requested that a protective guard should be assigned to the Legation. Statements by Pašić to newspaper interviewers were models of rectitude, though in his heart of hearts the Premier believed that the murders would mean war, and he did nothing to restrain press intemperance. For his inaction the Prime Minister pleaded the right of freedom of expression, and besides he feared that interference by the ministry would be effectively exploited by opposition elements in the parliamentary election campaign then in progress.

It has been argued, indeed, that in view of the domestic political turmoil, the Pašić ministry could not possibly

[32] Selections of inflammatory pieces from the Belgrade press are available in *Ö.-U.A.,* 9964, 9982, 10654, Beilage 9, 10437, and in Leopold von Chulmecky, "Österreich-Ungarn und Serbien," *ÖR,* XL (1914), 167–180.

have followed a course with reference to the Sarajevo conspiracy, whether in its preparation or in its execution, that might have culminated in an armed struggle with the northern Monarchy. This line of reasoning is reinforced by the persuasive logic that Serbia, only recently involved in the heavy fighting of the Balkan wars, was militarily incapable of a far more gruelling contest; dark spots in the evidence and several insoluble intangibles lend plausibility to that interpretation. Yet that viewpoint, however rational, neglects to weigh duly the soaring ambition of Serbian patriots promoting the Greater Serbia cause, confident of the help of the empire of the tsars, and regardless of consequences. As the diplomatic crisis with Vienna intensified, the electioneering was called off and deputies previously elected retained their seats throughout the war.

The Russian military attaché in Belgrade, General Victor A. Artamonov was well acquainted with the chiefs of the Black Hand and it is reasonably clear that he aided the society with cash, though it is more than doubtful whether he was informed in advance of the Sarajevo plot.[33] Policymakers on the Neva gave the Pašić cabinet firm promises of assistance should Serbia be attacked by the Monarchy and these pledges were supplemented by the completion of plans to furnish Russian military hardware to Serbia. Formally Tsar Nicholas II and his highest counsellors expressed horror over the murder of the Archduke, leading Russian dignitaries attended a memorial service for him, and important newspapers condemned the assassins as wild fanatics. Yet these gestures were surface phenomena; news of attacks upon Serbs in the

---

[33] Victor A. Artamonov, "Errinerungen an Meine Militärattachezeit in Belgrade," *BM*, XVI(2) (1938), 583–602. Only a thin harvest is offered in this piece, except in the closing paragraphs in which the author insists that he conferred only on official business with Apis. Cf. Albertini, *op.cit.*, II, 84–86. The theory that the tsarist intelligence service had in fact instigated the tragedy at Sarajevo would not down. See, for example, *Ukrainian Review*, XV (1959), 169–170.

Monarchy and of Viennese press charges that the Belgrade ministry was involved in the murder plot provoked a torrent of Russian newspaper vilification of Austria-Hungary.

Diplomatic waters were muddied by the dramatic passing on July 10 of Nicholas Hartwig, tsarist minister in Serbia. Death came while he was consulting with the Austrian minister, Baron Wilhelm Giesl, in the latter's Legation, and groundless gossip accused the Austrian diplomatist of poisoning his guest. Hartwig, an ardent Pan-Slav with a sinister reputation as a Hapsburgophobe, had great influence in the public life of Serbia. Very corpulent, the excitement of the hour had caused his heart to stop during the call upon Giesl, and he fell to the floor dead. It would seem, on balance, that his sudden departure removed a potential influence for moderation, or so at least it was reasoned by his Austro-Hungarian colleague; yet the London foreign office interpreted the death of Hartwig as an unqualified beneficence.[34]

11.

No European crowned head was so profoundly shocked by the Sarajevo crime as Emperor William II of Germany, for the Archduke was one of his choicest political companions. Putting aside an initial impulse to hasten to Vienna and express his grief, he dispatched warmhearted messages of condolence to Francis Joseph and to the orphaned children of Francis Ferdinand. Burning with indignation, William II called for measures to punish Serbia quickly. Solid, but imprudent promises were vouchsafed to the effect that Germany would stand by the Austro-Hungarian ally regardless of the policy that the Vienna cabinet might determine upon. The great German press responded to the tragedy at Sarajevo in

[34] *B.D.* nos. 48, 62.

much the same manner as its counterpart in the Monarchy. Papers with moderate traditions tended to ascribe the crime to Serbia under the inspiration at least of Russia. The conventional thesis of the menace of Slavdom to German Europe was harped upon,[35] but no paper advocated that the case against Serbia should be pressed to the point of war. As July moved along, however, and fuller knowledge of Serbian complicity in the assassinations became available, German press sentiment lurched sharply toward drastic treatment of the Balkan powerlet.

Official London condemned the Sarajevo gunmen as vehemently as official Berlin, and pity for the victims was widely expressed in Britain; as an earnest of fellow-feeling and respect, a British clergyman proposed that the familiar tune "Austria" should be used in all churches. Contrariwise, the very name of Serbia conjured up dark British memories of revolting brutalities in the regicide of the King and Queen a decade earlier. Before long the *Manchester Guardian*, which in reporting the murders had employed a double-columned headline for the first time, was writing, "If it were physically possible for Serbia to be towed out to sea and sunk there, the air of Europe would at once seem cleaner."

Leading papers leaned heavily toward sympathy with Vienna except for the London *Times*, and even its pro-Serbian inclination was scarcely explicit before July 22. To that point, articulate Britain was not much excited

---

[35] An informed British observer crystallized the German dread of Slavdom in this way: ". . . Austria is supposed to be the bastion that protects central Europe against the semi-Asiatic flood . . ." Many highly placed Germans thought "that the Serbo-Croats, and Slovenes and Ruthenians if they were wrested away from the Hapsburg Monarchy, would merely become Russian protectorates, if, indeed, they were not incorporated with the Muscovite realm . . . They [the Germans] have a vision of Bohemia, Ruthenia, Moravia established as Muscovite outposts, with the Cossacks overrunning Posen and Pomerania, and with Danzig and Stettin converted into harbors for the Czar's battleships." Sidney Low, London *Daily Mail*, quoted in *Literary Digest*, XLIX (Aug. 15, 1914), 409. It is interesting to compare this sketch of German prophecies with the situation that prevailed after the Second World War.

over the international implications of happenings in south-eastern Europe; an ugly turn of events in Ireland caused vastly more concern. That shrewd veteran of British diplomacy, Sir Arthur Nicolson, Permanent Undersecretary for Foreign Affairs and perhaps next to Foreign Minister Edward Grey himself the most influential brain in Downing Street, expected that the Balkan storm would blow over.[36] The usually well-posted London *Spectator* on July 11 casually commented, "The field of foreign affairs is this week barren of important events."

First reactions in France and Italy to the Sarajevo assassinations ran along comparable lines: sympathy for Francis Ferdinand and his wife coupled with the feeling that what had happened was devoid of major significance internationally. Yet weight-carrying publications of Paris, regardless of political coloring, maintained that Austria-Hungary in the past had been crudely insensitive to Serbian feelings. "It is the Serb idea which armed the hand of the murderer at Sarajevo," thought Georges Clemenceau, the "old tiger" of French politics. No doubt, many a Frenchman, interested in European affairs, shared the view of an author who later wrote that the murders were merely "a more or less commonplace anarchist plot, which owed its success to the imprudence of the victims and the absence of sufficient means of protection. Serbia's role in the event was nil." [37]

[36] *B.D.* no. 40.
[37] Jean Larmeroux, *La Politique Extérieure de l'Autriche-Hongrie* (2 vols., Paris, 1918), II, 437.

2. Summer, 1914

DESIGNED BY LUKAS VON HILDEBRANDT, A FAMOUS MASTER
of baroque architecture, the Ballhaus in downtown Vienna, within easy walking range of the Imperial Palace, had
served for nearly two centuries as the headquarters of
the Austrian ministry of foreign affairs. Here the diplomatic virtuosos Prince Wenzel Anton Kaunitz and
Prince Clemens Metternich had once toiled for the security and the prestige of the House of Hapsburg; here,
at the close of the Napoleonic warfare, crowned heads
and astute diplomatists had written the peace treaty of
Vienna. And here, in the turbulent summer of 1914, fateful decisions were taken that led into an armed conflict
between the Danube Monarchy and the kingdom of
Serbia, which in the twinkling of an eye, evolved into a
European and then into a global struggle.

Presiding at the Ballplatz (short for Ballhausplatz)
during the gravest crisis in the fortunes of the Hapsburg
Monarchy, was Count Leopold Berchtold. His previous
management of foreign affairs had created the image that

he was a vacillating dilettante, but that reputation was shattered in the tense, hectic July days of 1914. A strong sense of public duty had induced Berchtold in February, 1912, to take the helm at the foreign office and only devotion to crown and country had held him at the post. It may be presumed that the assessment of the diplomatic policies which the Foreign Minister pursued in 1914 will go on as long as this epochal era is studied. Peace he prized highly, but he laid still greater value on the preservation of the Danubian realm. Weeks before the tragedy at Sarajevo, he had decided that the next serious quarrel with Belgrade must be settled by military chastisement; only thus, he reasoned, could the multinationality Monarchy escape disruption. Recurrent provocations by Serbia and intrigues by Russian agents had worn the patience of an uncommonly patient man to the point where he had abandoned hope of peaceful coexistence. His conciliatory diplomacy, he later boasted, had staved off an armed clash with Serbia for two years.[1]

Spoken of as "the one man who must bear the guilt of the war above all others," Berchtold carried the awesome responsibility of Hapsburg statesmanship to a considerable extent by himself. Pace and procedure, though, were somewhat shaped by senior subordinates in the Ballplatz and by the impetuous war hawk, Conrad, who like nearly all European military pundits, fancied that fighting could not, would not, last more than a couple of months. Scarcely less influential in Hapsburg diplomatic

---

[1] On the public career and personality of Berchtold, see, Arthur J. May, *The Hapsburg Monarchy, 1867–1914* (Cambridge, Mass., new ed., 1965), 456–475. After the passing of the Monarchy, the Count, who lived until 1942, talked occasionally with scholars concerned with war origins, but rarely said anything for publication on the subject. As he requested, almost all of his personal papers relating to 1914 were destroyed. Alfred von Wegerer, "Graf Berchtold's Interview über den Kriegsausbruch," *BM*, XIII(2) (1935), 518–628; Hugo Hantsch, "Die Tagebücher und Memoiren des Grafen Leopold Berchtold," *Südostforschungen*, XIV (1955) 205–215; Karl A. Rohan, "Graf Leopold Berchtold," *BM*, XXI (1943), 31–34.

counsels was the strongest single political personality of the realm, Prime Minister Stephan Tisza of Hungary. Berchtold's share in bringing this masterful Calvinist around to his own thinking in essentials shows that the Foreign Minister possessed resources of strength not always or not adequately appreciated either by contemporaries or by historical writers.

The upper echelon of the Ballplatz hierarchy contained able, experienced, veteran diplomatists, whole-heartedly devoted to the welfare and integrity of their multinationality country.[2] Count Alexander Hoyos, chief of Berchtold's cabinet and his most trusted confidant, it appears, advocated swift application of force against Serbia with a minimum of diplomatic maneuvering; at first Berchtold hesitated, uncertain of popular backing and aware that Tisza would not consent to precipitate action. Undersecretary Count Johann Forgách, who like Hoyos belonged to the "Magyar clique" in the Ballplatz inner circle, had grown to hate Serbia while minister in Belgrade; he favored unsheathing of the sword in the belief that war upon Serbia would not involve serious European complications. The talented chief of the Near-Eastern Division of the foreign office, Baron Alexander Musulin, by birth a Croat and very hostile to a Greater Serbia, argued that punishment of Serbia (though not the invocation of armed force) must be undertaken to stop the unending challenge to the Monarchy.

In transactions with envoys of foreign powers during July, the men at the Ballplatz scrupulously adhered to classic traditions of calmness and courtesy in the diplomatic profession. They hearkened attentively to the German Ambassador Heinrich L. von Tschirschky, an unpopular and rather eccentric diplomatist, who had served

---

[2] Consult Ludwig Bittner, "Das Österreichische-ungarische Ministerium des Äussern, Seine Geschichte, und Seine Organisation," *BM*, XV(2) (1937), 819–842.

in Vienna for seven years, and who doubted the advisability of trying to bolster up a state which he thought was cracking asunder. Right after the Sarajevo murders, he implored the Ballplatz not to take hasty steps against Belgrade, but on orders from Berlin he shifted his ground and urged rapid chastisement of Serbia. Toward the end of July he failed to execute faithfully, instructions of a moderating character from the Berlin government and for that dereliction he has properly been censured by history.[3] For the most part, the ambassadors and ministers of Francis Joseph in the principal foreign capitals were talented gentlemen, acquainted with the traditions and languages of the countries in which they were stationed, and enjoying wide political and social contacts; of the ten ambassadors, six were Magyars.

2.

Vast erudition has been expended upon the veritable mountain of evidence concerning the evolution of European diplomacy during the five weeks following the Sarajevo tragedy. Taken all in all, the course of diplomatic exchanges, becoming feverish late in July, disturbs the facile theory that the First World War was the inevitable outcome of an insoluble European situation. The accent in the present exposition rests principally upon the line of behavior—and the thought animating it—followed by the cabinet of Vienna. The Ballplatz was convinced that the threads of the crime led directly into Belgrade even though full and unassailable proofs were not immediately forthcoming; revelations later substantially verified the

[3] Ludwig Bittner, "Graf Johann Forgách," *BM*, XIII (1935), 950–959; Alexander Musulin, *Das Haus am Ballplatz* (Munich, 1924); Felix von Oppenheimer, "Botschafter von Tschirschky," *ÖR*, XLIX (1916), 197–200. As an author, Hoyos wrote *Der Deutsch-englische Gegensatz und Sein Einfluss auf die Balkanpolitik Österreich-Ungarns* (Berlin, 1922).

Vienna hypothesis. Resolved though he was that the kingdom of Serbia should be punished physically, Berchtold was obliged to proceed cautiously and slowly for several reasons, prominent among them were the stern admonitions brought forward by Tisza against drastic action and uncertainty on the measure of support that Berlin would vouchsafe her Hapsburg ally. To clear up the second question first, the Foreign Secretary addressed a memorandum on the Balkan diplomatic panorama to William II of Germany and dispatched a personal communication from Emperor to Emperor in which the Sarajevo crime was charged up to the malevolence of Russian and Serbian supernationalism, bent upon the destruction of the multinationality Monarchy.[4]

Without disclosing with anything like precision how far the Ballplatz might go in the determination to wipe out "the nest of criminal agitation" in Belgrade, Francis Joseph (technically) asserted that further appeasement of Serbia was out of the question; for the integrity and peace of mind of the Monarchy, the bothersome little neighbor would have to be eliminated as a political factor of consequence. The bearer of these communications to Berlin, Hoyos, supplemented their contents by word of mouth, indicating that moving promptly against Belgrade without much diplomatic sparring was contemplated, and that once Serbia was overpowered, portions of its territory would be cut away.

Reading and hearing these views, William II and his Chancellor Theobald Bethmann-Hollweg, on the fateful fifth and sixth days of July, without inquiring whether adequate documentation of official Serbian complicity in the Sarajevo tragedy was at hand, gave assurances that Germany would stand by her ally without reservation. It was even urged that force should be applied upon Serbia, swiftly and decisively, while the murder memory was

[4] Ö-U.A., nos. 9978, 9984.

still fresh in the conscience of Europe, though the German policymakers recommended no time schedule.

As the men in Berlin appraised the prospects, Russian policymakers would declaim emphatically for the record against a declaration that Serbia was about to be trounced, and then they would draw in their horns. In spite of arrant boastings and blusterings by Russian militarists, German army technicians believed that the empire of the Tsar was unprepared for an arbitrament of arms on the grand scale. Should that calculation be falsified, the Germans pledged Vienna full backing, and in so doing they largely placed the fate of their country in the hands of the Ballplatz. Except for the Berlin assurances, it is unlikely that the cabinet of Vienna would have proceeded as brusquely against Belgrade as it did. Two considerations on the home front (and one abroad) compelled the Ballplatz to delay action; first, the stubborn resistance of Tisza to a line of diplomatic conduct that might explode in general war, and second, the unreadiness of the Hapsburg armies for a swift invasion of Serbia.

With the Berlin statement securely tucked in his pocket, Berchtold summoned, on July 7, a council of the leading political dignitaries of the realm—Prime Ministers Count Karl Stürgkh of Austria and Tisza, the two other common ministers of the Dual Monarchy, Biliński, finance, and Baron Alexander von Krobatin, war, and the chiefs of the army and navy, Conrad and Rear-Admiral Karl von Kailer.[5] Conversations in the council, lasting nearly seven hours with only a short recess, ranged over the whole gamut of the international problems of the Monarchy and its capacity to fight. Berchtold set out and defended his deep convictions: the very existence of the Monarchy stood in jeopardy; bloody events had upset the hypothesis that Serbia could be persuaded to live

[5] Ö.-U.A., no. 10118.

on terms of decency; therefore, that country must be rendered harmless. Implementation of this logic might lead Russia to fight, but whatever happened, Vienna could count without question upon the coöperation of Berlin. Other than Tisza, the principal advisers of the crown wheeled into line with Berchtold, dismissing the suggestion of mere diplomatic humiliation of Serbia as of no value, a mark, indeed, of weakness on the part of the Monarchy, which would invite an intensification of subversive activities.

No man could call Tisza a coward, but he was worried. In view of the dangerous international possibilities, in view of the deficiencies in the Hapsburg diplomatic posture in Balkan capitals, the Magyar thought an appeal to the sword would be wholly unwise and likely to bring on war with Russia; and so he argued to his fellow counsellors. He reiterated his fears to Francis Joseph and hinted that if his reasoning were disregarded, he would feel obliged to relinquish the premiership. The most that Tisza would concede—and this only in the shadow of the Berlin pledge of unrestricted support—was that demands upon Serbia should be exacting, yet of a character that would afford the Belgrade cabinet an opportunity to make amends without a threat of war. The Emperor-King, however, sanctioned the reasoning of the majority at the July 7 parley. That decision, together with the growing fury in the Serbian press against Austria-Hungary, appears to have converted Tisza to the Berchtold position; he entered a proviso, however, to the effect that once Serbia had been militarily chastised, only minor territorial rectifications, which would improve the strategic defenses of the Monarchy, should be exacted. He wanted no more Serbs in the Monarchy.

Given the Magyar's high sense of public duty, it is not difficult to understand the revision in his thinking, however much the change may be deprecated. Speaking to the Budapest parliament on July 15, Tisza frankly declared his alignment with policymaking colleagues. Relations with Serbia must be and would be cleared up, he explained, without disclosing how it was proposed to achieve that objective; reassuringly, he believed that Ballplatz diplomacy would not invite warlike complications, though every nation, as a last resort, must be ready to fight for its interests, he reminded the deputies. The serious press in both halves of the Monarchy warmly welcomed this statement, but a plea by Tisza that important newspapers should tone down their strictures against Serbia elicited only a limited response.[6]

At a second conference of Hapsburg senior statesmen on Sunday, July 19, final approval was given, quickly and without much controversy, to a severe set of demands to be made upon Belgrade. The phraseology of the note was largely devised by Musulin, the finest stylist in the foreign office, with certain touches contributed by Berchtold personally. It was agreed by the Austro-Hungarian policymakers that the demands upon Belgrade might lead to war, but if they were accepted the Monarchy would secure "certain guarantees for the limitation of Great Serbian intrigues" on its soil; Serbia would suffer "profound humiliation" and by the same token tsarist prestige in the Balkans would be diminished. If Belgrade refused to accede to the demands, armed force would be invoked. The council unanimously acquiesced in Tisza's stance that if war with Serbia came, only patches of frontier territory would be annexed by the Monarchy. Privately, however, Conrad and others contemplated much greater territorial subtractions,[7] and that much was suspected concerning Hapsburg intentions in European chancelleries. In the belief, it seems, that if fighting en-

[6] B.D., nos. 51, 65, 82.

[7] For a summation of the conference, see Ö.-U.A., no. 10393; Fritz von Reinöhl, Wien 19. July, 1914, BM, XVII(2) (1939), 676–678.

sued it would be no more than a short punitive operation, Emperor Francis Joseph stamped his approval upon what the officials had decided. Given a copy of the document to be sent to Belgrade, the German authorities did not recommend any modifications.

It was set out in the communication that the government of Serbia had flagrantly transgressed a pledge of 1909—after the Bosnian crisis—to live on good terms with her northern neighbor. Serbia was charged with tolerating subversive anti-Hapsburg agitation which had fructified on the Sarajevo street corner.[8] The dreadful conspiracy had been hatched, it was asserted, in Belgrade, and Serbian state officials had contributed crucially to its execution with guns, bombs, and freedom of transit over the Bosnian frontier for the assassins. In the face of that record, the Belgrade ministry was summoned to condemn and to repudiate anti-Hapsburg activities inside Serbia and to fulfill ten specific demands. The most drastic points called for the collaboration of Hapsburg representatives in stamping out Austrophobe sentiments and in tracking down and assisting in the trial of Serbian citizens believed to have been implicated in the conspiracy against the Archduke.[9] And, climactic, the cabinet

[8] Ö.-U.A., no. 10395.

[9] In framing this demand, the Ballplatz had in mind something of a precedent involving Serbia. On June 10, 1868 the enlightened Serb prince, Michael Obrenović, whose wife was a Magyar countess, was murdered by Serbs from southern Hungary. Not only did the Budapest government allow agents of Serbia to investigate the plot on Hungarian soil, but also to take part in the trial—a concession that did not seem to infringe upon the dignity or the sovereignty of a country considered a great power. Belgrade expressed lively appreciation for this cooperation; thirteen culprits were executed for complicity in the crime, "one of those dark and terrible tragedies," comments a sober British historian, "which throw into strong light the savagery which seems ingrained in the nature of the Balkans." Ö.-U.A., no. 10587; German embassy to foreign office, Oct. 12, 1918, P.A., Preussen, Varia, 1918; Jenö Horváth "Serbische Behörden in Ungarn 1868," BM, XIII(2) (1935), 690–698; "Eine Zuschrift von Dr. Jovan M. Jovanović und Erwiderung von Horváth, ibid., 876–885; Harold W. V. Temperley, History of Serbia (London, 1919), pp. 258–259.

of Serbia would have to respond to the note within forty-eight hours after delivery; if, by then, the demands were not accepted *in toto*, the Hapsburg minister would leave Belgrade at once.

Looked at in retrospect, and balancing matters as well as may be, the Vienna ultimatum must be adjudged rough and extravagant, and some of the terms were almost certain to be rejected, which is undoubtedly what the cabinet of Vienna desired and expected; the supposition cherished by Musulin that the Pašić ministry would acquiesce all down the line is unconvincing. When the admissable testimony has been weighed, it is as plain as a pikestaff that the Hapsburg chiefs of state were determined to humiliate Serbia militarily in the conviction that unless that were done the Monarchy was doomed to ruin. They trod a path which traditionalist statesmen of any great power of the twentieth century would have followed in anything like comparable circumstances.

Presentation of the ultimatum to Belgrade was postponed until a contingent of French public men, headed by President Raymond Poincaré, had departed from Russia; as had been planned for months, this delegation paid a state visit to St. Petersburg from July 20 to 23. If the contents of the note to Belgrade were divulged then, the Frenchmen might have encouraged their tsarist ally to stand up more stiffly on behalf of Serbia than otherwise would have been the case.[10] Beyond doubt, the spirits of the men on the Neva were lifted by the French visitation, although the implications of the Sarajevo murders seem to have entered into conversations only casually.

Not until six in the evening of July 23, after the French party had set off for home, did Minister Giesl launch his torpedo at the Serbian foreign office. It was nearly four weeks since the murders had been committed and

[10] *Ö-U.A.*, no. 10393.

the original indignation and horror which had surged across Europe had evaporated to a very large extent. At the same time that the note was delivered in Belgrade, the contents were communicated for the first time to Austria's Italian ally.[11]

3.

News of the ultimatum unloosed as terrifying and as complicated a diplomatic imbroglio as modern history has ever experienced. None but a superman could have followed the nuances of the rapid-fire telegraphic exchanges in all their amplitude—and in 1914 no Bismarck, no Richelieu, not even a Kaunitz or a Palmerston, sat in a seat of supreme authority.

How indeed did Europe respond to the peremptory demands presented to Belgrade? In the press of the Danube Monarchy the reception was mixed, positive approval predominating. Interpreting the ultimatum as evidence of the intention of the Ballplatz to put an end to the Serb menace once and forever, the bellicose *Reichspost* greeted the news with, "At last, at last." The *Neue Freie Presse* manifested fervent confidence in the fighting services of the House of Hapsburg and faith that a conflict would be restricted to the Monarchy and Serbia; even the traditional advocate of conciliatory treatment of Serbia, *Die Zeit*, endorsed the diplomatic note. Cacaphonous cries sounded, however, in Socialist quarters, which upbraided Ballplatz diplomatists for the harsh tenor of the note, pointed toward wanton infringement of the independence of Serbia. Papers in the Czech and South Slav tongues, which could have been expected to speak out on behalf of Serbia, were effectively muzzled.

Over in Budapest, leading organs of opinion univer-

[11] *ibid.*, no. 10526; Baron Wilhelm Giesl, *Zwei Jahrzehnte im Nahen Orient* (Berlin, 1927), ch. XII.

sally applauded the move of the Ballplatz, the temper of
the reaction being illustrated by condemnation of the
Serbian ministry in the *Pester Lloyd* as "a nest of pesti-
lential rats," which had exhausted the patience of the
long-suffering Monarchy; only the small voice of the
Hungarian Socialist press protested against the ultimatum.
In parliament, Tisza told fellow-deputies that the Vienna
action was a matter of life-or-death for the realm, though
not at all aggressive or provocative and he suggested
that a clash of arms would not necessarily ensue. Gripped
by patriotic emotionalism, opponents of the Prime Minister in the chamber pledged undivided cooperation and
willingness to bear whatever sacrifices might be necessary.
"For once," mused a British agent, "peace and unanimity
reigned in the Hungarian parliament." [12]

The ultimatum to Serbia excited a violent and internationally dangerous response among policymakers in St.
Petersburg. Foreign Minister Sergius D. Sazonov, a man
of moods, though stubborn once his mind had been made
up, was more suited for theology, his interest in early
manhood, than for the insensitive knockabout of international politics. His prestige was none too high, for influential personalities in the entourage of Tsar Nicholas
II and many deputies of the imperial Duma felt that he
had grossly mishandled diplomatic affairs during the recent wars in the Balkans. Of his devotion to the interests
of Russia there could be no question nor of his patronage
of Slavdom; and the obverse of that medal was profound
distrust of the managers of Hapsburg diplomacy. Nicholas
II heeded the several recommendations of Sazonov with
only slightly more reluctance than Francis Joseph had
shown in accepting the advice of Berchtold.

It is tolerably clear that policymakers on the Neva
were both surprised and shocked by the Austrian ultimatum, which was unhesitatingly branded as incompatible

[12] *B.D.*, nos. 106, 191, 242.

with the dignity of Serbia and entirely unacceptable. On learning the text of the note, Sazonov remarked, "This is a European war," and suggestions of a general nature on the content of the reply were wired to Belgrade. With an impulsiveness that was in character, the Foreign Secretary blurted out that the behavior of the Vienna cabinet was "provocative," designed to prepare the way for the absorption of the kingdom of Serbia and then a march onward to the Black Sea. His appeal for an extension of the time allowed Serbia to formulate an answer, corresponding with requests from the British and French foreign offices, elicited only a negative retort from the Ballplatz.[13] Unable to extract assurances of diplomatic solidarity from Britain, Sazonov succeeded in arranging a call up of part of the immense tsarist reserve forces, over the protestations of top Russian generals, on political and military grounds of a technical nature. This move signified that Sazonov had repudiated the proposition that the quarrel should be restricted to Austria-Hungary and Serbia alone.

When the ultimatum fury broke over Europe, Poincaré and other leading French statesmen were steaming home from their tour of duty in Russia and French diplomacy rested in the nerveless hands of the acting minister of foreign affairs, who counselled the Serbian cabinet to draft its answer to Vienna cautiously and with prudence. A wave of indignation swept over important French newspapers, which readily detected the sinister hand of Berlin steering the Hapsburg ship of state. By solid assurances of French backing, the ambassador at the court of Nicholas II, Maurice Paléologue, hardened the heart of the Russian decision-makers.

Speaking for official Britain, Foreign Secretary Edward Grey, after a day of hesitation and reflection, condemned the Vienna ultimatum as "the most formidable document

[13] *Ö.-U.A.*, nos. 10617, 10619.

ever sent by one state to another." Since the grave Ball-platz charges against Belgrade were not documented by impeccable proofs, citing chapter and verse, an understandable skepticism on the validity of the accusations prevailed in the London cabinet.[14] Using shrill and barbed language, Grey declaimed against the shortness of the time allowed the ministry of Belgrade to reply and against the demand that Hapsburg agents should take part in searching for the antecedents of the Sarajevo outrage on the soil of Serbia. Nonetheless, he advised Belgrade to offer the maximum acquiescence compatible with national honor; he still believed that if fighting started it might be confined to Austria-Hungary and Serbia.[15]

Even after the ultimatum, a large proportion of the responsible and moderate newspapers in the United Kingdom not only expressed lively sympathy for Vienna but quite a little frank approbation. Yet the London *Times* editorial leaders, while advising Belgrade to comply with such demands as were deemed reasonable and fair, admonished the Central Empires not to count on the neutrality of Britain if a war with Serbia should expand into a general European conflagration. Certain other influential Conservative papers predicted that the armed intervention of Russia would become a certainty unless the Vienna cabinet toned down its demands, though several major editors kept writing that warfare could be localized.[16]

The authorities in the Berlin chancellery heartily seconded the Vienna bill of indictment drawn against Serbia and believed that the quarrel would be restricted to the two principals; in a note to the other powers, the German foreign office contended that the controversy concerned only the Monarchy and Serbia and broadly hinted that

[14] *B.D.*, no. 91.
[15] *Ö.-U.A.*, nos. 10600, 10601.
[16] W. Zimmerman, *Die Englische Presse zum Ausbruch des Weltkrieges* (Charlottenburg, 1928).

other governments should keep hands off. Only outside help for Serbia, which the Germans dismissed as improbable, would entangle their country in hostilities, it was optimistically supposed. For the most part, the bourgeois press of Berlin welcomed the ultimatum, though with more restraint than by newspapers in Vienna.[17] As in Austria, German mirrors of the Socialist mind protested against the ultimatum in language akin to that of Sir Edward Grey; the most influential paper, the great and esteemed *Vorwärts*, denounced the note as designed to provoke war. "Shall an insane crime be overshadowed by a far more insane crime?" it asked. It was extremely irritating to the cabinet in Rome that it had not been vouchsafed advance notice of Vienna's intentions, as was implicit in the Triple Alliance Treaty dating from 1882; Rome calculated that Belgrade would not comply with all the demands nor should it.

Not a little mystery hovers over the precise manner in which the answer of the Belgrade ministry to the note from Vienna was composed.[18] It was a skillfully contrived document, calm and polite, and calculated to kindle sympathy in foreign parts for the little—and little known—Balkan land, and it was framed in full knowledge that Vienna would reject partial compliance as unsatisfactory. Pašić, who excused his talent for dodging crucial issues by the necessity of pressing on with the parliamentary election campaign, appeared in the capital on the morning after the presentation of the ultimatum looking "very anxious and dejected," to one impartial observer. Lengthy deliberations ensued in the Belgrade cabinet; at one stage serious consideration was given to unconditional surrender to the Vienna demands, only to be cast aside when

[17] Theodor Goebel, *Deutsche Pressestimmen in der Julikrise 1914* (Stuttgart, 1939).
[18] See, Slavko [J.] Gruić, "Persönliche Erinnerungen aus der Julikrise 1914," *BM*, XIII(2) (1935), 576–597. The author was general secretary of the Serbian ministry of foreign affairs.

the ministry felt absolutely sure that Russia would immediately and emphatically rally to the protection of
Serbia. If peace were ruptured, Nicholas II observed
shortly, Serbia could be certain that the empire of the
Tsar would not be indifferent to its fate. "Great, gracious
Russian Tsar," Pašić exclaimed jubilantly. Time and again
the tenor of the Serbian reply was revised, partly in keeping with advice privately proferred by Russian and French
masters of diplomatic technique. The finishing touches
on the document were not applied, it appears, until a
quarter-hour before its delivery.

The Serbian answer acquiesced in most of the items in
the Austrian note, but with a good few reservations and
ambiguities. It declined, moreover, to allow Hapsburg
officials to enter Serbia to collaborate in tracking down
the threads of the Sarajevo conspiracy; as a crowning
stroke, Belgrade proposed that if Vienna was not satisfied
with the reply the quarrel should be tossed into the lap
of the great powers or of the Hague Tribunal for ad-
judication.[19] Revealingly, before the reply was turned
over, the Belgrade cabinet ordered basic preparations for
war. It was not believed, in other words, that a soft
answer would turn away wrath. Upon receiving the note
from Pašić in person, Giesl tarried merely to glance at
it cursorily, recoiled at the qualified acceptance, and at
once entrained for home in accordance with instructions.
That same evening Hapsburg authorities ordered mobilization of the forces that were considered necessary to
conquer Serbia. Learning of what had happened in Belgrade, "Vienna burst into a frenzy of delight, vast crowds
parading the streets and singing patriotic songs till the
small hours of the morning." [20] So far as can be determined, articulate Vienna overwhelmingly and raptur-

[19] Ö.-U.A., Beilage to no. 10648.
[20] B.D., no. 676.

ously ratified war in order to inflict condign punishment upon the trouble-making southern neighbor.

The Serbian reply left the door open for further diplomatic parleying, but the Ballplatz abruptly slammed the door shut. Submission of issues rejected by the Belgrade ministry to the Hague Court or to a conference of the powers, as the Serbs proposed, would only have produced intolerable delay and procrastination. Taught by painful experience that paper pledges of Belgrade possessed little or no worth, the policymakers on the Danube made ready to exorcise the Serbian menace by force, and as they accurately divined, the prospect of military action appealed alike to the masses and to the classes of the Monarchy.

4.

Europe moved swiftly—inescapably, some writers insist —to the precipice. On July 28, the Vienna cabinet assumed technical responsibility for starting the epochal struggle by declaring war upon Serbia. "Serbia's fateful hour has struck," declared the *Pester Lloyd*; "Serbia willed war. Her will be done." Newspaper commentators, subject to official prompting, explained that the decision on whether the conflict would be localized or become general rested with the men on the Neva.

In the meantime, the Ballplatz, in communications to the leading European capitals, argued with no little verbal adroitness that the Serbian answer amounted to blank refusal to root out anti-Hapsburg subversion and sought approval of the determination to compel Belgrade "by the sharpest methods" [21] to change its tune. Surveying

---

[21] *Ö.-U.A.*, nos. 10714, 10780. As well as anything else, the furious tempo of diplomatic activity is illustrated by the decision of the editors of this collection of diplomatic papers to publish one hundred fifty-seven documents occupying eighty-four tightly-printed pages for the two days of July 27 and 28.

the immensely confused—and confusing—panorama on July 27, American Ambassador Frederick C. Penfield commented, "War certain and probably localized to the Balkans. Germany morally supports Austria but Italy is neutral, Montenegro and Rumania will aid Serbia, France will not participate but the Russian attitude is unknown. Vienna is anxious and hoping for a short conflict." This report by a detached observer was not particularly perspicacious.[22] Having blown hot ever since the Sarajevo murders, Conrad had turned cool concerning an immediate declaration of war, on the score that a fortnight would be required to put the Hapsburg armies in battle array, but the foreign office, excited by further ominous dispatches on Russian preparations to fight and wishing to preclude diplomatic maneuvers for a pacific settlement, insisted upon a prompt declaration against Serbia. Conrad reluctantly assented. With profound misgivings and under the erroneous impression that soldiers of Serbia had actually violated the frontier of the Monarchy, the octogenarian Emperor placed his signature on the war declaration. Chivalrous to the end, Francis Joseph granted permission to the Serbian Chief of Staff General Radomir Putnik, who happened to be in Budapest, to proceed unhindered to his homeland.

The Hapsburg war manifesto dwelt upon the ingratitude of Serbia, her faithlessness, her hostility. It had been the fond desire of the monarch to consecrate his remaining years to peaceful purposes, but the "malevolent opponent," which aimed at "destroying the foundations of public order" and had spurned "just and moderate demands," had compelled him to withdraw the sword from

[22] Penfield to Bryan, July 27, 1914, U.S., *Foreign Relations*, 1914, Supplement, p. 18. On the very next day, Charles Denby, consul of the United States in Vienna, finished off an extensive survey of business conditions and prospects with the observation: "It is felt that the chances for a permanent peace in the Balkans . . . are better now than for decades past . . ." U.S. Dept. of Commerce, *Daily Consular and Trade Reports*, 1914, pp. 529–544.

the scabbard. Serene in conscience, the old gentleman had "set out on the path which duty prescribes," trusting firmly in the sacrificial loyalty of his peoples and army, so often demonstrated, and "in the Almighty to confer victory on my arms." [23] Viewed in retrospect, this moving utterance proved to be the death-rattle of the strangest of European states.

Reiterated affirmations by the Ballplatz that no territorial aggrandizement at the expense of Serbia was contemplated failed to carry conviction in Entente foreign offices. In London, Grey felt that Serbia might be reduced to Hapsburg vassalage, even though the legal independence of the country was not infringed. Straightaway, Austrian gunboats rained shells upon Belgrade, creating popular panic; at midday of July 31, an order by Francis Joseph mobilized the whole armed resources of the Dual Monarchy, simply as a measure of precaution, the world was blandly informed. [24]

5.

Scarcely a week elapsed after Vienna threw down the gauntlet to Belgrade before Europe (and portions of the wider world) shivered in mortal combat. Country by country, foreign office by foreign office, policymakers by policymakers, each of the principal states must bear a greater or lesser share of responsibility for the transformation of an imbroglio in the Balkans into a global struggle. No country threatened the integrity of the empire of the Tsar, but Russian standing among the powers of the world was seriously engaged, as potent Pan-Slav newspapers thundered stridently. This fundamental facet of the July ordeal found crisp definition in the *Manchester Guardian* of July 30. "Is her [Russia's] national existence

[23] *NFP*, July 29, 1914.
[24] *Ö.-U.A.*, no. 11118.

threatened? Is any substantial interest of hers at stake
beyond the ambition to be regarded as the champion of
the smaller Slav states?" Yet the men on the Neva were
resolutely determined to stand four-square alongside their
Serbian kith and kin, as their predecessors, less confident
of the national capability for war, had chosen not to do
in earlier diplomatic disputes between Serbia and Austria-
Hungary.

After Hapsburg guns bombarded the Serbian capital,
the cabinet of St. Petersburg belligerently brushed aside
as deceptive and dishonest promises from Vienna that
Serbian territory would not be annexed. Certain that a
European conflict could not be avoided, the tsarist
supreme command pressed for immediate mobilization
of reservists; in the thinking of the military chiefs that
crucial leap was indispensable for victory. To these entreaties, Sazonov and his diplomatic advisers yielded, on
the supposition, perhaps, that full mobilization would con-
vince the Central Empires that Russia was really in
earnest. Many days would have to elapse before the
tsarist millions would be in shape to fight.

In the book of European military experts, however,
general mobilization was the veriest prelude to war itself.
On July 29, Nicholas II, nervous and uneasy in mind,
assented to the summoning of all the reserve forces to
the colors, then abruptly countermanded the order; on
the next day, in the language of an authority of unim-
peachable credentials, "the day of decision for Russia
and the world," [25] the Tsar dramatically reversed himself
again and restored the decree for general mobilization.
That verdict frustrated attempts belatedly made by Berlin
to restrain Vienna and to bring off a peaceful compromise. General mobilization meant that the gigantic
levies of Russia would be marshalled against Germany
as well as against Austria-Hungary. In the judgment of

[25] Gooch, *Before the War*, II, 366.

the veteran British military critic, Colonel Charles À. C. Repington, "In a very short time after Russian mobilization is announced it will be a miracle if all Europe is not aflame." [26] Resolved that the enemy should not achieve an advantage by beginning hostilities, professional soldiers in the tsardom and in other lands confirmed the observation of the American rhymster, Bret Hart:

> Blest is the man whose cause is just;
> Thrice blest is he who gets his blow in fust.

On the imperious bidding of the German supreme command, the cabinet of Berlin demanded that Russian preparations to fight should be suspended within twelve hours. When St. Petersburg failed to comply, Germany, on August 1, launched a thunderbolt of war against the eastern colossus.

In the decision-making quarters of Berlin, the Serbian reply to the Vienna ultimatum had elicited general satisfaction, William II remarking that every reason for war had been removed and that controversial questions still at issue could be smoothed away by diplomacy. Somewhat more reserved, Chancellor Bethmann - Hollweg thought that the wishes of the Vienna cabinet had been appeased, except on matters of secondary concern. But the men on the Danube, as has been explained, dissented radically from the Berlin interpretation, and no arts of persuasion could make them think otherwise. Even so, the Germans were ill at ease because of proposals for mediation between the two principals in the quarrel— Vienna and Belgrade—brought forward by London and St. Petersburg. Momentarily, no slight pressure was applied by Berlin upon the Ballplatz to accelerate plans to fight and so defeat possibilities of a peaceful settlement through the channels of diplomacy; yet on July 27, the German authorities, alarmed by the very real likelihood

[26] London *Times*, July 30, 1914.

that a conflict which started in the Balkans could not be
localized, but would flame into a general European conflagration, strongly advised the cabinet of Vienna to examine sympathetically proposals for direct diplomatic
conversations with the men on the Neva looking to a
peaceful adjustment; yet Berlin dropped no hint of de-
viation from its original promise to stand loyally at the
side of its Austro-Hungarian ally. The Germans recommended—and on July 30 the tone of communication took
on sharper urgency—that Hapsburg forces should occupy
a Belgrade enclave or other districts of Serbia, but nothing beyond that. The occupation should prevail, however,
only temporarily, while talks with the Russians proceeded.[27] Amid the encircling gloom, here was at least
a glimmer of hope for the preservation of peace.

The Ballplatz questioned, however, whether the Berlin
counsels were seriously intended, partly because of the
muddy language of Ambassador Tschirschky, but more
so because the German supreme command, probably without the knowledge of the statesmen, begged the Hapsburg military chiefs to concentrate their armies against
Russia and indicated that some German troops would
likewise be arrayed against the empire of the Tsar. Whatever the reasoning, the cabinet of Vienna was not at all
minded to consider a compromise by diplomacy, previously rejected as futile, and withheld its answer to the
German "Halt in Belgrade" gambit until too late to affect
the onrushing torrent of war. So, the tardy attempts by
Berlin statecraft to preserve the peace of Europe were
swept headlong into the mad whirlpool.

6.

Simultaneously with the summons to St. Petersburg to
revoke the decree for general mobilization, the Berlin

[27] *Ö.-U.A.,* nos. 11025, 11203.

foreign office called upon France, tsarist ally, to give concrete pledges of neutrality in case Germany and Russia should fight. Instead, the Paris ministry bluntly replied that France would act in accord with her national interests and began to call up the reserve forces; in point of fact, French diplomacy exercised only limited influence on the awesome cataract of events that followed the Hapsburg ultimatum to Serbia. Not until July 29 did Poincaré and his party return to Paris from their Russian excursion, and no significant moves were undertaken to restrain the Russians from general mobilization until it was too late. On the other side, as has been intimated above, French Ambassador Paléologue, a diplomatist of merely ordinary quality, egged tsarist policymakers on, imprudently if patriotically; and he neglected to keep the Quai d'Orsay accurately and punctually posted on trends in the thinking of the Russian foreign office.

At bottom, French policy was determined by the fixed idea that national security and welfare required full solidarity with the Russian ally; thus and thus only, it was reasoned, could the delicate power equilibrium in Europe be preserved. That fluid something called public sentiment, as exhibited in the French press and by deputies, adopted a fatalistic posture toward onrushing developments, as would be true again in the late 1930's. By the comparative test, belligerency in France was not widespread, though the ministry was ready to fight, however much it desired that the technical initiative for war should come from across the Rhine. Extreme caution was exercised to avoid any act that might legitimately be construed as provocative of the hereditary German antagonist.

On August 3, Berlin gratified the wish of the cabinet in Paris by issuing a formal declaration of war. Well-matured German plans of campaign—the Schlieffen Plan —in the event of war on two fronts prescribed that fighting should first be pressed with lightning speed against France, and once that country had been whipped, military resources would be shunted against the slower moving tsarist military machine. To implement that schedule with maximum expedition, the great armies of William II would crowd into France across neutralized Belgium, small but spirited.

German transgression of Belgian soil converted many a wavering Briton to the view that it was in the national and imperial interest to take up arms. As a country in which government by discussion and consent prevailed to a greater degree than anywhere on the Continent, the United Kingdom wheeled into the war more hesitantly than the other belligerents. Stage by stage, the British public awakened—slowly, yet nonetheless positively, to the prospect of involvement in the conflict. After the implications of the Viennese rejection of the Serbian reply had been fully digested, many a British journal, hitherto kindly disposed toward the Danube Monarchy or neutralist, sounded distinctly Austrophobe accents. Apprehensions multiplied with news of general mobilizations on the Continent, and the German threat to the internationally guaranteed integrity of Belgium swept fervor for intervention to a blazing climax. Grey personally belonged to that segment of British opinion which believed that moral alignment and diplomatic affinity with France and Russia must not be impaired, lest the balance of military strength should be dangerously tilted against the island kingdom and the British realm. While Grey, "an incarnation of negative goodness" in the suggestive appraisal of Beatrice Webb, Fabian sage, worked hard and honestly to stave off the catastrophe, he was resolved, as the crisis deepened, to resign if his ministerial colleagues should decide to hold Britain aloof from the impending struggle.

Scrupulously avoiding any utterance that might either

encourage or temper bellicosity in St. Petersburg or in Paris, the Foreign Secretary with equal care warned Berlin not to proceed on the hypothesis that Britain would stand on the side lines if fighting engulfed the Continent. Considerable flexibility and agility of mind and nearly superhuman patience were required to stay abreast of proposals for peaceful adjustment emanating from London. While one plan, for instance, invited Vienna and Belgrade to seek a settlement through diplomacy, another scheme contemplated a conference of the principal cabinets to hammer out a compromise, with the "Halt in Belgrad" concept as the point of departure for discussions. These and other British diplomatic proposals ran into sand, for the drift to war had advanced too far to be reversed. Significantly, the First British Fleet, which had been assembled for training exercises, was held together and at the ready.

Inside the British ministry, an irreconcilable division of mind on war or neutrality persisted—reflecting thought and emotion in the kingdom at large. Speculative intelligences have frequently contended that if the London cabinet had registered strong protests in St. Petersburg against concentration of military forces against both Central Empires, or if the ministry had been in a position to threaten with sufficient precision in the first stages of the crisis that in a European conflict British arms would be thrown against Germany, a general war might have been avoided. However that may be, the German violation of Belgium virtually unified sentiments in the island kingdom and provoked a quick declaration of war. Implicitly, the time-tested British doctrine of a "just equilibrium" in Europe, anathema though it was to many an idealistic, pacifically - minded Briton, had triumphed anew.[28]

---

[28] For an interesting synthesis on British policy, prepared by the Hapsburg Embassy in London, see *Ö.-U.A.*, no. 10974. In an address

The nominal third partner in the Triple Alliance, royal Italy, decided that its side in the war would be the outside—at any rate, for the time being. At the Consulta, presided over by the ailing Marquis Antonio di San Giuliano, less than three months removed from the grave, the studied secrecy of the Vienna cabinet in keeping its ally in the dark concerning intentions vis-à-vis Serbia irked and irritated. Appreciative that if a general war came, Italy might forsake allegiance to the Triplice, Berlin pleaded and pleaded again with the Ballplatz to purchase Italian loyalty by immediate and tangible concessions. Such counsels annoyed Vienna to the point of exasperation and went unheeded.[29]

As the international horizon darkened following the Serb rejection of the Austrian demands, the Italian foreign office brought out a meritorious formula for preventing an European conflagration whereby the Great Powers collectively would compel Serbia to yield without condition to the Austrian ultimatum and they would then supervise the execution of the demands. In spite of the sheer novelty of this plan—or just because of that—no chancellery responded appropriately, and the proposal was abruptly swept into the archives when Vienna proclaimed war upon Serbia. A second blueprint bearing the Roman stamp and contemplating an adjustment of the Austro-Russian phase of the complex quarrel expected too much of St. Petersburg, was maladroitly timed, and never so much as got off the drawing board. Denouncing the Austrian war upon Serbia as aggressive in intent and releasing Italy from treaty obligations to cooperate militarily with the Triplice if a European struggle ensued, the Italian ministry on August 3 proclaimed the neutrality of

---

to the Fisher Society at Cambridge University on May 7, 1914, the Ambassador, Count Albert Mensdorff, declared that he did not think "there had ever been a statesman who had inspired such absolute confidence abroad" as Grey. London *Times*, May 25, 1915.

[29] See, for instance, Ö.-U.A., nos. 10909, 10943, 10948, 10989, 11128.

their country, a verdict that occasioned no surprise in Central Power ministerial quarters, though it greatly disturbed German army chiefs.[30] Rumania imitated the example of Italy.

7.

On military grounds exclusively, the Ballplatz withheld formal announcement of war upon Russia until August 6 and was not technically at war with the western Entente powers for yet another week. Berlin besought Vienna to declare war on Britain and France at once and to order the Hapsburg fleet to cooperate with German naval units in the Mediterranean. Since Hapsburg seapower was not yet in fighting trim, the authorities in Vienna delayed a decision, but after ships of the Monarchy actually clashed with British naval forces and on the urgings of St. Petersburg, London and Paris declared war upon Vienna on August 12 and 13. Never before had the Hapsburg and British realms fought one another directly, although in the Seven Years' War of the eighteenth century, the ally of Austria, Bourbon France, warred upon the island kingdom and Vienna's enemy, Prussia benefited from British subsidies. Insisting that Britain had no quarrel with the Danube Monarchy, a London editor wrote, "We respect her and the last thing in the world that we desire is that she should commit suicide because Germany has got it into her head that it is a case of 'now or never.'"[31] This attitude prevailed widely in Britain, until the fearsome carnage had raged for nearly four years. In the light of the well-established tradition of Austro-British cordiality, it is not hard to understand an observation of Berchtold to Ambassador Sir Maurice de

[30] For a searing indictment of the diplomacy pursued by the Consulta, see Albertini, *op.cit.*, II, 245–253; III, 254–343.
[31] London *Spectator*, Aug. 1, 1914.

Bunsen at their farewell meeting. "It seems absurd," he said, "for good friends like England and Austria to be at war." "I did not argue the point, nor did he," Bunsen commented tersely. The two countries slipped into combat as a ship glides from her moorings on a fog-bound night.

On August 5, Montenegro, by verdict of parliament, in defiance of the neutralist wishes of King Nicholas, took up arms against Austria-Hungary. And before the month was over Vienna rounded out the orbit of conflict by declaring war on Japan, much against the will of Conrad, and on Belgium. Until almost the end of the war, the future of Belgium provoked unending friction and discussions inside the Central Powers bloc, Viennese leaders asserting time and again that German annexationist ambitions were an insuperable barrier to peace by negotiation with the western Entente.[32]

8.

For anything approaching an adequate appreciation of the coming of the War of 1914, it is necessary to cast the mind over the diplomatic environment in which the desperate Sarajevo crisis developed. For two solid generations, most of Europe had experienced a golden age of comparative peace, progress, and prosperity, which would later be looked back upon nostalgically; lasting peace had come to be taken for granted in the west of Europe, leastwise. War and revolution, massacre, fanaticism, and kindred manifestations of barbarism were widely regarded as monstrosities of an outmoded past; consequently, the outbreak of fighting in 1914 proved far more shocking than previous European struggles or

[32] Conrad von Hötzendorf, *Aus Meiner Dienstzeit, 1906–1918* (5 vols., Vienna, 1921–25), IV, 538–539; Hartmut Lehmann, "Österreich – Ungarns Belgienpolitik im Ersten Weltkrieg," *Historische Zeitschrift*, CXCII (1961), 60–93.

later ones. With the blessing of Hapsburg statesmen, detailed plans had been drafted for a big international pacifist conference to be held in Vienna in the autumn of 1914.[33] One historian, who in the fullness of time would rank among the eminent masters of the craft, closed a book published in 1912 by writing: "We can now look forward with something like confidence to the time when war between civilized nations will be considered as antiquated as the duel, and when the peacemakers shall be called the children of God." [34]

This judgment seemed fitting and proper, despite nearly a decade of wranglings and successive diplomatic crises involving the two great power blocks into which Europe had twisted itself: the Triple Alliance of Germany, the Hapsburg Monarchy, and Italy over against the Triple Entente, embracing France, Russia, and Great Britain. Nearly endemic quarreling had bequeathed to 1914 a combustible legacy of mistrust, suspicion, ugly streaks of resentment, humiliation; yet earlier crises had been surmounted in one manner or another without unleashing a conflagration. By virtue of the clearly demonstrated lukewarmness of Italy to her Triplice allies and of British moral commitments to hasten to the aid of France should the Third Republic become involved in war, it was a reasonable calculation that the Triple Alliance was the weaker of the two diplomatic combinations. Besides, the rising surge of nationalism among sections of the politically active national groupings in the Danube Monarchy, openly expressed desires for freedom and independence in instances, appeared to have diminished the stature of the Hapsburg realm as a power factor of front rank.

In fact, however, flames of dissatisfaction among na-

[33] Caroline E. Playne, *Bertha von Suttner* (London, 1936), pp. 231–237.

[34] George P. Gooch, *A History of Our Own Times* (London, 1912), pp. 248–249.

tionalities, whether in Austria or in Hungary, had not grown intense enough to burst into revolt. For years, the Ballplatz in chronic bickering and controversy with Serbia had striven consistently to shield the Monarchy against insidious external or externally-incited conspiracies and intrigues that might promote, if not unloose fatefully, centrifugal tendencies pointed toward national fulfillment. Viewed in historical perspective, Berchtold and his colleagues held unswervingly to that posture in the supreme crisis of 1914. Foreign observers who supposed that the venerable Monarchy was teetering on the brink of dissolution and that involvement in a major war would bring on immediate upheavals by discontented national communities were disappointed; Hapsburg soldiers of all languages and national dispositions obediently responded to the call to the colors. It is of more than passing interest that the eminent Czech politician, Professor Thomas G. Masaryk, who thought the prevailing Austro-Hungarian constitutional regime intolerable, when casting up a balance sheet on direct responsibility for war in 1914 placed Berlin, St. Petersburg, and even London, unexpectedly, ahead of Vienna.

In the east of Europe political tensions and uneasiness had been aggravated by the settlements effected after the fierce Balkan struggles of 1912–1913. And for a short spell early in 1914 Russian and German newspapers indulged in a passionately intemperate press polemic, in which some journals of the Dual Monarchy joined, but the feud ceased as suddenly as it had arisen. A budget of other outstanding sources of antagonism, such as has cropped up perennially in modern European history, and involving both stronger and lesser powers, seemed on the way to pacific adjustment or solution. On the surface at any rate, at the outset of 1914 the Old World appeared to be, if anything, calmer and more tranquil than for decades. French President Poincaré hit the nail squarely on the head when he wrote, " . . . the world was at peace at the time of the Sarajevo murder. The immediate determining causes of war must therefore be sought in the conduct of the various European nations after this tragedy." [35]

The aftermath of Sarajevo, thought Winston Churchill, loosed "upon mankind incomparably its most frightful misfortune since the collapse of the Roman Empire before the Barbarians." [36] An era of relative safety and comparatively cheerful living came to an end and no man could foretell whether it would be regained.

In deciding upon war the Vienna cabinet obeyed the iron law of self-preservation; specifically, policymakers on the Danube wished to retain for the Hapsburg Monarchy the South Slav-peopled areas. No self-respecting government could be expected "to stand quietly by" (as the phrase runs) and allow subversive poisons to eat away at its territories. Recklessly, the men in the Ballplatz, Berchtold leading, resolved to clear up relations with Serbia, though they coveted no Serbian territory beyond strategic rectifications along the borders. It would be wrong, however, to suppose that fault and folly lay solely on one side of the fierce Austro-Serb antagonism or the other. In the pattern of nineteenth-century Europe (with Italy as the closest analogue), prominent Yugoslavs, both in Serbia and in the Dual Monarchy, passionately desired the integration of all South Slavs in a united nation.

Patriotic aspirations, enshrined in an aphorism of Saint Sava, *Sama Sloga Srbina Spasova* (Union alone is the salvation of Serbia), could only be fulfilled at the expense of the Hapsburg realm, and even as Italian national-builders had relied heavily upon help from the

[35] Raymond Poincaré, "The Responsibility for the War," *Foreign Affairs,* IV (1925–1926), 13.
[36] *The World Crisis* (6 vols., New York, 1923–1931), VI, 82.

France of Napoleon III, so the Serbs found indispensable backing in the empire of the tsar. Time appeared to be working on behalf of the Yugoslav national ambition, unless South Slavs in the Dual Monarchy should be appeased; plans to that end had been simmering in the mind of the Archduke Francis Ferdinand, though whether they could have been implemented, in view of the stubborn antipathy of the Magyar ruling oligarchy especially, must seriously be questioned. From another angle, Serb patriots conjured up dreads, groundless or not, that the Vienna authorities had seized upon the Sarajevo tragedy as a handy pretext not only to despoil their kingdom but, in collaboration with covetous neighbors, to erase Serbia from the map.

3. The Eastern Wars

AFTER THE HAPSBURG MONARCHY WITHDREW THE SWORD from the scabbard, a prophecy ascribed to Prince Otto von Bismarck rang true. "If Francis Joseph mounts his horse, all his peoples will follow him." An overwhelming proportion of the citizenry in the multinationality realm rallied to the war effort with enthusiastic devotion, matching the response in other belligerent lands. Acute Russophobia of a character that would be better understood in western countries after 1945, gripped solemn and sober intellectuals of the Monarchy, and night after night enthusiastic Viennese on parade flaunted pictures of the Emperor, waved black-and-yellow Hapsburg flags, and chanted, "*Gott erhalte Franz der Kaiser*" or the stirring "Prinz Eugen Lied."[1]

Many an articulate Slav, who thought of the murdered

[1] See, Fritz Fellner (ed.), *Das Politische Tagebuch Josef Redlichs* (2 vols., Vienna, 1953, 1954) I, 240–242; echoing the appraisal of his British colleague, the Ambassador of the United States reported, "Public enthusiasm unbounded . . ."

Archduke as their special champion, wanted Serbia punished, and for a good part of the Roman Catholic clergy in South Slav areas and their flocks, the war possessed the quality of a holy crusade against Orthodox Serbia and Russia. Some Austrogerman progressives regarded the conflict as an instrument that would open the way to needed constitutional reform which would rejuvenate the realm, and Christian churchmen laid their peculiar interpretation upon the war. Gustav Cardinal Piffl, Archbishop of Vienna, for one, displayed the spirit of Urban II preaching the First Crusade—as related by William of Malmesbury—"Therefore go forward in happiness and in confidence to attack the enemies of God."

Some reservists were swept along by sheer fatalism. Others, convinced of the righteousness of the cause in hand, raised paeans of thankfulness to the God who had matched them with the hour. Many an ordinary citizen, wearied of a longish "cold war," of diplomatic tension and controversy heaved an immeasurable sigh of relief because war would write finis to endless fears. Besides, many a man revolted against the monotony and triviality of his daily round and the mood of the primeval hunter pierced through the thin wall of pacifism. When the tsarist colossus entered the lists, shattering the notion that fighting would be localized against Serbia, confidence in some Austro-Hungarian hearts sagged, but the Russian intervention assured the cooperation of the Socialist rank and file in the war effort. And it was widely assumed that the military strength and industrial productivity of the German ally guaranteed that the struggle would be short and successful; "Three months—then peace with glory," optimists murmured to one another.

Mobilization of Hapsburg soldiers, Viennese and Styrians, Czechs and Tyrolese, Magyars and Croats, Poles and Rumanians, Slovaks and Slovenes proceeded with remarkable smoothness. A poet of the hour sang:

> Das Heer des alten Kaisers schliesst den Reigen,
> Des grossen, schönen Ost'reichs letztes Heer,
> Geschmückt mit Eichenlaub und Tannenzweigen
> Ergriff es opferwillig seine Wehr.
> Vom Graubart bis zum Jüngling, flaumumsprossen,
> Eilt' es zur Fahne auf des Kriegsherrn Ruf,
> An Geist und Kraft aus zähem Erz gegossen,
> Wie niemals eine Zeit ein bess'res schuf.[2]

Anti-militarist Socialists and dissenting voices among national minorities were overwhelmed in a billowing wave of martial fervor; only Czech disaffection impeded the conduct of the fighting until well along in the second half of the war, and even Czech desertion was comparatively small when related to the number of Czechs in uniform. Weeks elapsed before popular exaltation at the opening of the war yielded to squalid horror.

Victory or defeat in very modern war hinges not only upon the fighting services, but upon the stability and intestinal fortitude on the civilian front, and for the armed forces the basic ingredients for success are morale, the quantity and quality of armaments and of transportation, and the capacities of commanders. Quickly the Hapsburg armed services expanded to 1,400,000 men, triple the peacetime strength; they embraced the regular joint army comprising reservists from Austria and from Hungary, and two militia forces, the Austrian Landwehr and the Hungarian Honvéd (Home Defense), both with reservists, and each contingent under the authority of its own government. Hungarian law prescribed Magyar as the official language of command for Honvéd levies, who would be justified in defying orders issued in German. The diversity of tongues spoken by the troops imposed something of a disadvantage upon Hapsburg armies, as indeed upon the Russian. Many an Austro-Hungarian private, and even some non-commissioned of-

[2] Rudolf K. Materna, "Alt-Österreichs Armee," quoted in Oskar Regele, *Feldmarschall Conrad* (Vienna, 1955), p. 517.

ficers, understood no German beyond about eighty words used in command; commonly, military orders published in German were accompanied by a Magyar translation. It was calculated in the official Hapsburg history of the war that of every hundred men called up in 1914, twenty-five spoke German as their mother tongue; twenty-three Magyar; thirteen Czech; four Slovak; nine Serbo-Croat; two Slovene; eight each Polish and Ukrainian, seven Rumanian; and one Italian. To a considerable extent, soldiers who spoke Slavic or Latin tongues were brigaded with troops of German or Magyar speech. Hearts beat in unison—or something approaching that—at the sound of the thrilling "Radetzky March" and other lusty martial airs. Uniforms, too, contributed to cohesion in the multinationality armies, though in a relatively few cases loyalty to the Hapsburg crown went no deeper than the clothes being worn. Certain regiments cherished great traditions which it was a matter of pride and of moral obligation to perpetuate. Chiseled into the façade of the War Ministry in Vienna was the Roman aphorism, "Si vis pacem, para bellum"—yet in the testing time the Dual Monarchy was far from ready to fight.[3]

[3] Basic works on the military aspects of the war are Edmund Glaise von Horstenau, *et al.*, *Österreich-Ungarns Letzter Krieg, 1914–1918* (15 vols., Vienna, 1930–1938) and Rudolf Kiszling, *Österreich-Ungarns Anteil am Ersten Weltkrieg* (Vienna, 1958). On the question of readiness for war, see Rudolf Kiszling, "Die Entwicklung der Österreich-ungarischen Wehrmacht seit der Annexionskrise 1908," *BM*, XII (1934), 735–749; Hugo Kerchnawe, "Feldmarschall Alexander Freiherr von Krobatin," *ibid.*, XII (1934), 313–318. Krobatin, war minister from the end of 1912 into April, 1917, has been dubbed the "Carnot" of the Hapsburg Monarchy. For the Hungarian side, an elaborate record was prepared by the War Archives of Budapest under the title *A Világ háboru* ["The World War"] *1914–18* (5 vols., Budapest, 1928–1932). The Archduke Joseph set out his impressions of the war in immense detail, *A Világ háboru ahogyan én lattam* ["The World War As I Saw it"] (7 vols., Budapest, 1926–1934). These works and other books on the war in the Magyar language to 1934 are surveyed in "L'Historie Militaire de la Guerre Mondiale en Hongrie," *Revue d'Histoire de la Guerre Mondiale*, XIII (1935), 313–324. See, also, Alexander L. P. Johnson, "The War Memoirs of Archduke Joseph of Hungary," *JMH*, VII (1935), 455–464.

Appraisals of the condition of the Hapsburg fighting services, their equipment and readiness for combat, diverge considerably. It is no surprise to learn that professional soldiers lamented that their pre-war recommendations had gone unheeded, so that the armed forces, due to the niggardliness of appropriations, were ill-prepared for the terrible rendezvous. Rifles, machine guns, and light artillery were not available in needed quantities, but heavy Škoda howitzers were turned over to Germany for use in smashing resistance in Belgium. These powerful Austrian weapons, capable of hurling armor-piercing shells as far as seven miles, could be quickly assembled and moved seventy-five miles and more in a day. Uniforms were in such short supply that many reservists, called from factory and farm, were transported to battle areas wearing black and yellow bands on the arms of their civilian coats. Transport and commissarist facilities were quite inadequate for the kind of war that was actually waged; carts and horses were freely commandeered from the peasantry.

2.

In the person of Conrad von Hötzendorf, Chief of the General Staff, the Hapsburg Monarchy possessed an able strategist, possibly the finest that the First World War turned up anywhere.[4] A professional soldier *par excellence* "grimly silent, watchfully alert," Conrad had built a great reputation for expertness in military planning and tactics. In appearance short and dapper, he resembled more a professor of philosophy, say, then a bellicose militarist, wedded to doctrines of the offensive in conducting war. His proficiency as a strategist, his courage and fortitude

[4] For a wartime sketch of Conrad, as the right man in the right place, see Artur Gaspar, "Conrad von Hötzendorff," *ÖR*, XLV (1915), 145–150. The standard biography has been written by Oskar Regele (Vienna, 1955).

long set a shining example for subordinate officers. He was also that dubious if not dangerous phenomenon, an intensely political general, who constantly dabbled in foreign policy, seldom to the advantage of the Monarchy. Though Emperor Francis Joseph had serious reservations about Conrad, he retained him as chief of staff; the general lost caste, however, with the old ruler, when in the second year of the war he married a divorcé, something repugnant to the Catholicism of the Emperor. The fiery Conrad quarreled not only with senior Hapsburg civilian officials, but also with top commanders of Germany; it was galling that campaigns which he devised were actually implemented by the Germans because Hapsburg resources alone were unequal to executing them.

Advanced as he was in years, the Emperor appointed his distant cousin the Archduke Friedrich as titular commander-in-chief, a post he held until "the little gentlemen in black velvet" carried Francis Joseph away. In keeping with family tradition, the Archduke had been trained for the military profession, though he was not fond of it, being reserved by nature and much preferring the leisurely existence of the grand seigneur. He and Conrad knew each other intimately, having served together as young lieutenants, and the Archduke tactfully allowed the Chief of Staff his head on military matters, so they got along quite well; Friedrich did much to soften frictions and bickering between the Austrian and the German supreme commands. For his services Friedrich was rewarded with a field marshal's baton, an honor also conferred on his younger brother, Eugene, who although educated in theology, distinguished himself as a commander in the Balkan theaters of war and subsequently against Italy. A third Archduke, Joseph Augustin of Hungary, achieved unusual popularity as a military leader and lasting renown for a huge history of the war in the Magyar language. Archduke Joseph Ferdinand won his spurs on the Russian front and eventually was put in charge of military aircraft.

At the side of Conrad in the Austrian high command (AOK) were several highly touted generals,[5] such as Oskar Potiorek, the ill-starred governor of Bosnia at the time of the Sarajevo tragedy, whose inability to produce victories was all too quickly revealed, and Moritz von Auffenberg, sometime imperial minister of war, whose initial successes against the Russians made him momentarily a popular darling, and his principal colleague in 1914, Victor Dankl, descended from the Tyrolese hero Andreas Hofer. Two generals of Croat stock, Svetozar Boroević and Stephan Sarkotić, whole-souled "black-and-yellow loyalists," attained high distinction as commanders and astute politicians.[6]

When the tocsin of war sounded, perhaps three of every four officers in the joint Austro-Hungarian army came from families of German speech, and many of the higher officers from Hungary were Germans from Transylvania. Authentic Magyars who hankered after an officer's career tended to pick the national Honvéd either out of patriotism or because of the language advantage; a large proportion of non-commissioned officers were Czechs. The Austro-Hungarian officers' corps, hardworking and technically well-schooled in general, was notably *Habsburgtreue*, and it was assumed that this professional class would compensate for the multilinguistic composition of the Austro-Hungarian armies. Yet many an informed German feared that the Hohenzollern Empire

[5] Theodor R. von Zeynek, "Über den Österreichisch-ungarischen Generalstab," *Militärwissenschaftliche Mitteilungen*, LXX (1939), 179–194.

[6] Edmund Glaise von Horstenau, "Feldzeugmeister Potiorek," *BM*, XII (1934), 144–148; Eduard Steinitz, "Moritz Auffenberg," *Neue Österreichische Biographie*, VI, 150–160; Glaise von Horstenau, "Svetozar Boroević," *ibid.*, I, 109–115; Rudolf Kiszling, "General Baron Stephan Sarkotić," *ibid.*, IX, 99–106.

was going to war "with a corpse hanging around its neck"!

3.

Before 1914, tentative, incomplete plans for joint campaigns against the empire of the Tsar had been prepared by the high commands of Vienna and Berlin.[7] While the bulk of the German armies would march against France, a small proportion of the German military resources, together with most of the Hapsburg forces, would strike at the Russians. The fate of the Monarchy, German military chiefs kept repeating, would finally be decided on the Seine, not on the Bug River. Austro-Hungarian regiments were divided into three army groups, the largest—thirty-nine infantry and ten cavalry divisions—being available for operations against Russia. The weakest—just over eleven divisions—would attack Serbia, and the third group would join in the drive against the Serbs if the fighting were localized, but otherwise would be dispatched against the Russians. In fact, when general mobilization was ordered, plans had advanced too far to switch the third army group immediately to the Russian front without causing calamitous confusion; in consequence, initial operations against Russia were greatly handicapped. "We hoped," Conrad later explained, "to fight Serbia without other complications. The endeavors of all powers to localize the war strengthened us in this belief."[8]

[7] Gerhard Seyfert, *Die Militärischen Beziehungen und Vereinbarungen zwischen dem Deutschen und dem Österreichischen Generalstab vor und bei Beginn des Weltkrieges* (Leipzig, 1934), 46–75. Consult Gerhard Ritter, "Der Anteil der Militärs an der Kriegskatastrophe von 1914," *Historische Zeitschrift*, CXCIII (1961) 72–91, esp. 81–91.

[8] Rudolf Kiszling, "Die Mobilmachung der Europäischen Mächte im Sommer 1914: Österreich-Ungarn," *BM*, XIV (1936), 189–224; Eduard Czekga, *Serbien und Montenegro, ibid.*, 3–23.

As has been intimated, Hapsburg and Romanov military experts envisaged a short, triumphant struggle, and in their planning both accented the offensive.[9] Austro-Hungarian divisions with modest help from Germany aimed at conquering Russian Poland, after which the tsarist troops would be rolled eastward into the Ukraine, so the blueprints read. But just as the German supreme command laid too high an estimate on the armies of Francis Joseph, so they had underestimated the fighting capacity of Russia. The Russians surprised the enemy by the speed of mobilization, and the rather small German forces in the east failed to swoop into the Polish salient as expected. Tsarist armies, indeed, crowded pell-mell into the province of East Prussia, obliging the Germans to appeal to Conrad for greater efforts and to shunt troops from France to the east—a diversion that helped to upset the program to knock the French out of the war swiftly. Not only did the Germans, Generals Paul von Hindenburg and Erich Ludendorff commanding, stem the tsarist pressure into East Prussia, but after the decisive battle at Tannenberg in August, 1914, the invaders were hurled from the province with immense losses.

Meantime, the Austrian phase of the campaign against Russia had favored the latter on balance. The Tsar thought only scornfully of the Hapsburg capacity to fight; he ordered the opening "at any price and as quickly as possible the road to Berlin. I attach only secondary importance to our operations against Austria." Yet Russian military specialists appreciated the material and strategic advantages that conquest of the province of Galicia would yield. About the size of New York State, and having a mixed population of eight million Poles and Ukrainians, Galicia was a leading granary of the Mon-

---

[9] The pertinent literature is comprehensively surveyed by Emil Franzel, "Politik und Strategie im Sommer 1914," *Neues Abendland*, XI (1956), 63–88.

archy and contained small, though productive oil-fields.[10]
If tsarist forces, moreover, could capture the province,
a thrust into Russian Poland from the south would be
next to impossible, while the Russians would be in a
position to press through Carpathian passes to the plains
of Hungary or to make a try for Berlin by way of Silesia;
and, besides, rapid conquest of Galicia would impress
wavering Balkan neutrals, Rumania above all.

The first fighting in the Galician theater possessed a
quality which soon became a mere memory by reason
of more lethal weapons and different tactical arrangements. Strategists were severely handicapped by the
limited transport facilities; picturesque cavalry charges,
cannon aligned in open position, and infantrymen fighting in close order typified operations in the summer of
1914. Intelligence services were of inferior quality, but
the Austrians and Germans had an edge in that department, and interception of tsarist military orders kept the
Central Powers reliably informed on Russian military intentions. Police in Galicia rounded up political suspects,
catching in their net a Russian idea-man of wily ambition
known as Vladimir Lenin; Austrogerman and Polish
Socialists contrived to have him set free.

At the outset Hapsburg arms scored heartening gains
and for a time they even threatened to ensnare an entire
Russian army; gradually divisions originally intended for
the Serbian front wheeled into battle array in the north.
But panic-producing thrusts by Cossack horsemen and
sheer weight of Muscovite manpower shattered the in-
toxicating dream of encirclement, necessitating retreat
by the Hapsburg troops, civilians in tens of thousands
fleeing with the soldiers. On September 2, the capital of
Galicia and key railway center, Lemberg (Lvov), fell

[10] On the economic importance of Galicia for the Monarchy, consult
Eugen von Philippovich, "Über die Bedeutung Ostgalizens für Österreich-Ungarn," ÖR, XLIV (1915), 105–111.

to the Russians with so little fighting that newspapers in the city which in the morning sang a Hapsburg tune appeared with a Russian slant in the evening. Steadily the Austro-Hungarian armies fell back, arriving at the San River on the 11th, while another Russian force plunged across the Bukowina capturing the capital Czernowitz (Cernăuti), which was destined to change masters over a dozen times before the close of the conflict. At that grim and desperate point in the war, the Ballplatz bluntly warned Berlin that unless more military assistance were forthcoming, the Dual Monarchy might be compelled to consider seeking peace.[11] Better than a third of the Hapsburg troops which had entered the struggle scarcely a month earlier had been lost; and the image of a Muscovite steam-roller, "like the flow of a great river in flood," danced in Entente headlines.[12]

Compared with the fearsome Hapsburg setbacks, the Russian disaster at Tannenberg seemed to be simply of local significance. Faint-hearted Viennese were heard to say that an armistice must be sought with the Slav colossus. Conrad in vehement language, and Francis Joseph more moderately, complained to Berlin because sorely needed help had not been forthcoming. Scanning the battle reports, Winston Churchill prematurely referred to "the collapse of Austria as a military factor, as the greatest feature yet apparent in the course of the war. That collapse appears irreparable," he supposed, "and that is a tremendous event in the history of the world." [13] Sanguinely, the French ambassador in Petrograd wagered a five-pound note with his British colleague that the fighting would be over before Christmas; in fact, before

[11]Berchtold to Hohenlohe, Sept. 8, 1914, P.A., *Geheim*, XLVII/ 3–1.
[12] Octavian C. Taslăuanu, *With the Austrian Army in Galicia* (London, 1918), vividly portrays battlefield realities. The author, a Hungarian officer of Rumanian speech, later deserted. *Salt of the Earth* (London, 1939), an unfinished novel by the Pole, Joseph Wittlin, points up civilian wartime experiences.
[13] London *Times*, Sept. 25, 1914.

that day arrived, Russian commanders were imploring both of the diplomatists to do all in their power to get desperately required rifles and ammunition shipped to the east.

By the end of September, a Cossack vanguard had penetrated to Hungary and the capture of Budapest appeared to lie within the range of the possible. These military developments were duly noted by watching-and-waiting policymakers in Rumania. Before long Conrad told General Erich von Falkenhayn, who had supplanted von Moltke as supreme German commander after the fiasco on the Marne, that unless appropriate help were dispatched the Hapsburg armies might be compelled to pull back to a "Danube line—Vienna—Budapest." In great anguish of spirit, his worst pre-war apprehensions coming close to reality, Tisza piteously begged the Germans to save imperilled Hungary; actually, the Russian sojourn on the soil of Hungary, though sweet, was short.

The Austro-Hungarian retreat westward continued apace, giving rise to a cynical Viennese witticism that the Hapsburg commanders desired simply to tire the invaders out. Planting a large garrison in the fortress of Przemyśl on the San River, the bulk of the Austro-Hungarian forces pulled into the far western sector of Galicia, enabling the enemy to advance within walking distance of Cracow (Kraków), ancient capital of Poland. Feeling that Vienna itself was exposed to mortal peril, the American ambassador ordered his staff to make preliminary preparations to depart. Imaginative minds in Western Europe pictured victorious Cossacks sweeping into Prague and even into Berlin.

Certainly the damage inflicted by the Russian hosts had been very extensive. Losses in battle are set in the official Austrian war history at 350,000, some of the best fighting material the Monarchy possessed; the material resources of almost all of Galicia had been lost, and refugees approaching the million mark had to be some-how cared for. Army morale had sagged, moreover, and grave shortages existed in military supplies, though prob-ably not so serious as on the Russian side. Sharp wran-glings, conflicting points of view on strategy, and recrim-inations afflicted the high commands of the Central Empires;[14] it wounded the sensitive soul of Conrad to beg the German ally for reinforcement, or indeed to see his beloved Monarchy dependent upon Berlin in any way. Each ally suspected that the other might seek a separate peace with the Russian bear. Before long Conrad wondered what "our secret foes, the Germans are doing? And what of that comedian, the German Emperor?" Ger-man military specialists, the Austrian complained, "sniffed about like spies." Proposals from Berlin that a unified command should be created in the east, which would have curtailed the authority of Conrad, so infuriated him that he threatened to resign; Francis Joseph brushed the German suggestions aside.

To reduce Muscovite pressure upon the Hapsburg troops, the Germans struck hard in the direction of War-saw. "Immediate help," Ludendorff averred in his mem-oirs, "had to be brought to the Austro-Hungarian army to avoid its annihilation"; that assistance threw the tsarist military machine off its stride. Throughout the winter sporadic fighting occurred in the Carpathian area, the Russians futilely squandering men and munitions in mountain warfare and in see-saw combat in western Gali-cia. Despite disheartening reversals the Danube Mon-archy had not collapsed like a pack of cards, as many a western pundit had optimistically prophesied.

[14] Egon C. Corti, "Die Uneinigkeit der Beiden Koalitionen im Welt-kriege und Ihre Folgen," in Otto Bruner, et.al., Historische Studien, A.F. Pribram (Vienna, 1929), pp. 257–269. The author, like many another student of strategy, castigates the Germans for driving hard to the west instead of concentrating against Russia with a view to knocking the tsardom out of the conflict quickly. Cf. Seyfert, op.cit., pp. 83–115.

The bleak situation of the Monarchy worsened when on March 22, 1915, a starving garrison in excess of 110,000 surrendered at Przemyśl after withstanding investment, siege, and the torments of typhus and cholera for almost four months. This setback was likened abroad to the French capitulation at Metz in 1870 or to the tsarist surrender at Port Arthur in 1905; and the Russian *Novoye Vremya* hailed the capture of Przemyśl as deciding "the fate of the whole Hapsburg Empire and consequently that of her ally, Germany." In other theatres, however, military stalemate prevailed, and Russian prospects of victory were bright only by comparison, which persuaded the statesmen on the Neva to pay most of the high price which the cabinet of Rome set for Italian intervention on the Entente side.

4.

Philosophically regarded, the reverses imposed upon Austria-Hungary by the vast manpower of Russia were understandable, but to suffer a series of defeats at the hands of little Serbia was gall and wormwood. Austrian gunboats on the Danube had opened the conflict, as has been seen, by lobbing shells into Belgrade and the Serbs retaliated by blowing up the railway bridge leading over the Danube to Hungary. Not once, but three times in 1914, Hapsburg armies struck against Serbia, achieved small gains, only to be hurled back ignominiously by South Slav veterans hardened in the Balkan wars of 1912–13; the director of Serb strategy was elderly General Radomir Putnik, whose father had emigrated from southern Hungary. Pitted against him was Potiorek, who, in collaboration with Conrad, had worked out military plans against Serbia in considerable detail, intending in fact to overwhelm the Serbs before their mobilization had been completed.

Instead of smashing frontally at Belgrade, the Austrian army on August 11 attacked from the west, crossed the Save River and stormed into Šabać, but Serb troops counterattacked, expelled the invader, and even advanced onto the soil of the Monarchy. Austrian strategy had gone awry and the diversion of troops to Galicia and some Czech troop disaffection had radically interfered with pre-war blueprints. At mid-September, with Austrian armies reeling backward in Galicia, a second offensive was unleashed upon Serbia. This campaign likewise speedily came to grief; yet Russian statesmen, aware of the shortage of military equipment in Serbia, wondered whether the Belgrade government might not find it politic to make peace with Vienna. France promised to send aid.[15] Attacking once more in November, a Hapsburg host of 200,000 hammered into Belgrade on December 2, anniversary of Francis Joseph's accession to the throne, but the Serbs stubbornly fought back, cracked the Austrian front, recovered Belgrade, and expelled the enemy from the kingdom. Austro-Hungarian losses ran a third higher than the Serb. It seemed to the British historian George M. Trevelyan that the success of the Serbs was "the most thrilling feat of arms that this war had witnessed . . . a victory in which Washington and Garibaldi would have loved to take part . . . "

In a clever cartoon, "Austria beaten by the Serbs," the Dutch satirist, Louis Raemaekers, portrayed a stalwart Serb, gun and bayonet in hand, with a woman and child crouching behind him. A heavily bandaged Austrian stood beside a helmeted German who asked, "Why didn't you use *franc tireurs* more, as I did in Belgium?" The famous cartoonist followed up this piece of propaganda with another just before Christmas showing the venerable

Francis Joseph, wearing his imperial robes, and offering the Christ-child a cannon as a gift; the Austro-Hungarian minister protested to the Netherlands government over this ghoulish creation.[16]

For Serb patriots, it appeared that the prayer enshrined in the national hymn of their people was being answered.

> God of Justice, thou who didst save
> From downfall the Serbian People.
> Hear henceforth our voice, we pray Thee
> Be forever our salvation!
>
> By Thy mighty hand guide, direct
> The vessel of our future
> God save, God protect
> The Serbian King, the Serbian People.

On the other hand, the small Socialist party of Serbia set up a clamor for peace in its press, though blank spaces often revealed the hand of censorship. In parliament, Socialist deputy Laptsčhević shouted that his fellows had "enough of subservience to Russia. Will you make a second Belgium of Serbia?" He seems to have escaped punishment, though other protestants were clapped into jail.

Accompanied as the Austro-Hungarian expulsion from Serbia was by large losses in manpower and material, the turn of events in the south increased the sense of moral depression in the Monarchy. The American ambassador reported that military fervor in Czech and Hungarian circles had already touched the vanishing point and that the financial and commercial classes of Vienna desired a quick restoration of peace. The evacuation of Belgrade, lamented the representative of Francis Joseph in Madrid, had reduced the prestige of the Monarchy almost to zero;

[16] Giskra to Burián, Ap. 19, 1915, P.A., Haag, *Berichte*, 1915.

"I could scarcely appear on the street out of shame," he commented.[17]

Blamed for the catastrophes in the south, Potiorek was replaced as supreme commander in that theater by Archduke Eugene. Along the battle front, quiet prevailed until the autumn of 1915, while the Serbs grappled with an adversary far more destructive than the guns of the secular foe—a terrible typhus epidemic which carried off about 150,000 soldiers and civilians, as well as some 70,000 war captives, in the space of six months.[18] Meantime, the military energies of Austria-Hungary were fully engaged against the Russians and against Italy.

5.

Under circumstances to be examined farther along, the kingdom of Italy declared war upon Austria-Hungary in May of 1915. Not only were the battle lines of the Monarchy thereby extended by nearly two hundred and seventy-five miles, but the naval challenge in the Adriatic assumed a rather different complexion. At the outset of the fighting only about 100,000 Hapsburg troops were posted along the borders of Italy, mainly in two sectors—the tongue of southern Tyrol, known as the Trentino (Generals Krauss and Dankl) and eastward in the valley of the Isonzo (Boroević), and the region leading down to Trieste. In both areas, military science and nature herself favored a defensive posture for the Austrians. In no other war zone was the natural environment more forbidding or harsher: rough, mountainous terrain, which engineers had rendered still more impregnable with gun emplacements; in wildernesses of rock and ice, communication was restricted to pack mules, dog sleds, or aërial

[17] Fürstenberg to Berchtold, Jan. 4, 1915, P.A., Madrid, *Varia*, 1915.
[18] Richard P. Strong, "The Anti-typhus Campaign in 1915 in Serbia," *International Journal of Public Health*, I (1920), 7–33, 188–210.

railways. "It was more the setting of an opera," an Austrian civilian-soldier recorded, "than a potential battlefield." Duels between cannon mounted on towering summits lent a certain picturesqueness to what otherwise was monotonously dull warfare. Innovations in training made possible fighting above the snow level, something never attempted in previous wars; this sort of fighting, which netted only slender gains for either side, contrasted sharply with Bonaparte's dashing Italian campaign of 1796–97.

Aside from inferiority in number of divisions, Austria was handicapped by transport problems in switching reserves from one front to the other, while the Italians enjoyed the very real advantage of operating on interior lines. It was a rather lighthearted Roman cabinet which had thrown down the gauntlet to Vienna, for it was believed that the Italian sword would quickly tip the scales to the Entente side and that peace would be restored within six months. Though one Italian general described the national army as "a ship lost in the Dead Sea," other military chiefs, scornful of the fighting capabilities of Hapsburg armies, talked glibly of occupying Trieste in a matter of days, storming into Vienna, and feeding Italian troops from the wheatlands of Hungary. It was assumed that the Russian steam roller would conduct a powerful offensive in the north, while the Serbs stabbed vigorously from the south. Events shattered both of these optimistic hypotheses.

Directing the military resources of Italy was General Luigi Cadorna of Piedmontese noble stock, an army man by family tradition, training, and temperament. A keen student of military affairs, he was internationally respected for his knowledge of war in all its branches, especially artillery. Rising fast in the military hierarchy, Cadorna had been appointed chief of staff in June, 1914 and immediately set about, as he recounted in his memoirs, improving the poorly disciplined, bady paid and inadequately equipped troops and nerving them for contemporary styles of warfare. Devout Catholic that he was, energetic and strong-willed, he encountered personal and professional difficulties with suspicious anti-clericals in high Italian civilian posts. Since the Italian forces were insufficient to mount an offensive against Austria-Hungary all along the line, he chose to stand on the defensive to the north in the Trentino and to attack boldly in the east.

Taking Trieste and Laibach (Ljubljana) as his larger goals, Cadorna, late in June, 1915, struck resolutely toward the Isonzo River—the first of four assaults delivered there that year, the first of eleven battles of the Isonzo to be waged before the war was over. Soldiers of Francis Joseph, notably South Slavs, fought spiritedly against perfidious Italy and gave up only strategically inconsequential positions. By the end of 1915 Italian casualties were twice as large as the Austro-Hungarian, and though the red, white, and green tricolor pinned down large bodies of Hapsburg troops, the fighting had not prevented Central Power conquest of Russian Poland and of Serbia and Montenegro. Yet, considering all theaters of the war, by January of 1916 Hapsburg losses approached three and a half millions, of which 10 per cent had been killed, nearly a third wounded, an equal proportion sick, and almost a million listed as prisoners or missing. To satisfy manpower needs the military service law had been broadened to embrace males in the age range from fifteen to fifty-five years.

Before the war Conrad had worked out with meticulous exactitude a brilliant thrust against Italy from the Trentino, and in May of 1916 the blueprint was put to performance. To knock Italy out in one massive offensive—and the objective was nothing less than that—Conrad required reinforcements from Germany. "I regard the offensive against Italy," he jotted down in his diary, "as the final decisive contest in which for many urgent and imperative reasons, the Austro-Hungarian Monarchy must seek to win success before the year 1916 closes." Unconvinced of the validity of the Conrad project, and determined to conquer French Verdun in 1916, the Berlin strategists, Falkenhayn leading, turned down the Austrian appeal. Victory would come quickest and most surely, Falkenhayn and his advisers calculated, with hard blows in the west to the very heart of France. All other theaters of war were subsidiary to this supreme purpose; the Italian front, Falkenhayn bluntly remarked, lay beyond the range of Germany's direct concern. Believing an offensive in France to be impracticable until the enemies in the east had been humbled, Conrad had clamored for German soldiers and supplies, and painful clashes of judgment, as in the very first months of the struggle, reappeared. By its adverse decision, the German high command missed what seems to have been a singularly propitious chance in 1916 to remove Italy from the formidable list of opponents.

Without revealing his timing to the Germans, Conrad resolved to deliver a surprise assault from the Trentino upon the detested Italians relying solely on Austro-Hungarian divisions. Heavy falls of snow, however, necessitated delay in operations until mid-May, and by then Cadorna had made ready to withstand attack. The new heir of Francis Joseph, the Archduke Charles, was given nominal command of the troops in the Tyrol; initially, the Austrians, including divisions pulled down from the Russian front, carried all before them, thrusting eastward of the Adige River and even seizing the Asiago Plateau, no more than an hour's march from the open plain of Lombardy. If that region were taken, Hapsburg armies might then sweep to the Adriatic and cut off the Italians in the Isonzo theater; to escape disaster Cadorna rushed in reinforcements from the east. Under the shock of the Austrian advance, Premier Antonio Salandra, who had steered Italy into the war, was obliged to resign; he had quarreled with the high command over strategy, but more important, doubtless, his estimate of a short war had been rudely falsified. The Danube Monarchy had demonstrated afresh that it possessed fighting qualities and a will to win that foreign experts had not anticipated. Fortunately for Cadorna, the empire of the Tsar responded to appeals for help with a sensational drive—the Brusilov offensive, recounted below. Without that assistance, and if Germany had furnished support as requested, it seems not improbable that Italy could have been broken in 1916. As matters worked out, the lightning Brusilov stroke necessitated transferral of Hapsburg troops from the Italian zone to the north. Faced by little more than rearguard contingents, Cadorna counterattacked, recovering half the area that had recently been lost, and forcing the Austrians to take cover in prepared positions. Once more the Trentino district settled into comparative somnolence.

On August 6, 1916, Cadorna mounted yet another major offensive in the Isonzo sector, and, after skillful and stubborn resistance, the Austrians were compelled to evacuate Gorizia (Görz), a key army base on the Isonzo, splendidly protected by natural defenses and elaborate fortifications, though no Hapsburg "Verdun" as romantic military critics were wont to call it. While the community itself was abandoned, the Italians were unable to seize the heights overlooking the town; and the capture, the first considerable setback administered to Austria by Italy, did not throw open the route to Trieste, as Italian strategists had fancied would come to pass. True enough, the terrain intervening was frightfully rugged, the rocky, treeless, waterless Karst (Carso) district, with enemy gunners concealed in hollows, and mountains in places as steep as the side of a house—all made the worse by the ruthless *bora*, a wind that carried along clouds of dust or rain, sleet, or snow. Three times late in 1916 Austrian troops halted heroic Italian thrusts, which netted only scanty parcels of ground.

6.

In the Russian theater, meanwhile, the pendulum had switched unmistakably to the Central Empires. After the loss of Przemyśl, the Hapsburg armies pursued "a gentlemanly routine," a defensive posture, and again Russians opened a path into the Hungarian plain. Jubilant western newspapers hazarded the guess that Muscovites would garrison Budapest by June, 1915. On the Austrian side, in reality, it was the calm before the storm. Conrad devised an imaginative plan to break through the enemy lines at Gorlice-Tarnow, directly north of the Carpathian mountains, wheel behind the Russians if possible, and sever their communications with the east. It was a gigantic enterprise, worthy of the first military brain of the day, but too big for Hapsburg divisions to carry out unaided. The German Chief of Staff Erich von Falkenhayn assented to the project—assented reluctantly, for he thought the war could only be won in France, and agreed to furnish German soldiers and guns. At the beginning of the massive drive eastward, red-trousered Hapsburgers and German troops participated in about equal proportions, and the German commander August von Mackensen had general supervision of the campaign.

On May 2, 1915, the vastly superior artillery of the Central Empires unloosed a murderous barrage between Gorlice and Tarnow which caused the tsarist defenses to crumble. Although insufficiency of transport slowed up the pursuit, the Central Allies swept the enemy from nearly all of Galicia, the Bukowina, and Russian Poland in under four months, capturing hundreds of thousands of prisoners and quantities of military supplies in the process. Galician oil-wells, put out of commission by the retreating Russians, were rapidly restored to production. These glittering successes wonderfully inspirited morale on the Austro-Hungarian home front; in a succession of special editions, the *Neue Freie Presse* interpreters and military correspondents such as the Hungarian playwright, Francis Molnár, lauded the exploits of the armies of the Central Empires and so helped to offset the feeling of depression induced by the intervention of Italy and a grave diplomatic quarrel with Washington following the destruction of the "Lusitania." Upon news of the recapture of Przemyśl and Lemberg (Lvov), Hapsburg cities and hamlets staged boisterous mass celebrations; in Vienna a solemn *Te Deum* was sung in St. Stephen's Cathedral to mark the recovery of Lemberg. Certain Hapsburg diplomatists thought the time now ripe to consider seeking a separate peace with the battered tsardom.

Entente writers, on the other hand, sought to explain —or explain away—the terrible Russian débâcle without mentioning controversies in the tsarist high command or dwelling much on the cruel shortage of rifles and munitions. It was recalled, for instance, that the Muscovites had fallen back before the onslaught of Napoleon I, but had kept the fight going until the invader had been decisively thrashed. This chapter of the past would be duplicated, it was confidently predicted—the disciplined, patient endurance of the inexhaustible Russian manpower, the constant attrition of the armies of the Central Empires ensured, it was said, the military recovery of the Slav colossus. Learning that the Austrians had hacked their way back into Lemberg, the London *Times* marvelled, not that the Russians had been expelled, but that they had achieved so much against enormous odds. "The reverse will only strengthen the indomitable resolution of the Russian army," it was ventured consolingly, "and of the Russian nation to maintain an unyielding resistance to the foe." [19] Early in August, great Warsaw fell to the Central Empires, but expectations of a gigantic envelopment of tsarist divisions were not realized; in the ensuing two months Austrian arms were routed more than once, but the episodes possessed only local importance. The approach of winter soon called a halt to campaigning, and by then the battlefront had been pressed to a line running roughly from Riga to Czernowitz (Cernăuţi) in the Bukowina, and the empire of the Tsar had suffered disasters from which it would never recover.

Highly pleased with the swift march of events Hindenburg observed, for consumption in the Monarchy, "This war must not come to an end without just punishment being inflicted on the three chief criminals—England, Serbia, and Italy." He recalled that he had first met Austrians as an enemy on the battlefields of 1866. "It was in that campaign that I first learned to know Austrians—and to appreciate them"; whether his tongue was in his cheek the interviewer neglected to note.[20]

By the autumn of 1915, better than 8,000,000 Russians had been called to the colors, and the losses verged on the fantastic: approximately 1,400,000 had been killed or wounded, 1,000,000 had been taken captive, and huge quantities of irreplaceable military supplies had fallen to the Central Empires. In a manner that would become more vehement in the Second World War, Russian spokesmen protested that Britain and France "sat still like rabbits," obliging their country to shoulder the entire military burden; propagandists of the Central Powers naturally strummed upon this theme in psychological warfare addressed to the tsardom. On September 8, 1915 Nicholas II took over the supreme command in the stead of the discredited Grand Duke Nicholas, a change in

[19] June 24, 1915.
[20] *NFP*, Dec. 5, 1915.

leadership that identified the Tsar more intimately with military catastrophes and accompanying human misery.

7.

Even more cheering to many an Austro-Hungarian heart than the striking progress against Russia was the subjugation in 1915 of Serbia and Montenegro. To carry out that objective, Bulgaria was wooed and won to the Central Powers bloc, and the Germans promised assistance, though in defiance of the counsels of Hindenburg and Ludendorff. Apart from erasing the political and military humiliations at the hands of the Serbs in 1914, Vienna and Berlin were anxious to open a throughway for supplies to Turkey and to exert a decisive influence upon uncommited Balkan cabinets.

On October 7, 1915, armies of the Central Empires struck southward across the Danube, subjecting Belgrade to terrific bombardment, and forcing it to capitulate. Thereupon, Bulgarian divisions, in tune with agreement, pressed into southern Serbia, cutting the vital railway supply line down to Greek Salonica. Anglo-French troops, shipped into Salonica, advanced to the relief of Serbia, but they were no match for the Bulgars and soon pulled back to their starting point. Conrad pleaded with characteristic earnestness for the seizure of Salonica, but German commanders imposed a veto, arguing that the undertaking would possess little strategic value and might persuade Greece to team up with the Entente—something Anglo-French diplomacy had been assiduously striving to accomplish, London even dangling Cyprus as bait before the ministry at Athens. Except for occasional sorties into Bulgaria, the Entente garrison stationed in Salonica remained immobile until the autumn of 1918; Central Power wits jibed at Salonica as the largest of all concentration camps.

Squeezed between Hapsburg and German divisions on the north and Bulgars on the east, the Serbs, Putnik in command, fought gallantly, and contrived to escape encirclement, but assistance promised by the Entente powers failed to come up to expectations. The Viennese were informed that Serbia was the victim of a gross betrayal—"The Entente has tossed Serbia aside like a squeezed lemon . . . the strong man protects his friends; the weak man [i.e. the Entente] lets them sink without stretching out a hand to save them." [21]

In November, 1915, the battered Serb troops started across the rough, heartless terrain of Albania and Montenegro to the Adriatic coast where Entente seapower would afford protection. It was a ghastly exodus, civilians mingling with soldiers, some 25,000 Austrian prisoners of war going on before, not less dramatic than the famous march of Xenophon's Ten Thousand; in the motley array were about 3,000 Montenegrins who had deserted from the Austrian army. Under the influence of Austrian Catholic propaganda and armed with Austrian rifles, Albanian tribesmen were far from friendly to the refugees. Upon arrival at the harbors of Durazzo (Durrës) and Scutari (Usküdar), about 150,000 destitute Serbs were hauled away to the Greek island of Corfu (Corcyra), which the French had seized in January, 1915. After a sharp encounter with Entente warcraft off Durazzo, the Hapsburg fleet hardly interfered with the transit to Corfu; there the cabinet of Nikola Pašić set up shop, and the remnants of the Serb armies were re-equipped and trained by a French military mission before being transferred in the summer of 1916 to Salonica. Hundreds of Serb and other Yugoslav refugees preferred to take up residence in Switzerland, where fierce feuds over the political future of the South Slavs flared up between partisans of the Greater Serbia formula and friends of a

[21] *NFP*, Nov. 10, 1915.

federalized Yugoslavia who saw eye-to-eye with a South Slav Committee in London.

By reason of the victories in the south, the channels of Central Power communication ran uninterruptedly from the North Sea to Mesopotamia. In high spirits, Professor Hans Uebersperger of Vienna rejoiced that "next to the fundamental satisfaction of seeing the crime of June 28, 1914 atoned for by the total annihilation of the Russian vassal on our southeastern frontier, we must place the joy of direct and secure communication with the Turkish ally. All this means that the Entente has lost the war," but other blows would need to be delivered, he warned, before the enemy would concede the point.[22] "Dreams beyond attainment a short time ago are becoming realities," exulted the Vienna *Reichspost* when a new bridge was thrown across the Danube at Belgrade.

Occupation of Serbia and of Montenegro, which followed shortly, stirred up debate on the disposition of the conquered countries. Conrad and those who shared his views desired to divide up Serbia with Bulgaria, annex Montenegro bodily, and establish effective Austro-Hungarian control over Albania. These and other possibilities were sharply assailed by Tisza, who stood firmly on the position that only strategically useful border areas of Serbia should be taken over; he proposed that after the parcels of Serbia promised to Bulgaria had been cut away, a section should be assigned to Albania and the remainder of Serbia should remain free but linked to the Dual Monarchy by economic bonds. "The continuance of the war does not depend on us," the Magyar statesman told a reporter, "it does not rest with those who are only defending their territory to say when the war shall end . . . Serbia will be curtailed and weakened . . . She must not be left in such a position that she can be . . . the permanent source of danger that she has been

22 *NFP*, Nov. 7, 1915.

till now . . ." "We do not ask for the complete destruction of our enemies," said Count Julius Andrássy of Hungary, "but would be content with such guarantees as would preserve the position we have at present, while the Entente wishes to annihilate Central Europe." [23] Appraising the sentiments of ordinary folk in the Hapsburg realm, on the war, it seemed to the American Embassy in Vienna that the dominant feeling was that fighting should now stop, inasmuch as the Monarchy had taken up arms solely to punish Serbia. How some of the Austrian fighting men felt about the purposes of the war was reflected in the letter of a soldier, opened after his death. "We go to battle for freedom and justice and we struggle for a lasting peace. This is what the priest said today in his sermon. . . . If this is really attained, then I shall not have yielded my young life in vain . . . My spur to endurance is the thought of world peace which is to follow this world war." [24]

On the heels of the conquest of Serbia, Montenegro succumbed to the greatly superior Austrian forces after a fortnight of hard fighting on land and with naval support. The little Slav kingdom had joined in the struggle on August 5, 1914, only after a good deal of pressure from St. Petersburg and somewhat to the astonishment of the Ballplatz, which had been secretly negotiating with the king for neutrality. Before the war King Nicholas had manifested complete distaste for schemes to unite Montenegro with Serbia, which, if consummated, would rob him of his crown. The bulk of the Montenegrin armed forces, instead of fighting shoulder to shoulder with the Serbs, had been dispatched into Albania, where the Montenegrins vied with several competitors to win control.

Early in January, 1916, the Montenegrin ministry was apparently much divided on the question of surrender,

[23] *NFP*, Nov. 3, Dec. 21, 1915.
[24] *AZ*, Dec. 19, 1915.

but on the 17th, Nicholas formally capitulated, yielding up territory never fully overpowered by ancient Roman legions, by Turkish conquerors, or by the armies of Napoleon I. Austrian occupation of Mount Lovčen, over-hanging the key harbor of Cattaro (Kotor) and often saluted as the Adriatic Gibraltar, touched off popular ex-uberance in the Monarchy. "We now feel for the first time," exclaimed the *Neue Freie Presse,* "that the Bay of Cattaro and the southern coast of Dalmatia really belong to us." Over in Rome it was said that the Hapsburg suc-cess had put Italy's position in the Adriatic in dire jeopardy.

To the amazement of the Ballplatz, King Nicholas and his faithful first minister Lazar Miuškovic fled to Italy. Foreign Secretary Burián remarked that the king had agreed to negotiate on terms of peace, but that when Aus-trian diplomatic agents reached Montenegro they dis-covered that Nicholas had run away.[25] Yet his second son, Prince Mirko, drifted to Vienna avowedly to obtain treat-ment for tuberculosis, though it was unclear whether he was in fact a guest or a prisoner; an Austrophile at heart, the Prince intended perhaps to promote the political in-terests of his family should the Central Powers win the war. Until the death of Mirko at Vienna in March, 1918, stories circulated that Hapsburg policymakers wished to seat him on a South Slav throne annexed to the Mon-archy; in any event, he was the recipient of substantial sums from the Ballplatz, which fancied Montenegro would become a Hapsburg satellite after the war.

The picturesque "peasant king" Nikita took up resi-dence in France, where he lived modestly on Entente subsidies and dreamed of a federal Yugoslavia in which his dynasty would continue to rule Montenegro; but a

[25] Penfield to Lansing, Jan. 27, 1916, U.S., *National Archives,* 763.72/2357. See also, Alexander Devine, *Montenegro* (London, 1918), and Harry Hanak, *Great Britain and Austria-Hungary during the First World War* (London, 1962), p. 64.

faction of exiled Montenegrin politicians, led by ex-Premier Andrew Radović—"my fourth son," Nikita once called him affectionately—advocated unrestricted integration of Montenegro in a Yugoslav state. Wherever possible, Radović spread the charge that the king had treacherously broken off armed resistance to the Hapsburg invader—and the accusation, groundless or not, stuck. Entente sentiment came to favor the merger of Montenegro with Serbia.

Until the end of the war, Hapsburg and Bulgarian officials governed Serbia with the Morava River as the line of demarcation between the two zones. The Austrians strove to merit the good-will of the native population; foreigners working in a Serbian hospital commented upon "the excessive politeness" of the occupying authorities. Properties that had been damaged in the fighting were repaired, schools and public welfare institutions were reopened, health facilities were improved, and the deadly typhus peril was effectively combatted—all financed for a time by Austria-Hungary. Newspapers, appearing under the auspices of the occupation officials, diffused sentiments sympathetic to a South Slav state inside the realm of the Hapsburgs.[26] As a constant reminder of the brutal murders of King Alexander and his wife in 1903, the Austrians raised a monument over their graves, explaining that they were victims of "criminal hands." Quite probably appeasing gestures made little impression upon the Austrophobe heritage of the Serbs; so often were Serbian infants surnamed *Slobodan* (freeman) or *Nadezhda* (hope) that Hapsburg officials advised the clergy that such names should not be permitted at baptism. And Serbian guerrilla fighters everlastingly tormented the army of occupation.

In July of 1917 the Hapsburg military government in Serbia was given a stronger civilian character; more care

[26] Ernst Klein, *The Road to Disaster* (London, 1940), p. 156.

was paid now to bettering agriculture and stock-raising, and plans were devised to extend railways. When the occupation came to an end in 1918, the Austrian zone of Serbia was materially better off than before the war; more children were in school and cultural activities had been somewhat "Europeanized." All in all, the occupation authorities could take pride in the results of their administration, and much the same record was written in primitive Montenegro but there, too, partisan warfare harried the alien occupiers.[27]

8.

Austrian forces also marched into the kingdom of Albania, a synonym for instability since its creation in 1913, and took control of approximately three-quarters of the country. Neighboring states, one and all, coveted sections of Albania, and exploited the opportunity which the war provided to nail down their claims. In the autumn of 1914 Italians seized the island of Saseno at the mouth of the Bay of Valona (Vlone) and shortly thereafter they moved into Valona itself. Greek troops set up a military administration in the extreme south—northern Epirus—and in June of 1915, Montenegro and Serbia assumed control in the northern and central areas respectively. The following January, Hapsburg commanders, upon entering Albania, proclaimed that their troops came as liberators and as such they were welcomed by some native leaders. The Austrians courted with especial finesse youthful Ahmed Zogu, a restless tribal chief who was placed in charge of a contingent of volunteer Albanian soldiers, until his loyalty was suspect—

[27] The realities of the Austrian administration of Montenegro have been divertingly sketched by Milovan Djilas, *Land Without Justice* (New York, 1958), pp. 60–90.

then he was whisked off to Vienna. After the war Zogu became in quick succession prime minister of Albania, president, and then king.

Not a little in the Hapsburg administration of Albania merited applause, and almost no trouble was experienced from rudimentary native nationalism. Schooling and economic life were moderately improved and narrow guage rail lines were laid down. It was announced in January, 1917, that the Monarchy intended to preserve the independence of Albania under the tutelage of Vienna; and in June the Italian commander to the south, on the authority of the cabinet in Rome, countered with a similar declaration, naming his country as the guardian angel. Coming as it did without consultation with allies, the Italian manifesto on Albania stirred up angry flutterings in Entente dovecots.

9.

In waging offensives against Serbia and Montenegro, the armies of the Central Empires benefited from the cooperation of Hapsburg seapower. Thanks to the driving dynamic of Archduke Francis Ferdinand, who, like William II of Germany, but unlike Francis Joseph, believed profoundly in the influence of seapower upon history, the fighting capacity of the Hapsburg fleet had been virtually doubled between 1906 and 1914. Promoters of the navy had Italy in mind as the potential enemy in pushing expansion, and yet in 1914 the Austrian seaforces would doubtless have been no match for Italy in open combat. An Austrian Navy League of some 50,000, presided over by Count Alfred Liechtenstein, waged a whole-souled crusade for an ever greater battlefleet; on the death of Francis Ferdinand, the new heir-apparent, Archduke Charles, took over the dignity of supreme patron of the League, which, early in the war, was reinforced by a like organization in Hungary, solidly backed by Premier Tisza.

When the war began, the Monarchy boasted three Dreadnaughts and a fourth slid down the ways at mid-1915.[28] Three new and six older battleships of the pre-Dreadnaught class and half a dozen small submarines of limited cruising range rounded out the principal units of the navy; glaring deficiencies existed in auxiliary craft such as cruisers and scouting vessels incorporating the latest innovations in naval architecture. At Pola (Pula), on the tip of the Istrian peninsula, and at Cattaro (Kotor), the Monarchy possessed its best naval stations, with Spalato (Split), Trieste, and Fiume (Rijeka) of secondary significance. By reason of the screen of islands fringing the Dalmatian coast, reinforced by coastal artillery and an elaborate tracery of minefields, Hapsburg men-of-war could pass with comparative immunity from sea base to sea base.

Commanding the Hapsburg naval forces was Admiral (Grand Admiral in May, 1916) Ante Haus, a Dalmatian farmer's son, and sometime professor of oceanography at the Austrian Naval Academy. Haus attracted the admiration of Francis Ferdinand and in 1913 had been promoted to the post of chief of the navy department in the joint Austro-Hungarian ministry of war and appointed an admiral. Crews of warships were recruited mainly from coastal-dwelling South Slav youths of the Monarchy. Uncertain as to which way Italy would jump, after assuming a neutralist stance in 1914, Haus, as cautious as he was capable, decided to husband his resources and hold to an essentially defensive policy in the Adriatic,

[28] On the naval aspects of the Monarchy at war, consult Hans H. Sokol (ed.), *Österreich-Ungarns Seekrieg, 1914–1918* (2 vols., Vienna, c. 1933); A. Thomazi, *La Guerre Navale dans l'Adriatique* (Paris, 1925); S. W. Gould, "Submarine Warfare in the Adriatic," *U.S. Naval Institute Proceedings*, LXX (1944), 683–689.

however untoward the effects upon morale of the naval personnel. Guardianship of the Adriatic approach to the Mediterranean was entrusted by the Entente to the French navy (Admiral Boué de Lapéyrère), Britain furnishing a few units.

Barely had the war started than Entente vessels began to blockade the Strait of Otranto, forty miles across, so as to prohibit communication by the Monarchy to or from the Mediterranean. Next a string of drifter vessels was stretched across the Strait, each ship being equipped with a steel net, extending as much as 180 feet beneath the surface of the water, to intercept submarines. A few U-boats were ensnared, but far more sallied into the Mediterranean and exacted an impressive toll of Entente cargo shipping. U-boats of Germany, working in the Mediterranean, sometimes hoisted the Hapsburg ensign, and by the end of 1916 about twenty German submarines had lairs in the splendid harbors of Cattaro Bay.

In the Adriatic itself, Hapsburg seaforces protected coastal shipping and sought to wear down the French watchdog by submarine action. On Christmas Day of 1914, a U-boat damaged the new French battleship "Jean Bart" near Otranto Strait, and on April 26, 1915, the "Léon Gambetta," an armored cruiser, proceeding in bright moonlight without a destroyer screen, was hit twice by torpedoes and sank in ten minutes with heavy loss of life. Thereupon, the French Admiralty pulled capital ships out of the dangerous Adriatic, though repeated assaults were made upon Pola (Pula) and the principal Austro-Hungarian submarine rendezvous, Cattaro (Kotor), without, however, doing much harm.

When in May, 1915, Italy became a belligerent, Austrian naval strategy underwent no little revision. German and the Pola shipyards had turned out several new warcraft, among them the "Novara," captained by Nicholas Horthy, a resourceful scion of Magyar gentry stock, once aide-de-camp of Francis Joseph and destined for highest responsibility in the Hapsburg naval arm. Upon the entry of Italy, the "Novara" delivered surprise raids upon towns and cities along the east coast of the kingdom, until driven off by shore batteries. Presently a daring Austrian U-boat sank the British cruiser, "Dublin," in spite of protecting destroyers, and another eliminated the older Italian "Giuseppe Garibaldi" and the battleship "Regina Margherita." These achievements evoked rapturous applause in the great press of the Monarchy. But the naval ledger had another side, for the Entente forces, now under the direction of Italian Vice-Admiral the Duke of Abruzzi, accounted for at least two enemy submarines, and bold Italian torpedo boats—the *bersaglieri* of the Adriatic—carried on guerrilla fighting, which cost the Monarchy both naval and merchant craft. Yet, on balance, in the first half of the war, sea warfare in the Adriatic clearly favored the Central Empires.

10.

So drastic had been the punishment inflicted in 1915 upon the armies of the Tsar, so seemingly insurmountable the débâcle, that commanders of the Central Empires, not to speak of laymen, might be forgiven for supposing that only defensive operations could be expected from Russia in the future. Amidst destruction and carnage, elements of humanity still persisted among troops on both sides of the trenches, as the following graphic portrayal of "An Easter Celebration" sufficiently attests.

Evening comes on; the frogs begin their nightly concert . . . It is 11 o'clock at night. Suddenly great masses of white and red and green rockets shoot up from the Russian trenches. At the same moment on the whole enemy front, a clear song rises, broken by occasional cheers. Over there, too, Easter has come. Soon quiet prevails again, and nothing is heard except the mighty blows of our men who are somewhere raising wire entanglements . . . Hardly is it light when a white flag is seen waving in the breeze, and is eagerly greeted from our side. Presently gangs of men emerge from trenches and make gestures. It is the same on our side; slowly they move forward on both sides to meet each other. Cautious men voice warning, but to no avail, for the soldiers want to meet. They halt on opposite sides of a river and can go no farther. Men laughed, chatted in Polish and made jokes. When an Austrian pulled out a cigarette and some cigars, a young Russian pulled off his boots and swam across the river . . . Handshaking. Others came over in a boat and greetings turned more cordial. Even Russian officers came across, bringing bacon and eggs. "We have enough of these things," they said, "but no bread to go along."

Friendly exchanges ran on for hours—peace seemed to have come. Suddenly, booming in the distance, and the soldiers dispersed hurriedly. Two grenades fly over the river and crash. Easter messages from the Russian artillery . . . our heavy guns reply. Soldiers hasten through the barbed wire . . . a crash before the trench and a man, horribly mangled, whirls through the air. Pieces of ragged flesh hang on the entanglement . . .[29]

Throughout the winter of 1915–16 and into the spring, the empire of the Tsar made intensive, wide-ranging preparations to resume the offensive. Greatly to the astonishment of the Austrian Command, on June 4, 1916, Russian forces struck hard into eastern Galicia and the Bukowina, whose defenses had been weakened by the diversion of regiments to Conrad's Trentino adventure. This ferocious Russian lunge, which ground fully to a stop only in October, carries the name of its principal commander, Alexei A. Brusilov, optimistic, talented, short in stature, peppery, resembling in truth the Austrian Conrad. On a wide front of three hundred miles, Brusilov unleashed four great armies in direct response to an

[29] AZ, May 14, 1916.

Italian appeal for an offensive which would compel the Hapsburg forces to reduce the suffocating pressure out of the southern Tyrol.

Although Brusilov possessed only a slight superiority in manpower, his soldiers surged forward hurricane-like, smashing three tiers of trenches in as many days and bagging 44,000 prisoners and their equipment. Once more Conrad cried aloud for help from Germany; the answer came promptly, but not in the quantity desired, and Hapsburg reserves had to be shunted from the Italian front to oppose the Muscovite onslaught. Within little more than a fortnight after the Brusilov drive began the Austro-Hungarian armies in the Bukowina had virtually disintegrated, and, as in the Galician theater earlier, desertions ran high. Again tsarist troops swept close to the Carpathian passes leading into Hungary and the whole eastern front of the Central Empires seemed imperilled; again the imagination of Europe danced, the Entente hoping, the Central Powers dreading. Professor Redlich, for instance, thought the end was in sight for the Monarchy; *Punch* brought out a fresh "steam roller" cartoon: from the funnels of the monster smoke gushed forth, while ruined trenches and broken barbed wire was strewn around. Francis Joseph rushed wildly about, and as his cap fell to the ground, he shouted to Russia, "I say, you know, you're exceeding the speed limit."

Measured by territory seized and prisoners and guns captured, the Brusilov offensive was not only the outstanding military adventure of 1916, but one of the striking achievements in the martial annals of imperial Russia. For the last time though, the lumbering Slav colossus had responded heroically to the plea of an ally for assistance. Yet Russian sacrifices soared to appalling dimensions—possibly more than 700,000 killed and wounded, an even larger host of deserters, and reservists to take their places were insufficient; despite rising shipments from factories in Japan and the United States, Russian armaments ran short, and that handicap, together with sorry transport, caused the massive campaign to peter out. What westerners eagerly interpreted as the regeneration of the empire of the Tsar proved in fact to be its death-knell. Morale at the front and in the Russian cities sagged, while gathering urban privations intensified discontent and revolutionary stirrings. For those with ears to hear, the roar of the avalanche sounded clearly and ominously.

As the Russian peril abated, war correspondent Francis Molnár could report that the Austro-Hungarian soldiers were more worried by approaching autumn rains and the frost and snow of winter than by Cossack shot and shell. Actually, so greatly had Hapsburg manpower resources been depleted that the bottom of the barrel had to be scraped. Falkenhayn attributed the Brusilov gains to the incompetence of Conrad, called for his demotion, and for the unification of the Central Powers' command in the east. The cabinet of Vienna reluctantly complied, and Emperor William II assumed the dignity of generalissimo in the east on September 6, 1916, but the arrangement came to an end with the death of Francis Joseph two months later.[30]

11.

In the meantime, the ever more popular giants, Hindenburg and Ludendorff, the latter an able commander but stupidly ambitious and politically obtuse, had superceded Falkenhayn in supreme command, and the dramatic Brusilov advance had induced the hesitant cabinet of Rumania on August 27, 1916, to cast the national

---

[30] Gisbert Beyerhaus, *Einheitlicher Oberbefehl* (Munich, 1938), a short, but competent treatise. Hermann von Kuhl, "Unity of Command among the Central Powers," *Foreign Affairs*, II (1923–24), 130–146.

sword onto the Entente side of the scales. 600,000 fresh troops faced the Central Empires, but the Rumanian officers corps left much to be desired. Popular Rumanian hatred of the Magyar foe found fierce, belligerent expression in poetry:

> Hungarian, thou mad dog, thou hast made me suffer; the time has come to avenge me.

> Hungarian with the long mustache,
> I have called on death to pursue thee, on flame
> to burn thee, on the cross to hang thee. La hora!
> May I dance to the flames of that fire.[31]

Blissfully assuming that territorial promises enshrined in a secret treaty with the Entente would be swiftly realized and at modest cost, Rumanian divisions dashed headlong into coveted Transylvania. Only about 34,000 Hapsburg soldiers, not of first quality at that, offered resistance; they were commanded by General Artur Arz von Straussenburg, himself as Transylvanian Saxon, and a future chief of staff of the Hapsburg armies. A section head in 1914 in the ministry of war, Arz had been entrusted with the task of mobilization planning, and on duty with troops, he had distinguished himself as a division and a corps commander.[32] If the Rumanian campaign had been unloosed two months earlier and if the Rumanian troops had been better equipped, the Hapsburg cause might well have suffered irretrievable disaster. Outnumbered ten to one, the Arz forces fell back and were joined in retreat by multitudes of refugees. Fierce protestations in the Budapest parliament and press over the management of diplomatic and military affairs prompted Tisza to implore Berlin for help, and the Germans responded rapidly and effectively.

---

[31] Quoted in *Literary Digest*, LIX (Jan. 13, 1917), 71.
[32] Artur Arz von Straussenburg, *Kampf und Sturz der Mittelmächte* (Vienna, 1935), thin but revealing reminiscences and reflections.

On September 25, 1916, the Central Powers commenced to roll hard against the Rumanians, with Falkenhayn pushing from the north and Mackensen commanding German, Bulgar, and Turkish regiments attacking on the south—both armies pointed for the capital city, Bucharest. After five days of fighting, Transylvania was cleansed of Rumanian troops and Hapsburg and German divisions advanced through supposedly impregnable Carpathian passes onto the flat lands of Rumania. Stocks of Rumanian munitions and food ran low and facilities to care for the wounded were incredibly bad; salvation must come, if it came at all, chiefly from Russia. Yet assistance from the east fell way below expectations and Entente assurances that troops from Salonica would checkmate the Bulgars turned out to be paper thin. Late in November, the northern and southern armies of the Central Empires clasped hands, and on December 6, barely three months after fighting had started, Bucharest, glorified as "the Paris of the East," capitulated and the valuable oilfields of nearby Ploesti were seized. Better than half of the Rumanian soldiers had been taken captive, killed, or were reported missing; the fragment that was spared concentrated in the north, where it kept the fight going at a modest tempo with limited help from France.

The condign thrashing administered to Rumania lifted spirits in the Danube Monarchy, not alone because the punishment was an appropriate sequel to baseless diplomatic treachery, but also because foodstuffs and oil, it was imagined, would presently be flowing from the conquered kingdom. Straightaway the Central Powers set about extracting the maximum economic aid from Rumania as fast as possible. Workmen in town and countryside were subjected to military discipline and strictly rationed, but corruption and evasion of regulations ran rampant; wily peasants, for example, concealed grain in coffins which were lowered into graves with traditional

ritual and solemnity. Food exports to the Central Empires
from the occupied areas of Rumania never reached really
substantial levels and a full year elapsed before appre-
ciable quantities of oil were available.

12.

Now that Rumania had been largely overrun, all of
the Balkan peninsula, save for neutral Greece, had been
drawn into the orbit of the Central Empires, either by
alliance or conquest. At the end of the first half of the
war the only portions of the Dual Monarchy in enemy
possession were the Gorizia (Görz) sector held by Italy
and a small parcel of the Bukowina in Russian occupancy.
Over against that, Hapsburg troops, either alone or in
conjunction with their allies, exercised mastery over Russian Poland, most of Rumania and Albania, and all of
Serbia and Montenegro. It is stated in the official Austrian
history of the war that by the end of 1916, 7,500,000 men
had been enrolled in the fighting services; a minor sensation was created in Hungary that year when roving
gypsies were summoned for military duty. To satisfy
manpower needs, army physical standards had been
steadily lowered. Something like a million and a half
Austro-Hungarians had been taken prisoner and nearly
as many more were either missing, incapacitated beyond
further service, or killed.

Few were remembered in obituary notices such as that
of Lieutenant Theodor Schwerwacher, son of the sacristan
of Vienna's Votivkirche, who met death on the plains of
Poland. "His life was dedicated to duty; his death to the
Fatherland and God. His body rests far from home—the
memory of him will live shining in our hearts. In heaven
his soul will glory in the revelation of the greatness of
God. . . . Let us learn from the horrors of this war that
it is our duty to promote with all our power the cause

of compulsory international jurisdiction for the defense and protection of Christian civilization." [33]

At the end of 1916 Hapsburg military prospects looked as bright as at any time since the drums started to beat. Serbia and Montenegro lay prostrate and Rumania nearly so; Italy, after twenty months of war, had made no substantial progress in the rough country above the Adriatic and the Russian bear prowled in vain against the Carpathian barrier. Resounding Austro-Hungarian military successes tended to gild over humiliating defeats in the early stages of the struggle,[34] and troop morale in general held up remarkably well. Apart from ordinary patriotic spurs and a soldierly sense of duty, Catholic chaplains contributed uniquely to "chins up" attitudes. They offered a religious interpretation of the hard, boring contest, teaching that soldiers were doing the will of the Almighty, which would merit a suitable reward, and that "the Lord of Hosts is our Shield." Dedicated churchmen, in addition to conducting divine services, ministered to the wounded and to war prisoners; and scores of priests fell victim to shot and shell on the battlefields.[35]

For unusual valor Hapsburg soldiers were decorated with silver or gold "Courage Medals." Among the higher honors were the Great Cross Order of Leopold, *Pour la merité*, the Order of Stephen, and the much coveted Order of Maria Theresa, reserved for officers of extraordinary distinction; recipients of this last award were admitted to an élite fraternity whose grand master was the Emperor himself, were assured of modest pensions and patents of hereditary nobility. It was estimated that by 1917 upwards of three million medals of all grades

[33] *Illustrierte Wiener Extrablatt*, Nov. 20, 1914.

[34] Politicus, "The Plight of Germany's Dupes," *Fortnightly Review*, CVI (1916), 375 ff.—a lugubrious survey, though instructive as showing what outsiders were thinking.

[35] Viktor Lipusch, *Österreich-Ungarns Katholische Militärseelsorge im Weltkriege* (Graz, 1938). This agreeably detailed survey contains a wealth and variety of documentary materials.

had been handed out, consuming, as someone captiously observed, tons of sorely needed metal and thousands of yards of silk ribbon.

Up to a point, prisoners of war compensated for shortages of Austro-Hungarian civilian workers and they were freely transferred from place to place to meet demands for labor. Russians formed the great majority of the captives, the figure soaring by July, 1916 to 800,000, many of them deserters. Under detailed regulations, multitudes of prisoners were put to work on the land or in building roads for which they were paid pittances. Very large camps existed at Theresienstadt (Terezin) and Eger (Cheb) in Bohemia and at Györ in western Hungary, where Russian and Serb prisoners engaged in murderous feuds. It was reported in the *Retch* of Petrograd late in 1915 that escaped prisoners brought home stories of their fellows being shipped to Italian theaters to dig trenches or being placed in front of Austrian troops under fire of the enemy; similar stories, susceptible neither of proof or disproof, circulated in other countries as well.

The American Ambassador and his colleagues, who periodically inspected prison camps in the Dual Monarchy, concluded that the inmates were decently treated; for instance, some 90,000 prisoners incarcerated near Linz lived "in comfortable buildings erected in a 'town' laid out in squares, with cook-houses and other necessary adjuncts" such as Orthodox churches and sanitation was systematically looked after. "Pretty garden plots are laid out before some buildings . . . Running water is laid on at most of the camps and buildings are equipped with electric lights." Many Russian prisoners indicated a desire to stay in Austria-Hungary after the war was over.[36] These general impressions of the humane treatment of prisoners were reiterated by Penfield early in 1917 when

[36] Penfield to Lansing, July 30, 1915, U.S., *National Archives*, 763.72/2041.

war captives had risen to 1,100,000. Investigations of alleged abuses of prisoners revealed, he stated, that the
charges had been based upon misinformation. It gratified
the heart of the Ambassador that the American YMCA
started in 1916 to make existence a little more tolerable
for prisoners, organizing and setting up clubs and schools,
shows, games, and religious services. "The joy of a Russian of middle age writing the first letter of his life to his
family in the homeland, cannot easily be described," the
Ambassador observed.[37] Proposals for distribution among
Russian prisoners of a newspaper calculated to foster
anti-tsarist sentiments were turned down at first by the
Hapsburg military authorities:[38] but at least from January,
1917 onward, the ministry of war published a weekly in
the Russian language containing excerpts from Russian
newspapers, peace rumors, and related information.

Hapsburg soldiers taken captive by the Russians were
rather strictly segregated in keeping with the language
they spoke. Austrogerman and Magyar prisoners, for instance, were likely to be hauled off to the Siberian vast-
ness, (the prison eventually of more than a million), and
watched carefully, while Czechs, Slovaks, and even Poles
were allowed a good deal of freedom and kept mostly in
European Russia until after the March Revolution of
1917. Camps ranged anywhere from a few score men to
as high as 35,000. "Each was a Robinson Crusoe and
Siberia was the desert island," one captive dryly commented. Many private soldiers took employment as farm
workers, road builders, and the like. Food and clothing
seldom if ever exceeded minimum necessities, and the
incidence of illness stood high; in one prison installation
during the winter of 1915–16, 17,000 out of 25,000 inmates died of typhoid fever. Austrian physicians ex-

[37] Penfield to Lansing, Jan. 31, 1917, U.S., *National Archives*,
863.50/34.
[38] Von Gagern to Burián, June 21, 1915, July 8, 1915, P. A., Schweiz,
Berichte, 1915.

changed from Russia in 1916 reported that a sixth of the officers had perished because of unsanitary conditions in camp; wooden huts in Siberia had no illumination in the winter and instances of death by freezing occurred.[39]

The dreary daily round of the prisoner was enlivened by newspapers, now and then, music, lectures, language studies, or a chance Red Cross packet.[40] Russian propaganda, both before and after the Bolshevik seizure of power, played upon the minds and emotions of the captives. Among Czechs and Slovaks visions of national freedom were modestly fostered, and the unguarded remark of Bethmann-Hollweg that the war represented a contest between Germanism and Slavdom was strummed upon. After the November, 1917, *coup d'etat* emissaries of Bolshevism endeavored to attract prisoners to the Marxist analysis of society, and converts carried the Leninist gospel back to army camps or to their native cities and villages. Some prisoners grew fond of Russia and chose to remain permanently, while others, because of the revolutionary turmoil, had to wait years after the war before returning home.

Among these last were Hapsburg prisoners sequestered in Siberia east of Lake Baikal, whose hopes of getting back to Europe were interrupted by fighting Czechs and Slovaks. Armed clashes occurred between prisoners from the Monarchy who were not Czechs and Slovaks, equipped with weapons by Bolsheviks, and Czechoslovaks furnished guns by the Japanese. It was a situation that largely inspired a momentous decision of July 6,

[39] *Vossische Zeitung,* July 29, 1916.

[40] Burghard Breitner, *Unverwundet Gefangen* (Vienna, 1921), a revealing, detailed diary by a Viennese physician imprisoned near Vladivostok; Emil Lengyel, *Siberia* (New York, 1943), pp. 186–211; Gustav Krist, *Prisoner in the Forbidden Land* (London, 1938), lightweight, but not uninteresting; Elsa Brändström, *Among Prisoners of War in Russia and Siberia* (London, 1929), the author was dubbed "the angel of Siberia." Heinrich Benedikt, *Die Friedensaktion der Meinlgruppe 1917–18* (Graz, 1962), pp. 263–266.

1918, in Washington to collaborate with the Japanese in aiding the Czechoslovaks. Ripe scholarship has cast grave doubt upon the wisdom of dispatching American troops to Siberia to help the Czechs, who in fact fought Bolsheviks, hoping to throw down the infant Red regime far more than they did Hapsburg war prisoners, but that was unknown to senior officials in Washington.[41] War captives especially skilled in crafts, who were imprisoned in Italy, were set to work building up glass, leather, and toy industries.

13.

As part of the war on the psychological front, both sets of belligerents published accounts of bestial inhumanities commited upon soldiers and non-combatants alike. It was charged by Serbs, for example, that Austrians and their even more vicious Hungarian partners were guilty of putting the torch to hospitals, maltreating prisoners and innocent women and children, firing dumdum bullets, and kindred atrocities. Following a journey to Serbia early in 1915, British historian George M. Trevelyan reported on ghastly outrages perpetrated by Hapsburg soldiers, such as the murder in cold blood of upwards of 2,000 civilians. "The Serbs are less barbarous than their great 'civilised' neighbor," affirmed the distinguished biographer of Garibaldi. To investigate and report on Austro-Hungarian barbarism, the Serbian government employed R. A. Reiss, reputedly a distinguished Swiss professor of criminology, though in reality a slick journalist endowed with a fertile imagination. Through public lectures and pamphlets he depicted horrors in Serbia no less gruesome than the atrocities of which the Germans were accused in Belgium, and the assumed profes-

[41] George F. Kennan, *The Decision to Intervene* (Princeton, 1958), pp. 400–403.

sional standing of Reiss invested his narratives with special credibility. "I shall continue to fight," said he, "for the fair land of Serbia till the moment arrives when the red, blue and white tricolour . . . shall wave wherever the Serbian tongue is spoken . . . "[42]

With a preface by the eminent British barrister William Joynson-Hicks, a searing indictment of *Austro-Magyar Judicial Crimes* (1916) was published in London. Although he could not accept at face value all the statements in the pamphlet, Joynson-Hicks nonetheless believed that the Hapsburg Monarchy conducted warfare as cruelly as its German partner and that the published summaries of horrors committed in the name of law should disillusion those of his countrymen who conceived of Austria-Hungary as a civilizing asset and needful for the security of Europe. The Entente press carried long accounts of heartless deportations of Bosnian Serbs, who were accused of treason, and it was also charged that Austrian troops employed a kind of mace, studded with iron spikes, to kill injured Italian soldiers.

Italian psychological warfare accented the theme that the Monarchy as in previous wars conducted the fighting with no less bestiality than the Germans; it was juvenile superstition to suppose that Austrians were good-natured and chivalrous. "In trickiness and low cunning," declared an Italian propaganda piece, "the Prussian is a clumsy amateur when compared with his Austrian brother-in-arms." Not only were prisoners maltreated, but civilian populations in invaded areas were brutally plundered, young women sadistically ravaged, and in payment for outrages of frightfulness cheques were cir-

[42] *The South Slav Bulletin*, Feb. 21, 1916; R. A. Reiss, *Austro-Hungarian Atrocities* (London, 1916) was a representative product. In the nature of a reply to such outpourings was a booklet, Erwin Janischfeld, *Kultur . . . drei Briefe an Professor Reiss* (Zürich, 1915). See, also, C. Langfeld (ed.), *Gegen Lug und Trug, Deutschlands und Österreich-Ungarns Schicksalstunde in Wort und Bild Ihrer Feinde* (Leipzig, 1915).

culated "payable by Cadorna" or "payable by Jesus Christ." "Austria," it was stated, "acted on the principle of wholesale extermination" of Italians in conquered areas.[43]

Propaganda from Hapsburg sources equally reminded citizens of atrocities by the enemy; horror stories and pictures made a morbid popular appeal in all warring countries not unlike unadulterated pornography. Following an official investigation, the Vienna Foreign Office issued a fat *Red Book* in April of 1915, citing enemy enormities, Serbs being excoriated as even more infamous than Cossacks.[44] Presently a supplement appeared and in the autumn of 1916 a companion Austrian *Red Book* relating violations of customary laws of war came off the press. As examples of cruelty, it was said that Serbian "women bring water, milk or wine for the thirsty—all poisoned"; or women carrying infants approached knots of Austro-Hungarian soldiers, and dropped the babies—which in fact were lethal bombs. The military press bureau in Vienna published a large collection of documents concerning Cossack atrocities in invaded districts, especially cruelties inflicted upon families of the Jewish tradition. Hot indignation swept the press of the Monarchy in March, 1916, when the hospital ship "Electra" was torpedoed by an enemy submarine, presumably French, and two persons were carried to watery graves. Plenty of cases of man's inhumanity to man occurred wherever fighting took place, but a good few of the atrocity tales must be dismissed as purely fabrications designed to generate mass loathing of malevolent, sadistic foes. From one angle

[43] I. I. B., "Austrian Frightfulness," *Anglo-Italian Review*, I (1918), 62–70; Luke Hansard, "Early Austrian Frightfulness," *ibid.*, III (1919), 82–86; C. E. Prato, *Life in the Trentino Under the Austrian Heel* (London, 1918); cf. E. C. Crosse, *The Defeat of Austria As Seen by the Seventh Division* (London, 1919), pp. 92–93.

[44] *Sammlung von Nachweisen für die Verletzungen des Völkerrechtes durch die mit Österreich-Ungarn Kriegführenden Staaten* (Vienna, 1915).

of vision, the invocation of the submarine weapon by the Central Empires was the answer "to the greatest atrocity of the whole struggle"—the relentless efforts of the British blockade to starve out the enemy.[45]

[45] *NFP*, Jan. 9, 1916.

4. Uneasy Partners

FIRMLY ALLIED THOUGH THE CENTRAL EMPIRES WERE, sharp discords and endless divergences cropped up, as is the way with coalitions. For public consumption, it is true, the fiction of monolithic solidarity was proclaimed by top officials, and the press of the two countries sang of mutual respect, affection, and loyalty. After all, the partners were quite unequal, and the martial prowess and inner strength of Germany were a source of gratitude in the Monarchy, not untinged with envy. Many an Austrogerman was positively hypnotized by the achievements of the great northern ally, while Hapsburg court circles, jealous for the prestige of the Monarchy, smarted under the military and economic dependence upon Germany, and arrant boasting in the German press of military triumphs ruffled tempers in the official world of Vienna. As was repeatedly noted in the dispatches of Prince Gottfried Hohenlohe, appointed Austro-Hungarian ambassador to Germany just after the onset of war, lively doubts accumulated in Berlin as to whether the alliance with the Danubian Monarchy represented the quintessence of wisdom in foreign policy or indeed whether Austria-Hungary would in fact survive the struggle as a great power.[1]

William II astutely endeavored to deepen the sense of Nibelungen solidarity; on a visit to Vienna, for instance, he wrote in the war album of the municipal council, "Demnoch" (come what may). "A strong word for hard times," observed Mayor Richard Weiskirchner, "But we will hold to it." Agencies of propaganda shouldered the responsibility of uplifting hearts and minds and cementing inter-allied fraternity; highly placed personalities in each country showered allies with fulsome flattery and hearty assurances that their combined efforts would produce victory in the fullness of time. In leading cities of the Central Empires, chapters of a league of brothers-in-arms were established, and each ally praised the supreme commanders of the other. Remarked the *Süddeutsche Zeitung* of Stuttgart, "If it is true that Hindenburg's name inspires confidence in the Danube Monarchy, it is not less true of Conrad's name in Germany."

The centennial of the birth of Prince Otto von Bismarck elicited a spate of essays in newspapers of the Monarchy lauding the Iron Chancellor for his work in forging the Austro-German alliance of 1879, which for two generations had kept Europe at peace and in war was conclusively proving its worth. Equally, the birthday of William II was commemorated in 1915 throughout the Monarchy. At a gala party in Schönbrunn, Francis Joseph arrived in the uniform of a Prussian officer; in the Protestant church of Vienna the pastor invoked divine blessings upon the Hohenzollern Emperor, and the congregation sang the spirited "Heil dir im Siegers' Kranz." Austrogermans and to a degree Magyars looked upon William II, as the personification of Germany, with emotions akin to veneration. As a mark of friendliness, on the an-

[1] For example, Hohenlohe to Burián, Sept. 13, 1916, P.A., *Geheim*, III/173.

niversary of the death of the ill-starred and popular former Crown Prince Rudolph, the German ambassador placed a memorial wreath at his tomb.

Much was said and written about *Nibelungentreue*, fidelity of the allies each to the other, until all enemies had been humiliated. A poet of modest talents framed his emotions in verse form, under the title "Bis zum Ende":

> Mit Gift und Verleumdung geifert der Feind
> Wir aber stehen fest vereint
> Und reichen von Kampf uns die Hände.
> Das Schwert ist gezogen, die Fahne weht!
> Ob eine Welt auch gegen uns steht,
> Wir halten die Treue zu Ende.

Friendship and comradeship with allies served as the leitmotiv for a "Liebesgaben" by German authors to the influential journal *Österreichisches Rundschau*.[2] Professor Ernst Haeckel, one of the most respected of German intellectuals, in his contribution—"Dauern der Friede"— emphasized that the Central Empires must win a decisive victory in order to ensure their own independence, break the tyrannous grip of Britain upon the Continent, restore justice and law in international affairs, and create conditions of enduring peace. To broaden understanding and heighten solidarity, the Budapest government established a chair in the Magyar language and Hungarian history at the great University of Berlin. "Never has the meaning of our alliance been more beautifully brought home to us than by your music," commented an elderly German general, emotionally uplifted by a Berlin concert of the Vienna Philharmonic Orchestra.

2.

On many issues of international policy Vienna and Berlin were in fact far apart and so they remained to

[2] XLII (1915) the entire issue of March 15.

the end. No firm meeting of minds was ever reached, for instance, on the objectives, beyond the range of mutual self-preservation, for which the gruelling contest was being waged. Frequently in the first half of the war the two cabinets exchanged views on war aims, without arriving at clear-cut conclusions; it was agreed, however, that a public bid for discussion of peace terms would be rejected by the Entente and would simply fortify the will to win in enemy countries. Time and again the Ballplatz proposed to Berlin that it could foster peace sentiments in the United Kingdom by openly promising to restore Belgian independence at the close of hostilities.[3] Tisza was an early exponent of a compromise peace, though he repudiated any suggestion that the Monarchy should independently seek a settlement with the Entente; on errands to Berlin he unsuccessfully tried to smoke out senior officials on conditions of peace. So far as Serbia was concerned, Tisza held to his July, 1914, opinion that the Monarchy should restrict annexation to slight frontier rectifications; in his more sanguine moments he desired the enlargement of Galicia at the expense of Russia, and he favored setting off the predominantly Ukrainian-speaking portion of the province as a separate crownland of Austria.

A small but assertive twenty-year-old Austro-Hungarian Colonial Society, presided over by Dr. Ernst F. Weizl, raised demands for the acquisition of overseas possessions in the eventual peace settlement. The organ of the Society, *Kolonial Zeitung*, set forth conventional arguments for a place in the colonial sun by the only major power of Europe without holdings in underdeveloped regions of the globe. For Austro-Hungarian industry fresh sources of raw materials were required, it was urged, and outlets for manufactured wares, and colonies would afford places of settlement for emigrants, the point

[3] Burián to Hohenlohe, Nov. 26, 27, 1915, P.A., *Geheim*, XLVII/3-10.

being stressed that since 1880 upwards of four million sons and daughters of the Dual Monarchy had moved away and their skills and brawn were lost forever to the Fatherland. If colonies were procured in Africa, or even South America, the doctrine ran, emigrants would take up homes there, and the Hapsburg achievements in Bosnia demonstrated the capabilities of the Monarchy in improving underdeveloped areas, it was contended.[4]

3.

In spite of glowing public utterances, breathing the ardent faith of the Nibelung, painful disharmonies existed between the two supreme commands on strategy and related problems. It was easy for the men in Vienna to blame the German ally for military reverses and find a measure of solace therein; these matters have been touched upon in the preceding chapter. Asperities were tempered, to be sure, by the breath-taking battlefield successes of 1915–1916, but the soul of the spunky Conrad was not appeased. Following the triumphant offensive against Rumania in 1916, Hindenburg wired Conrad a telegram of warm praise, which inspired the Austrian to remark wryly to his wife, "if you like, keep this. It is an historic document—a recognition of Austria's services."

On one standard assignment of diplomacy—the winning of neutrals to intervention or, failing that, working to hold them neutral—the cabinets of Vienna and Berlin were generally agreed, though at times they were at variance on the precise means to the end. At the outset of the war the Central Empires scored a resounding coup by wheedling Turkey into their coalition—the state whose menacing military pressure centuries before had con-

---

[4] Tschirschky to Bethmann-Hollweg, Dec. 21, 1915, memorandum by Richard Seyfert, *et. al.*, Vienna, 1916, F.O. 553/329; London *Times*, Aug. 11, 1916.

tributed so crucially to the making of the Hapsburg Monarchy. For years, Central Power statesmen, tradesmen, and military men, Germans in the van, had been assiduously courting the friendship of the ruling authorities of Turkey, and when war approached in 1914 Hapsburg diplomacy initiated overtures in Constantinople for a formal alliance. Looked at in isolation, this move by the Ballplatz had a brash appearance, since the Turks had not forgotten how the Monarchy had in 1908 arbitrarily annexed their erstwhile province of Bosnia.

At mid-July 1914, the Marquis Johann Pallavicini, seasoned Hapsburg ambassador at the Porte and esteemed by Emperor Francis Joseph as one of the most competent officials in the diplomatic corps, felt that the odds inclined to the Entente, thanks to the activities of the Russian and French envoys and to Turkish suspicion of Italian ambitions in Asia Minor; yet, if the Monarchy pursued a vigorous policy against Serbia, as Pallavicini had been pleading, the tide of sentiment in Turkey might swing, for policymakers nurtured rooted distrust of the tsardom and its "historic mission" in the Strait area. He reminded the Ballplatz that if the Porte's request for an alliance before the Balkan wars of 1912–13 had been met, the stream of events in southeastern Europe would have run into radically different channels, and he reported that he was striving to effect a reconciliation between the Turks and Bulgaria, at war a year earlier.[5]

Initially, German diplomacy reasoned that the condition of Turkey, which had just fought three wars in as many years, would oblige the country to refrain from international commitments; one day, however, if war came, Turkey would align herself with the coalition that appeared to have the better prospect of winning. As the price of an alliance the Turkish cabinet, it was thought

[5] Ö.-U.A., nos., 10083, 10217, 10410; Pallavicini to Berchtold, July 25, 1914, P.A., 941, Krieg, 21a, Türkei.

in Berlin, would insist upon an iron-clad guarantee of protection against "the bear that walked like a man," and that seemed too much to pay. If Turkey stood on the side-lines, Russia would need to post troops along the borders as an assurance against abandonment of neutrality and that in itself would prove beneficial to the Central Empires.[6]

But on July 24, 1914, Emperor William II spoke up vigorously for a pact with the Turks, and Ambassador Baron Hans von Wangenheim, against his better judgment, obeyed instructions from Berlin. Conversations were immediately initiated with Turkish officials for an alliance which would remain in force until the end of 1918, in the event of hostilities with Russia. On the insistence of Vienna, the cabinet there was kept fully posted on the trend of the negotiations; Pallavicini generally worked hand-in-glove with the German ambassador at the Porte. With German General Liman von Sanders, chief of a military mission made up of two-score experienced German military specialists, exercising potent influence in Turkish army circles, Wangenheim appealed to Berlin for the dispatch of men-of-war which, together with the Turkish fleet, would outmatch Russian seapower in the Black Sea. In total secrecy, an alliance was drawn up and signed on August 2; not half a dozen Turks knew about the treaty which commited their country to fight shoulder to shoulder with the Central Powers against the empire of the Tsar.[7]

Since German-Russian fighting had already started, pressure was applied upon the Turks to draw the sword from the scabbard at once, but they dilly-dallied due to military and economic unpreparedness, uncertainty regarding Bulgaria and Rumania, dire threats by the En-

[6] For a sheaf of informative documents, see Ernst Jaeckh, *The Rising Crescent* (New York, 1944), pp. 9–24, 112–118.
[7] *Tagesbericht* (Berchtold) Aug. 1, 1914, P.A., XLVII, *Krieg*, 8 a-b, Türkei; Pallavicini to Berchtold, Sept. 9, 1914, ibid.

tente, and fundamental cleavages in the Turkish ministry over policy.[8] Four Turkish ministers resigned, actually, in protest over the Central Power diplomatic orientation. Throughout this delicate period the decisive Turkish personality was Enver Pasha, who would presently rise to unchallengeable authority in the public life of his country. From obscure origins, he had pushed to a place of distinction in politics and war; a quiet, dapper little man, he burned with an ardent passion to revive the fallen fortunes of the Ottoman Motherland. In appearance resembling the young Napoleon, Enver had become a strong Germanophile while serving in Berlin as military attaché, and he had also been Turkish minister of war. Undercover, he engaged in farcical conversations with Russian agents, looking toward Turkish cooperation with the Entente. Extravagant bait dangled before his eyes by the Russians excited nervous apprehensions in London and Paris, but the Turk distrusted the men on the Neva and their lucrative promises.

Popular Turkish sentiments were enflamed against Great Britain when the London ministry tactlessly commandeered two warcraft being built in British shipyards for the Turkish navy. Counterbalancing that loss in a sense, two German cruisers, the "Goeben" and the "Breslau," which had eluded Entente patrols in the Mediterranean, pulled into Constantinople on August 11, and through fictional purchase were acquired by the Turkish government. That transaction has been judged by a British diplomatic underling on the spot as "the most disastrous incident in the whole war," since these ships solidified the Turkish military alignment with the Central Empires.[9] To all intents and purposes, German naval officers took

[8] Pallavicini to Berchtold, Aug. 20, 28, 29, Sept. 9, 13, Oct. 12, 1914, P.A., 941, *Krieg*, 21a, Türkei.
[9] Telford Waugh, *Turkey, Yesterday, To-day and To-morrow* (London, 1930), p. 147; David Woodward, "The Escape of the *Goeben* and *Breslau*," *History Today*, X (1960), 232–246.

command of the Turkish fleet. The Ballplatz turned aside requests for the dispatch of Hapsburg war-vessels to reinforce the German and Ottoman elements. Toward the end of August, Turkey began calling up army reservists and requisitioning supplies, while a small stream of technicians, cash, and military hardware flowed down from Germany and Austria.

As a harbinger of things to come, on September 26, the Turks closed the Strait to commerce carriers. Time and again the ambassadors of the Central Empires begged the Porte to commence fighting, and on October 19 Pallavicini was authoritatively assured that military intervention impended.[10] With the explicit approval of Enver Pasha, on October 24, 1914, German and Turkish ships, German Rear-Admiral Wilhelm Souchon commanding, shelled Odessa and other Black Sea ports of Russia and sank several Russian vessels at sea. Even after the bombardments a cautiously minded coterie in the Turkish cabinet still wished to avoid conflict with the Entente;[11] but the decision no longer rested with the Porte, since Russia and the western Entente unhesitatingly picked up the gauntlet.

For the Central Powers, Turkey as a belligerent brought the inestimable advantage of closure of the Strait to traffic in and out of the Black Sea to Russia, and it obliged the tsardom to concentrate more of its army resources against the Turk and diverted some Anglo-French military and naval forces from the west of Europe. Not least in value, the entry of Turkey might induce neutralist Balkan cabinets to team up with Austria and Germany or, failing that, to hold strictly to a neutralist posture. On the other side, the problem of transporting war materials

[10] Pallavicini to Berchtold, Oct. 19, 24, 1914, P.A., 942, *Krieg*, 21a, Türkei.

[11] Pallavicini to Berchtold, Oct. 29, 31, Nov. 1, 5, 1914, P.A., 942, *Krieg*, 21a, Türkei; Ulrich Trumpener, "Turkey's Entry into World War I," *JMH*, XXXIV (1962), 369–380.

to the reluctant Turkish ally posed very serious problems for Vienna and Berlin. And the Young Turk militarists, by their hazardous adventure, involved their country in nearly four years of exhausting strife, at whose close large stretches of Turkish territory in Asia would be cut away. "We steered for the abyss," cried Marshal Izzet Pasha in his memoirs, "till the world war came and gave us the *coup de grâce*."

But Turkey had been won to the Central Power bloc and at a minimum of friction between the cabinets of Vienna and Berlin. Yet, the activities of the Germans to purchase the continued neutrality of Italy at the expense of Austria-Hungary aroused righteous indignation in Vienna, as is explained in another context.

4.

In the realm of economics in general and finance in particular, wartime bonds between the Central Empires were less effectively coordinated than between the principal Entente belligerents, though the weaker ally leaned steadily upon Germany for aid. Prior to the war, no plans had been devised for economic collaboration, and at the start of the fighting, Germany clamped down on the export of goods, depriving the Danube Monarchy of raw materials and foodstuffs from northern neutrals and normal sources of overseas commodities by way of the Netherlands or Germany. Large quantities of goods owned by nationals of Austria-Hungary were impounded in German warehouses until the autumn of 1914 when the ban on the transit trade was lifted. Under pressure from the Ballplatz the Germans turned over a portion of the war materiél and rawstuffs, such as rubber, that was seized in Belgium and northern France or captured from the Russians, but Vienna was not satisfied with the quantities allotted. In the course of the fighting, inter-allied understandings were achieved on the allocation of goods imported from neutral or occupied countries. After the spring of 1915, the Monarchy recurrently called upon Germany for shipments of food—and not always in vain.

Beginning in November of 1914, both the Austrian and the Hungarian governments obtained loans from a German banking consortium to cover purchases from German concerns; once started, the lending operations continued steadily, so that by October of 1917, the debt of the Monarchy to German interests exceeded five billion gold marks. Thereafter, the tempo of borrowing slackened, due to the unwillingness of German financiers to accept more Austro-Hungarian paper.

Growing economic perplexities in the Central Empires, aggravated by the shortage of provisions from overseas because of the British blockade, inspired the resurrection of schemes for the consolidation of the economies of the two allies. Resurrection—for the original advocates of Central European integration had appeared in the forepart of the nineteenth century, and once the idea had been raised it had never wholly been forgotten. The exigencies of the war era quickened interest in economic integration both for the immediate advantages it would yield and as an assurance that standards of living would be raised after the war. That prospect possessed immeasurable propaganda value in fostering faith and hope among central European peoples tormented by the hardships and privations which the war entailed.

The basic idea of economic unity between the Central Powers was the subject of an immense volume of wartime literature, learned and popular. More than fifty specific projects for integration appeared and many of them were analyzed and debated in specialist clubs and journals. From press and forums, suggestions on integration passed to official circles, which reviewed them languidly; but the proposals yielded no positive results until the last stage of the war—and then it was too late. By and large, programs for economic unity envisaged either a customs union between the two Central Empires, more or less on the pattern of the German *Zollverein* of the nineteenth century, or a schedule of tariff preferences akin to arrangements within the British Commonwealth; subsidiary features concerned the merger and expansion of transport facilities and of lesser aspects of the two economies.

Economic integration was widely identified with the term "Mitteleuropa." That term was in fact a coat of many colors, had a formidable number of variants, implying, for instance, a free trade community wider than Austria-Hungary and Germany, connoting to some minds a solid and lasting political confederation, and to others merely more intimate cultural associations than had hitherto prevailed.[12]

Of all the wartime literature on the integration theme, the book *Mitteleuropa* (1915) by the German Friedrich Naumann easily excited the broadest and longest interest. Sometime a Luthern pastor concerned with social applications of Christian ideals, Naumann had traveled extensively and had read history to good advantage; for many years he had interested himself in the Hapsburg Monarchy and the peculiar problems growing out of its multinationality complexion. Gifted with the pen and as an orator, Naumann also displayed surpassing skill as a polemicist. The principal paper of the German Socialists, *Vorwärts*, described him as something between an early Hebrew prophet and the director of the statistical bureau

[12] Henry C. Meyer, *Mitteleuropa in German Thought and Action, 1815–1945* (The Hague, 1955), a standard treatise; Jacques Droz, *L'Europe Centrale: Evolution Historique de l'Idée de "Mitteleuropa"* (Paris, 1960), Chap. VII; Rudolf Wierer, *Der Föderalismus im Donauraum* (Graz, Böhlaus, 1960), pp. 136–138; Paul Sweet, "Recent German Literature on Mitteleuropa," *Journal of Central European Affairs*, III, (1943–44), 1–24; Dwight C. Long, "Efforts to Secure an Austro-German Customs Union in the Nineteenth Century," in *University of Michigan Historical Essays* (Ann Arbor, 1937), pp. 45–74.

of a great industrial corporation! Turning to politics
Naumann had been elected as a Reichstag deputy, where
he espoused bourgeois liberalism and a genial humani-
tarianism.[13]

Composed in the spring and summer of 1915, following a period of study and of conversation with significant
politicians and intellectuals in Austria-Hungary, *Mitteleuropa* came off the press precisely at the time that
the Central Powers were thrusting the Russians out of
Poland and had overpowered Serbia. Extensively translated, *Mitteleuropa* was a literary sensation and provoked
a flood of commentary, sympathetic and hostile, in Central
Europe and in Entente countries. Just as German historical writers of the nineteenth century had shaped a climate
of opinion sympathetic to German national unity, so Naumann, admirers insisted, had smoothed the road to economic consolidation of Central Europe.

With sobriety, grace, and infectious enthusiasm, Naumann presented as his central and vital thesis a loose-
jointed economic partnership of Germany and Austria-
Hungary; a customs union, he contended, would form
the logical pendant to the collaboration of the two
countries in the war. On a longer view, the Naumann
formula promised to raise material standards of living
and to temper strife between disparate nationalities, for
Naumann genuinely respected the cultural and political
sensibilities of the non-German national communities in
the Danube Monarchy. He approached public questions
from the standpoint of a "good central European," not at
all as a purely German nationalist. Once the two Central
Empires were associated economically, neighboring states
might be drawn into the combination to the common gain
of all concerned, Naumann argued, and the end result
would compensate, up to a point, for the rigors and
horrors of the war. Naumann was convinced—and rightly

[13] Theodor Heuss, *Friedrich Naumann* (2nd ed., Stuttgart, 1949).

so—that in the future large states alone would possess importance in terms of power and material prosperity; in the existing world only the British and Russian Empires and the United States qualified as authentically free states. Mitteleuropa, were it created on the Naumann pattern, would embrace the largest single market of white consumers on earth, and would compare favorably with the three truly great powers. Naumann advocated, not a supranational federation but rather a league of two sovereign states, without a common ruler or common parliament. The general affairs of the union would be administered by technical experts of the two countries, and problems having to do with education, language, and religion would lie quite outside the scope of the combination.

With a view to disarming a fundamental criticism of his blueprint, Naumann proposed that industrial methods in the Dual Monarchy would have to be raised to the German level in order to compete effectively; undeniably Germany would be the stronger member of the combination, but the alternative for the Monarchy would be to sink to the plane of an inconsequential Balkan state. The menace of the Russian colossus, Naumann stressed, made it imperative for Austria-Hungary to line up economically with Germany for security and self-preservation.

Public reaction to the Naumann program or variants thereof, ran the gamut from hearty approval to total condemnation with diverse shades of response lying between. To generalize, the Naumann vision evoked more adverse criticism in Germany than applause; press mouthpieces of German commerce and industry sharply chided Naumann on the score that Mitteleuropa would constitute extremely poor compensation for the inescapable loss of foreign markets. For economic health, the industries of Germany required outlets all over the globe, it was reasoned; in point of fact, Russia before the war absorbed a larger volume of German manufactured products than the Hapsburg Monarchy. Academic opponents of Naumann, such as Professor Friedrich Förster of Munich, condemned Mitteleuropa as inviting commercial warfare after the war of steel had ceased, unless the partnership were the forerunner of a universal league of European nations. Spokesmen of left-wing Socialism in Germany denounced integrating schemes as shrewd stratagems to fortify the dominance of big business, and their counterparts in Austria-Hungary echoed that interpretation.

Within the Monarchy backing for a Central Power customs union came from certain university professors, influential bureaucrats, and publicists, from Christian Socialist politicians representing the interests of Austrogerman peasants and small businessmen, and from the section of the Socialist party which followed the leadership of Dr. Karl Renner, a convinced and persuasive exponent of economic integration. Many an ordinary Austrogerman bourgeois looked upon close unity with Germany as an asset in preserving ascendancy over the smaller national communities, while among intellectuals, the historians Heinrich Friedjung, Alfons Dopsch, and Richard Charmatz and the geographer Hugo Hassinger, all warm friends of Germany, propagated Mitteleuropa doctrines. On the other side of the controversy, the weight of opinion in Austro-Hungarian industrial and commercial circles reacted belligerently against integration; the powerful Bohemian industrialist, Baron Emil Škoda, for instance, preferred a customs union with the Balkan countries, feeling that after such a combination had operated for fifteen years, Germany might perhaps be invited to enter. In the main, large Austrian manufacturers smothered the idea of integration with the contention that their establishments could not compete with the technically more advanced industry of Germany; efforts by proponents to dissipate that apprehension by the argument that manufacturing firms in the smaller states of Germany had prospered after national consolidation failed to convert skeptics.

Emperor Francis Joseph doubtless reflected the dominant views in court and aristocratic quarters on the Naumann program when he blurted out, "They're talking too much about this business, and that's too bad." It was easy to imagine, in the light of the political sequel to the formation of the *Zollverein* of German states in the nineteenth century, that the House of Hapsburg would be subordinated indefinitely to Germany if a tight economic community were established. Among articulate Slavs of the Monarchy the certainty of German supremacy in any commercial and industrial partnership provoked unqualified opposition. In the Magyar governing élite, opinion was sharply divided, with Premier Tisza, consistent admirer of Germany though he was, antipathetic on competitive grounds and because he suspected infringement upon Hungary's constitutional integrity; his political opponent, Count Albert Apponyi, however, aligned himself with the partisans of Mitteleuropa, which included a substantial section of the Magyar landed proprietors, who stood to profit from easier access for their agricultural products to the markets of Germany.

Naumann's *Mitteleuropa* greatly stimulated discussion of the general theory of economic coördination.[14] Meetings of a *Mitteleuropäische Wirtschaftsverein* (Economic League for Central Europe), held in various German and Austro-Hungarian cities, earnestly debated the advantages and the drawbacks of amalgamation. Deputies of the two countries and representatives of commercial organizations and of the Socialists likewise conferred, published resolutions, and appointed committees to explore the problems of integration methodically. In a resolution of October

[14] The more important pamphleteering and press activities are reviewed in Meyer, *op. cit.*, pp. 148–158.

21, 1915, adopted unanimously by the Vienna chamber of commerce, it was asserted that Austria-Hungary and Germany should regulate their commercial policies according to a unified plan and act together in negotiating commercial treaties; this body favored a limited customs union, allowing for disparities in the techniques of production in the two countries, and wanted other nations given an opportunity to enter the partnership. Realistically, the resolution stated that the ten-year economic pact between Austria and Hungary, due to expire in 1917, would first have to be renewed "for without that no comprehensive change in economic relations with Germany is possible." Weighty volumes appeared, such as Richard Charmatz, *Minister Freiherr von Bruck: Der Vorkämpfer Mitteleuropas* (1916), Joseph Szterényi, *Mitteleuropa in Ungarischer Beleuchtung* (1916), and in Germany, Ernst Jaeckh, *Das Grössere Mitteleuropa* (1916). Support for the general principle of economic unity probably attained its peak before the first half of the war had run its course.

Official circles in Vienna and Berlin manifested little concern in the idea of Mitteleuropa before the appearance of Naumann's book, and even then the interest was scarcely more than tepid. In July 1915 the semi-official *Fremdenblatt* of Vienna had flatly voiced disapproval of economic unity save as the object of private study and discussion, but on the initiative of Germany, diplomatic exchanges on closer economic community started in the autumn of 1915, and with this suggestion were linked proposals for more intimate and enduring diplomatic and military bonds.[15] Economic integration by means of preferential tariffs and joint arrangements for transport by rail and water, it was urged by the cabinet of Berlin, would consolidate the existing alliance and yield material advantages for both partners. On November 10 and 11,

[15] Hohenlohe to Burián, Oct. 25, 1915, P.A., *Geheim*, XLVII/3–10.

1915, the Hapsburg foreign secretary, Baron Stephan Burián engaged in three lengthy conversations with Chancellor Bethmann-Hollweg covering a wide range of topics of mutual concern, pertinent to war and peace, including future economic relationships. It was accepted in principle that a common commercial policy would be mutually beneficial and that the proposition should be carefully examined. In harmony with his promise, Bethmann presently supplied Vienna with a sketch of German official thinking, which favored a commercial treaty to run for thirty years, beginning in January 1918, and subject to revision at the end of ten years of experience; in essence the German memorandum envisaged only sharp reductions in tariffs, not a rounded customs union, and provided that other states should be allowed to join the combination. Secondary features contemplated an understanding on the railway leading to the Ottoman Empire and on ship traffic on the Danube and the Elbe. Joint commissions, it was proposed, should be set up to work out the technical aspects of the arrangements.

The Ballplatz responded sympathetically, though without enthusiasm, to this elaborate program, and assented to further talks; at the end of November, the entire subject was ventilated afresh while William II was in Vienna for conversations with senior statesmen of Austria and Hungary. Sentiment generally favored discussions on broader economic intimacy, though there was no support for a customs union, and intertwined were problems bearing on the continuation of the economic pact (*Ausgleich*) between Austria and Hungary. In line with the understanding between the Berlin and Vienna cabinets technicians wrestled assiduously on problems of economic integration for months, producing eventually a draft agreement, but the policymakers pigeonholed it.[16]

[16] Burián Memorandum, Nov. 14, 1915, *Promemoria* by German Foreign Office, Nov. 13, 1915, Burián to Hohenlohe, Nov. 22, 1915,

Persuaded of the desirability of some sort of commercial union with Germany, the *Neue Freie Presse* declared that "those who fought together during the deadly struggle will not separate with the return of peace—will not, cannot, dare not"—yet the paper pointed out, however, that irreconcilable divergencies on the way to unity existed. The idea of a customs association, it believed, had been abandoned because of difficulties that could not be surmounted and "is no longer advocated by any responsible authority." A Hungarian Social Democrat journalist, Josef Diner-Dénes held that the war was promoting economic centrifugalism not only between the Central Empires but also between the two states in the Dual Monarchy themselves.[17]

In Entente countries, interested intellectuals and in time some politicians equated the basic idea of Mitteleuropa with ambitious German designs for lordship over Europe. Exploited by Entente psychological warfare, Naumann's book and kindred writings were pointed to as proofs of a long-range Pan-German ambition to achieve world hegemony with the Hapsburg Monarchy as the veriest puppet and the enslaved vassal. What in fact was essentially a product of the war period was interpreted by Entente publicists as a facile explanation of why there was war at all; and, if Mitteleuropa were shaped into reality, it would render all of Europe subservient and would constitute a formidable peril for the rest of the globe, it was argued. "Mitteleuropa," wrote a British scholar, "is primarily a political postulate, but is represented in the guise—or rather the disguise—of an economic

---

Hohenlohe to Burián, Nov. 24, 1915, P.A., *Geheim*, XLVII/3–10; Stephan Burián, *Drei Jahre aus der Zeit Meiner Amtsführung* (Berlin, 1923), Eng. trans., *Austria in Dissolution* (London, 1925), pp. 327–328; cf. Paul R. Sweet, "Germany, Austria-Hungary and Mitteleuropa," in *Festschrift für Heinrich Benedikt* edited by Hugo Hantsch and Alexander Novotny (Vienna, 1957), pp. 197–204.
[17] *NFP*, Feb. 17, Mar. 22, 1916; *AZ*, Ap. 1, 1916.

scheme." [18] True enough, Entente voices contended that economic amalgamation, as well as Mitteleuropa in its political and military conceptions, could not be achieved in practice. "There is a tendency in many of the Allied countries, and most of all in our own, to magnify the importance of Naumann's schemes," commented one Englishman, while the "Radical" publicist Henry N. Brailsford adopted a clearly tolerant position on the Naumann plan for central Europe in the future. [19] Yet as the fighting raged on, the feeling spread in Entente capitals (and in Washington) that if Mitteleuropa were realized, it would ensure German hegemony over Europe. That interpretation persisted in the west even after the idea of economic integration had declined as a practical proposition in the Central Empires.

5.

Throughout the years of the war the future of Poland was an apple of discord, a standing obstacle to fully harmonious collaboration between the Monarchy and Germany as well as the subject of competition between the two belligerent coalitions. [20] Scarcely had the fighting

[18] Lewis B. Namier, "The Old House and the German Future," *Nineteenth Century*, LXXX (1916), 160–190. See, also, Robert W. Seton-Watson, "The Pan-German Plan and Its Antidote," *Contemporary Review*, CIX (1916), 422–428, and Sidney Low, "Peace and Settlement," *Atlantic Monthly*, CXX (1917), 39–50.

[19] J. M. Kennedy, "The Failure of Central Europe," *Fortnightly Review*, CVI (1916), 990–1002, p. 1002; H. N. Brailsford, "The Shaping of Mid-Europe," *Contemporary Review*, CIX (1916), 338–349.

[20] Internal aspects of the Polish question in the Monarchy are treated in Werner Conze, *Polnische Nation und Deutsche Politik im Ersten Weltkrieg* (Cologne, 1958); Arthur Hausner, *Die Polenpolitik der Mittelmächte und die Österreichisch-ungarische Militärverwaltung in Polen während des Weltkrieges* (Vienna, 1935). This author, who participated in the administration of the Austro-Hungarian zone of Russian Poland, presents a detailed and orderly account; Richard Perdelwitz, *Die Polen im Weltkriege und die Internationale Politik* (Leipzig, 1939), in which extensive use has been made of original Polish documents; Charles Appuhn, "Le Sentiment Nationaux Polonais

started than a propagandistic bid to the Poles of Austria and of Germany was issued over the signature of the Russian generalissimo, the Grand Duke Nicholas, vaguely promising autonomy to a united Poland under the scepter of the tsar. In the nature of a counterblast to the Russian gesture, the cabinet of Vienna published a skillfully phrased appeal to the Poles, asserting:

"Poles! The moment of your liberation from the Muscovite yoke is nearing . . . We come to you as your friends! Trust us! . . . We bring you liberty and independence for which your fathers suffered so much. Let eastern barbarism step back before western civilization, common to you and us! . . ."[21]

At the very beginning of hostilities lively interest in the destiny of the Poles was manifested in political circles of the Monarchy, much support being shown, then and persistently, for an "Austro-Polish" solution, whereby a Polish state, undefined geographically, would be attached in some fashion to the realm of the Hapsburgs. Back in 1863 the vivacious Empress Eugénie of France had recommended to the Austrian ambassador at the court of Napoleon III that the three fragments of Poland should be combined under the kingship of a Hapsburg archduke, and certain Polish publicists before 1914 had advocated a Polish state tied in with the Danubian Monarchy. Time and again in the war era, it was proposed in various quarters that the historic crown of the Jagellonians should be conferred upon the Hapsburg Archduke Charles Stephen, two of whose daughters had married Polish aristocrats, and who had himself effectively cultivated the good will of the Poles. It was said that the blood of six-

---

et les Empires Centraux pendant la Guerre," *Revue d'Histoire de la Guerre Mondiale*, VII (1929), 98–124; consult also Imanuel Geiss, *Der Polnische Grenzstreifen, 1914–1918* (Lübeck, 1960).

[21] Quoted in Harold H. Fisher and S. Brooks, *America and the New Poland* (New York, 1928), p. 71.

teen kings of Poland flowed in the veins of the Archduke and that he spoke the Polish language flawlessly.

Within Hapsburg official circles thinking on the Austro-Polish formula underwent ups and downs. On August 13, 1914, the Austrian ministry approved a draft proclamation on Poland, which Francis Joseph, coached by Leon R. Biliński, the outstanding Polish public man of the Monarchy, was willing to sign. This document contemplated a Polish kingdom, embracing Galicia and Russian Poland, linked to the Monarchy. The new Poland would have a ministry of its own and a parliament sitting in Warsaw.[22] Eager to obtain more Polish soldiers, Conrad immediately gave the project his hearty blessing, though Foreign Minister Berchtold frowned upon the formation of a full-fledged Polish army. On the optimistic assumption that Russian Poland would swiftly be overrun by the Central Empires, the Foreign Secretary urged that a detailed plan should be devised for the administration of the area, else Polish partisans of national unity and freedom might vault into the political saddle. Tisza, effectively reinforced by policymakers in Berlin, resisted an Austro-Polish arrangement, and, in defense of his position, the Magyar exposed two lines of thought: first, to take away the Polish holdings of the Tsar would kill all chances of a compromise peace with Russia, and, second, the creation of a Polish state in the Hapsburg complex would upset the dualistic pattern of the Monarchy, to which Tisza was immovably wedded. If Russia were shorn of Polish territory, he thought at another time, the area should be linked to the province of Galicia and the Ukrainian-peopled eastern section of Galicia should be organized as a new Austrian crownland; by way of compensation, Bosnia-Herzegovina and Dalmatia should be

22 Titus Komarnicki, *The Rebirth of the Polish Republic* (London, 1957), p. 100.

assigned to Hungary.[23] A Polish state as a third member of the Monarchy was completely anathema to Tisza; on one occasion he likened adding a third partner to bringing a mistress into a home and thus creating calamitous complications. It was opposed, too, by Count Alexander Hoyos, on the grounds that a third unit would be economically disruptive, impair military solidarity, and would tend to strengthen Austrogerman elements which were desirous of very close political communion with the German Empire; he preferred the union of Poland with the empire of Austria, compensating concessions being given to Hungary.[24] Tisza's inveterate political adversary, Count Julius Andrássy, persistently backed the Austro-Polish formula, believing that Poland as a third member of the Monarchy would surely align with Hungary on controversial questions; Burián, foreign minister after January 1915, oscillated in his thinking, coming down finally on the side of the Austro-Polish plan. But to all arguments and entreaties, Tisza, confident of backing from Berlin, returned a flat negative.

6.

After the Central Empires conquered Russian Poland in 1915, two proposals for the region, aside from the Austro-Polish formula, came under debate. Under a plan espoused by the German high command, the entire district would be turned over to Germany, which would probably have meant that Austrian Galicia, sooner or later, would be drawn as by a magnet into this German-connected Poland; alternatively, Russian Poland might be

[23] Berchtold to Szögyény, Aug. 16, 1914, Pro domo, 4023, Aug. 20, 1914, an essay prepared apparently by Baron Leopold von Andrian, former Austrian consul in Warsaw, on "Die Frage Österreichischen Gebietserwerbe im Nordosten im Falle eines Glücklichen Krieges der Zentralmächte gegen Russland," P.A., XLVII, *Krieg*, 8b-11, Türkei.

[24] Memorandum by Count Hoyos, Aug. 12 (?), 1914, *ibid.*

placed under the administration of both Central Powers, with implications of a fresh partition. Up to a point, a settlement of that character was embodied in a Convention of Teschen (Český Téšin), signed on December 14, 1915. Thereby Russian Poland was split into a German zone of occupation, centering upon Warsaw, and an Austrian zone to the south and east, containing a population of about four and a half millions, with headquarters at Lublin, an arrangement that did not exclude the possibility of using conquered Poland as a pawn in peace talks with Russia, and which lasted in fact until the end of hostilities in 1918.

While the Germans subjected their area of occupation to severe requisitioning and hauled off machinery and men, the Hapsburg administrators, more experienced and more considerate in dealing with Polish sensibilities, tried intelligently to merit the good-will of the inhabitants. In the absence of a prepared plan, administration of the Austrian zone was patterned upon models applied in conquered provinces by Prince Eugene of Savoy early in the eighteenth century; until April, 1916, the stern Baron Erich von Diller served as governor-general, when he was supplanted by General Carl Kuk. To a considerable extent, Poles, either native to the area or recruited in Galicia, were appointed as civil servants and several municipal governments were set in operation.

Polish and German were the official tongues, and, though a rigorous censorship kept watch and ward over the press, three dozen newspapers were permitted to be printed. Polish schools and churches, many of them rebuilt after destruction in the fighting, performed their appointed tasks in a manner that was singularly gratifying to the Roman Catholic clergy who tended to be pro-Hapsburg in sentiment. Public health services—sanitation and hospitals—were improved, as was transport; and provision was made for the care of destitute refugees. Before the war, Russian Poland had normally exported commodities to the Monarchy, and the urgency of getting food, as well as coal, timber, and horses played its part in the gentleness displayed by the Hapsburg administration.[25]

In the summer of 1915, meanwhile, Chancellor Bethmann-Hollweg tentatively consented to an Austrian solution of the Polish problem with certain economic and political reservations to safeguard German interests. At that point, Andrássy commenced a vigorous propaganda in the press and in the Hungarian parliament for the attachment of Russian Poland to the Monarchy and against its partition between the Central Empires; the settlement which he advocated would convert Poland into a bastion of defense for central Europe against the empire of the Tsars, Andrássy kept saying. While this campaign elicited a chorus of applause from many Austrian Polish politicians, it aroused undisguised displeasure in Berlin, above all in military quarters, whose gaze was primarily focused upon the reservoir of Polish military manpower in the occupied zones. Under Ballplatz auspices a comprehensive blueprint to integrate the Polish area of Russia with the Monarchy was worked out and at a Hapsburg crown council it was carefully examined. Shifting his ground, Tisza now spoke up for the Austro-Polish formula on the understanding, however, that Hungary should be rewarded with Bosnia and Dalmatia.

Slightly revised, the Austrian draft was passed along to the cabinet in Berlin; once more, Bethmann responded sympathetically and promised to prepare a memorandum on war aims in general as a starting point for discussions with the authorities in Vienna. At a conference in Berlin,

---

[25] Hugo H. Kerchnawe, *et.al.*, *Die Militärverwaltung in den von den Österreichisch-ungarischen Truppen Besetzten Gebieten* (Vienna, 1928), pp. 8–33.

in November, 1915, the Chancellor nodded approval of
the Austrian solution on Poland, but raised basic questions on whether that program would not mean the
submergence of the Germans in Austria and Slavic pre-
ponderance in the public affairs of the Hapsburg Monarchy. Germany would require, he disclosed, solid
assurances that her business and transport interests in
Russian Poland would be protected, and also strategic
frontier modifications; without at all commiting himself,
Burián listened attentively.

But early in 1916, under goading by the military
hierarchs, the Berlin ministry reversed its stand and flatly
vetoed the Austro-Polish formula. Slavs, it was urged,
must not be permitted an opportunity to attain ascendancy in the Monarchy, and, besides, Germany must
acquire Russian Polish territory commensurate with the
annexations it was assumed the Monarchy contemplated
making in the Balkan peninsula. This radical revision
in German policy thoroughly incensed the managers at
the Ballplatz; yet nothing could budge Bethmann. Burián
pressed for a definitive understanding on Poland, pointing out that clamor for unfettered national independence
was rising among Poles who counted. It was his considered judgment that the Austro-Polish solution, far from
curtailing the political influence of the Austrogermans
would in fact enhance their position, inasmuch as no
Poles would thereafter sit in the parliament at Vienna;
and he was entirely agreeable to reasonable frontier rectification and to guarantees for German economic interests in Russian Poland.[26] For a time, discussion of
Poland's future was prohibited in the press of the Hapsburg zone of occupation, but later allowed on the supposition that newspapers would propagate the Austro-
Polish formula.

[26] Ballplatz Memorandum, Ap. 1916, P.A., *Geheim*, XLVII/3–12;
Hohenlohe to Burián, Ap. 10, 1916, *ibid*.

Support increased in German quarters for a condominium settlement, in effect, authorizing each ally to retain its zone of occupation permanently; Bethmann seems to have wheeled around to that view, and at a mid-April meeting, 1916, with Burián he set out his reasoning in detail. With no little spirit Burián upheld the Austrian solution and combatted the German alternatives and their supporting arguments; in the end, both parties agreed to disagree, Burián observing that he could not compromise without conferring first with other senior officials of the Monarchy.[27]

Due to intransigeance in Berlin, Ballplatz experts now advised that the Monarchy should advocate an independent Poland, extending over almost the whole of Russian Poland, and headed by a Hapsburg Archduke; each of the Central Empires would enter into long-term treaties with this free Polish state, prescribing and guaranteeing economic and military rights. To heighten the distress of Vienna, the news leaked out in Berlin that the cabinets of the Central Powers were squabbling over the disposition of conquered Polish territory and that the Germans yearned to establish an autonomous state under the aegis of Berlin; an American journalist wrote a dispatch on the subject which the German censorship refused to pass. Burián, regarding these reports as a betrayal of trust, appealed to the Berlin cabinet to issue an official communiqué stating that nothing on Russian Poland had as yet been decided; unless that were done the Ballplatz, to protect the interests of the Monarchy, would be obliged, he warned, to reveal openly its firm adherence to the Austro-Polish solution.[28] Another set of Berlin proposals restricted the projected Polish state to the German occupied area, while the House of Hapsburg, if it wished,

[27] Aufzeichnung über die Beratungen in Berlin am 14. und 15. April 1916, P.A., *Geheim*, XLVII/3–12.

[28] See, for example, Burián to Hohenlohe, Ap. 20, 1916, P.A., *Geheim*, XLVII/3–12; *ibid.*, May 12, 1916, *ibid.*

might merge its zone with Galicia; Burián stood pat, however, on the full Austrian formula.[29] Andrássy in the Budapest parliament deplored the unwillingness of the Ballplatz to reveal its position on the Polish question publicly; and he wanted an unequivocable statement against a new partition of Poland. "We must remember," he said, "that if we desert the Poles, they will turn against us with all their strength." "If we succeed in keeping the Russian armies from Polish soil," added Apponyi, "it must be done not to conquer but to liberate."

Presently, on the morrow of the reversals suffered by the Austro-Hungarian armies in the slashing Brusilov campaign of 1916, Field Marshal Conrad pleaded for a joint Central Power pledge of independence to Russian Poland, on the conditions laid down by Berlin; only then, he argued, would it be feasible to try to enroll Polish soldiers, which the Central Empires would imperatively need in 1917. Besides, by going along with Berlin on the Polish issue, Austria-Hungary could count more certainly upon German backing, Conrad thought, for its purposes in the more vital Balkan peninsula and in peace-making with Italy.[30]

Reluctantly, the prime ministers of Austria and of Hungary acquiesced in the reasoning of Conrad. What the German military mind was thinking was disclosed in a letter of July 17, 1916, by Ludendorff: "There is no end to the dirty tricks of the Austrians. The troops are no longer holding their ground . . . Poland catches my eye again. The Pole is a good soldier. If Austria fails us, we must get hold of other forces. Let us make a grand-duchy of Poland out of Warsaw and Lublin and then a Polish army under German command . . ."[31] Military planners estimated that Russian Poland contained 1,000,000 men

[29] Burián to Hohenlohe, June 15, 1916, *ibid.*
[30] Conrad to Burián, July 12, 1916, *ibid.*
[31] Ralph H. Lutz (ed.), *The Causes of the German Collapse* (2 vols., Stanford, 1934), I, 281.

of military age, another 400,000 lived in adjacent provinces, and about 100,000 Russian Poles were in the prison camps of the Central Empires.

At precisely this point, Polish officers and soldiers fighting under the Hapsburg flag openly manifested disappointment and impatience over the fabian tactics on Poland's destiny being pursued in Vienna and Berlin; and they demanded release from the armed forces. Appeasing concessions to the protestants by Conrad enflamed emotions in the German high command. Beset behind and before, the Ballplatz grudgingly pigeonholed the Austro-Polish scheme and consented, under certain reservations, to an independent Poland, embracing the former Russian Poland and sections of Lithuania (Vilna included) and of Byelo-Russia, peopled by Polish-feeling folk. This Polish state would be allied militarily to the Central Empires, would accord them preferential tariff rates, and would proceed to enroll a national army, which would be bound to impress the Entente and neutrals and might conceivably hasten the coming of peace.[32]

7.

Against that background, diplomatists of Vienna and Berlin, after parleys on August 11 and 12, approved a secret convention concerning Poland, in which both parties yielded ground on some points. The agreement stipulated that an independent Polish state would be set up as an hereditary kingdom, though the boundaries would not be fixed nor a constitution prepared until after the war; from this new Poland, Galicia and the Polish-peopled districts of Prussia would be excluded. The frontiers of both Central Empires, moreover, would be rectified for strategic purposes primarily, at the ex-

[32] Aufzeichnung by Burián, toward the end of July, without a definite date, P.A., *Geheim*, XLVII/3–12.

pense of Russian Poland; each ally would retain control of its zone of occupation until the Polish kingdom was a going concern. A commission composed of military experts would plan the organization of the Polish army, which would operate under German direction. Since no understanding on tariffs could be reached, that subject was left in abeyance. A Hapsburg crown council strongly urged that the projected Polish state should remain wholly outside of German political jurisdiction.

Baseless rumors got around that a manifesto promising the establishment of a Polish kingdom would be issued on August 18, 1916, the birthday of Francis Joseph. In fact, a fresh quarrel between the Central Powers emerged over the timing of the independence announcement, Vienna insisting on promptness lest tsarist Russia should publish more attractive terms of freedom; the Germans, however, preferred delay while the chances of making a separate peace with the men on the Neva were decided one way or the other. Suspicions cropped up in Vienna that the Germans might scrap the August understanding and tension was further accentuated by reports that officials of Germany in occupied Poland were murmuring that Galicia would be drawn into the projected Polish kingdom. Before the end of August the entry of Rumania into the war increased the urgency of recruiting an army of Russian Poles.[33]

As the next gambit in the extremely involved Polish tale, the German high command brought forth a plan for merging the two zones of occupation in the name of greater efficiency and tidiness and to facilitate military recruitment, but the cabinet of Vienna, on grounds of strategic and military interests, as well as of prestige, and almost neurotically sensitive to the drift of Polish political

[33] Burián to Hohenlohe, Aug. 20, 21, 23, Sept. 13, 1916, Hohenlohe to Burián, Aug. 25, Sept. 16, 1916; and Conrad to Hindenburg, Sept. 2, 1916, *ibid.*

sentiments, looked askance at this obvious attempt to diminish the role of the Monarchy among the Poles. Acerbities reached a point where the Germans threatened to cancel the August bargain and to proceed unilaterally to raise an army in their own area of occupation; rather than relinquish the Hapsburg zone, the Ballplatz was not unwilling to see Germany go it alone. After that an army would be organized in the Austro-Hungarian zone, and the two Polish forces might then be combined.[34]

Nonetheless, Burián pressed for an early public statement on independence for Poland, without disclosing anything on the national army contemplated until the climate of Polish opinion was propitious. He requested one more conference with Berlin to deal with a broad range of problems of common concern, and he had his way, for on October 18, civilian and military leaders of the two allies met at Pless, headquarters of the German army. The impassioned debate on Poland was resumed, German commanders arguing forcefully for the immediate consolidation of the two zones of occupation as the indispensable prelude to building a great Polish army, but the men from Vienna stood their ground doggedly, convinced that what the Germans really had in mind was the total elimination of the Monarchy from conquered Poland. After no small travail, a fresh agreement was hammered out that satisfied the fundamental claims of Austria-Hungary.[35] To the Russian Poles would be given a solemn pledge for an independent, hereditary kingdom, in which natives would manage domestic affairs generally, but control over foreign relations and the fighting services would rest with the Central Empires. In the near future a proclamation on this understanding would be issued.

---

[34] Burián-Tschirschky, Oct. 13, 1916, *ibid.*
[35] *Aufzeichnung über die Unterredungen im Deutschen Hauptquartier am 18. Oktober 1916, ibid.*

Intending to forestall Polish agitation for the union of Galicia with the proposed kingdom of Poland, the cabinet of Vienna revealed on November 4, 1916, that Galicia would enjoy as full freedom in transacting internal business as was compatible with membership in the Austrian empire, an announcement that provoked resentment in Berlin which had no intention of according home rule to Prussian Poland and it also antagonized articulate Ukrainians of the Monarchy who desired a distinct Ukrainian crownland in eastern Galicia.

On November 5, amidst much pomp and circumstance a joint manifesto was issued stating that the rulers of the two Central Empires "guided by the wish to lead to a happy future the Polish districts taken away from Russian domination . . . have agreed to form out of these districts an independent state with an hereditary monarchy and a constitution." Free Poland, boundaries unsettled, would lead a national existence of its own, govern itself by elected representatives, and possess a national army, linked up with the Central Powers.

Echoing the views of many Austrogermans, the *Neue Freie Presse* ecstatically welcomed "a nation of twelve millions into the circle of the Central Empires." But in Paris *Le Matin* recoiled in alarm at the prospect of a Polish army of possibly 700,000 to strengthen the enemy coalition; under the caption, "The Independence of Poland," London *Punch* pictured a huge Teutonic warlord brandishing a brutal whip, while a host of young Poles marched to a structure labelled "cannon fodder department." The *Corriere d'Italia* likened the Central Powers' pledge of Polish independence to "the deception of the boy who freed a sparrow to whose leg he had previously attached a string."

Yet the proclamation of the Central Empires elicited loud applause from many Polish patriots, if only as an installment on the road to a genuinely independent national life. For the first time in the war era a belligerent coalition had deigned to acknowledge openly the Polish right to national freedom. The more sanguine Polish spirits heaped praise upon the Central Empires, which they assumed, were by way of resurrecting their beloved land, entombed since the downfall of Napoleon. At Warsaw an excited popular celebration was staged, public buildings beflagged, and noisy demonstrations formed on the main squares and thoroughfares; church altars of Our Lady of Poland were festooned with offerings of gratitude.

On the other side, Polish elements that preferred organic integration with the Hapsburg state scarcely concealed their disappointment, while Polish opponents of the Central Empires denounced what had been promised as solely a transparent stratagem to entice young Poles into army uniforms. Revered Professor Casimir Morawski of the University of Cracow in a press contribution compared the day when the Central Power independence manifesto appeared to the same date in 146 B.C., when conquering Romans under cover of a declaration of freedom for Greece had ultimately enslaved the country. At just this time, disturbing food riots rocked the miserable city of Lemberg (Lvov), shops were plundered and savage outcries were raised against German soldiers in Polish areas who were shipping food home to their families. It was imagined in Polish émigré circles that the proclamation of the Central Empires would at long last awaken Entente statesmen to the importance of Poland in the destiny of Europe. Foreign newspapers envisaged the Hapsburg Archduke Charles Stephen as the future ruler of the Polish kingdom to come, which in some respects recalled the Grand Duchy of Warsaw erected by Napoleon.

As had been accented by the governor-general of the German zone, Eric von Beseler while reading the procla-

mation of independence in Warsaw, the Central Empires
—Germany far more confidently than Austria-Hungary—
fancied that the pledge of Polish freedom would induce
multitudes of young men to volunteer for military service.
Under official prompting doubtless, a Warsaw paper
described the proclamation as "crowning the work of
the great Polish patriot—that is, Joseph Pilsudski—who
was the true creator of the Polish Legions and who would
be the father of the Polish army." But enrolling Poles
for military service proved in fact scarcely easier than
plowing sand, and fewer than two thousand actually
volunteered. Ludendorff, whose influence had been cast
so decisively on the side of the Polish independence
gesture, ascribed the frustration of the military expectations to the preference of patriotic Poles for a settlement
of the Polish question under Entente auspices. War weariness, more likely, and vehement aversion to German
authority weighed more decisively with Poles of military
age.

To stimulate enlistment the Central Powers rounded
out their Polish program by organizing a provisional
council of state composed of fifteen Poles from the German zone and ten from the Austro-Hungarian. Although
this body possessed only advisory functions and was subject to the occupying authorities, it represented a step
toward a government for the promised Polish state; to
the council was assigned nominal responsibility for drafting a constitution, tuning up the administrative machinery, improving economic conditions, and for promoting the creation of an army. The legend-encrusted
Pilsudski, a member of council, was set in charge of the
department of military affairs.

Certain Austrophile Poles agitated for the appointment
of a regent for the kingdom. Among the candidates
spoken of were the Archduke Charles Stephen, who
would probably have faced a veto by Germany, and

Count Agenor Goluchowski, sometime foreign minister of Austria-Hungary, an experienced and esteemed statesman of Austrophile convictions and not unfavorably regarded in Berlin. While not averse to serving as regent, Goluchowski had opinions of his own about the character of a new Poland; the regent, he thought, should be responsible to the emperors of the Central Empires, and should be invested with broad authority, including the selection of a ministry. That body should move forward in the framing of a constitution, with the advice of the council of state, and should supervise the civil administration in both zones of occupation; in raising a national army, voluntary enlistment should be relied upon exclusively.[36]

What the Central Powers had done and were doing in Russian Poland caused no little consternation in Entente chancelleries, notably in Petrograd. The western Entente governments united with Russia in a solemn protest denying that the enrollment of Russian Poles for military purposes would become legal simply by virtue of the proclamation of a Polish kingdom, and reviling the Central Empires for transgression of "the most elementary principle of justice and morality."

[36] Von Gagern to Burián, Dec. 22, 29, 1916, submitting memoranda by Ladislaus Skryziński, an officer in the embassy and a whole-souled Austrophile, P.A., Schweiz, *Berichte*, 1916.

5. The Spreading Flame

SCARCELY HAD THE CABINET OF ITALY PROCLAIMED ITS neutrality on August 2, 1914, than the future policy of that government became the subject of intense concern in Vienna—and as well in the other European capitals. In the days of August, the streets of Vienna resounded to effervescent pro-Italian demonstrations; crowds appeared before the Italian embassy chanting the national anthem of the Latin ally, while Austrian army officers ostentatiously saluted the Italian flag, and the great press of Vienna shouted "*Evviva l'Italia.*" But the popular emotionalism was not matched in the sober, gray council rooms of the Ballplatz. Men with longish memories properly appraised the depth of irredentist sentiments in Italy and the legacy of antagonism and rivalry which colored feelings in wide circles of the Italian governing classes, despite the surface cordialty embodied in the Treaty of the Triple Alliance, last renewed in 1912.[1] The

[1] Pre-war Austro-Italian relations are analyzed in a thoroughly documented essay by William C. Askew, "The Austro-Italian Antagonism, 1896–1914," in Lillian P. Wallace and W. C. Askew (eds.), *Power, Public Opinion, and Diplomacy* (Durham, N.C., 1959), pp. 172–221.

aphorism that a seed of irredentism existed in every Italian heart may well have been valid, and yet it seemed improbable that the seeds would yield a harvest of rifles and bayonets.[2] Only irrational romantics in the Monarchy, however, could have imagined that Italy would fight shoulder to shoulder with the Central Empires. The most that could be realistically anticipated was the neutrality of Italy; at worst, the country might seize the opportunity created by the war to deliver a staggering "stab in the back," so as to acquire areas of the Monarchy peopled by Italian-speaking folk—the Trentino or south Tyrol region, Trieste and its environs—to establish hegemony over the Adriatic Sea, and to advance national ambitions in the western Balkans, in the Ottoman realm, and in Africa.

To Austria belonged a critical sector of the natural strategic bastion to the north of Italy, which had been rendered the stronger by impressive fortifications, leaving the plain of Lombardy open to comparatively easy penetration. Had not Petrarch written:

> Well did Nature for our state provide,
> When the bulwark of the Alps she put
> 'Twixt us and German fury?

While Italian dialects predominated in the southern district of the Tyrol—the Trentino—a minority of the articulate citizens there certainly had no hankering for incorporation in the kingdom of Italy. Politically passive, many a peasant household blissfully ignored clamor for unity with Italy, though most of them would probably have welcomed "redemption." [3] And the flag of the Hapsburg waved, as it had since 1382, over the harbor of Trieste, essentially a creation of Austrian enterprise, and

[2] Cf. Florence S. Speranza, *The Diary of Gino Speranza* (2 vols., New York, 1941), I, 11.

[3] Archibald C. Coolidge, "Nationality and the New Europe," *Yale Review*, IV (1914–15), 447–461, esp. 460.

the entrepôt for a large share of the foreign trade of the Dual Monarchy; Austrian publicists were wont to describe the port as "the lung" of the Hapsburg realm, which was no mere figure of speech. Shipping at Trieste just before the war was not much below Genoa in volume, far ahead of Venice, and ninety per cent of the vessels were Austrian owned. "If the Danube is the Hapsburg Monarchy's spinal cord," commented a Briton, "Trieste is the sensory organ through which it communicates with the rest of the world." [4] The language spoken in the city was overwhelmingly Italian, with Slovene the tongue, in the main, of newly come proletarians; for Italian patriots Trieste constituted the moral capital of the unredeemed territory. They wanted the city detached from Austria; they wanted it kept out of the hands of the South Slavs; they wanted Trieste for Italy on both economic and sentimental grounds.

And the concept of Italia Irrendenta soared eastward beyond Trieste and its surrounding area. In a brochure, *Trieste e la Sua Fisologia Economica* (Rome, 1915), Mario Alberti, a not untypical ideological champion of Italian expansion, sketched this image:

> Trieste is a very important factor for the solution of the Adriatic problem. But Trieste is only one factor. Side by side with Trieste we must have several other factors, if we wish to make a lasting and successful effort: Istria, Fiume, and Dalmatia—with Trieste these are links in one and the same chain . . . The problem has to be solved integrally or not at all . . . There can be no two masters of the Adriatic.

Irredentist orators were known to claim the Austrian province of Dalmatia "by both divine [strategic?] and human right." Truly the Dalmatian coastline, indented by many bays and inlets and shielded by a screen of island chains, contained bases for potential enemy naval sallies

[4] Arnold J. Toynbee, *Nationality and the War* (London, 1915), p. 111.

against the eastern flank of Italy; by contrast, on the Italian shore of the Adriatic sandy beaches stretched almost unbroken from Venice to Brindisi. The "human right" to Dalmatia—or to part of it—consisted of a thin, town-dwelling population of Italian speakers—less than five per cent of all, immersed in a sea of Southern Slavs. Not one of the eleven deputies elected in Dalmatia to the parliament at Vienna was of Italian speech, and Italians controlled only a single municipal council in the province—Zara (Zadár). Italian pretensions to Dalmatia inescapably cut athwart the aspirations of Yugoslav patriots and invited their relentless hostility.[5] Symbolical of the dreams of Italian irredentism was a golden lamp burning night and day before the marble tomb at Ravenna holding the remains of the poet Dante; five massive figures of enchained women on the lamp personified the Trentino, Trieste, Gorizia (Görz), Pola (Pula), and Zara.

2.

Trends of thinking in the Consulta, it was appreciated by the Vienna cabinet, would be shaped significantly by the swing of events on the battlefields. Since it was almost uniformly supposed that the war would be of short duration, it was a reasonable hypothesis that Italy would not forsake its posture of aloofness. Reinforcing that calculation was the condition of the Italian fighting services, which had not regained their breath since a brief, triumphant war upon Turkey in 1911–1912, and substantial contingents of troops were engaged in subduing recalcitrant guerrillas in the recently annexed

[5] Representative impartial and contemporary assessments of the problem are Coolidge, *op. cit.*, p. 461; Marion S. *Newbigin*, "Italy and the Adriatic," *Scottish Geographical Magazine*, XXXII (1916), 466–477; Douglas S. Freshfield, "The Southern Frontiers of Austria," *Geographical Journal*, XLVI (1915) 414–433; Arthur Evans, "The Adriatic Slavs," *ibid.*, XLVII (1916), 241 ff.

African colony of Libya. Although it was customary for European statesmen in after dinner speeches to laud Italy as a great power, its capacity to fight hardly warranted that distinction.

While the impact of imperial Germany upon Italian affairs has often been exaggerated, it was nonetheless weighty and ramified. Commercial and financial ties between business houses of the two countries were extensive and intimate, and many an Italian intellectual, distinguished and otherwise, cherished affectionate recollections of his student experiences at the great shrines of German learning and research. Business concerns which prospered on wartime sales to the Central Empires (frequently imported goods ostensibly destined for consumption in Italy) exerted subtle pressures on behalf of neutralism. Countervailing these assets for the Central Powers were varied Italian economic and intellectual bonds with France and to a lesser extent with Great Britain. If Germany, moreover, had stood forth as a kind of paternal guardian of its Italian ally for better than a generation, the Consulta dared not overlook in its political calculations the naval superiority of Britain and France on the blue Mediterranean.

Among Hapsburg senior officials, none surpassed Count Stephan Tisza in determination to keep Italy neutral. Not only did he dread the addition of Italian military resources to enemy strength, but he quite properly reasoned that the policy of Italy would exert a considerable if not a decisive influence upon the cabinet of Rumania. He begged Berlin to inform Rome that if the Monarchy were attacked, German troops would promptly be thrown against Italy; yet he adamantly rejected any suggestion that Italian neutrality should be purchased by the transfer of Hapsburg territory, knowing full well that a concession of that sort would sharpen appetites in Bucharest for

Hungarian soil.[6] Count Andrássy undertook to persuade the Italians that national aspirations would best be served by loyal cooperation with the Central Empires; as rewards, the Italian empire in Africa would be enlarged at the expense of France and Britain, Andrássy wrote, Corsica and even coveted portions of France proper would be acquired, and predatory Russian ambitions in the Near East inimical to Italian interests would be thwarted, putting the kingdom in the way to assume mastery over the Mediterranean.[7] Italians were steadily admonished that victory for the Entente might convert the Adriatic into a Slavic lake.[8] It was cold comfort for the Ballplatz to learn that the ministry in Rome had declined to respond to agitation in influential newspapers for the formation of a Balkan league of nations, Bulgaria among them, under the aegis of Italy.[9]

The cabinet of Berlin, more than that of Vienna, was concerned to hold Italy neutral, out of the embrace of the Entente if that were at all possible. For months the German contention that Italy was entitled to territorial compensation under Article VII of the Treaty of the Triple Alliance was intransigeantly rejected by the Ballplatz; as construed in Rome, this tricky article meant that if the Dual Monarchy occupied any portion of Serbia even temporarily or improved its position in the Balkan peninsula by virtue of the war, Italy was entitled to compensation in the form of Hapsburg territory Italian in speech. Denying that it contemplated changing the status quo in the Balkans, the Ballplatz repudiated the claims of Rome. After the German military setback at the

[6] Oskar von Wertheimer, "Graf Stefan Tisza und der Eintritt Italiens in den Weltkrieg," *Preussische Jahrbücher*, CCXV (1929), 54–76.

[7] *NFP.*, Aug. 19, 1914.

[8] Berchtold to Macchio, Sept. 25, 1914, P.A., Italien, *Weisungen*, 1914.

[9] Macchio to Berchtold, Nov. 18, 1914, P.A., Italien, *Berichte*, 1914.

Marne in September, 1914, pressure by Berlin upon the Hapsburg cabinet to purchase Italian neutralism by appeasing territorial concessions mounted in tempo, and pressure was intensified in the winter and spring that followed. Furious though the Ballplatz was over the imperious urgings of the northern ally, it was obliged to yield league by league in the face of Austro-Hungarian military reversals at the hands of Russia and of Serbia and of increasing dependence upon Germany for military and economic help.

3.

At mid-August of 1914, Baron Karl von Macchio, veteran Hapsburg diplomatist, replaced the ailing and woefully tactless Kajetan von Mérey as the representative of Francis Joseph at the court in Rome.[10] Himself a native of "unredeemed" Italy but devoted to the Monarchy, Macchio executed his delicate responsibilities with exemplary patience and firmness; to German charges of indolence, obstinacy, and lack of initiative in transactions with the Consulta, Macchio hotly retorted that he evaluated the Italian situation more accurately than his colleagues from Germany and that he was necessarily bound to proceed in accordance with instructions emanating from Vienna.[11]

The Baron peppered dispatches to his superiors with authoritative paragraphs on the irredentist ferment in Italy. At Milan, for instance, an impassioned theater audience ripped an Austrian flag to shreds, and at Florence, the showing of a film, "L'Italia si Desta," touched off a

[10] Maximilian Claar, "Die Römische Mission . . . von Merey," *BM,* X (1932), 245–257; *ibid* "Zwanzig Jahre Habsburgische Diplomatie in Rom (1895–1915)," *ibid.,* XV(2) (1937), 539–567, esp. 558–567 —mostly based on a diary by Claar, who was attached to the Hapsburg embassy in Rome.

[11] Karl von Macchio, *Wahrheit! Fürst Bülow und Ich in Rom* (Vienna, 1931).

volcanic street demonstration punctuated with shouts of *"Abbasso l'Austria."* Following formal Austrian protests at the foreign office, Italian prefects clamped down on popular exuberance of this character.[12]

Extremist Italian journalism in prose and poetry portrayed the patriarchal Francis Joseph with obscene vulgarity; an especially vicious cartoon depicted the Emperor dangling from a gallows with his crown hanging from his feet. On adjacent gallows swung a string of heroic Italian irredentists executed by black-and-yellow hangmen, and vivid accounts of the death of these patriots were published. Official Vienna ruled out legal action against loathsome irredentist papers, lest trials in court would pile fuel upon flame. Press stories of the arrest in Austria of Italian businessmen and of their enforced labor on defenses along the border of Italy or exaggerated accounts of rebellious outbreaks in Bosnia and elsewhere fed Italian hostility to the Monarchy. And, the Italian ambassador in Vienna frequently complained that Italian citizens, nuns among them, had been thrown into jail on groundless accusations of espionage.[13] The funeral of Bruno Garibaldi, grandson of the legendary hero of the Italian *Risorgimento*, killed on the battlefields of France, degenerated into a noisy anti-Hapsburg uproar; the ambassadors of France and Great Britain walked in the mourning procession. Italian irredentists organized, moreover, a league of friendship with their Rumanian counterparts and also established a "Comitato Italiano pro Polonia," as instruments in a crusade against the House of Hapsburg.[14] Until stopped by the minister of the interior, inflammatory anti-Austrian pamphlets—

---

[12] Macchio to Berchtold, Sept. 16, 1914, Dec. 12, 1914; Ambrózy to Berchtold, Dec. 30, 1914, P.A., Italien, *Berichte*, 1914.

[13] Macchio to Berchtold, Sept. 29, 30, Oct. 6, 1914, Nov. 18, 1914, *ibid*.

[14] Macchio to Berchtold, Jan. 13, 1915 (two reports), Macchio to Burián, Feb. 3, 1915, P.A., Italien, *Berichte*, 1915.

"L'Agonia di Trieste," "Guerra di Popolo"—were peddled on the streets of Italian cities, and propagandistic maps, extensively circulated, dramatized the disparity between the ethnic-linguistic frontier of Italy, which extended to the Alps, through the western side of the Istrian peninsula to beyond Fiume, and the existing political boundaries of the kingdom.[15]

As best they could, Austrian agents strove to enhearten and stiffen the forces of Italian neutralism. Respected Social Democrats of Vienna, for example, visited Italy and conferred with kindred spirits, and subsidies were handed out to newspapers, such as the *Mattino* (Naples), the *Popolo Romano*, the *Il Giorno* (Rome), and possibly others to diffuse the gospel of neutrality.[16] Generous distribution was made of pieces of Austro-Hungarian propagandist literature, including an analysis of responsibility for the war written originally by Count Albert Apponyi for consumption in the United States, and a brochure "Italia e la Guerre," prepared in the Hapsburg embassy in Rome with the object of fostering pacifism. Articles by Andrássy expressing fellow feeling for Italians and dwelling upon the dangers to the kingdom of an Entente victory were published in the press of Rome as of Vienna.[17] Similarly, the German embassy in Rome set up an energetic bureau of public enlightenment which spread lurid tales of Entente atrocities and tried to enlist

[15] Macchio to Burián, Ap. 7, 1915, *ibid.* Accompanying this dispatch was a lengthy and very informative analysis of the progress of Italian speech northward in the Tyrol and samples of irredentist tracts and maps circulating in Italy. For a contemporary survey of Italian press propaganda against the Monarchy, see Josef Hirn, *Die Kriegshetze der Reichsitalienischen Presse* (Innsbruck, 1915); somewhat amusing, with a taste for the bizarre is Ludwig Müfflemann, *Die Italienische Freimauerei und Ihr Wirken für die Teilnahme Italiens am Kriege* (Berlin, 1915).

[16] Ambrózy to Berchtold, Aug. 29, 1914, Macchio to Berchtold, Nov. 9, 1914, P.A., Italien, *Berichte*, 1914; *ibid.*, Jan. 13, 1915, P.A., Italien, *Berichte*, 1915.

[17] *NFP*, Jan. 26, Feb. 28, 1915.

respectable newspapers and journalists in the interest of the Central Empires.

Contracts for goods were awarded to Italian firms whose managers were known to espouse neutralism, and cash was passed out to Austrophile politicians. The cause of neutrality profited, too, from the work among Catholic press associations of Dr. Alcide de Gasperi, Reichsrat deputy from the Trentino and a Hapsburg loyalist, who, after the Second World War, distinguished himself as prime minister of the Republic of Italy. Undercover Austrian emissaries and spies carried on clandestine activities, pushing propaganda, and accumulating military and political information of value.[18]

4.

At the Consulta, meantime, the management of foreign affairs rested in the supple hands of Marchese Antonio di San Giuliano. Reputedly a partisan of the Triplice and a man of unusual personal charm, San Giuliano had achieved distinction as an author, and he was well-known for an urchin's gift of wit and fun. Of Norman-Sicilian stock, his not unkindly disposition toward the Central Empires diverged considerably from the outlook of many Italian leaders coming from the northern provinces. Detractors unhesitatingly tagged the foreign minister an Austrophile, which was as inaccurate as it was injudicious; in reality, San Giuliano steered a diplomatic course of calculated ambivalence.

For reasons not peculiar to themselves, the ambassadors of Italy stationed in Vienna and Berlin, Duke Giuseppe Avarna di Gualtieri and Riccardo Bollati pleaded for strict adherence to neutrality. Representative

[18] Wolfram W. Gottlieb, *Studies in Secret Diplomacy During the First World War* (London, 1957), pp. 194–195; Macchio to Burián, Jan. 27, 1915, P.A., Italien, *Berichte*, 1915; von Gagern to Burián, July 1, 5, Sept. 6, 1915, P.A., Schweiz, *Berichte*, 1915.

of the Consulta at Vienna for better than a decade, Avarna, belonging to a Sicilian patrician family, had shown merely modest talents as a diplomatist.[19] Except for the ambassadors in Paris and London, the professional diplomatic corps of Italy generally approved the neutralist posture; unless the Danube Monarchy were preserved, some of them argued, the Slavic-speaking nationalities would gravitate into the orbit of Russia, and Italy would then be confronted by a far more formidable menace.

Outstanding clerical personalities of Italy, likewise spoke up for neutrality—men who looked affectionately upon the Hapsburg Monarchy as the most reliable daughter of Mother Church and whose detestation of anti-clerical France and the schismatic empire of the Tsar matched their aversion to the kingdom of Italy, despoiler of the papal temporal domains.[20] Sympathy for the Central Powers prevailed widely, too, in the lingering fragments of the Italian aristocracy, and at the opposite side of the social spectrum, doctrinaire Marxists in the international, pacifist wing of Socialism vociferously expressed attachment to neutralism. The chances are that the *Osservatore Romano*, official organ of the Vatican, was not wide of the mark when it asserted that, "the great majority of the country regards with manifest aversion anything that tends to disturb the neutrality policy." These currents by no means passed unnoticed in policy chambers of the Central Powers.

For all his professions of allegiance to the Triplice, San Giuliano was keenly alert to the Italian national interest. At the end of August, 1914, he recorded his intention to resist expansion of Hapsburg power in the Balkans, and more specifically, to uphold the territorial integrity

---

[19] Siegmund Münz, "Herzog von Avarna," *ÖR*, LII (1917), 197–205.
[20] Macchio to Berchtold, Nov. 10, 1914, P.A., Italien, *Berichte*, 1914; Friedrich Engel-Janosi, *Österreich und der Vatikan* (2 vols., Vienna, 1958, 1960), II, Chap. X.

and political independence of Serbia. On September 23, he signed an understanding with Rumania looking toward a common course of action in dealings with the two belligerent camps. Responding to bids from Entente cabinets for the sword of the kingdom, San Giuliano spelled out his price in several communications, the most comprehensive being drafted late in September. First of all, he wanted the Italian-speaking districts of Austria (to the north as far as the principal watershed of the Alps and eastward to Quarnaro, as a minimum); next, Albania should be parcelled out among her neighbors, Italy obtaining the port of Valona (Vlone) and its hinterland. Besides, Italy must obtain unfettered sovereignty over the Aegean islands, which had been occupied since a war with Turkey in 1911–12, and if the Ottoman realm was dismembered, Italy must be accorded an appropriate share of the spoils. Finally, if Italy experienced trouble with Ethiopia, adjoining her African empire, the Entente must promise to support Rome.[21]

During October conversations with Jules Cambon, last French ambassador in Berlin, San Giuliano ruminated on three strands of logic that prevented his government from breaking with the Central Powers. On the side of morality, Italy could not in good conscience hastily desert allies of more than thirty years standing; economic conditions made it impossible for Italy to wage a long war, and the army was not ready for effective fighting. Nonetheless, at some time in the future, San Giuliano seems to have hinted Italian policy might switch Ententeward. At that point, the Entente cabinets laid aside the Italian price for intervention as exhorbitant, yet in truth the terms that San Giuliano had put forth closely approximated the content of the Treaty of London of April 26,

[21] San Giuliano to Tittoni, Sept. 25, 1914, *Documenti Diplomatici Italiani*, Quinta Serie, I (Rome, 1954), no. 803. George M. Trevelyan, *Grey of Fallodon* (Boston, 1937), pp. 331–332.

1915, under which Italy eventually enlisted on the side of the enemies of the Central Empires.

Along in September, 1914, the patent failure of the German war machine to achieve its targets in France gave a fillip to pro-Entente sentiments in Italy. Prime Minister Antonio Salandra recounted in his book of memories that the German setback at the Marne convinced him that the hour had arrived for Italy to push out her frontiers to the limits "consecrated by nature and tradition." [22] On October 16, 1914, a heart attack carried off San Giuliano and the spirits of pro-Entente interventionists bounded upwards.

Baron Sidney Sonnino was now placed in command of the Consulta. Trained in law and diplomacy, he had served more than once as prime minister in the whirligig of national politics, and he had boundless confidence in his own diplomatic judgments. Tall and spare he was, serious, stern, and stubborn, and during the Sarajevo crisis of 1914 he inclined to alignment with the Central Empires, as a matter of honor becoming to an ally. German official circles respected him and, upon his accession to the foreign office, Berchtold saluted him as a man who would hold his country to neutralism, but, after the Marne, as has been indicated, Salandra had definitely moved to an interventionist position. A university professor of no special eminence, Salandra delighted to refer to himself as "a modest burgher of Apulia," the province that had given the glorious Horace to world literature. Before long, he announced to the chamber of deputies, convened for the first time since the beginning of the war, that Italians "must have no other thought than exclusive and unlimited devotion" to their country—to "sacro egoismo nazionale," a famous utterance that re-

Antonio Salandra, *Italy in the Great War* (London, 1932), which combines his *La Neutralità Italiana* (Milan, 1928) and *L'Intervento* (Milan, 1930).

flected the calm, cold, calculating realism, not unmixed with pugnacity, of the premier. Of like mind was the Francophile Ferdinando Martini, shrewd son of Tuscany, and minister of colonies; along with Sonnino, these two statesmen practically determined the shape of Consulta diplomacy.

Broad sections of the Italian press with varying degrees of intensity advocated fighting on the side of the Entente.[23] Leading the pack was the *Corriere della Sera* of Milan, internationally the most prized paper of the kingdom with a deserved reputation for sobriety and balance; in a series of articles as early as August of 1914, the *Corriere* expatiated on the unwisdom of absolute neutrality.[24] Soon the paper was teaching that "the public conscience must be made clear to those who govern"—which meant in truth the Entente convictions of the directors of the *Corriere*. Lesser bourgeois journals with passionately nationalistic traditions such as the *Idea Nazionale*, jingo paper *par excellence*, trumpeted aloud for collaboration with the Entente, and they were joined by the *Secolo* (Milan), which often expressed the viewpoints of Leonida Bissolati, a moderate Marxist, and by the tepidly collectivist *Il Popolo d'Italia*, edited by one Benito Mussolini, renegade pacifist. On the eve of the European war, the Fascist dictator of the future had espoused absolute neutrality, threatening a proletarian rebellion if San Giuliano lined up with the Triplice; Mussolini's hatred of Austria, with whose prisons he was not unacquainted, verged upon the pathological. In October 1914, he published in the *Avanti*, official paper of

[23] Gottlieb, *op. cit.*, pp. 188–189. Cf. Mario Toscano, "Italiens Eingreifen in den Weltkrieg," *BM*, XIII(2) (1935), 737–752.

[24] The editor, Luigi Albertini, spent his enforced leisure during the Fascist era in composing his *magnum opus* on the coming of war, published in English dress as *The Origins of the War of 1914* (3 vols., London, 1952–1957). Although generally fair and judicious, this work reflects up to a point the wartime predilections of Albertini for the Entente.

Socialism, an interventionist piece extolling relative or conditional neutrality "in a war to end war" crusade, and for his audacity he was expelled from the Socialist party. Possibly with French financial backing, the apostate launched his own paper, whose editorials were a daily and violent incitement to intervention as the prelude to tearing down the degenerate and moribund institutions of capitalism. Shouted Mussolini, "Neutrals have never dominated the future."

One day Salandra would explain that without the interventionist press Italy would never have taken up arms. Aside from journalists, many Italian intellectuals and patriotic nationalists identified themselves with the interventionist cause; a slim minority in the chamber of deputies and a larger contingent, doubtless, in the senate adopted a pro-Entente position. The range of interventionist opinion swept all the way from the purest patriotic idealism, harking back to Giuseppe Mazzini, to crude chauvinism, naked and unashamed.

Giovanni Giolitti personified supremely that segment of opinion which wanted Italy to stay out of the war on condition that negotiation with the cabinet of Vienna netted some gains. Time and again premier and minister of the interior, ringmaster without peer in the parliamentary arena, and very nearly the uncrowned monarch of the peninsula, Giolitti could confidently rely upon the backing of a substantial majority of his colleagues in the deputies. A novice in diplomacy, and never one to care much about *haute politique*, Giolitti was nonetheless very much the patriot, albeit intelligently cautious, and he was steadily guided by the basic principle of the best interests of his country as he understood them. It seemed to him that the Ballplatz had precipitated the war in a "brutal" manner; he felt, too, that Italy had no treaty obligation to stand by the aggressor, and that Hapsburg war aims were dangerous for Italy. And yet, as he related in his uninspired autobiography, Giolitti believed that involvement in a prolonged war would have dire consequences for his beloved Motherland and he felt sure that the Hapsburg Monarchy could be induced to concede quite a lot—*parecchio*—in order to hold Italy to neutrality. In his estimate the European struggle would rage on for three years at the least; by diplomatic bargaining Italy could spare itself the horrors and sacrifices of war and still add something to its patrimony.[25] Beyond that, he reasoned that centrifugal contentions inside the multinationality Hapsburg realm would produce a smash-up, sooner or later, and in that event Italy could peacefully pick up districts coveted by irredentism. Banner-holders of the views of Giolitti for public consumption were the *Stampa* (Turin) and the *Tribuna* (Rome), once the chosen mouthpiece of San Giuliano.[26]

5.

As has been intimated, the Germans toiled more assiduously than the Ballplatz to hold Italy on the side-lines—much more. To that end,[27] the Berlin cabinet, in defiance of the judgment of some senior officials, dispatched Prince Bernhard von Bülow, sometime chancellor of the Empire, on a special mission to Rome; although greeted rapturously in the Vienna press, the appointment was distasteful to the Ballplatz.[28] Before becoming

[25] Giovanni Giolitti, *Memoirs of My Life* (Eng. trans., London, 1923), pp. 354–401, esp. 385–6.

[26] *Manchester Guardian*, Oct. 21, 1916.

[27] The analysis of this theme in Gottlieb *op. cit.* may be warmly recommended.

[28] Hohenlohe to Berchtold, Nov. 20, 24, Dec. 5, 1914, P.A., Preussen. *Berichte*, 1914. Bülow, in his reminiscences, presented a highly colored account of his mission. Bernhard H. von Bülow, Denkwürdigkeiten (4 vols., Berlin, 1930–31), III, 193–244. For searching criticisms, see Botho von Wedel, "Fürst Bülow und Österreich," Süddeutsche Monatshefte, XXVIII, (1930–31), 396–398, 405–410, and Hans von Flotow, "Um Bülows Römische Mission," *ibid.*, 399–404, a caustic indictment by an embittered man. Both of these writers insist that Bülow imagined he

chancellor, Bülow had served as ambassador to Italy, and he was married to an Italian aristocrat, whose brother was a senator. Bülow, who spoke Italian fluently, often resided in a sumptuous villa in Rome; he possessed intimate knowledge of Italian politics and he enjoyed friendly relations with many public leaders, Giolitti and Sonnino among them. On December 14, 1914, he set off on his errand, the plaudits of German newspapers ringing in his ears.

With gloom encircling the Ballplatz by reason of humiliations on the fields of battle and the dispatch of Bülow to Rome, Berchtold reluctantly consented to talks with Italy on cession of districts of Italian speech as the price of neutrality. Hoping that the Consulta would be content with the Trentino alone, the Foreign Minister was prepared to see that area turned over; diplomatic haggling, which started on December 9, 1914, proceeded intermittently into May of 1915. Sonnino invited "an exchange of views" to be followed by a binding engagement on territorial compensation, in keeping with his reading of Article VII of the Treaty of the Triple Alliance; his gambit, Macchio accurately advised Vienna, would be to threaten to join the Entente in order to exact the maximum territorial advantages. Concurrently with the diplomatic exchanges between the Ballplatz and the Consulta, Bülow conferred with Sonnino, who on January 4, 1915, disclosed that as rewards for neutrality, Italy must obtain the Trentino and Trieste. Sympathetic to the Italian pretension in the Trentino, the German took a decidedly negative stand on Trieste, where, to be sure, his own country possessed commercial interests. The most that the cabinet of Vienna could yield or should yield concerning Trieste, Bülow thought, was a generous

---

could bring off a glittering diplomatic coup in Rome which would smooth his path to the German chancellorship again; Bülow's political opponents in Germany shared this viewpoint.

measure of home rule; nonetheless, he apprized the Ball-platz of what Sonnino had in mind.

To canvass the problem of Italy a crown council was convened in Vienna on January 10 with Berchtold, Baron Stephan Burián, joint minister of finance, and Prime Ministers Stürgkh and Tisza in attendance. Berchtold proposed that the Trentino should be ceded, remarking that unless that were approved he could not accept responsibility for keeping Italy out of the embrace of the Entente; but the premiers violently dissented, Tisza out of fear that this concession would whet appetites in Rumania for Transylvania, and Stürgkh stressing that the loss of the Trentino would further depress public morale and might inspire Bavaria to reach out for the rest of the Tyrol. Berchtold's recommendation and the opposing viewpoint of the prime ministers were laid before Francis Joseph, who thought the cession of the Trentino would be suicidal; in his judgment, the Consulta was indulging in beastly blackmail to which he would not yield, and he did not think if the demand were denied Italy would forsake neutrality. Crown Prince Charles, on order of the Emperor, rushed to Berlin to explain that the Trentino meant as much to the Hapsburg Monarchy as Alsace-Lorraine did to Germany. William II suggested that in return for the surrender of the Trentino, Germany might transfer small parcels of land to Austria; but the Vienna cabinet responded unsympathetically.[29]

6.

At this juncture, a change in the top echelon took place at the Ballplatz, Berchtold relinquishing his onerous burden to a Magyar veteran of public life, Count Stephan Burián. Never really happy as foreign secretary,

[29] Arthur C. Polzer-Hoditz, *Kaiser Karl* (Vienna, 1928), pp. 213–214.

a post he had undertaken only with extreme misgiving and in response to the importunities of the crown, Berchtold had held the diplomatic tiller for nearly three years; more than once he had asked to be relieved of his duties. Resentful of exhortations on Italian policy emanating from Berlin, he felt that he lacked the personal qualities necessary to carry on maneuvres with Rome successfully; and that view was shared by influential policymakers such as Tisza and Conrad. The Emperor agreed that a more energetic, more resourceful personality should be installed as head of the foreign office and desired Tisza himself to take charge, but the tough-textured Magyar declined, saying that it was indispensable that he remain at the helm in Budapest. He urged the appointment of Burián, his political intimate, and Francis Joseph, after debating alternative candidates, acquiesced.

Announcement of Berchtold's resignation on January 13, 1915, unleashed all manner of gossip on why he had done so. The American ambassador, for instance, thought he had been dismissed because of his stand on the future of Albania, while other observers attributed his replacement by Burián to Magyar restiveness or to a feeling in Berlin that Budapest ought to cut a broader swathe in Hapsburg foreign affairs. As for Berchtold, he was pleased no end to be freed from the wearisome tasks at the Ballplatz; later he returned to the public stage as a trusted counsellor of the heir-apparent.

Taken unawares by the change at the Ballplatz, the great press of the Monarchy nevertheless welcomed Burián cordially, the *Neue Freie Presse* remarking that he had to shoulder more challenging responsibilities than any predecessor since the age of Napoleon. German circles, likewise, applauded the selection of Burián in testimony to his capacity and political talents. As a young man, the new foreign minister had worked in the Hapsburg consular and diplomatic services, and he was esteemed as an expert on Eastern Europe; in the office of Austro-Hungarian finance minister, he had earned high marks for ability and trustworthiness, and his advice on foreign affairs had often been solicited. Less an imaginative statesman than an industrious, cautious, plodding servant of the crown, Burián was a lacklustre personality, short on personal magnetism. After he had thought his way to a conclusion, he was apt to hold tenaciously to it, and he was not easily swayed by the judgments of colleagues in the Ballplatz; in fact, only Musulin and von Merey of the foreign office staff carried much weight and even they were not consistently consulted.

No question could be raised of Burián's native intellectual quality, but he resembled an ivory-tower scholar more than a rough-and-tumble man of the world. He "is capable of giving one a two hour lecture," a high and captious German judge remarked, "very learned and interesting, but nothing comes of it. He cannot make a decision. He is no statesman, but a professor who belongs in a University." [30]

Sponsored though he was by Tisza and in communication with him almost daily, Burián was no mere puppet of the Magyar Premier, as critics often and angrily charged. At his accession, Burián, not ordinarily given to euphoria, interpreted the military prospects hopefully. "The shock of the enormous forces of the Russians," he later remembered, "was being broken by the heroic defence in the frontier mountains of Hungarian Galicia. The road to Budapest was blocked. After this failure . . . our enemies could no longer hope that the mighty struggle would be decided in a short time by the mass effect of the Russian armies, by the 'steam roller' crushing every-

[30] Ralph H. Lutz (ed.), *The Fall of the German Empire* (2 vols., Stanford, 1932), I, 831.

thing in its path." His "first grave anxiety" was to keep Italy neutral by a minimum sacrifice of Hapsburg soil.[31]

On precisely the day that Berchtold retired, a terrible earthquake devastated a wide Italian area to the east of Rome, killing about forty thousand and causing heavy material losses. Clumsiness in the administration of relief work provoked questions in the press on how Italy would fare if the kingdom became a belligerent; and the suggestion was made that the earthquake had cooled somewhat the ardor of the pro-Entente interventionists. Sure that Italy would never abandon neutrality, Tisza, in a moment of inexplicable aberration, was shortly writing, "After many sleepless nights, I feel that the war is over." [32]

Soon after assuming his diplomatic duties, Burián told the Italians, in effect, that they should seek compensation in Albanian Valona (Vlone), which Italian troops had already occupied,[33] and in the Dodecanese, but that proposal the Consulta gruffly brushed aside. Undoubtedly confidence in Vienna was nourished by the belief—or at any rate the hope—that the Salandra ministry might shortly be overthrown by the followers of Giolitti.[34] Bülow worked furiously to that purpose exploiting his personal prestige and charm, entertaining handsomely, and distributing funds with a lavish hand.

Presently he was reinforced by Matthias Erzberger, able, aggressive, and the outstanding figure in the German Center or Catholic party; he was often employed by the Wilhelmstrasse on wartime errands, propagandistic and diplomatic, where it was believed his Catholic affiliations would be of value. In Vienna, Erzberger had many important acquaintances, and he thought that an

---

[31] Burián, op. cit., pp. 17, 19.

[32] Macchio to Burián, Jan. 17, 1915, P.A., Italien, Berichte, 1915.

[33] Called a Gibraltar on the Adriatic for Italy, Valona was admirably adapted for a large fleet base and might serve as a springboard for penetration into the Balkans.

[34] Macchio to Burián, Jan. 24, 1915, P.A., Italien, Berichte, 1915.

attractive future awaited the great Catholic Monarchy.
A commoner not notably discreet in politics, Erzberger
had often fought with the aristocratic Bülow on public
issues, yet in Italy the two men allowed by-gones to be
forgotten and worked harmoniously at the desperate
game of keeping the kingdom neutral.[35] After consultations with representative Italians, Erzberger concluded
that neutrality could be ensured "at the price of relatively
small Austrian offers," and he implored the Vatican and
the Berlin cabinet to do all in their power to secure
acquiescence in Vienna. By way of payment, he recommended that Germany should offer economic concessions
to the Monarchy.

More than inklings of the maneuverings of the Germans in Rome spread across Europe. A Dutch newspaper
cartoon slyly depicted William II holding part of a leg
sawn from the prostrate form of Francis Joseph. Handing
the limb to King Victor Emmanuel, the Kaiser says:
"Don't hesitate. Would you like another piece?" A witticism in Vienna inquired, "Was ist der Dreibund? Ein
Zweibund und ein Vagabund."

7.

Thinking about Italy by Hapsburg senior officials,
meanwhile, had undergone revision. Even Tisza now
acknowledged that territory would have to be ceded and
he told the Emperor just that. As talks proceeded, Sonnino decided that the men in Vienna were not bargaining
in good faith, and published utterances by officials of
the Monarchy, not to speak of reports in the press condemning the very idea of transfers of land, cast grave
doubts on the sincerity of the Ballplatz desire to come to

[35] Matthias Erzberger, *Erlebnisse im Weltkrieg* (Stuttgart, 1920),
pp. 21–41; Klaus Epstein, *Matthias Erzberger . . .* (Princeton, 1959),
pp. 72–73, 79–86, chap. VI, *passim*.

an understanding. Consequently, Sonnino resumed conversations with the Entente bloc, mainly through the
British cabinet, but at the same time—and deceptively—
the Consulta held open the line to Vienna, which, under
German pressure, made fresh offers. It was devoutly
hoped in influential Austro-Hungarian circles that a striking military success over Russia would put the Monarchy
in a position where it could deal appropriately with
the avaricious Italian "ally."

At mid-February, 1915, the Consulta handed over new
claims to Hapsburg land, warning that unless they were
satisfied "serious consequences" might ensue, and on
March 4, the territorial compensations were more precisely defined, and it was made clear that the coveted
areas must be occupied by Italy immediately. Just then
tsarist armies were tightening the noose around Przemyśl
and pushing hard toward Hungary; the zero hour had
arrived Berlin told Vienna, and responsible German newspapers injudiciously summoned the House of Hapsburg
to make real sacrifices to keep Italy out of the war. The
Vatican prompted Catholic dignitaries and Erzberger
urged Austrian Catholic politicians to exert influence to
get the Ballplatz to meet Italian claims. By now Sonnino
had moved into formal negotiations with the Entente for
intervention. At an auction sale the seller customarily
seeks the best price.

In a Hapsburg crown council on March 8, Francis
Joseph presiding, the principal statesmen of the realm—
Burián, Tisza, Stürgkh, Conrad, Krobatin, and Koerber
—debated the delicate Italian problem in detail and in
the end unanimously assented in principle (no more) to
hand over the predominantly Italian-speaking Trentino.
Informed of that decision, Sonnino responded that the
offer was too vague to satisfy, and assurances by Berlin
that Germany would oblige Vienna to fulfill any promise
failed to carry conviction in Rome.

Burián then countered in positive language with an

offer of the Trentino, though the precise extent of the cession would be subject to negotiation. For this parcel of land Italy would have to pledge benevolent neutrality and grant the Monarchy freedom of action in the Balkans, save for Albania. But the Consulta dismissed this bid as quite insufficient since the Trentino alone would not provide strategic security and Italian claims along the eastern Adriatic had not even been mentioned. Burián considered dispatching Crown Prince Charles to iron out the wrangle with the Italian king, but decided that nothing of value would result; instead, he requested the ministry in Rome to spell out its expectations once more.

Accordingly the Consulta on April 8, complacently re-affirmed its terms, never imagining that they would be accepted. Apart from the south Tyrol up to the Brenner Pass, Italy asked for the districts of Gorizia (Görz) and Gradisca (Gradiška), the Curzola (Korčula) archipelago in the Adriatic, the conversion of Trieste and the adjacent area of Istria into an autonomous province, and if Vienna accepted, the areas in question should be transferred at once; Sonnino also demanded a free hand in Albania. In his delayed reply of April 16, Burián renewed the offer to cede the Trentino, though not until the war was over, rejected the rest of the Italian demands with no little asperity, and proposed that the status of Albania should be threshed out in an international conference. This communication was an exercise in futility.

In the nature of a diversion, Sonnino tried fantastically to wheedle Tisza into cutting Hungary loose from Austria. The Magyar Premier, very much worried by the possibility that Italy and Rumania might unleash war upon the Monarchy simultaneously, thought in that eventuality the Central Empires would be obliged to seek a compromise peace, with either Sweden or Denmark an intermediaries.[36]

[36] Arthur Weber, "Graf Tisza und der Eintritt Italiens in den Welt-krieg," *BM*, V (1927), 608–632.

On May 3, the Consulta openly declared that it had withdrawn from the Triple Alliance, and about then it was known in Vienna that the cabinet of Rome had signed the so-called Treaty of London (April 26, 1915) with the Entente powers. "This will be the end of us, I fancy," cried the heart-broken Francis Joseph, yet Macchio optimistically supposed that another bid to hold Italy to neutrality might prove fruitful, not least because the fortunes of war against Russia had begun to swing to the Central Empires. Berlin repeatedly implored Vienna to accept the Italian claims, Falkenhayn, chief of the general staff predicting, it was reported, that if Italy fought alongside of the Entente, the Central Empires could not win the war. As anxious as Berlin to keep Italy neutral, the Vatican pleaded with the authorities in Vienna to meet the wishes of the Consulta.

The final Hapsburg communication, dated May 9, offered Italy the whole Trentino district, a small strip west of the Isonzo River, control over Albania; and promised that Trieste would be granted autonomy, within the Hapsburg realm. Beyond that, Vienna stood ready to examine amicably Italian wishes on Gorizia and on Dalmatian islands; the execution of the engagement with Italy, the note explained, would be guaranteed by Germany. Sonnino remained mum; yet the Ballplatz terms, which abundantly satisfied Giolitti's *"parecchio,"* were printed in Italian newspapers and were appreciatively welcomed by most of the Italian deputies, seemingly, and by many senators. It was an open question whether the Salandra-Sonnino ministry would remain in power.

8.

Italian negotiations with the Entente and the impact of Entente propaganda upon the mind and emotions of Italy can not be examined here. It is sufficient to note that the Consulta insisted that the talks must be carried on in London where the likelihood of "leaks" was decidedly slighter than in Rome, and that British and French statesmen were now prepared—as they had not been ready in the preceding autumn—to pay the price of the Consulta for intervention, steep though it was. But Russian diplomacy forced the Italians to shave down their pretensions in the Adriatic region, especially in Dalmatia, which clashed with Southern Slav aspirations. Far more tenaciously than many a westerner outside of the chancelleries imagined, the men on the Neva fought to protect the interests of their Slav brothers.[37] British and French pressure upon the Muscovite ally to modify its stand rather resembled that of Germany upon the Hapsburg Monarchy to buy the neutrality of Italy.

"The memorandum on Italian rights and obligations," completed on April 26, prescribed that Italy should take up arms against the Central Empires within a month. As rewards, Italy would obtain the south Tyrol up to the Brenner Pass, Trieste and its environs, Gorizia, the northern half of Dalmatia, most of the Adriatic islands lying off that province, northern Albania, and Valona and its environs. These pledges, if integrally carried out, would diminish the Danubian Monarchy, but it would still remain a considerable power, potentially an obstacle to Russian, British, or French pretensions to hegemony in the Balkans, and to the political consolidation of the

[37] These matters are treated in Gottlieb *op. cit.*, esp. pp. 312–358. An interesting Italian version has been composed by Mario Toscano, *Il Patto di Londra* (rev. ed., Bologna, 1934); see also C. Jay Smith, Jr., *The Russian Struggle for Power* (New York, 1956), pp. 242–272; René Albrecht-Carrié, *Italy at the Paris Peace Conference* (New York, 1938), pp. 24–34; Emile J. Dillon, *From the Triple to the Quadruple Alliance* (London, 1915) presents an on-the-spot assessment of currents in Italy by a veteran British watcher of the international scene. On Entente propaganda, see Carl Mühling, "Italiens Eintritt in den Weltkrieg," *BM*, XIII (1933), 411–433. See also W. O. Pitt, *Italy and the Unholy Alliance* (London, 1915), a contemporary analysis by an ardent Italianophile, which seems to have attracted a large audience.

South Slavs—and these long-range calculations were never out of the mind of the Consulta. On the other hand, the commitments that had been given would furnish Italy with a splendid strategic frontier from Switzerland to the Adriatic and would convert that sea essentially into an Italian lake.

Apart from Italian-speaking folk, the promised lands contained hundreds of thousands of Austrogermans and South Slavs. Other clauses in the April memorandum assured Italy of full sovereignty over the Dodecanese archipelago and territorial aggrandizement in Turkey and Africa; more, the Vatican would be excluded from the peace conference, and a loan for Italy would be floated on the London money market—its small size, about $450,-000,000, reflected the belief that Italian intervention would bring the war to a speedy conclusion. French Foreign Minister Delcassé aptly summed up the transaction by saying that the Italian cabinet had "put a pistol to our heads," but the help of a million Italian bayonets and an additional six hundred thousand expected soon from Rumania were worth the price.[38]

9.

The bargain with the Entente having been sealed, it remained for the Salandra-Sonnino ministry to carry the kingdom into the conflict. And that was no light challenge, not least because the last proposals of Vienna held out impressive gains without the sacrifice of any Italian blood or any treasure whatsoever. In consultations with the king and Salandra, Giolitti resolutely stood out against going to war, but the Prime Minister revealed that the cabinet had already decided to fight, and if parliament balked, he would resign; in an adroitly dramatic maneuver of May 12, Salandra in fact presented his resignation,

[38] H. W. Steed, *Through Thirty Years* (2 vols., London, 1924), II, 66.

provoking a national and an international sensation. But meantime, he had played a shrewd card by bringing a famous Italian man of letters, Gabriele D'Annunzio, back from Paris, where he had grown into a passionate Francophile and champion of thorough-going cooperation between the Latin sisters.

Hailed alike as "the poet laureate of Italian unification," and "the last *condottiere*," this picturesque demagogue lashed huge Italian audiences in Genoa and Rome into an interventionist frenzy with flamboyant oratory; his performance impressed a British observer "as effective as Mark Antony's less sincere rhetoric" in old Rome. D'Annunzio painted a lush image of a greater Italy, enriched by territorial and industrial expansion, and he hotly repudiated the popular, foreign conception of his beloved country as a land of antique ruins, palaces, and moonlight. "We are not," he screamed, "and we will not be, *a pension de famille*, a museum, a hotel, a summer resort, a horizon painted with Prussian blue for international honeymooners—but a living nation!" Austrian censorship restrained the press from denunciation of D'Annunzio's coarse-grained zealotry; the orator never recovered his equipoise after the immense enthusiasm which greeted his bellicose harangues.

Pro-interventionist newspapers in Italy waged a fierce feud with neutralist sheets. Street-fighting between rival partisans, excited demonstrations and parades for and against going to war, strikes by anti-war Socialist wageworkers churned up the cities of the kingdom in the turbulent days of late April and May. No fewer than sixty Roman Catholic bishops placed their signatures on a manifesto opposing intervention. In the midst of this furious ferment, this trial of strength, news reached Italy of the destruction of the "Lusitania" by U-boat savagery, which quickened interventionist passions. Mussolini's *Popolo d'Italia* shouted "war or a republic," and before long it was urging that a public monument should be raised to the sacred memory of the murderers of Archduke Francis Ferdinand! Nationalistically-intoxicated journalism slurred Giolitti as an "ignoble traitor," cravenly serving an alien master who, allegedly, had suborned him with a fabulous pile of cash, and threats upon the lives of "neutralist" lawmakers persuaded many of them to desert to the interventionist camp. In the face of violent and irresponsible denunciations, Giolitti withdrew with dignity from public life, though a mere five years later he reappeared as prime minister.

Emboldened by the street effervescence, and perhaps fearful that he would jeopardize his own life or his dynasty if a neutralist were appointed premier, Victor Emmanuel II, a calm, retiring man, declined to accept the resignation of the Salandra ministry. On May 20, the parliament, almost unanimously in the senate and by 407 to 74 in the deputies, voted full power for war to the ministry; it was exactly thirty-three years since Italy had signed the first edition of the Triple Alliance Treaty. Three days later, Italy was at war with Austria-Hungary, though it refrained from declaring against Germany, and so failed to execute wholly the contract with the Entente.

Whether the verdict for intervention tallied with "the will of the Italian people," as the phrase goes, has been the subject of prolonged and acrimonious controversy; the weight of the evidence inclines to the negative, Salandra himself estimated that at the time he handed up his resignation more than two-thirds of the deputies wished to keep out of the fighting. So convinced an exponent of *interventismo* as the left-wing democrat, Leonida Bissolati, a politician of sterling honesty, believed that most Italians preferred neutralism. "The majority hopes and dreams," confessed an interventionist historian, "that Italy may watch the terrible conflict with folded arms, to the end." [39]

War upon the House of Hapsburg meant indeed that a pugnacious, noisy, patriotic minority had triumphed. Italy embarked upon the terrible adventure radically divided in mind and purpose, and the schism never healed; speaking for the majority Socialists, their leading spirit declared they would neither collaborate in the war effort nor sabotage it. With no little reason, Mussolini in the 1930's commemorated the day when Italy plunged into war as the beginning of the Fascist era.

10.

Responding to the Italian war declaration, a manifesto issued over the signature of Francis Joseph, but written by Baron Alexander Musulin, condemned a "perfidy of which history knows not the like"—in a way the intervention of Italy resembled the Japanese malevolence at Pearl Harbor in another decade. The imperial message alluded in general phraseology to the willingness of the Monarchy to make "great and painful sacrifices" in order to preserve peace with Italy, but to no avail. It was recalled, too, how Hapsburg arms had trounced Italian forces in the past, a record that would be speedily vindicated. "A wonderful composition," commented the American ambassador in Vienna, "vibrant with the pathetic reproach of one stricken by what he called the 'perfidy' of a king who had been a long trusted ally."

Sidewalks of Vienna resounded with exultations and marching throngs cheered the prospect of military punishment for the faithless former friend. Newspapers carried

[39] Leonida Bissolati, *La Politica Estera dell'Italia dal 1897 al 1920* (Milan, 1923); Guglielmo Ferrero, "Italy's Duty," *Atlantic Monthly*, CXV (1915), 559–568, esp. 566. See also, W. Petzold, *Italiens Eintritt in den Weltkrieg* (Leipsig, 1934).

editorial leaders and contributions from eminent Austrian and Hungarian personalities heartily seconding the language of Emperor Francis Joseph and boasting sanguinely that Italy would be thrashed in short order. "The Monarchy has no fear of this war," observed the *Národni Politika* of Prague, "which it will wage victoriously and gloriously, and with all the more certitude because of the loyal assistance of Germany." In the estimate of the Vienna correspondent of the *Frankfurter Zeitung* Italian treachery had provoked popular contempt and loathing in the Monarchy beggaring description; senior officials of Italy, to be clearly distinguished from the rank-and-file of the peace-loving citizenry, were hated, he reported, with a profound and honest hatred terrible to behold.

Fairly accurate information spread about on the wide-ranging territorial pledges which Italy had extracted from the Entente, and Hapsburg propaganda embellished that intelligence to intensify martial ardor among Tyrolese and South Slavs in particular. Croats, Slovenes, and Serbs in the armies of Francis Joseph fought Italians with un-exampled resolution and passion. Many a Yugoslav politician, conspicuously exiles from Dalmatia, who nursed black memories of controversies with Italians in coastal communities, despised the kingdom of Italy even more than they detested Austria-Hungary, and a manifesto by South Slav émigrés bitterly protested that "the dismemberment of the Adriatic littoral would be a terrible injustice, especially during a war for the liberation of nations . . ." [40] It was appreciated in some Entente quarters at the time of the intervention of Italy, and more poignantly later, that the commitments that had been made rendered it next to impossible to inveigle the cabinet of Vienna into a compromise peace. The Conservative London *Morning Post* argued that the entry of Italy would in fact prolong, not shorten, the war, and

[40] London *Times*, May 13, 1915.

frustrated any chance of detaching the Danube Monarchy from the German ally.[41]

Unlike many a Hapsburg journalist and politician, the Austro-Hungarian supreme command did not think the armies of Italy would collapse like the proverbial house of cards. When war seemed imminent, commanders anxiously debated denuding the district down to and including Trieste of defense forces, but to have done so would have grievously hampered communications with the fleet and would have had untoward consequences upon the war spirit; so the idea was vetoed.

Here and there the Ballplatz was subjected to acrid criticism for the manner in which diplomatic relations with Italy had been handled. In rebuttal Burián begged to point out that at no time had the men in the Consulta honestly desired to reach an accommodation; rather they had perfidiously dragged out conversations so as to gain time for preparations to fight. Having lost in the competition for Italy, the Ballplatz now focused upon holding Rumania to neutrality. It is perhaps not surprising that Bülow claimed—arrogantly and unconvincingly—that his labors had staved off the Italian decision to fight for five months. Until early May, 1915, it appears, he imagined that Vienna and Rome might strike a mutually acceptable bargain, and he ascribed the failure of his mission to twin evils: pride, ignorance and obstinacy at the Ballplatz, and the neglect of Berlin to apply as heavy pressure upon the cabinet of Vienna as it should have done.[42] Hapsburg officialdom, on the contrary, was sure that Bülow had sown extravagant ideas in avaricious Italian heads which had yielded a most miserable harvest.

[41] *Literary Digest,* L, (June 5, 1915), 1320.
[42] Bülow, *op. cit.,* III, 243; for Erzberger's blistering memorandum on Ballplatz tactics and Burián's defense, see Dionys Jánossy, "Erzbergers Denkschrift über der Eintritt Italians in den Weltkrieg und die Replik Buriáns," *Ungarische Jahrbücher,* XIII (1933), 54–72; Epstein, *op. cit.,* pp. 139–140.

The entire episode left a bitter taste in the mouth of Vienna, where the very name of Bülow became anathema. When the belligerency of Italy seemed to be only a matter of days, Bülow adjured the cabinet in Berlin to prevent an outburst of anti-Italian passion in the German press by strict censorship. "We must keep open the possibility," he counselled, "of concluding a separate peace in case of a change of ministry, which is easily possible here." [43]

As for the course steered by the Salandra ministry, no more judicious appraisal could be expected than that of the Philadelphia *North American*. ". . . Every other nation involved in the war," it explained, "is actuated in just the same way, by the spirit of nationalism, which is simply selfishness on a sublime scale. Italy alone is bold enough to declare that she fights to advance her own interests, and not from motives of altruism or in the cause of humanity." [44]

11.

To a modest extent, the military collaboration of Bulgaria with the Central Empires, commencing in the autumn of 1915, compensated for the entry of Italy into the enemy coalition. When the war in Europe started, Bulgarian patriots nursed burning grievances over the territorial arrangements fixed at the end of the Balkan convulsions of 1912–13. National ambition coveted most keenly Macedonian soil that had passed under the flag of Serbia, but territorial aspirations extended to Rumania —to southern Dobrudja wrested away in 1913—and to Greece as well. King Ferdinand, German by origin, personified the vision of a "big Bulgaria" and the conviction

[43] Hohenlohe to Burián, Sept. 7, Dec. 22, 1916, P.A., Preussen, *Berichte*, 1916. Bülow to Wihelmstrasse, May 7, 1915, in Lutz., ed., *op. cit.*, I, 754.

[44] Quoted in *Literary Digest*, L (June 5, 1915), 1314.

that Serbian power in the Balkan peninsula must be curtailed. Exhausted though Bulgaria was by the strain of recent warfare, the country commanded a strategic geographical position investing it with diplomatic importance out of all proportion to its resources; and Sofia became a marketplace of acute competition between the rival belligerents.[45]

Even as the Entente bid for Italy with Hapsburg territory, so the Central Empires held out Serbian soil as bait to Bulgaria. Before the war, Vienna had won golden opinions in Sofia by gestures of good-will and assistance, including support in Germany for a loan. Indeed, talks for an alliance had advanced by August of 1914 to the point where it seemed that a treaty could quickly be drafted; on August 2, the ministry of Sofia set as prerequisites for a pact solid assurances of aid in realizing irredentist ambitions. With alacrity Berlin acquiesced and urged Vienna to approve, but most senior officials there kept debating, out of fear that a contract with Bulgaria might widen the chasm with Rumania; Tisza, however, argued for a mutually profitable alliance. Then the Sofia cabinet temporized, trying to puzzle out how the war would end, waiting until the intentions of Turkey and Greece took on sharper clarity, a non-commital posture that persisted for months, while the Central Empires promoted an efficient press campaign for intervention.

The inability of Entente arms to smash through the Turkish Strait in the spring of 1915 and the lethal blows rained upon the empire of the Tsar by the Central Powers persuaded the Bulgarian court clique, to which the crafty and German-educated Premier Vasil Radoslavov belonged, that the laurel of victory, sooner or later, would rest on the brows of Austria-Hungary and Germany. Even the journalistic mouthpiece of the parlia-

---

[45] Noel and Charles R. Buxton, *The War and the Balkans* (London, 1915) pp. 72–77, 83–101.

mentary opposition, the *Mir* of Sofia, exclaimed on May 29, 1915, "If Bulgaria remains neutral to the end of the war, she runs the risk of being condemned to live forever within the narrow limits she has today, hemmed in on every side." Considering the source, this viewpoint could not fail to stimulate the ardor of interventionists; in fact, the Central Powers had promised Bulgaria, just as Italy was entering the fray, its maximum pretensions to Serbian land,[46] simply for holding to neutrality, and offered bits of Greece and Rumania in payment for intervention. In July, diplomatic conversations which had proceeded without interruption, entered the decisive stage.

Astute, not to say brilliant diplomacy, by Berlin and Vienna facilitated a Bulgar-Turkish rapprochement in that month whereby the Turks consented to a frontier rectification in Thrace, extending Bulgarian sovereignty to the Maritza River and embracing a region traversed by a railway to the Aegean. Assessing this transaction, Andrássy described it as "an ever shining example of political wisdom and insight," and he added that a Bulgarian attack upon Serbia "would be wholly justified on grounds of prudence and morality alike," and would bring the attacker impressive winnings.[47]

Meantime, late in August, as an indication of the direction in which the diplomatic wind was blowing, Russophiles in the Sofia ministry handed in their resignations, and in a matter of days—September 6—the rump Radoslavov cabinet signed a treaty and military convention

[46] Certain Bulgarian official papers, translated by Stoyan Stoyanoff, appeared in *Revue d'Histoiré de la Guerre Mondiale* IX (1931), 257–298, 392–420. Radoslavov offered his version of what happened in *Bulgarien und die Weltkrise* (Berlin, 1923), pp. 132–194; Carl Mühlmann, "Der Entritt Bulgariens in den Weltkrieg," *BM*, XIII (2) (1935), 829–844; K. Kratchounov, *La Politique Extérieure de la Bulgarie, 1880–1920* (Sofia, 1932), pp. 61–73, a documented treatment by a native scholar; George C. Logio, *Bulgarian Problems and Politics* (London, 1919), pp. 50–80, 131–152, by the lecturer on Bulgarian affairs in King's College.
[47] *NFP*, Sept. 22, 1915.

with Austria-Hungary and Germany. By then it had become reasonably clear that Turkey would retain command at the Strait and that Russia might before long be reduced to military impotence. In return for cooperation in fighting Serbia, Bulgaria was promised its full claims upon that country, possibly territory belonging to Greece and Rumania if they should align with the Entente, and a substantial loan. Entente agents, both official and unofficial, strove feverishly to keep Bulgaria out of the conflict, but these maneuvers lie outside the range of the present work and it is only necessary to remark that Serbia was the insurmountable stumbling block, unwilling to sacrifice territory that might have appeased the Radoslavov ministry. Bulgarian parliamentary resistance to intervention, never so vigorous nor so large as in Italy, could not stem the Ententophobe tide; the more outspoken opponents of ministerial policy were clapped into prison, among them the youthful Gheorghi Dimitrov, who one day would be honored as the hero of heroes by Communist Bulgaria.

Avowing that mobilization was essential to preserve neutrality, the Bulgarian cabinet on September 22, 1915, suddenly summoned some 300,000 troops to the colors. Pointed warnings sped from Entente foreign offices to Sofia not to take the last fateful step, but they were barren of result. On October 14, Bulgaria, alleging that Serbian soldiers had violated its frontier, joined in an offensive against Serbia, which armies of the Central Empires had already launched from the north. In a proclamation explaining its policy, the Radoslavov ministry predicted that the total collapse of tsarist Russia impended and that France, Italy, and Serbia would walk the same road. "Bulgaria would commit suicide, if she did not fight on the side of the Central Powers," the document affirmed, "which offers the only possibility of realizing her desire for the union of all Bulgarian peoples."

Unsheathing the sword against Serbia, King Ferdinand proclaimed:

"I call the armed Bulgarian nation to the defense of native soil defiled by its felonious neighbor; we shall fight the Serbs together with the brave Central Empires. May our soldiers fly from victory to victory . . . God bless our armies!" [48]

The intervention of Bulgaria materially profited the Central Powers and rounded out their coalition. Not only was Serbia rapidly overrun, but a clear channel to Turkey was opened through which streamed soldiers, supplies, and munitions to keep that ally going; and the entry of Bulgaria strengthened resolves in Greece and in Rumania not to team up against the Central Powers' bloc. On a courtesy call to Vienna, King Ferdinand was awarded the baton of a Hapsburg field marshal and he engaged in talks to cement the alliance by the marriage of his heir, Boris, to an Austrian archduchess—of whom there were "eight or ten charming girls" with no suitors on the horizon. Ferdinand brought along in his luggage a blueprint to remove Serbia from the map, Bulgaria to annex two-thirds of the kingdom and the region fronting on the Danube to go to the Hapsburg realm. Official circles in Vienna greeted the Balkan monarch without particular warmth, for he had a merited reputation for duplicity and unreliability, and his adoption of the Orthodox Eastern faith was resented at the Hapsburg court.[49]

12.

Given its geographical location, its resources of grain and oil and its military manpower, Rumania was a prize eagerly sought by both belligerent groups. The Entente governments, whose diplomatic, commercial, and propa-

[48] John C. Adams, *Flight in Winter* (Princeton, 1942), p. 67.
[49] Penfield to Lansing, Feb. 21, 1916, U.S., *National Archives*, 874.001, F 37/44½.

ganda representatives laid down a persistent barrage of persuasion, finally convinced the cabinet of Bucharest— in August, 1916—that the national interest would best be advanced by making war upon Austria-Hungary. As with Italy and Bulgaria, the Rumanian decision for war climaxed months and months of blowing hot and cold, backing and filling, of debate and controversy.

It was not known by the general public of Rumania or even by most ministers of state that as far back as 1883 the crown had negotiated an alliance with the Hapsburg Monarchy and Germany; that treaty, which commited Rumania to fight in the event of an unprovoked attack upon the other signatories, had been renewed on five occasions, most recently in 1913. It was the custom of the king, under a pledge of total secrecy, to acquaint each new prime minister with this pact, which had been signed when the kingdom was embittered by the cession under duress of a portion of Bessarabia to the empire of the Tsar. The dream of recovering that lost province, along with profound mistrust of the Slav colossus, had dictated the thirty-year alignment with the Central Empires. But Rumanian nationalism possessed a second and grander irredenta—lands to the west of the Carpathians inhabited by some 3,500,000 brothers and sisters, nearly double the number under the flag of Russia. The coveted areas included mainly Transylvania and the Banat of Temesvár (Timișoara) in the kingdom of Hungary and the Austrian province of the Bukowina.

Just before 1914, official antipathy in Rumania toward Russia had diminished, and affection for France and somewhat less so for Britain had increased in Rumanian intellectual and political quarters. On the other side of the shield, enmity toward the Danube Monarchy had grown more intense and widespread, due to unenlightened, oppressive Magyar policies in handling the Rumanian minority, especially in Transylvania, the very cradle of the nationality, and to burgeoning irredentist fervor in the kingdom of Rumania—the Regat. These considerations had produced a shift in the climate of national diplomacy, and striking Rumanian military and political triumphs in Balkan warfare of 1913 had fostered a false conception of the armed strength of the kingdom; the rather friendly posture of Vienna toward Bulgaria, moreover, during the turmoil of 1913 fed resentment in Bucharest. The last ambassador of Francis Joseph at the court of Rumania, Count Ottokar Czernin, a cosmopolitan Bohemian aristocrat well known for sympathy with the Rumanian minority of Hungary, repeatedly warned the Ballplatz that in the testing time of a general European war the loyalty of Rumania to the alliance would be dubious at best. Policymakers in Berlin thought, however, that in any eventuality the kingdom would at least remain neutral.[50]

When war broke over Europe in 1914, William II addressed a series of dispatches to King Carol I pleading with him as a Hohenzollern and a monarch to cooperate in the spirit of alliance engagements; Francis Joseph dispatched a similar appeal. From Berlin went offers of Bessarabia and maintenance of territorial integrity if the kingdom would mobilize immediately against Russia, and information was also vouchsafed to Bucharest on the newly contracted secret alliance with Turkey. The men on the Neva, backed by the western Entente capitals, countered with a tempting agenda of expansion and promises of military assistance if Rumania would cast its sword on the Entente side of the scales.[51]

On August 3, 1914, King Carol I convoked a crown council comprising the ministry, spokesmen of the parliamentary opposition, and selected royal advisers. After a reading of the text of the alliance treaty with the Central

[50] May, *The Hapsburg Monarchy*, pp. 448–449, 469–472.
[51] Leonid C. Sonevytsky, "Bukovina in the Diplomatic Negotiations of 1914," *Annals of the Ukrainian Academy*, VII (1959), 1586–1629.

Powers, all agreed that under the existing circumstances, the letter of the document imposed no obligation to render support; a searching debate ensued on the policy to be followed. Befitting a Hohenzollern scion, who in his youth had worn a Prussian army uniform, the venerable and venerated Carol earnestly pleaded for war upon Russia in league with the Central Empires, and his views were reinforced by a fiery, old Conservative leader, Peter Carp, an unregenerate Russophobe, and less militantly by ex-Premier Alexander Marghiloman, a moderate conservative.[52] Fidelity to contract and dread of the consequences of a Russian victory formed the principal argumentation of the interventionists, but politicians who were inclined to be Ententophile, best represented by another former prime minister, Take Jonescu contended that the kingdom should stand on the sidelines, and that policy was advocated likewise by Premier Jon I. C. Brătianu, son of the statesman who had originally signed the alliance with Vienna and Berlin. A cautious individual, astute, calculating, and very ambitious for the greater glory of Greater Rumania, Brătianu boasted a personal and family prestige rivalling that of the reigning dynasty itself. His thinking on policy was somewhat colored by the Italian declaration of neutrality and by the conviction that in time the iron dice of war would roll to the Entente corner; consequently, he proposed that the kingdom should imitate Italy, wait watchfully, strengthen the fighting services, and alert the nation for whatever might come to pass. Much to the mortification of Carol, a large majority of the council, approved the logic of Brătianu.

[52] Georges Fotino, "Une Séance Historique au Conseil de la Couronne 3 Août 1914," *Revue des Deux Mondes*, LVIII (1930), 527–541; Alexander Marghiloman, "L'Intervention Roumaine," *Revue d'Histoire de la Guerre Mondiale*, VI (1928), 157–166, being accounts of the crown council of 1914 and of another on August 27, 1916 drawn from his elaborate *Note Politice* (5 vols., Bucharest, 1927).

Wittingly or otherwise, Rumania obeyed the counsel of Otto von Bismarck. "Rumania ought to cultivate cordial relations . . . with all her neighbors," he observed in 1868, "and await with patience until the ripe fruit of the European tree drop of themselves on her table . . ." So profoundly did the King dislike the neutralist decision that he regretted that he had lived so long, and he seriously considered giving up the crown, as, indeed, he had threatened to do in 1870, when leading Rumanian public men showed a preference for France during its war with the German states.[53] Privately Carol assured the cabinets of the Central Empires that so long as he was the ruler, the arms of Rumania would not be turned upon them, and he even recommended that Vienna and Berlin should persuade Bulgaria to state publicly that it would fight Rumania, if the latter intervened on the Entente side.

For a short time, Ambassador Czernin and the Ballplatz wishfully imagined that Rumania might join the Central Empires in war, yet the tide of military developments, west and east, speedily forced the abandonment of that fancy. Throughout the devious maneuverings of the next two years, Czernin properly reiterated the obvious in dispatches to Vienna: the diplomacy of Bucharest would be fundamentally determined by what happened in the theaters of fighting.[54]

In the first stage of the war, as tsarist armies advanced successfully against Austria-Hungary, the German au-

[53] Carol's diary of the period mirrored the agony of his spirit; broken in health he soon took to his bed. C. J. Diamandy, "La Guerre Mondiale Vue de Versant Oriental," *Revue des Deux Mondes* XLIX (1929), 815–820.

[54] Czernin to Berchtold, Aug. 4, 6, 1914, and Berchtold to Pallavicini, Sept. 23, 1914, P.A., *Geheim*, XLVII/7a. For a representative selection of the diplomatic correspondence involving Rumania, see *Diplomatische Aktenstücke Betreffend die Beziehungen Österreich-Ungarns zu Rumänien* (Vienna, 1916). This collection presents, of course, only a fraction of the pertinent archival records; in the main, passages in the original papers, excised from this "Red Book," relate to third countries or to prominent political personalities, still living at the time of publication.

thorities implored the Hapsburg ally to make concessions to Rumania that would at the minimum hold it to neutralism. By his generosity in dangling parcels of Hapsburg soil before Rumanian politicians, the newly appointed German ambassador, Hilmar von der Bussche, a diplomatist of about the third magnitude, antagonized Czernin who regarded his partner as naive, the victim of irresponsible optimism, and von der Bussche, for his part, held the Bohemian grandee in low esteem. Even so, Berlin let it be known in Bucharest that war upon the Monarchy would involve, *ipso facto*, fighting Germany as well.[55]

With the military horizon of the Central Powers darkening in 1914, Conrad lent his weighty voice to the idea of ensuring the neutrality of Rumania by a territorial grant, urged that means must be found of satisfying Rumanian nationalism. But all such pleas the Ballplatz turned aside, aware that Tisza would never consent to the loss of land belonging to the crown of St. Stephen, and certain that a concession to Rumania would quicken appetites in Rome, as well as being interpreted as a confession of weakness that would adversely affect soldier and civilian morale. True enough, on urgings from Berlin, Tisza promised improvements in the treatment of the Rumanian minority in Hungary, but these pledges left leading irredentists cold; he vetoed recommendations from Berlin that a Hungarian-Rumanian should be brought into his ministry and that some Rumanians should be appointed as provincial prefects.[56] Czernin personally favored granting Transylvania autonomy, but Tisza adamantly resisted any change in the status of "the pearl of the Hungarian crown," as he phrased it.

Only extensive concessions of land, if indeed that,

[55] Pro domo, no. 4315, Sept. 3, 1914, P.A., *Geheim*, LXVII/3; Hohenlohe to Berchtold, Sept. 23, 1914, *ibid.* / 7c.

[56] Tisza to Berchtold, Aug. 22, 1914, P.A., *Geheim*, XLVII/7a; *ibid.*, Sept. 24, 1914, *ibid.* /7c.

would have mollified Rumanian Magyarophobes and the most that the Ballplatz ever offered was certain districts of southern Bukowina; Vienna was, of course, quite willing to see Rumania annex all of Bessarabia and even Russian territory extending off to Odessa. The cabinet of Bucharest kept an eye cocked on Bulgaria, properly calculating that this neighbor would seize any propitious opportunity to reclaim the southern Dobrudja, snatched away by Rumania in the Balkan struggle of 1913. It is reasonably certain that if Rumania had joined the Entente coalition early in the war, Bulgaria would straightway have aligned with the Central Empires. After Turkey became a belligerent, the Central Allies applied every available form of coercion, short of war, upon Bucharest, to secure unimpeded transit for military supplies across the kingdom, but without success. At the outset of 1915, when the Entente mounted an ill-starred offensive against the Turkish Strait, agents of the Central Powers ingeniously contrived to smuggle small quantities of badly needed war goods through Rumania to the Turks.

Inside the kingdom, Central Power and Entente emissaries struggled furiously to win friends and influence people, both competitors blending blandishments with bullying. Keen contention raged over the purchase of surplus grain, which pushed prices upward to the unconcealed delight of boyar and peasant. Gold was generously distributed to the notoriously venal press of Bucharest and of other substantial communities to publish news and views sympathetic to one belligerent or the other, and atrocity tales figured conspicuously in propaganda literature.[57] Funds were also spent to suborn Rumanian deputies and other key personalities; at one point, Czernin even supposed that the highly vocal Entente partisan, Take Jonescu, whose personal finances were shaky, could

---

[57] Czernin to Burián, Mar. 22, 1915, P.A., Rumänien, *Berichte*, 1915, a detailed accounting of Austrian work.

be bought. From the Hapsburg embassy money flowed to the small Socialist party to agitate against the empire of the Tsar and against war in general; it was intended thus to offset parallel activities organized by friends of the Entente. Mob fury on occasion rose to such a pitch that a security guard had to be thrown round the residence of Czernin; quaintly enough, the Ambassador reported, hired claques demonstrated for the Monarchy in the morning and after lunch against it.[58]

Both belligerents exploited Rumanians in their propaganda in the Regat, the Entente doing a more effective job of it. For the latter, a valuable asset were impassioned, patriotic speeches by Professor Nicholas Jorga, foremost historian and intellectual Nestor of Rumania, hailing the approach of "the hour for which we have lived our whole life as a nation, for which we have written, worked, and fought." [59]

13.

At the death of broken-hearted and childless King Carol in October of 1914, his nephew, Ferdinand I assumed the crown, though neither by endowment nor taste was he well suited for the august responsibility. Understandably, he did not command the respect enjoyed by his predecessor, whose whole mature life had been devoted to the welfare of his adopted land; lacking force of character, too, Ferdinand was more easily swayed by the counsels of Brătianu. Yet his inner emotions lay with his native Germany, which he believed deep-down would eventually carry the Central coalition to victory. His attractive wife, Queen Marie, a British princess and grand-

[58] Czernin to Berchtold, Nov. 23, Dec. 7, 8, 1914, P.A., *Krieg,* 6A, Rumänien.
[59] John C. Campbell, "Nicholas Jorga," *Slavonic Review,* XXVI (1947–48), 44–59, p. 55; Nicholas Jorga, "La Problème Danubien et les Roumaines de 1913 à 1918: Czernin contre Tisza," *Revue d'Histoire de la Guerre Mondiale,* XII (1934), 105–126.

daughter of Alexander II of Russia, cherished strong affections for the Entente, loathed neutralism, but chose to stand above the battle, save as her views were solicited by Ferdinand.[60] Badgered by pressures from both warring blocs, Brătianu felt his health was long being so dangerously undermined that he ought to relinquish office; and in such ways as were open to them the Central Power ambassadors worked to have a friendly statesman take over as premier.[61] Time and again Czernin predicted that if Italy lined up with the Entente, Rumania would forthwith imitate her, and Conrad shared that judgment.[62] Arguably, the most opportune occasion for Rumania to have entered the titanic struggle was March, 1915, when the Galician stronghold of Przemyśl fell to the Russians —but the chance was passed by. When Austro-Italian diplomatic relations approached the breaking point, martial excitement gripped Bucharest partly because representatives of Vienna banking houses made ostentatious preparations to go home; it was assumed that they felt certain that Rumania intended to march hand-in-glove with Italy. To calm apprehensions, Czernin requested the Ballplatz to prevent the withdrawal of the bank officials. But the massive Central Power offensive of 1915 against Russia temporarily chilled the martial passions of Rumanian Ententophiles. Smarting under the defection of Italy, Berlin intensified pressure upon Vienna and upon Tisza to offer concessions that would bring Rumania in as an ally or at least would induce it to remain neutral, but the Magyar Premier derisively pushed the requests aside, and pleaded for greater diplomatic activity in

[60] Queen Marie of Roumania, *Ordeal* (New York, 1935), pp. 5–52.
[61] Czernin to Berchtold, Nov. 17, 1914, Hohenlohe to Berchtold, Nov. 21, 1914, P.A., *Krieg*, 6A, Rumänien.
[62] For example, Çzernin to Berchtold, Jan. 9, 1915, P.A., *Geheim*, XLVII/7d. Wartime understandings between Bucharest and Rome, of which Czernin may have had knowledge, implied that the two cabinets intended to pursue parallel diplomatic policies. C. J. Diamandy, "La Grande Guerre Vue du Versant Oriental," *Revue des Deux Mondes*, LX (1930), 425–32.

Sofia, contending that Rumania would keep the peace, if Bulgaria hooked up firmly with the Central Empires. Prominent newspapers of Germany protested loudly that the Ballplatz was handling the Bucharest problem maladroitly.

In the late summer of 1915, Rumanian emotions turned jittery when it appeared that Bulgaria was making ready to enter the Central Alliance and Hapsburg troop movements stirred fears of an impending invasion; Czernin toiled at pouring oil on the troubled waters. Pro-Entente interventionist feelings mounted, as the Central Powers swept ahead in the conquest of Serbia, but Brătianu defiantly repulsed demands for war upon Austria-Hungary, made by Hungarophobes and Entente diplomatists alike.[63] "The defeat of Serbia," lamented the Bucharest *Adeverul*, "means that we Rumanians are completely encircled; . . . it means that in the future, when the Allies are defeated by the Germans, we shall become a German province—alas! worse than that, a Hungarian province."

Feverish competition for the wheat of Rumania proceeded apace. In January, 1916, Vienna and Berlin were highly incensed when British agents brought off a contract for a large quantity of grain which could not possibly be gotten out to the island kingdom and must therefore be allowed to rot. Aside from diplomatic protests, Czernin revived maneuvers to overthrow Bratianu and kept them going for weeks; in these efforts he had the full cooperation of his German colleague. By frontal pressure, Czernin managed to force Rumanian refugees from Transylvania, who aspired to seats in the Bucharest parliament, to withdraw their candidacies. More than that, in March, 1916, the Central Powers completed deals for Rumanian grain, providing for shipments which would run almost twice as high as the purchases recently made

[63] Tisza to Czernin, May 23, 1915, P.A. *Geheim*, XLVII/7d; Burián to Czernin, May 30, June 1, 1915, *ibid.*; Hohenlohe to Burián, June 2, 1915, *ibid.*

by the British. Many an observer construed the transaction to mean that the protracted vacillation of the Brătianu ministry was nearing the end and that it would soon enter the war as the ally of the Central Empires!

Yet, in fact, the pendulum in June sharply swung the other way in response to "Brusilov's immortal days." The hour had struck, the premier at last decided, to join the Entente, but he dilly-dallied while the terms of intervention were bolted down in black and white. Somehow or other Czernin got wind of the Bratianu conditions and forwarded them to Vienna.[64] Thoroughly alarmed by the prospective intervention of Rumania, Tisza demanded that military reinforcements should be posted along the frontier, else, if war came, the enemy would march into Transylvania, as though on parade; and Sofia, he implored, should state unequivocally that if Rumania fought the Monarchy it would be involved in war with Bulgaria as well; repressive regulations upon the Rumanian minority in Hungary, particularly controls on the press, were tightened. His hands more than full with the Brusilov challenge, Conrad piteously appealed for the expenditure of whatever sums as bribes were necessary to hold Rumania to neutrality, and the cabinet of Berlin again made it pellucidly clear to Brătianu that German guns would be turned against Rumania if its troops attacked the Danube Monarchy.

Inside Rumania opponents of intervention clashed violently with Austrophobes. Troops broke up rioting by anti-war Socialists, killing several and wounding more, and their newspapers were muzzled. "Give us war and sacred union," staunch interventionist Take Jonescu shrieked to the crown, "that together we may make a

---

[64] Czernin to Burián, June 28, 1916, P.A., *Geheim,* XLVII/7g. On the devious dickerings of Brătianu with the Entente, Russia principally, see, Sherman D. Spector, *Rumania at the Paris Peace Conference* (New York, 1962), pp. 21–39.

greater Rumania, for in a small Rumania, there is room
neither for you nor us."

Czernin could not make up his mind on how precisely
Brătianu intended to behave; one dispatch assumed that
belligerency on the Entente side would follow the har-
vesting of crops, but another argued that if the Brusilov
offensive were stopped, neutralism would prevail. Toward
the end of July, it was learned in Vienna that war supplies from the west had begun to trickle into Rumania
by way of Russia, that reservists were being called to the
colors, and that children living near the Hungarian border were being evacuated to the interior of the Regat.
Certain now that Rumania would shortly join the Entente, Tisza and Conrad pressed for a sudden, surprise
attack before preparations to fight had been completed,
but they could not impose their wills on the Ballplatz;[65]
the semi-official *Fremdenblatt* of Vienna revealed, however, that plans had long since been devised for thrashing
Rumania, if it became a belligerent. Yet, as late as August
19, Czernin reported that a new ministry, pledged to
neutralism might take office, and the day before the
actual decision to fight was taken Ferdinand and Brătianu solemnly assured the Austrian that the kingdom
would stay out of the war, the King observing that nine
out of ten of his subjects subscribed to that line. But the
last diplomatic records on Rumania bear witness that
Czernin and his superiors in Vienna accurately divined
the ultimate Rumanian policy even to the time when the
verdict for intervention was made.[66]

In the meanwhile, on August 17, the principal Entente
ministries had definitively accepted the price that the
Prime Minister set for the sword of his nation, though
the Russians and the French agreed in a secret reservation that the bargain would be fulfilled "only to the

[65] Conrad to Burián, Aug. 12, 1916, P.A., *Geheim*, XLVII/7g.
[66] Czernin to Burián, Aug. 19, 20, 26 (two despatches), *ibid.*

extent that the general situation permitted." What territorial promises, in fact, did Brătianu exact? All of Transylvania, the Banat of Temesvár (Timișoara), and the Bukowina to the Pruth (Prut) River—pledges which grossly
contravened the principle of self-determination, for although many Rumanian-speaking folk lived in the promised lands, so did relatively large groups of Magyars,
Ukrainians, South Slavs, and others. Against the pleadings
of the Entente cabinets, Brătianu stubbornly insisted that
his country would fight only Austria-Hungary, not Germany. It was stipulated that the signatories would not
make separate peace settlements with the enemy and that
at the eventual peace conference Rumanian delegates
would rank on a footing of equality with the major allies.
Military prescriptions of the treaty obligated Rumania to
begin fighting before the end of August; Bucharest was
promised substantial military assistance from Russia and
was assured that the Entente forces cooped up in Salonica would checkmate Bulgaria, if the latter warred upon
Rumania. It was imagined, however, by Brătianu, in the
light of secret, soothing phrases from Sofia, that Bulgaria
would remain quiet.

In the testing time, these pledges and prognostications
turned out to be illusory: Russian aid and help from
Salonica were inconsequential, and Bulgaria attacked
fiercely. Seldom in modern times has a nation been so
miserably deceived, and yet it must be said the diplomatic
behavior of the Brătianu ministry fell below model standards of rectitude and fidelity. Moreover, in spite of the
lessons of more than two years of war in Europe, the
Rumanian armies were incapable of anything more than
limited campaigns, and soldier morale, at the boiling
point so far as Magyars were concerned, evinced only
passive hostility toward the armies of Germany.

With the Entente treaty in hand, Brătianu convened

a fateful crown council on August 27 attended by Ferdinand, ministers of state, and other weight-carrying politicians. King and Prime Minister defined the case for going to war, Ferdinand tortured in mind at the sacrifice which patriotism required of his personal convictions. As at the crown council of August, 1914, the old Russophobe, Peter Carp stood alone, this time in resisting an armed struggle with the Danube Monarchy; to the king he boldly declared that intervention would cost him both his throne and his country. Although Marghiloman preferred that Rumania should stick to neutrality, out of patriotic sentiment he went along with the majority of the council. Not for the first time, the crucial decision for war was taken without any consultation whatsoever with parliament. Of its own choosing and on its own terms, Rumanian statecraft after long and anxious deliberation launched the kingdom on a veritable life or death struggle.[67]

In the call to arms King Ferdinand asserted that Rumania had patiently waited two years and more for betterment in the treatment of national kinsmen living in Hungary, but in reality tyranny had grown more intolerable. "It is given us," he proclaimed, "to assure unshakeably and in its fulness . . . the union of the Rumanians on both sides of the Carpathians." In accepting the challenge, the cabinet of Vienna likened the conduct of Bucharest to that of Rome, to that of Judas, and soon published a *Red Book* of diplomatic documents to "prove" its case. The leading Social Democratic organ of Vienna stridently reviled perfidious Rumania, and proceeded to deliver a sermon on the worthlessness of secret treaties such as the Central Empires a generation and more be-

---

[67] Marghiloman, *op. cit.*, pp. 161–166. Queen Marie recorded in her diary, ". . . I have known [what is coming to pass] for many weeks . . . I know it is going to be war . . . Are we right? Are we wrong? I know not, but the moment has come . . ." *op. cit.*, pp. 49–50.

fore had negotiated with the new adversary.[68] Deprived of Transylvania, declared Count Andrássy, Hungary could not exist, "We must fight to the last man to avenge this terrible treachery." "We will fight like bears," echoed the *Pester Hirlap*, "tigers, hyenas, lions."

14.

By way of illustration of the manner in which journalism oscillated amidst the ordeal of war, the interpretations of Mussolini's *Popolo d'Italia* on Rumanian policy deserve to be tagged a classic. While the Bucharest cabinet held to neutrality the paper pulled no punches:

Italians must cease describing the Rumanians as our sister nation. They are not Romans at all, however much they may claim this noble title. They are a mixture of barbarous aborigines, conquered by Romans, and Slavs, Kazans, Avars, Tartars, Mongols, Huns, and Turks. It is easy to imagine what a brood of rascals has emerged from such origins. The Rumanian of today is still a barbarian . . . who apes the Parisian . . .

But after Rumania plumped for war, the *Popolo* told readers:

The Rumanians have now proved in the most striking fashion that they are worthy sons of the ancient Romans, from whom they, like ourselves, are descended. They are in fact our nearest brethren, who with courage and determination are fighting with Latin and Slav against German—in other words, in the battle for freedom, civilization and right against Prussian tyranny, domineering, barbarism and egotism . . . In the face of Austro-Hungarian barbarism and uncivilization [the Rumanians will] throw their sharp sword into the scales and weigh them down. Nothing other indeed

[68] *AZ*, Sept. 5, 1916.

could be expected from a people which has the honor of belonging to that Latin race which once ruled the world.[69]

Upon morale in the Hapsburg Monarchy the intervention of Rumania exerted a double impact: exhilarating in the longer term, but initially disheartening. Once more, as with Italy, a major diplomatic gamble had gone awry, and Hungary, Turkey, and Bulgaria lay open to attack by presumably powerful Rumanian-Russian armies, imports of grain and oil ceased, and Austro-Hungarian battle lines were extended about five hundred miles. Furious outbursts over alleged mismanagement of relations with Rumania and neglect by the military authorities to provide adequate defenses for Transylvania rocked the parliament and press of Budapest; but Tisza contrived to silence the storm. The Austro-Hungarian mood of pessimism deepened during the first encounters of the war, as Rumanian armies tempestuously charged into Transylvania; yet the stay however sweet was short, and in a few weeks Central Power troops had conquered the choicest portions of the Regat.[70]

Four days before the involvement of Rumania, Italy declared war upon the German Empire. Up to a point that announcement merely came to grips with reality. Rigorous censorship had excluded discussion of relations with Germany from the Italian press, many spokesmen of the commercial class wished technical neutrality to be maintained, and fear was expressed that if war were declared, German armies might strike at the peninsula by way of Switzerland. But such counsels were submerged by the ministry in Rome, which recited deeds of German hostility, assistance rendered the Danube Monarchy, and

[69] Quoted in *Frankfurter Zeitung*, Sept. 11, 1916.
[70] Gogu Negulescu, *Rumania's Sacrifice* (New York, 1918), a piteous lament, addressed to Americans, dwelling on the themes that the kingdom was the innocent victim of unscrupulous allies and that the country would have been better off if neutralism had been preserved.

maltreatment of Italian nationals in Germany as enemy aliens. By entering the lists against Germany, Italy tardily fulfilled her pledge in the Treaty of London.

The spreading flame had now enveloped Europe entirely save for the fringes in the southwest and in the extreme north.

6. Entente Opinion and the Danube Monarchy

ENTENTE CHANCELLERIES REVEALED PRECIOUS LITTLE IN THE first half of the war on the objectives of the fighting so far as the Danube Monarchy was concerned, and encouragement of revolutionary sentiments as a weapon of victory received scant attention. But unofficially, and markedly in Great Britain, debate on the future of the Hapsburg realm started virtually with the beginning of hostilities. British intellectuals who wished the Monarchy preserved might have drawn sustenance from the pronouncement of the eminent Lord Palmerston, "It is greatly for the interests of Europe," he affirmed on January 1, 1859, "that Austria should continue to be a Great Power in the center of the Continent," or of Lord Salisbury (October, 1879) who believed that "in the strength and independence of Austria lie the best hopes of European peace and stability." [1]

[1] Quoted in William H. Dawson, *Problems of the Peace* (1917), p. 148; see also Pribram, *Austria-Hungary and Great Britain*, p. 42. British knowledge of the Monarchy before the war is surveyed by Harry Hanak, *Great Britain and Austria-Hungary During the First World War* (London, 1962), Chap. I.

Hardly had the war begun than the London *Nation,* which considered Serbia "the basest member of the European family," recommended only minimum alterations in the Hapsburg patrimony in the peace settlement. Apprehensive of possible tsarist aggrandizement in the Polish area of the Monarchy, this mouth-piece of Liberal opinion reminded readers that Austrian Poles enjoyed considerable home-rule and were reasonably contented. If Galicia were taken away and the Trentino were awarded to Italy and Transylvania to Rumania, in return for neutrality, then Austria-Hungary, it was asserted, would be indistinguishable from one of the larger Balkan kingdoms; as sequels the power equilibrium of Europe would be disrupted and cultural levels would be lowered. Seeking to calm the dreads which tsarist Russia aroused in Liberal and Labour breasts the Fabian novelist, H. G. Wells, dismissed such apprehensions as due to "extreme ignorance of Russian realities." At least two centuries would have to elapse, Wells supposed, before the Slav colossus could become an authentic menace to the West of Europe. "When Russia has the will to oppress the world," Wells explained, "she will never have the power; when she has the power she will cease to have the will." So he was prepared to see Russia annex all Polish districts and Austria-Hungary dissolved. The creator of *The New Machiavelli* lashed out scornfully against Labourites who were against the war because of "some fancied diabolical quality of our ally Russia," and he poked fun at the "penny dreadful idea of Russia," contending that the tsardom had in fact turned "liberal," willy-nilly, by virtue of alignment with Britain and France.[2] Equally, the influential Catholic writer, Gilbert K. Chesterton, contributing to the *Daily Mail* in the autumn of 1914, strove to

---

[2] Anon., "The Future of the Poles," and H. G. Wells, "The Liberal Fear of Russia," *Nation,* Aug. 22, 1914; Wells to the editor, London *Times,* Sept. 22, 1914.

smooth away misgivings about the empire of the Tsar with the logic that it was much less menacing for the security of Europe than Prussia.

Some leftward oriented British publicists, Henry N. Brailsford for one, argued that talk of dismembering Austria-Hungary justified the German doctrine that vast armies were necessary to protect the security and integrity of the Central Empires. He predicted that the Dual Monarchy might suffer considerable amputations along the frontiers, yet he felt that on economic and political grounds it would be desirable for the Hapsburgs to reign over Hungary and Bohemia. The Danube Monarchy, he observed, "inspires no love, but it arouses only local hates. It will survive as a convenience." He did not exclude from his calculations the possibility of a speedy termination of the war on the basis of a federal union along the Danube in which the South Slav districts would be fully autonomous.[3]

In point of fact, the disposition of Brailsford toward the Monarchy, as also of Noel and Charles R. Buxton, stemmed in part from the conviction that Bulgaria, their Balkan pet, had been robbed of land in Macedonia by Serbia in the warfare of 1913. Earlier Brailsford had written, "Servia is not exactly a credit to civilization, and one cannot say that her political extinction would be a serious loss to Europe."[4]

If the cabinet in Vienna adopted a policy of wisdom, mused an anonymous British writer, and broke loose from imperial Germany, the House of Hapsburg might emerge from the conflict bigger and more influential internationally than ever; what he had in mind was the addition

---

[3] H. N. Brailsford, London *Nation*, Aug. 29, 1914; *ibid.*, "Hungary and Independence," *New Republic*, II (Feb. 13, 1915), 44–45; *ibid.*, to Seton-Watson, undated, but probably 1915, Seton-Watson Papers; see, Hanak, *op. cit.*, pp. 136–144.

[4] *Macedonia* (London, 1906), p. 319.

of Silesia, Saxony, and southern Germany to the Monarchy.[5] If Britain honestly believed in the much-discussed principle of the balance of power in Europe, commented the *Economist*, the foreign office would repudiate crude projects to tear Austria-Hungary apart. In an unusually perspicacious analysis of the future of the Monarchy, Sydney Brooks, a leading journalist who wrote frequently for periodicals in Britain and in the United States, likened the nationality wrangle in Bohemia to the strife in Ireland and insisted that leaders of the Hapsburg national communities agitated simply for autonomy, not for secession. Expressing a viewpoint that popped up many times, it seemed to him initially that dissolution of the Monarchy would mean that Russia would attain mastery over Hapsburg Slav-speaking populations, but shortly, astonished by the military disasters which befell Hapsburg arms in the east, Brooks fancied that the realm was on the brink of utter collapse, and that partition impended along lines of nationality. The Magyars might be allowed to form an independent state, confined to areas of Magyar speech, he suggested, while the Austrogermans would gravitate into the empire of the Hohenzollerns.[6]

Best known as an African specialist, Sir Harry H. Johnston wished the Monarchy to resume after the war a solid place among civilized countries and opposed wresting away any land that rightfully belonged to Austria or to Hungary or which preferred to remain with them. Yet Herzegovina should be given to Serbia, he believed, the Cattaro (Kotor) enclave to Montenegro, and these south Slav kingdoms should be permitted to decide the status of Albania, except for the southern zone. Johnston also proposed that Galicia, and predominantly Ukrainian-peopled portions of the Monarchy should go to Russia,

[5] "V," "What will be Austria's Future?" *Fortnightly Review*, CIV (1915), 55–69.

[6] Sydney Brooks, "The Future of Austria-Hungary," *North American Review*, CC (1914), 194–202; *ibid.*, "The New Europe," *ibid.*, 670–672.

provided that Galicia were combined with Russian Poland as an autonomous state ruled by a tsarist prince.[7]

As the fighting dragged along, Johnston urged that the cabinet of Vienna should be persuaded to pull out of the war in exchange for the right to annex southern Germany; the Monarchy in turn would have to yield "some degree of satisfaction" to "reasonable Italian and Rumanian aspirations," sacrifice territory to the south Slav states, and cooperate in the making of an independent Poland. With a Monarchy, thus revamped, the Entente could "live on brotherly terms," Johnston reasoned, for Vienna was not hated, as Berlin would be hated for generations to come.[8] Thinking along somewhat kindred lines, the Oxford historian J. A. R. Marriott questioned whether the Monarchy on the Danube had outlived its usefulness and doubted whether it would be judicious, even if it were possible, to annihilate it. By sacrificing peripheral provinces, which were a liability for internal health and international stability, the Hapsburgs could continue to fulfill their historical mission and to play a worthy role in the affairs of Europe, Marriott believed.[9]

Dispassionately surveying the horizon of southeastern Europe, Marion L. Newbigin, geographer, imagined that the Monarchy could save itself by realistic adaptation to a changed political environment. "Perfection is an attribute of machinery," it was sagely observed, "not of living organisms." The union of Serbia and Montenegro was bound to come about, Newbigin thought, and he was disposed to gratify the Serbian ambition for an outlet on the Adriatic by way of northern Albania and to attach parts of Bosnia-Herzegovina to Serbia; on the other hand, to incorporate Dalmatia and Croatia in Serbia would be

[7] Harry H. Johnston, "Germany, Africa, and the Terms of Peace," *Nineteenth Century*, LXXVII (1915), 752–767.

[8] Harry H. Johnston, "Austria and the Way Out," *Living Age*, CCXC (1916), 629–631.

[9] J. A. R. Marriott, "Some Issues of the War," *Nineteenth Century*, LXXVI (1914), 1377–1394.

"a hazardous experiment," and to deprive Hungary of the seaport of Fiume would spell disaster for all concerned.[10]

Certain that the war was both a folly and a crime, the Cambridge don, G. Lowes Dickinson, favored allowing the South Slavs in the Monarchy to decide their political future in a plebiscite. He shared the rather widespread dread of imperial Russia and felt that if tsarist ambition to expand westward were frustrated, Europe entire would benefit. Warmly sympathetic to ideas of self-determination and of a post-war league to maintain peace, Dickinson argued that application of these principles would alleviate human antagonisms even in European areas which were "an almost inextricable tangle of nationalities"; he and others like him conducted a continuous and vigorous propaganda on the theme of democratic control of foreign policy, insisting that "the time had gone by for entrusting the destinies of nations to the supposed wisdom of experts." [11]

An editorial leader, "Our friend, the enemy," appearing in the Conservative *Morning Post*, well-known for Magyarophile predilections, elicited a spate of commentary on both sides of the debate concerning the Hapsburg realm. Voicing pity for the Magyars, the editorial regarded them as enemies solely because they were fighting alongside of Germany, and the British government, it was recommended, should bend every effort to wheedle the leadership of Hungary into a compromise peace. Letter-writers strongly endorsed the opinions in the editorial, and showered praise upon Hungary and the Hungarians, with an important reservation on Prime Minister

[10] Marion L. Newbigin, *Geographical Aspects of Balkan Problems* (New York, 1915), pp. 232–236.

[11] Goldsworthy Lowes Dickinson, "The War and the Way Out," *Atlantic Monthly*, CXIV (1914), 820–837; *ibid.*, CXV (1915), 516–524, 691–700; *ibid.*, CXVIII (1916), 145–152.

Stephan Tisza, who, it was charged, had foully betrayed the splendid traditions of his Motherland. Contrariwise, Alfred Noyes, poet of the "Barrel-Organ," penned a blistering indictment of the Magyars for atrocities in the war, citing as proof stories put about by the Swiss pseudo-scholar, R. A. Reiss, and he earnestly protested against all thought of a separate peace or pledges of Hungarian territorial integrity. Seconding that point of view, Dr. R. W. Seton-Watson, militant spokesman of the *Austria delenda* school, insisted that the current conflict was "quite as much a Magyar war" as a German war, for crude and cruel Magyar racist policies had led inevitably to the struggle, and he begged to point out that Hungarian politicians irrespective of party had enthusiastically acclaimed the decision for war and still pressed for its vigorous prosecution; only by a total Entente victory, he wrote, could the corrupt and benighted Magyar ruling caste be thrown down and abused national communities liberated.

Almost from the onset of the war, the right-wing *Morning Post* set itself up as the champion of Hungary in British journalism. Though it published a few pieces favoring dissolution of the Monarchy into its national components, these contributions were smothered by a running barrage of pro-Hungarian articles. They portrayed the land of the Magyars as peace-loving, fond of England and things English, yearning for release alike from the Hapsburg connection and German lordship, and wishing to lead an independent national existence. British partisans of the Hungarian national minorities struck back vigorously, accusing the Budapest ministry of special responsibility for the coming of the war and upbraiding it for brutal oppression of the minorities. Yet the *Morning Post* campaign was waged vigorously until the summer of 1916, when one Joseph Szebenyei, a Magyar residing in London who had written many of the pieces, was imprisoned as an enemy alien.[12] At about the same time, Sir William R. Robertson, chief of the British general staff, urged that the Monarchy should be perpetuated since it checkmated the power of Russia and prevented France or Italy from transforming the Mediterranean into a private preserve, which would work disadvantageously for the imperial interests of Britain.

These representative specimens of British thinking indicate that a good deal of support existed for the maintenance of the Monarchy, in harmony with the views expressed by Palmerston and Salisbury. A fervent advocate of the destruction of Monarchy charged that greedy international financiers, myopic Roman Catholics, and benighted scions of British high society, all cherishing kindly sentiments for the Hapsburg dynasty, maliciously interfered with the logical processes of history.[13]

2.

In British intellectual circles a not inconsiderable heritage of anti-Hapsburg sentiment prevailed, reaching back to the age of Prince Clemens Metternich, a black ogre in the scales of liberalism. Hostility had been nourished by and during the tumultuous reception accorded in 1851 to Louis Kossuth, leader of the less than liberal Magyar revolt of 1848–49 against the rule of the Hapsburg. Gladstonians kept recalling the famous—and injudicious—utterance of their master made in 1880 to the effect that in the whole world it was impossible to place a finger on a spot and say, "Here Austria did good." At the turn of the twentieth century the Dual Monarchy was indicted for real and fancied oppression of minority

[12] *Morning Post*, Aug. 22, 23, 24, 28, Sept. 1, 1916; cf. Hanak, *op. cit.*, pp. 164–173.
[13] H. W. Steed, *Through Thirty Years*, 1892–1922 (2 vols., London, 1924), II, 129.

populations, for the arbitrary annexation of Bosnia-Herze-govina, and because of the feeling that national self-de-termination harmonized with the loftiest principles of the democratic creed.[14] Multinationality Austria-Hungary was derided as an anomaly and an anachronism which ought to be swept into the spacious dust-bin of history. When the war started in 1914, it was freely charged, as indeed it had been before, that the Monarchy was little other than the supine marionette of the mighty, aggressive Ger-man Empire, a pawn in the desperate game of Berlin to establish hegemony over the Continent.[15]

The distinguished Cambridge historian, George M. Trevelyan, whose writings on Garibaldi had earned him enviable international acclaim, and who had worked at civilian relief in war-wracked Serbia, proclaimed on both sides of the Atlantic that Europe would never know peace until the national communities of the Monarchy had secured self-government and freedom for their languages and schools. On a trip to the United States, Trevelyan blended harrowing tales of bestial savageries committed by Austro-Hungarian soldiers with moving appeals for humanitarian assistance to the Serbs.

To the contention that the Monarchy must be main-tained as a post-war counterpoise to the empire of the Tsar, Professor J. Ellis Barker, specialist on German af-fairs, retorted that dread of Muscovite expansion was a bogey, since the war would exhaust the eastern colossus for decades to come. "Nature and natural evolution," he thought, could be relied upon to raise an effective barrier against Russian aggression. Not only had the Danube Monarchy degenerated into an enslaved vassal of Ger-many, but Austrian and Hungarian soldiers were guilty

[14] Pribram, *Austria-Hungary and Great Britain,* a convenient survey, which disputes the theory of a "traditional friendship" between the two countries and then proceeds to demonstrate that interpretation.

[15] Arthur J. May, "R. W. Seton-Watson and British Anti-Hapsburg Sentiment," *American Slavic and East European Review,* XX (1961), 40–54.

of hideous atrocities, the teachers of the Germans in bestial enormities. Yet before long, Barker was writing that if the tiring Monarchy would quickly agree to a separate peace, her territorial losses would be limited to a section of Galicia, which would pass to a resurrected Poland, and to Bosnia-Herzegovina, which would be assigned to Serbia; in compensation, Austria might obtain the Roman Catholic districts of southern Germany. Barker prophesied civil conflicts in the Slav provinces and in Hungary and predicted that if the cabinet of Vienna did not come to terms promptly with the Entente, Italy and Rumania would take up arms to secure Hapsburg territories they coveted. "It is therefore conceivable," he wishfully reasoned, "and is indeed only logical, that Austria-Hungary will conclude overnight a separate peace." Barker rather liked the idea of a reconstructed Hapsburg realm embracing the German-inhabited areas of Austria, the Catholic states of southern Germany and possibly Prussian Silesia, or, alternatively, a federal union to replace the discredited and tottering Austro-Hungarian dualistic structure.[16]

Without particular intensity Lord James Bryce leaned toward the disruption of the Monarchy, though he doubted whether all of the South Slavs desired to merge with Serbia. He was generally sympathetic to Czechoslovak national ambitions, and to a free Poland, save for the Ukrainian area of east Galicia; the Magyars should be allowed to decide their own fate, and Italy should be accorded the Trentino. Wisely Bryce wrote, "leaders, especially when they are also exiles, naturally tend to attribute their own ardent convictions to their fellow-

[16] J. E. Barker, "The Ultimate Disappearance of Austria-Hungary," *Nineteenth Century*, LXXVI (1914), 1003–1031; *ibid.*, "The Chances of Peace and the Problem of Poland," *ibid.*, LXXVII (1915), 84–114; *ibid.*, *The Great Problems of British Statesmanship* (London, 1917), 105–145; see, Hanak, *op. cit.*, pp. 98–99.

countrymen at home, many of whom may be but faintly interested in nationalistic aspirations." [17]

For sheer resourcefulness and sustained labors to bring to pass the destruction of the Monarchy and the creation of an independent Czechoslovakia and a united Yugoslavia, very high marks must be awarded to the British publicist, H. Wickham Steed. Often called a "statesmanjournalist," Steed ranks among the shrewdest and most persuasive molders of British sentiment on international affairs of his generation; well has it been said that he "not only influenced world policy but actually made history." Tall, spare, elegant, with pointed mustache and Vandyke beard, charming in manner and of commanding personality, Steed reminded contemporaries of Cardinal Armand Jean du Plessis de Richelieu. He gave the impression of being more the seasoned diplomatist than a workaday newspaperman.

Steed benefitted from a cosmopolitan education, and, as correspondent for the London *Times* in Berlin, Rome, and Vienna, where he was stationed for more than a decade, he fashioned a European reputation. He left Vienna in 1913 "with the relief a man feels when he escapes from a vast edifice that is tottering to its fall." An indefatigable traveller and an engaging, brilliant conversationalist, he had built up personal acquaintanceships with the principal nationality leaders of Austria-Hungary, above all with the Czech Professor Thomas G. Masaryk, and gained their confidence.

In 1913, Steed was appointed chief of the foreign department of the *Times* and that year his "long essay" on *The Hapsburg Monarchy* came off the press; it was translated into several languages and several times reprinted. A work of lasting merit, it revealed remarkable

[17] James Bryce, *Essays and Addresses in Wartime* (New York, 1918), pp. 156, 162–163.

familiarity with the realities of the Danubian realm, and reflected Steed's deep detestation of the existing regime and his passionate love of liberty. He was profoundly convinced that the Monarchy would bring disaster upon itself and upon Europe unless the "crazy" dualistic framework of government was replaced by some scheme of federal unity. A trialistic reconstruction, putting the southern Slav areas on a plane of equality with Austria and Hungary, Steed rejected as unacceptable, tagging it a clerical stratagem to exploit the Roman Catholic Croats in bringing the Orthodox Serbs under Hapsburg authority. On the ground that the book insulted Emperor-King Francis Joseph, it was banned by the Austrian government, which intensified the author's aversion to the dynasty. To the very close of his lengthy, versatile, and distinguished career, and despite the horrors and tragedies that befell Europe after 1914, Steed still firmly believed that in Austria-Hungary "no ostensible fact corresponded to any obvious or tangible reality." [18]

Touched with the spirit of the knight-errant and not above indulging in venom, sensationalism, and fantasy, Steed thought and preached, sincerely no doubt, that the dissolution of the Monarchy was the indispensable prerequisite for lasting peace and stability in Europe. He dedicated his admittedly immense energies to the promotion of the centrifugal work of secessionist forces in the Danubian realm and won golden opinions from national patriots there. In the war years, he entertained at his London residence weight-carrying men of many tongues, who, in that congenial environment, devised ways and means of achieving freedom for their co-nationals. On Steed, the Czech politician Eduard Beneš

[18] For appreciations of Steed at his death, see, London *Times*, January 14, 17, 18, 1956. His experiences of the war are recorded in the second volume of *Through Thirty Years*. See also *Slavonic and East European Review*, XXX (1952), 334–335, and Hanak, *op. cit.*, pp. 11–20.

wrote, he "has and always will have a place of honor in the history of our liberation." While Professor Trevelyan hailed Steed as "the evil genius" of the Hapsburg House and "the avenging angel" of the smaller nationalities, friends of the Danube Monarchy have classified him among its principal grave-diggers.[19]

For readers of the *Edinburgh Review* Steed sketched his thinking on the objectives of the war in no small detail. Germany, he contended, benefitted far more than Austria-Hungary from their alliance, and he summoned the Entente powers to disrupt the realm on the Danube beyond repair. "The Hapsburg Monarchy," he eloquently declared, "must be broken into and broken up from outside by detaching from it those elements, which, ethnically, belong elsewhere." Specifically, he wanted a strong, united kingdom of South Slavs, a unified and autonomous Poland under the scepter of the Tsar, a Czechoslovakia, which would enjoy home rule, or, best of all, untrammeled independence, and the cession to Rumania of preponderantly Rumanian-peopled districts—provided that the cabinet of Bucharest cast its sword on the Entente side of the war scales; except for Dalmatia, Steed was prepared to satisfy the well-known pretensions of Italian irredentism. Altogether, his wide-ranging agenda, if implemented, would clearly spell the doom of the Hapsburgs.[20]

Convinced of the righteousness and the political rightness of his crusade to destroy the House of Hapsburg, Steed was not one to suffer opponents gladly, nor was he above giving less informed associates what he called his

[19] Éduard Beneš, *Souvenirs de Guerre et de Révolution* (2 vols., Paris, 1928), I, 174–175; Adolf Dresler, "Henry Wickham Steed, der Gekaufte Hetzjournalist," *BM*, XX (1942), 546–551; *ibid.*, "Lord Northcliffe's Generalstabchef," *Süddeutsche Monatshefte*, XXII (1924–25), 41–45, 72–73; Enrico Serra, "Ricordo di Henry Wickham Steed," *Nuova Antologia*, CCCLXXXIII (1956), 575–582.

[20] H. W. Steed, "A Programme for Peace," *Edinburgh Review*, CCXXIII (Ap. 1916), 373–392.

Child's Guide to Knowledge. Optimistically, Steed felt sure that British public sentiment was wheeling round to the cause of dismemberment, and on July 16, 1915, he wrote: "The foolish doctrine that it may be to our interest to spare Austria-Hungary as much as possible is giving way to the sounder doctrine that our vital interest is to aid in the creation of as many moderately strong states as possible in Europe . . ." [21]

3.

In the person of Robert W. Seton Watson, Steed had an ally not less knowledgeable on the affairs of south-central Europe than himself, and a tenacious, resourceful and indefatigable crusader in the war years on behalf of the South Slavs, the Czechoslovaks, and the Rumanians, whom he knew so well and admired with lively, though not uncritical affection.[22] He had a decided preference for the westernized Croats under the Magyar yoke rather than for the Serbs.

Educated at Oxford, Berlin, Paris, and Vienna Universities and widely traveled in the Hapsburg Monarchy and in the Balkans, Seton-Watson was a prolific author of articles and books bearing on these areas. As a young man, he contemplated writing a history of Austria or of Calvinism in Hungary, but he switched to the contemporary scene, and, under the pen-name of "Scotus Viator," "bent on the study of history and politics," he gave wide circulation to the abuses inflicted upon national minorities in Hungary, more particularly the Slovaks and the Croats. His *bête noir* was the Magyar ruling caste, even though he appreciated the stern virtues of Count Stephan Tisza,

---

[21] *The History of the (London) Times* (4 vols., London, 1935–52), IV, 237.

[22] For the career of Seton-Watson, consult Hanak, *op. cit.*, pp. 20–35, and Arthur J. May, "Seton-Watson and the Treaty of London," *JMH*, XXIX (1957), 42–47, n. 1.

a zealous Calvinist like Seton-Watson himself. Imbued with a Gladstonian, liberal outlook on human affairs, Seton-Watson fought unflinchingly and nobly for causes he believed to be true and right and generous. In his approach to the problems of Central Europe, a deeply emotional quality was apparent with morality—grounded, perhaps, upon religious convictions—as guide and mentor. " 'Scotus' was a dear soul," Steed said of him, "tender and sensitive, tenacious and righteous, prudent and brave." Comfortably off financially, and a remarkable linguist, he enjoyed an extensive acquaintance with nationality spokesmen of the Monarchy, especially with Masaryk whom he met in 1910; thereafter, the wandering Scot developed an active interest in the Bohemian question.

Before the war, Seton-Watson pleaded for the conversion of the Danube Monarchy into a tripartite realm, a Yugoslav partner taking its place alongside of Austria and Hungary. Such an arrangement, he believed, would form the starting point for the evolution of the Hapsburg dominions into a multinationality federal union, and he dismissed suggestions that the Monarchy should be broken up into a bevy of national states as not only impracticable but impossible. Yet, after fighting commenced in 1914, he thought the Monarchy neither could nor should survive the conflict and worked for its complete disruption. It is evident that it was only with supreme reluctance that Seton-Watson abandoned his faith in a trialistic reconstruction of the Monarchy and came out in advocacy of dissolution.[23]

With surpassing industry Seton-Watson toiled to mold British public thinking and diplomatic policy to his point of view by means of articles in periodicals, books, and

---

[23] R. W. Seton-Watson to Lord Cromer, Sept. 12, 1915. Seton-Watson Papers. In this note appeared the observation ". . . I can never cease to regret lost hopes which I had centered upon the late Archduke and his genuine determination to work for internal reform."

propagandistic societies. As a literary stylist, he wrote with gusto, born of deep conviction, and he could be—and frequently was—ironical and intensely polemical. For him and like-spirited British intellectuals, interpreting their idealism in transcendental fashion, the war took on the complexion of a holy struggle.[24] Seton-Watson was often reproached as irresponsible, as a dangerous immoderate agitator who was entirely willing to prolong the miseries of the war so that his convictions on central Europe might assuredly be translated into realities. On the other side, Scotus Viator endeared himself in a lasting way to the politically articulate among the smaller national communities of the Dual Monarchy.

It is not necessary to recount in detail the varied and ceaseless wartime labors of Seton-Watson, a record that awaits the completion of a biography of the man and his work. Shortly after the onset of the fighting he acted as intermediary for Masaryk in placing the views of the eminent Czech on the existing situation in Central Europe and the prospects for the future before the foreign offices of Britain, France, and Russia.[25] He also journeyed to Serbia to collect information with which to rally British support for that war-ravaged land, and on returning he delivered (March 30, 1915) an address in London calculated to kindle enthusiasm for the political consolidation of the South Slavs. To permit Serbia merely to wrest Bosnia away from the Monarchy, he explained, would settle nothing; unless all the Yugoslavs were united around Serbia as a nucleus, it would be better if Serbia and Montenegro were annexed to the realm of the Haps-

---

[24] His major books of the war era were *Roumania and the Great War* (1915), *The Balkans, Italy, and the Adriatic* (1915), *German, Slav and Magyar* (1916), and *The Rise of Nationality in the Balkans* (1917), the last a work of solid learning which lacked a preface and conclusion due to the fact that the author was hurriedly called up for military duty.

[25] R. W. Seton-Watson, *Masaryk in England* (Cambridge, Eng., 1943), pp. 33–50, *ibid.*, "President Masaryk As I Knew Him," *Review of Reviews* (London), LXVIII (1923), 185–190.

burgs. He accumulated information on the making of the secret Treaty of London with Italy in 1915, so damaging to South Slav aspirations, and then "left no stone unturned" in trying to dissuade the British foreign office from signing the document.[26] As one aspect of his publicity work for the Czechs he enlisted a score or more of prominent Oxford scholars to join in a letter of praise for the heroic John Hus on the quincentenary of his death, and he organized a Hus celebration at King's College, London, chaired by Lord Bryce. For an address on "the future of Bohemia," in which he expounded the theme that the Czechoslovaks passionately desired freedom and the destruction of Austria-Hungary, Seton-Watson took as a text the verse of the Psalmist, "Thou shalt break them with a rod of iron; thou shalt dash them in pieces like a potter's vessel."

Busy though he was in the interest of the "Bohemians," Scotus Viator by no means neglected his first love, the South Slavs, whose independence he deemed vital for the welfare of the British Empire. Slowly but surely, he believed, Britain had awakened to the necessity of a united Yugoslavdom to prevent German mastery over the Continent; this state would serve as a major link in a *cordon sanitaire* embracing Bohemia, Poland, an independent Hungary, and an enlarged Rumania.[27] At a reception in London in April, 1916, for Crown Prince Alexander of Serbia, Seton-Watson, speaking in Serb, saluted the guest as the personification of South Slavdom, united in suffering and confident that a brighter future lay ahead. A steady stream of articles from his pen publicized the doctrine that lasting European tranquillity depended upon the parcellation of the Dual Monarchy into its national components; after that the Austrogerman provinces, he felt, would merge with Germany. "No

26 May, "Seton-Watson and the Treaty of London," *op. cit.*
27 Remarks on January 10, 1916 by Seton-Watson, reported in *Geographical Review*, XLVII (1916), 261–262.

power on earth," as he put it, "could keep the Germans of Austria and the Empire apart, if once they determined to unite." It seemed to him stupid to imagine that a separate peace could be negotiated with the cabinet of Vienna or that Hungary could be lured into the embrace of the Entente. "The twentieth century," he asserted, "is the century of the Slav and it is one of the main tasks of the war to emancipate the . . . Slavonic democracies of central and southern Europe . . . The supernation must follow the superman into the limbo of history." [28]

4.

As a special vehicle to diffuse his own viewpoints and those of kindred minds and thereby to arouse public interest in central and eastern Europe, Seton-Watson founded, financed, and largely edited a periodical carrying the optimistic title, *The New Europe*. The basic idea of a journal of that sort had been brewing in his mind before the war. At that point he was thinking of a quarterly publication to deal primarily with nationality questions on the Continent; articles would be contributed by recognized experts from many countries. The outbreak of war forced the abandonment of the original project, but it was revived in broad outline under the strident urgings of Masaryk, who had himself thought of launching a journal of opinion in Britain, and because the London *Times* declined to print certain pieces submitted by "Scotus" and Steed.[29]

The first issue of the review, appearing on October 17, 1916, defined the objectives. It would "provide a rallying ground for all those who see in European reconstruction, on a basis of nationality, the rights of minorities, and the

[28] R. W. Seton-Watson, "The Pan-German Plan and Its Antidote," *Contemporary Review*, CIX (1916), 422–428.
[29] Seton-Watson, *Masaryk in England*, pp. 35–36, 84–88. Hanak, *op. cit.*, pp. 174–192.

hard facts of geography and economics, the sole guarantee against an early repetition of the horrors of the present war." *The New Europe* would seek to unmask German war objectives, elucidate the historical, nationality, and strategic background of current problems, and emphasize the urgency of a definite Entente blueprint for victory and peace. The approach of the journal would be "frankly critical and vigilant, reading the meaning of history out of the brutal logic of facts" and it would plead the necessity of an "integral" Entente victory, in order to vindicate national rights and public law and to emancipate subject nationalities from German and Magyar rule. For these purposes, *The New Europe* would strive to stimulate an "alert, organized, and eager" public understanding which would buttress statecraft in the exacting task of arranging settlements in Europe once victory had been achieved. Taking as its battlecry, *Pour Une Victoire Intégrale, The New Europe* selected Abraham Lincoln as its inspiring patron.

The collaborators in this enterprise were not numerous, but they included savants and publicists from Britain and the Continent who commanded attention and respect, and who held positive convictions on what ought to be done in peacemaking. All alike were dedicated to the proposition that any peace settlement would be fragile and impermanent unless the realm of the Hapsburgs was torn to pieces. Articles tended to be brief, engagingly written, and more often than not they were unsigned; efforts to secure contributions by publicists in Russia proved fruitless, but authoritative treatments of Russian affairs were presented by Bernard Pares and Harold Williams, probably the most knowledgeable British private citizens on the tsardom at the time. Writers struck out belligerently against British authors who with varying shades of sympathy wished to preserve Austria-Hungary more or less—more rather than less—intact.

The principal sponsors of *The New Europe* consulted frequently on lines of policy to be pursued, emphases to be diffused. They included Seton-Watson and Steed, of course, and their intimate colleague Sir Arthur J. Evans, best known as the discoverer of Cnossus, but also a specialist on the South Slavs; his enmity toward the House of Hapsburg reached back at least to 1882 when he had been unceremoniously expelled from Bosnia. The ardent philhellene, Ronald A. Burrows, principal of King's College in London, and the historians, J. Holland Rose, Ramsay Muir, George W. Prothero, and W. Alison Phillips were active participants, as was Alexander F. Whyte, member of parliament, who occupied the editorial chair of *The New Europe* during the short period that Seton-Watson was in military service, and H. M. Hyndman, prominent spokesman of a democratic version of the Marxist creed.

Invited to share in *The New Europe* undertaking, George P. Gooch, editor of *The Contemporary Review* and one day to be honored as a Nestor of British historians, chose to hold aloof, for "while sympathizing with the aspirations of the Czechs for independence and the desire of the Southern Slavs for political unity, I felt that the Hapsburg Empire represented, however imperfectly, a unifying force in the Danubian lands, and I could not entirely rule out the possibility of a loose federation." [30] Masaryk composed the very first piece to be printed in *The New Europe* and many later ones, stressing the menace of Mitteleuropa, Pan-Germanism, and the absolute necessity of gratifying the patriotic longings of the Slav nationalities for liberation from the Hapsburgs. [31] Noted French collaborators were Professors Louis Eisenmann, Charles Seignobos, Ernest Denis and the journalists Auguste Gauvain, André Chéradame, André Tardieu;

[30] Gooch, *Under Six Reigns,* p. 178.
[31] Seton-Watson, *Masaryk in England,* pp. 88–96.

from across the Atlantic, Professor George B. Adams, Yale medievalist, and Elmer Davis, newspaperman, submitted articles.

Circulation of *The New Europe* ranged from only three to four thousand, but the journal was read by many members of parliament interested in foreign politics and by molders of public sentiments on both sides of the Atlantic; since *The New Europe* spoke with the voice of authority it was listened to—the New York *Times*, for instance, frequently quoted or paraphrased materials that appeared on its pages. "*The New Europe*," remarked the *Spectator*, "excites controversy almost every week, but it is doing excellent work in promoting interest in foreign politics," [32] and *Punch* paid the publication an astonishing compliment by writing that if it had been in existence before the war, the conflict itself might never have come. Grossly exaggerated though that appraisal was, it is nonetheless true that *The New Europe* remains an indispensable quarry of information on currents of thinking among an important segment of Entente intellectuals on the future and fate of the Hapsburg Monarchy—as well as on Germany, the Mitteleuropa mirage, and associated themes.

With the two hundred and eleventh number of October 28, 1920, *The New Europe* ceased publication. By then the editor and financial angel had plunged something like $37,500 into the publication and with the deficit running at about $5,000 a year he was unwilling to keep the subsidies flowing. Somewhat disillusioned, he confessed, too, that he was "fed up with the role of the disinterested philanthropist in politics," and he chafed under the taxing, restrictive chores of an editor; he often toyed, later on, with the notion of reviving the journal, but a multitude of other interests dissuaded him from doing so. What Seton-Watson had expended on *The New Europe* in

[32] *Spectator*, CXVIII (1917), 306.

energy and in money he patriotically considered his contribution to the Entente triumph.[33]

5.

Argument for argument, French expressions of view on the destiny of the Monarchy matched opinions given currency in the United Kingdom. An economist of Poitiers, Professor Arthur Girault, wanted Austria-Hungary largely preserved as a counterpoise to Russia and Germany alike; while he favored the detachment of lands on the fringes of the Monarchy inhabited by non-Germans or non-Magyars, save for the Czechoslovaks, he also recommended the annexation of Prussian Silesia and the south German states by Austria-Hungary. After these transactions had been effected the population of the Hapsburg realm would be very nearly as large as before the war.[34]

Newspapers such as the *L'Écho de Paris*, a widely circulated conservative daily, edited by the intense nationalist, Maurice Barrès, and the *Action Française*, organ of extreme French clericalism and royalism, pleaded for the maintenance of the Danube Monarchy as a bulwark of Roman Catholicism and on the score that if the realm were split into several small countries they would be impotent to resist conquest by Germany. Jean Herbette, editor of the *Écho*, agreed with Girault that the south Germans should be conjoined to Austria to form a great German Catholic state which would be a barrier to Protestant Prussia, yet he felt that French public sentiment sympathized with the creation of a Yugoslav state as a second rampart against German "access to the unexploited lands . . . in the Orient. . . . We will support our Slav allies in their utmost demands." [35] On the ground

[33] Seton-Watson to Steed, Oct. 8, 1920. Seton-Watson Papers.
[34] Yves Guyot, *The Causes and Consequences of the War* (New York, 1916), pp. 303–304.
[35] *L'Écho de Paris*, Mar. 30, 1916.

that the languages and cultures of the smaller nationalities of the Monarchy were only feebly developed, Charles Maurras, a political director of *Action Française*, spoke out for the perpetuation of Austria-Hungary; disruption would represent retrogression in the affairs of Europe, he believed.

Among influential press antagonists of Austria-Hungary were *Le Temps* and *Le Matin*, which, well along in 1916, unleashed a veritable crusade for the destruction of a state which was pictured as the veriest marionette of Germany. Magyar chauvinism, they contended, bore a heavier measure of responsibility for the coming of the war than the cabinet of Vienna and they laughed to scorn the hypothesis that the Monarchy of its own volition would break away from Germany. "If Austria's end has come," commented *Le Temps*, "it is better to defeat her completely than to patch her up. . . . To reach Germany by destroying Austria—that is the proper way."

French partisans of the dismemberment of the Dual Monarchy completely disregarded the admonition of that far-seeing statesman, Charles Maurice de Talleyrand, who, on the morrow of Napoleon's smashing victory over the Austrian and Russian armies at Austerlitz in 1805, adjured his imperial master not to partition the realm of the Hapsburgs. "The Austrian monarchy," he explained, "is a combination of ill-assorted states, differing from one another . . . and having only one thing in common—the identity of their ruler. Such a power is necessarily weak, but she is an adequate bulwark against the barbarians— and a necessary one. . . ." Napoleon rejected the advice.[36]

Slavs in general, Hapsburg Slavs in particular had few, if any, more tenacious champions in France than Auguste Gauvain, editor of *Le Journal des Débats*, oldest Parisian daily. An acute analyst of international affairs and equipped with a wealth of first-hand knowledge about

[36] Duff Cooper, *Talleyrand* (London, 1932), pp. 149–151.

eastern Europe, this "general of the pen" consistently and courageously proclaimed *Austria delenda* and the liberation of the national communities; his editorials, catering to the well-informed in French academic, financial, and political circles, were subsequently reprinted in book form (*L'Europe au Jour le Jour*), and in 1920 grateful Yugoslavs named Gauvain an honorary citizen of Belgrade.[37] Among French academic scholars, the most respected Slavophile perhaps was Ernest Denis, Professor at the Sorbonne, a Protestant and a progressive. Coming to Slavic studies at the time of the tragic French humiliation of 1870, Denis wished to demonstrate to his countrymen how another people, the Czechs, had resisted successfully the harsh yoke imposed upon them by Germans, a theme that infused his doctoral dissertation on John Hus and his followers and larger historical studies devoted to Bohemia. Denis's son was killed in the forepart of the war and thereafter he dedicated his immense learning and his talent for popular writing to the cause of freedom for the Slavs and the disruption of the Hapsburg realm.

Not long after the fighting commenced, Denis drafted an agenda for far-reaching reconstruction of the Monarchy. Specifically, he envisaged an extensive Hapsburg confederation of four components: a Czechoslovak state, a German-Austria, a Hungary confined to areas of Magyar tongue, and a Yugoslavia including Carniola (Kranj), southern Carinthia, portions of Styria and Croatia, with Trieste as a free port. The central government would exercise authority in military and diplomatic affairs, in transport and communication, but other matters of public concern would be entrusted to the individual states. Beyond all that, Rumania would acquire Transylvania and a portion of the Bukowina, Serbia would be enlarged by

[37] Anon., "La Mort d'Auguste Gauvain," *L'Europe Centrale*, VI (1931), 257 (357).

Bosnia, Dalmatia, and part of Croatia, and, in return, would grant concessions to Bulgaria in Macedonia; Italy would obtain the Trentino and Valona (Vlone) on the Albanian coast.[38] Denis's wartime craftsmanship was shown in *La Grande Serbie* (1915), marred by venomous personal assaults upon the octogenarian Francis Joseph, and *La Question d'Autriche: les Slovaques* (1917); at Geneva in July, 1915, he shared speaking honors with Thomas G. Masaryk at a celebration of the five-hundreth anniversary of the death of John Hus.

To familiarize Frenchmen with the Czechoslovaks and their political aspirations, Denis founded and edited *La Nation Tchèque*, which at the end of the war was converted into the official organ of the Czech government. Contributors included Louis Eisenmann, another respected expert on Central Europe, professor of Hungarian literature and culture at the Sorbonne, and intellectual refugees from the Dual Monarchy, among them Masaryk, co-founder of the periodical, and Eduard Beneš, who had once studied under Denis. He also edited *Le Monde Slave*, put out by the Institute of Slavic Studies, and a Yugoslav publication, *Le Revue Yougoslave*, likewise carried articles by Denis; without let or halt the dynamic Sorbonne historian propagated the gospel of *Austria delenda*. So popular did he become in Czech patriot circles that a movement developed to make him the head of Czechoslovakia, and in 1928 at the tenth anniversary of the proclamation of the Republic a statue to his sacred memory was raised in Prague.[39]

A widely known French publicist, Guyot, who described the Hapsburg realm as "a polyglot polyarchy," argued that it would be as futile and as dangerous to try to save Austria-Hungary as to shore up the Ottoman Em-

[38] Seton-Watson, *Masaryk in England*, pp. 52–53.
[39] For an illuminating set of articles and addresses on Denis, his career and writings on the Slavs of central Europe, see *Le Monde Slave*, V (1928), 161–320.

pire; not only did he want a South Slav federal union, but also an independent Czechoslovakia, and he believed that the Austrian province of Vorarlberg should join Switzerland. While Guyot was ready to accept Italian acquisition of the Austrian region south of the Brenner Pass, his viewpoint was not clear-cut on the destiny of Trieste or of Dalmatia; he favored a greatly extended Rumania as a "balancing force" in the Balkans, and a free Poland which would embrace most of Galicia. The German-speaking districts of Austria proper should either be formed into a separate political community or linked to Bavaria. In short, Guyot proposed that the peace settlement "must substitute voluntary groupings for the compulsory associations of the past." [40]

6.

Out in Russia, certain Duma deputies belonging to the Constitutional Democratic party, above all Professor Pavel Miliukov, advocated the detachment from Austria-Hungary of its Slav-speaking districts. On a visit to England this eminent intellectual declared that only by dismemberment of the Monarchy could the problems of Poland, of Serbia, and of Rumania be solved, and he was a stalwart exponent of a free Bohemia and "Slovakia," a "Slavic outpost," in his phrase, which would protect southeastern Europe from spoliation by Germany. As Miliukov read the signs of the times, a set of national states would succeed the House of Hapsburg, and he ardently desired precisely that. [41] Members of the Russian Orthodox Church hierarchy pleaded for the destruction of Austria-Hungary and the setting free of the nationalities within

[40] Guyot, *op. cit.*, pp. 250, 277, 301–302, 308, 316.
[41] Merritt G. Abrash, "Entente Policy Towards Austria-Hungary, August 1914–March 1917," an unpublished thesis for the Certificate of the Russian Institute, Columbia University (c. 1958), pp. 121–138, 26–33.

her borders. It was the judgment of the chauvinistic *Novoye Vremya* that the liberation of the Hapsburg Slavs was a Russian obligation on a par with freeing the Slavs in the Balkans; it advanced the familiar argument that durable peace in Europe required the fragmentation of the Monarchy into half a dozen independent states and the cession of Serbian, Rumanian, and Ukrainian-speaking areas to "their respective nations." [42]

A conservative Russian clique which clustered around Count Sergius Witte in the first months of the war, and which looked upon the struggle against the Central Empires with undisguised aversion, nonetheless wanted the Danube Monarchy broken into its component national fragments. Russia would annex Galicia and a slice of the Bukowina, while the balance of that province and Transylvania would be added to Rumania; Italy would get the Trentino and western Istria, and a new state of Yugoslavs would cover eastern Istria, the area of the Slovenes, Croatia, Dalmatia, and a section of Bosnia. Serbia would acquire what remained of Bosnia, while Bohemia and a rump Austria would be set up as independent countries.[43]

[42] *Literary Digest*, L (1915), 1184–1187.
[43] Hoetzsch, *op. cit.*, vol. VII (1), no. 37.

7. Entente Cabinets and the Danube Émigrés

EXCEPT FOR RUSSIA AND MUCH LATER ITALY, THE DIPLOMATIC secrets of the Entente cabinets in the First World War have not yet been revealed. It needs hardly be said that the western Entente powers regarded the realm of the Hapsburgs as a side-show diplomatically no less than militarily compared to the Hohenzollern empire. In so far as the views of Entente policymakers on the future of Austria-Hungary have been disclosed, they diverged widely and were steadily revised in accordance with the fortunes of the fighting. In the language of Sir Edward Grey, "the skein of Allied diplomacy was so tangled and confused that to unravel it and show it as a consistent whole is not possible"; and, he continued, "a consistent policy was impossible. Circumstances were always changing . . . Diplomacy had to adapt itself to what happened at the battle front . . . in war words count only so far as they are backed by force and victories." [1] Any attempt,

[1] Edward Grey, *Twenty-five Years* (2 vols., New York, 1925), II, 157–158, 165. Seldom were the aims of the war ventilated in the British House of Commons; debates on aims on November 11, 1915, February 23, 1916, and May 24, 1916 side-stepped the problem of Austria-Hungary.

250

therefore, to reconstruct official Entente currents of thought on the Hapsburg Monarchy can only be of a tantalizingly tentative character.

As First Lord of the Admiralty, Winston S. Churchill asserted when the struggle was quite young that the transfer of southern provinces from the Monarchy to Balkan neighbors, in accordance with nationality, would be highly desirable, and would assuage the memory and the evil consequences of former quarrels forever. No skepticism troubled his ample mind concerning the ultimate outcome of the conflict. "England has always won in the end," he wrote, "and Russia is unconquerable"; after the tocsin of war ceased sounding, Austria-Hungary would be resolved into its component parts. The Entente must press for "the liberation of the imprisoned nationalities in the grip of the Hapsburg." "We may see a Poland," declared the outstanding Briton of his century, "united and in loyal and harmonious relations with the Crown of Russia. We may live to see a federation of the Christian states of the Balkans. . . . We may see an Italy whose territory corresponds with the Italian population." Later on, Churchill told a reporter, "We want this war to settle the map of Europe on national lines and according to the true wishes of the people who dwell in the disputed areas. . . . We want a natural and harmonious settlement which liberates races and restores the integrity of nations." These points of view, it may be interjected, diverged radically from Churchill's reflections during the Second World War when he repeatedly lamented that the realm of the Hapsburgs had been riven asunder, removing an obstacle to possible aggression from the East.[2]

On the basis of informal conversations with British ministers and weight-carrying Conservative politicians, the Russian ambassador in London, Count Paul Bencken-

[2] Noel Buxton and C. Leonard Leese, *Balkan Problems and European Peace* (New York, 1919), pp. 70–72; *Literary Digest*, Oct. 24, 1914, 781–782; London *Times*, Sept. 25, 1915.

dorff, summed up British war aims as they affected Austria-Hungary this way: Russia would obtain the Polish-speaking area of Galicia, preferably as part of an autonomous Polish state: the tsardom would annex outright the Ukrainian districts of Galicia and of the Bukowina; Rumania might take over Transylvania, if she fought alongside of the Entente; Bosnia and Dalmatia would be divided between the southern Slav states and Italy (the latter would also secure the Trentino, provided she became a belligerent). Benckendorff was sure that British sentiment desired a settlement based upon ethnography, as essential for maintaining peace in the future.[3]

Prime Minister Herbert H. Asquith, no specialist on foreign affairs, let it be known that he considered application of the principle of self-determination a necessity for a peace that would endure, yet understandable imprecision marked his public pledge of November 9, 1914, that Britain would go on fighting "until the rights of the smaller nationalities of Europe are placed upon an unassailable foundation." By signing the secret treaties under which Italy and Rumania took up arms against the Central Empires, the British cabinet, of course, assented, albeit somewhat reluctantly, to peripheral amputations of Austro-Hungarian territory, and Foreign Secretary Grey disclosed in September, 1915, that if agreeable to the ministry of Serbia, the inhabitants of Bosnia, southern Dalmatia, and Croatia should be permitted to determine their future themselves, and that British policy on these areas would be guided by the wishes of the populations involved.[4]

On October 4, 1916, as the first half of the struggle was grinding to a close, Arthur J. Balfour, then First Lord of the Admiralty, set down "some stray reflections" on the

---

[3] Benckendorff to Sazonov, Sept. 28, 1914, Hoetzsch, *op. cit.*, Vol. VI (1), No. 329.
[4] David Lloyd-George, *The Truth About the Treaties* (2 vols., London, 1938), I, 39.

peace that-was-to-be. Approving a European settlement attuned in principle with nationality, he favored enlargement of Italy, Serbia, and Rumania, and home-rule for the Poles. His image of a new Poland incorporated the tsarist ruled districts and as much of Austrian and Prussian Poland as possible; yet he did not want the Polish kingdom of the eighteenth century revived, holding that a state of that dimension would be provocative of German-Russian antagonism and strife rather than an asset for tranquillity. Wisdom dictated, he believed, the creation of an autonomous Poland, as an integral segment of the tsardom. No little ambiguity attached to Balfour's thinking on Bohemia, which his heart told him should be free, but his head questioned whether an independent state would be capable of resisting absorption by Germany; the destiny of the Czechs, he philosophically concluded, should be given "very careful consideration." For the rest, he desired to see the German-speaking provinces of Austria proper remain with the Magyar areas of Hungary, though he acknowledged that the war might lead to the total disruption of the Monarchy; should that come to pass, the German-peopled districts would coalesce, he imagined, with imperial Germany, making her potentially more formidable than in 1914.[5]

About two months before, on instructions from Prime Minister Asquith, two senior officials in the foreign office, Sir William Tyrrell for one, drafted a secret memorandum on the territorial desiderata in the peace settlement. Grounded upon self-determination, this document contemplated the dissolution of Dual Monarchy. "The survival of Austria-Hungary," the authors reasoned, "could not be reconciled with the objects for which the Allies went to war"; in its particulars, the paper proposed a large Polish state, including the coalfields of Silesia, linked to

[5] Blanche E. C. Dugdale, *Arthur James Balfour* (2 vols., London, 1936), II, 435–439.

Russia merely by the person of the Tsar. For Bohemia a variety of alternatives was studied: an independent state, and a Bohemia combined with either Yugoslavia or Poland. In the end, the foreign office experts recommended the latter possibility as in conformity with the wishes of "farseeing Czechs and Poles"; the Slovaks appear to have been quite forgotten. To Rumania should pass the Rumanian-speaking sections of Transylvania and of the Bukowina (substantially less than was secretly awarded Brătianu in August, 1916). Territorial pledges to Italy, it was recommended, should be faithfully implemented, even though that involved placing many Austrogermans and South Slavs under the flag of Victor Emmanuel. As for the other Yugoslavs, the memorandum proposed a strong federation combining Serbia, Montenegro, and the Croats and Slovenes of the Monarchy, though with reservations regarding the South Slavs of southern Hungary. This state would stand as a barrier to any attempt at a *Drang nach Osten* by Germany. German-Austria should be allowed to amalgamate with imperial Germany—a gain for Berlin that would be more than counter-balanced by detachments of territory from Germany; it was argued that an increase of Roman Catholics in Germany, by virtue of the incorporation of German-Austria, would strengthen the non-Prussian population in a desirable fashion. The Magyar area of Hungary would be constituted as an independent country with assured access to the sea at Fiume.

The framers of this memorandum appreciated that their recommendations might have to be modified in deference to the wishes of Petrograd and in the light of geographical and military considerations. Grey circulated the document among cabinet colleagues without comment and it was not formally examined by British policymakers until well along in 1917. At least one other memorandum on war aims prepared in the London foreign office did not contemplate the destruction of the Dual Monarchy.[6]

2.

More than a year before the European war commenced, Nicholas II of Russia ventured the opinions that the realm on the Danube was on the verge of disintegration, that independent kingdoms of Bohemia and Hungary would return to the map, and that the southern Slavs would probably merge with Serbia, Transylvania with Rumania, and the Austrogermans with the Hohenzollern Empire.[7]

Vague manifestoes of September, 1914, over the name of the tsarist generalissimo, the Grand Duke Nicholas, could be interpreted as meaning that a united Poland would be accorded autonomous status in the empire of the Tsar and that eastern Galicia would be annexed to Russia outright.

This Russian declaration was designed to encourage separatist sentiments in the enemy camp—a relatively novel device of war in which Russia was the first of the belligerent countries to indulge. Drawn up in the foreign office by Gregory Trubetski, a staunch apostle of Slav solidarity and of Russia's Slav mission, the document may have been somewhat edited by the Grand Duke, who personally considered haste on the Polish question unnecessary, and he frowned upon commitments likely to benefit

[6] Lloyd-George, *op. cit.*, I, 31–50; *History of* (London) *Times*, IV, p. 320.

[7] George W. Buchanan, *My Mission to Russia* (2 vols., Boston, 1923), I, 182. Back in 1896, Nicholas II had displayed considerable hostility to the Monarchy and envisaged the possibility that one day the Slav-peopled areas might seek union with the tsardom, but he emphatically repudiated the idea that Russia would hasten dissolution by force of arms. Margaret M. Jefferson, "Lord Salisbury's Conversations With the Tsar at Balmoral, 27 and 29 September 1896," *Slavonic and East European Review*, XXXIX (1960), 216–222, esp. 219–220.

Roman Catholicism. "Poles! the hour has struck," the proclamation asserted, "in which the sacred dreams of your fathers and forefathers must find fulfillment. . . . May that nation [Poland] reunite into one body under the scepter of the Russian emperor. . . . Under this scepter Poland will be reborn, free in her faith, in tongue, and in self-government. . . . The dawn of a new life is breaking for you. May there shine, resplendent above that dawn, the sign of the Cross, symbol of the suffering and Resurrection of your people!" [8]

Circulated in millions of copies, the Russian manifesto elicited a good deal of applause from romantic lovers of freedom. Politicians from four parties of Russian Poland gleefully welcomed the proclamation professing to believe that the promise of autonomy for a united Poland would be faithfully carried out at the end of the war. In the West the document was praised as "a masterpiece of imaginative statecraft," "sanctification of the war"; "Poland rises miraculously like Lazarus from the grave," declared Georges Clemenceau's *L'Homme Libre.*[9] Yet in reality the tsarist pledge was transparently a progagandistic stratagem, never intended to be applied except possibly in areas conquered by Russian arms. Poincaré wryly alluded to the proclamation as "an announcement of disguised annexation," not sanctioned by the Third Republic.

After the armies of the Tsar had driven onto the soil of the Monarchy, a second manifesto signed by the Grand Duke Nicholas, appeared in nine tongues, asserting that Russia was seeking only "the reestablishment of right and justice . . . liberty and realization of national dreams." Each nationality of the Dual Monarchy, the text read, would preserve its own language and faith and live

[8] Robert W. Coonrad, "The Duma's Attitude Toward War-Time Problems of Minority Groups," *Amer. Slavic and East European Review,* XIII (1954), 29–46, esp. 39–40.

[9] *Literary Digest,* XLIX (1914), 401, 499–501, 566.

in peace and friendship. On its face, the proclamation seemed to assure national freedoms, but the ruthless Russification of Ukrainians in occupied Galicia illustrated in fact what Cossack conquest meant.

It was policymakers in Petrograd who first raised within the Entente bloc the issue of post-war territorial changes in the Central Empires. Little or no credence, however, can be placed in the memoirs of Sazonov in which he remembered that he desired the break-up of Austria-Hungary; avowedly he wanted the status of Bohemia altered, though whether he was thinking in terms of independence is unclear, and he disapproved incitement of Hapsburg minorities to rebel, aware that if revolutionary currents were unleashed they might leap over the wall into the tsardom itself. At mid-September of 1914, when Russian soldiers were marching across Galicia and the German advance in France had been stopped, Sazonov sketched for the French and British ambassadors what he picturesquely called "a tapestry the woof of which is not yet woven"; therein he expressed lively personal sympathy with the principle of self-determination. Russia would annex eastern Galicia and other territory up to the river Niemen (Neman); a Polish state would be created under the Tsar and would cover eastern Posen, Silesia, and western Galicia, as well as Russian Poland. The Hapsburg realm would be converted into a triple monarchy; Austria (including the Slovene districts), Hungary, which would retain Croatia, and Bohemia, which would include the Slovak counties of Hungary; Rumania would be allowed to annex part of Transylvania, while Serbia would acquire Bosnia, Dalmatia, and northern Albania, Greece getting the southern strip, except for Valona (Vlone), which would be allotted to Italy. The Monarchy on the Danube would be required to pay reparations. So far as is known the French and British ministries never registered judgments on this wide-ranging agenda. Tsarist cabinet discussions on Poland yielded an extremely tentative plan for the establishment of an autonomous state under a Russian viceroy.[10] Going well beyond his superior, the Russian ambassador in Paris, Alexander Iswolsky, tried to persuade the French ministry that the Hapsburg "anachronism" should be replaced by independent national states, except in the case of Poland. A sincere partisan of Serbia, he wished it to annex Istria and Dalmatia; it seemed to him that French senior officials were dismally lacking in familiarity with the perplexities of central and eastern Europe.[11]

Saying that the Entente must dictate the peace, Nicholas II on November 21, 1914, defined Russian objectives relating to Austria-Hungary as acquisition of Galicia and the western reaches of the Bukowina, which would extend his empire to the Carpathian Mountains, her natural frontier. His views on Poland, Rumania, Yugoslavia, Albania, and Transylvania closely resembled those of the foreign minister; Bohemia and the Slovak counties should be granted unrestricted home-rule at a minimum, and Austria should be confined to German-speaking areas. This program profoundly disturbed the French ambassador, Paléologue, who felt that the preservation of the Monarchy accorded with French national interest and who fancied that by a mixture of force and persuasion Vienna could be detached from the ally in Berlin.[12] On his own initiative, the Frenchman proposed to Sazonov that a bid for a separate peace should be proffered to the Ballplatz; as conditions of a settlement, the Monarchy would be required to cede Galicia to Russia and Bosnia to Serbia; but by now, the thinking of Sazonov on Austria-Hungary had undergone radical revision. The notion of

[10] Hoetzsch, op. cit., vol. VI, (1) no. 256; see also, Frantz Gunther, "Die Wiederstellung Polens im Rahmen der Russischen Kriegsziele," BM, VIII (1930), 1156–1163.

[11] Hoetzsch, op. cit., no. 386.

[12] Maurice Paléologue, La Russie des Tsars pendant la Grande Guerre (3 vols., Paris, 1921–1922), I, 199–201.

a triple monarchy had been discarded; briefly he favored dismemberment, then reverted again to the view that Russian interests, on balance, would best be served if the Monarchy were kept basically intact. None of the Entente cabinets cared much for the idea of a compromise peace or at the time would even consider the problems of Austria-Hungary, and Paléologue was sharply reprimanded by Paris for his audacious, unauthorized proposals to Sazonov.[13]

From time to time officials in the tsarist foreign office hammered out memoranda on the peoples of Austria-Hungary, notably the Czechs and the Slovaks, though whether these papers affected the outlook of policymakers remains shrouded in uncertainty. In any event, on instructions from Nicholas II, Sazonov in 1916 had a definite scheme for an autonomous Poland inside Russia worked up, which the Tsar sanctioned and ordered to be printed; sinister, dark forces around the throne, however, intervened, and Sazonov was soon obliged to relinquish the foreign secretaryship. Following the November, 1916 declaration by the Central Powers of independence for Russian Poland, the men on the Neva reasserted that Russia was explicitly committed "to create a complete Poland, embracing all Polish territories, which will enjoy the right when the war is ended of freely regulating their national, intellectual, and economic life on the basis of autonomy, under the sovereignty of Russia, and of maintaining the principle of a united state. This decision of His Gracious Majesty remains unshakable," and on Christmas Day, 1916, Nicholas II, less than three months before he was forced to abdicate, reiterated assurances of a Polish state inside the tsardom. These affirmations called forth hearty approbation in Polonophile circles in the West, and Entente governments, whose behavior in all matters concerning the Poles was still dictated for prac-

13 *Ibid.*, I, 245–247.

tical purposes by the empire of the Tsar, hastened to en-
dorse the principle of a united Poland under Russia as
an objective of the war.

3.

Only the foggiest notions prevailed at the Quai d'Orsay
on French war aims involving Austria-Hungary, though,
at that, they may have been clearer than in London. It
was fully appreciated by Théophile Delcassé, foreign
minister almost from the beginning of the war until
October, 1915, that makers of French public opinion were
sharply divided against and for the breaking-up of the
Danubian realm; on the delicate question of Poland, he
was extremely careful to assure the men on the Neva that
Paris would follow their lead, and as has been mentioned,
he rebuked Paléologue for talking of a compromise
peace.

It appears that the Paris cabinet regarded the general
concept of self-determination with disapprobation, although on occasion Delcassé brooded on the desirability
of transferring peripheral zones of the Monarchy to adjoining states and of organizing the remainder as a realm
of three members. Toward the end of 1914, Aristide
Briand, minister of justice at the time, supposed that the
war could be rapidly won if combined Anglo-French
forces struck at the Danube Monarchy by way of the
Balkans and if the Slav communities were incited to revolt. Becoming premier and foreign minister in October
of 1915, Briand avowed that freedom for the Yugoslavs
was a French aim of the fighting, and he was the first
Entente statesman to receive officially the Czech Éduard
Beneš, representing the Czechoslovak cause. Personally,
Briand sympathized whole-heartedly with unqualified
Polish independence, but since the Russian ally opposed
that, he tactfully held his tongue.

Polish politicians in Russia, in the meantime, who had been working for autonomy under the Tsar, came to doubt the wisdom of that policy. Dreams of home-rule had been quickened, it is true, by the manifesto of the Grand Duke, but the terrific tsarist military reversals of 1915 had wrought with disenchanting impact upon Polish cooperationists. Persuaded now that the future of the Poles would be decided in western capitals, their leading spirit, Roman Dmowski, a Duma deputy, left Russia and pitched his tent in November, 1915, in London; he maintained close contacts with Polish émigré groups in other cities of western Europe, and pressed forward with propaganda for Polish independence among Entente public men and editors. He found British politicians, who knew little about the Polish problem, particularly receptive to his pleadings. On February 28, 1916, he addressed an appeal to Russian Ambassador Iswolsky in Paris for unfettered Polish independence. In August of the following year Dmowski assumed the chairmanship of the Polish National Committee which one day would be recognized by the Entente as the authoritative representative of Polish interests.

At Vevey, Switzerland, a company of Polish patriots foregathered around the towering personality of Russian-born Henryk Sienkiewicz, whose fictional writings on Poland's past had contributed to keeping faith and hope in the future green. He acted as chairman of a Vevey Committee, which aided children and others in war-ravaged Polish areas, and branch offices were set up in western Europe and the United States. "It frequently happens," he wrote in anguish, "that when the Red Cross goes out to collect the wounded from a battlefield they lift from a heap one man in German uniform, another in Austrian, and a third in Russian, and discover that they are all—Poles." To anyone who cared to listen, Sienkiewicz pleaded for a reunited Poland, and he had many disciples among Austrian Poles; his death in 1916 was a calamity for the Polish national cause.[14]

Among the Poles at Vevey was the internationally renowned pianist, Ignace Paderewski, also born on Russian soil, who soon moved off to Britain, where he learned that the official world was extremely reserved on the subject of a free Poland; but his special sphere of activity was the United States, where he toiled among public leaders and men of Polish ancestry. He was named honorary chairman of the Polish National Department of Chicago, which eventually contained representatives of practically all Polish political societies in the United States, and by his astute labors Paderewski awakened interest in the resurrection of Poland in American quarters that counted.

In London a Polish Advisory Council was organized, made up mostly of British intellectuals. The Council had a chequered history, several members resigning over the question of propaganda on behalf of Polish freedom which they felt would greatly offend the empire of the Tsar and impose a fresh strain upon the Entente coalition; it looked as though the Council might dissolve with untoward consequences for pro-Entente Poles everywhere and a corresponding gain for the Polish element that leaned toward the Central Powers. Thanks to the intervention of Seton-Watson, the London Poles decided to eschew independence propaganda—at least for the time being.[15]

4.

Arguably, Austria-Hungary could have been deprived of Galicia and other peripheral areas and still have remained a considerable factor in the high politics of Europe. But if Bohemia and the Hungarian counties of

[14] Von Gagern to Burián, Nov. 24, 1916, P.A., Schweiz, *Berichte*, 1916.
[15] R. W. Seton-Watson to J. Holland Rose, Dect. 2, 5, 1916, and J. Holland Rose to Seton-Watson, Dec. 3, 1916. Seton-Watson Papers.

Slovak habitation were lost the Monarchy would cease to count for much, and therein lies the supreme importance of the Czechoslovak question and Entente attitudes on it. Of all the émigré politicians and publicists who worked abroad to destroy the Hapsburg Monarchy and to secure freedom for his co-nationals, a place apart must be reserved for Czech Professor Thomas G. Masaryk, whose glittering achievement made him the *beau ideal* of campaigners with similar objectives in the future. It has been said of Masaryk that if any one man might claim credit (or discredit) for the ruin of the Monarchy, this Czech savant was the man, and another judge who knew the Czech intimately, observed, "the Austro-Hungarian mosaic was broken into bits by Masaryk's gigantic personality."

Son of a humble Slovak coachman, Masaryk had chosen an academic career, advancing to a professorship in the Czech section of the University of Prague. Meditative, reserved, grave as a Roman senator, he was an inspiring teacher and writer, but his mind was never fully dedicated to the calling of scholarship; his tastes lay more in the arena of politics. Richly talented with the pen and effective on the platform, he did not shrink from assuming responsibility, as has been true of some other men of thought; for a personal philosophy that was not translated into deeds Masaryk had only contempt. Leader of the tiny Czech party of Realists and the sturdy champion of the welfare of Slavs generally in Austria, he had attained a considerable reputation in his home country before 1914, though he was not well known outside. A devout Czech patriot, though not at all a chauvinist, and a foe of romantic Pan-Slavism, Masaryk may be called a tolerant humanist, who conceived of the resurrection of his nation in terms of an ethical-religious challenge.[16]

---

[16] Eugen Lemberg, "Die Historische Ideologie von Palacký und Masaryk und Ihre Bedeutung für die Moderne Nationale Bewegung," *Historisches Jahrbuch*, LIII (1933), 429–457. This essay is faithful to its title.

When war started in 1914, the Professor, sixty-four at the time, cast away his former ideal of converting the Monarchy into a co-partnership of nationalities—a monarchical Switzerland—and decided to labor for an independent state of Czechs and Slovaks, or, as he was wont to say, of Bohemia. To that purpose he held unswervingly through all vicissitudes, and he fully understood that his vision would be more likely to become reality if armed contingents of Czechs and Slovaks were organized and marched into battle. He realized, besides, that the task of propaganda (or education) would require a fairly long period of time, and more than once he was alarmed by the possibility that the war might cease before the propaganda seeds he was sowing had matured; Masaryk's own book, *The Making of a State* is the classic account of his unflagging toil to build Czechoslovakia.[17]

After laying preliminary plans for a revolutionary conspiracy in Bohemia and arranging what should be done in the event that Cossacks crowded into the province, the elderly professor left home in December, 1914 on what turned out to be an amazing, lengthy, adventuresome, and triumphant odyssey. Stopping first in Italy, his initial intention was to go back to Prague once propaganda activities for a free Czechoslovakia had been fairly launched abroad; at Rome he entered into plans with South Slav émigrés for coordinated efforts to gain mutual freedom. Reluctantly, but on the urgent advice of his lieutenant, Beneš, Masaryk decided to stay away from the long arm of the Austrian police, and not until 1918 did he return to his homeland, coming back as President of the

---

[17] Thomas G. Masaryk, *The Making of a State* (London, 1927). Cf. Wenzel Jaksch, *Europas Weg nach Postdam* (2nd ed., Stuttgart, 1959), pp. 120–190, a critical analysis. For a succinct exposition of Masaryk's case for the dissolution of the Monarchy, see, T. G. Masaryk, "The Czecho-Slovak Nation," New York *Nation*, CVII (1918), 386–388. On the spelling of the name of the projected state, see Alois R. Nykl, "Czechoslovakia or Czecho-slovakia," *Slavonic Review*, XXII (1944), 99–110.

Czechoslovak Republic and installing himself in the ancient royal palace of Prague. While abroad he spent himself unsparingly in Europe, Asia, and America, warming his colleagues and co-nationals by his own inner fire, spreading simple, sincere, serious propaganda on the themes that Central Europe must be radically reconstructed and that the Czechoslovaks had a right to a political destiny of their own.

Unlike a Russophile branch of the Czech patriotic movement, Masaryk, who himself looked to the tsardom as liberator well into 1915, some snippets of evidence suggest, eventually pinned his faith for freedom upon the parliamentary West.[18] He was rootedly mistrustful of Russia and her habits—of which he possessed a precise, profound understanding by reason of prolonged and penetrating researches, and his distaste increased because of Russification tactics in occupied Galicia. Even so, Masaryk could write early in 1915, "Bohemians are . . . strongly Slavophile . . . thoroughly Russophile. A Russian dynasty, in whatever form would be most popular . . . the Bohemian politicians wish the establishment of the kingdom of Bohemia in full accordance with Russia. Russia's wishes and plans will be of determining influence." Only after the revolutionary Russian convulsions of 1917 did Masaryk espouse a Czech republic and feel confident that such a state could make its way unaided by the Slav colossus.[19]

On the other side, highly placed tsarist policymakers thoroughly resented the pro-western orientation adopted by Masaryk and his Czech and Slovak followers living in Russia; more exactly, the Russians dreaded the possibility

[18] Paul Molisch, "Zur Tschechischen Frage in Weltkriege," *Zeitschrift für Politik*, XIX (1930), 690–699; Ludwig Bittner, "Zur Geschichte der Tschechisen Umsturz Bewegung in den Jahren 1914 und 1915." *Mitteilungen des Österreichischen Instituts für Geschichtsforschung*, LII (1938), 417–429, based heavily on testimony from tsarist foreign office archives.

[19] Seton-Watson, *Masaryk in England*, pp. 124, 133.

of Czechoslovakia becoming a client of Great Britain in the heart of Europe. National interest and Russian authority with other Slavic-speaking groupings outside of the tsardom dictated support of a program for an autonomous Czechoslovakia, as part of the Russian realm under the governance of a Romanov viceroy.[20] It was understood in Petrograd, however, that a settlement of that character would be stiffly resisted by the western Entente, unwilling to see Russian power thrust far into central Europe.

Among Czechs in the Monarchy, as will be explained later, secessionists, operating through the underground *Maffia*, smuggled messages to the men of the emigration, and spies in Vienna picked up valuable military and related information which was transmitted to appropriate Entente quarters. Patriotic Czech gymnastic societies, called *sokols*, were envisaged by Masaryk as a national guard, to be set in motion if Russian troops invaded Bohemia, and as the hard core of a Czechoslovak army of tomorrow. Funds to promote the revolutionary conspiracy were largerly furnished by Czechs and Slovaks who had emigrated to the Americas; in August of 1915 Vojta Beneš, brother of Eduard, was dispatched to the United States to perfect machinery for raising cash.

5.

Since Masaryk headed only a small party in Bohemia and possessed no mandate whatsoever from his co-nationals to toil in foreign parts for a free Czechoslovakia, it was sheer audacity—and high conviction—for him to proceed as he did. The opening gun of the independence

---

[20] Anon., "La Russie Tsariste et la Question Tchècoslovaquie," *Le Monde Slave*, I (1924), 124–138, 294–300, an elaborate treatise on the past, present, and destiny of the Czechs and Slovaks.

campaign was fired at Geneva on July 6, 1915, when Masaryk delivered a commemorative oration on the five hundredth anniversary of the death of the Czech hero of heroes, John Hus; he spoke in the Hall of the Reformation where a few years later the first meeting of the League of Nations convened. The *Neue Freie Presse* of Vienna accurately characterized the address as a declaration of war upon the House of Hapsburg.

In the meantime, Masaryk had been in intimate touch with friends in Britain. A small company of Czech patriots, residing in London, artisans mostly, organized a Czech National Committee and linked up with Wickham Steed and other British Czechophiles. At mid-September, 1914, an emissary from Masaryk, Emanuel V. Voska, an American citizen though born in Bohemia, handed Steed a letter beseeching him to intercede with Petrograd so that Russian soldiers would not fire on Czechs and Slovaks deserting from Hapsburg armies.[21] Steed complied. Presently Masaryk and Seton-Watson—the father and the midwife of the Czechoslovak Republic they have been called—conferred secretly and at length in Rotterdam, and the Czech Professor set out his views on the post-war settlement, devoting particular attention to Austria-Hungary naturally; at the time he was thinking along the lines of a kingdom of Czechoslovakia ruled by a western prince, Danish or Belgian preferably, yet under the military shield of the Tsar.

With Seton-Watson as go-between, Masaryk's plans were passed on to the principal Entente foreign offices. Before long, Masaryk selected London as the headquarters of his activities, and there in April, 1915 he sketched

---

[21] An indefatigable and astute henchman of Masaryk, Voska, who had amassed a small fortune in the United States, subsequently turned his talents to espionage in combatting agents of the Central Empires in the United States. Emanuel V. Voska and Will Irwin, *Spy and Counterspy* (New York, 1941), a lurid and far from accurate account.

out his vision of an independent Bohemia in a detailed memorandum.[22] Seton-Watson arranged for the Czech to lecture on Slavic affairs at King's College in London, as one means of stimulating British interest in and support for Czechoslovakia; on October 19, 1915, Masaryk presented his first lecture on "The Problem of Small Nations in the European Crisis." A large audience listened and Lord Robert Cecil occupied the chair in the stead of Prime Minister Asquith, who had consented to preside, but illness prevented him from doing so; the presence of Cecil, undersecretary for foreign affairs, invested the gathering with something approaching an official quality. Thenceforward, Masaryk converted his lecture stand into a pulpit from which he declaimed about the "Pan-German menace" and preached that if Europe were to know peace, national states would have to replace the multi-nationality realm of the Hapsburgs. His tireless pen contributed to several journals of opinion and he kept open channels of communication to co-conspirators on the Continent and in America. Near Picadilly Circus a Czech press bureau, directed principally by Vladimir Nosek, was established to supply British newspapers with information on conditions inside Austria-Hungary and to foster sympathy for Czech freedom, but it is improbable that these labors made much impression upon the general public.[23]

For the herculean task of bringing the cause of Bohemia before the mind and emotions of the West, Masaryk possessed two resourceful and dedicated young collaborators—Eduard Beneš and Milan Štefánik, both of

[22] All aspects of Masaryk's work in the United Kingdom are authoritatively recounted by Seton-Watson, *Masaryk in England*. The April, 1915, memorandum occupies pages 116–134; see also, Anon., "Masaryk und Seine Aktion während des Krieges," *BM*, XV (2) (1937), 1000–1020; Hanak, *op. cit.*, pp. 100–110, and Zeman, *op. cit.*, pp. 76–82.

[23] For the Czech colony in Britain and its allies, see, Hanak, *op. cit.*, pp. 110–127.

whom lived in Paris, but allotted some attention to Rome. Once a student under Masaryk, Beneš, grew into his devoted political disciple, sharing his pro-western orientation and outlook; mutual admiration facilitated magnificent teamwork throughout the critical era of the war— and later. If Beneš lacked the personal magnetism and generosity of spirit of his master, he nonetheless was endowed with a perceptive intelligence, the hard practicality and courage of a peasant, and a passion for infinite detail. His easy ascent up the Czechoslovak ladder of politics proved in the supreme testing time of his career to be more a liability than an asset.

When the European war started, Beneš, who had dabbled a bit in local politics, was still an obscure lecturer on social questions at Prague University; he and Masaryk put their heads together and mapped out general ways and means of winning freedom for the Czechs and Slovaks. A physical disability exempted Beneš from service in the Austrian army, and he proceeded to build up the Czech revolutionary conspiracy until Austrian guardians of the law threatened to arrest him. Travelling by way of Germany in September, 1915, he escaped abroad, settling down finally in Paris. France was well known to him, for he had studied and earned a doctorate there—in his dissertation he had argued persuasively for the reorganization of the Hapsburg Monarchy as a federal union.[24] Around Beneš rallied a contingent of other Czech refugees, among them Lev Sychrava, lawyer, politician, and selfless Czech nationalist; before even Masaryk, he had fled abroad and commenced to propagate the Czech national faith, and in Paris he performed yeoman service as an editor, organizer of underground communication

[24] Beneš' personal record has been published in several tongues, in a western language the French version is the most complete and reliable. Éduard Beneš, *Souvenirs de Guerre et de Révolution* (2 vols., Paris, 1928).

with Prague, and adviser in the building of Czechoslovak armed forces.

6.

Forever memorable in the annals of free Czechoslovakia will be November 14, 1915, for on that day Czech and Slovak refugees published in Paris a manifesto boldly deposing the Hapsburg dynasty and declaring national independence. After excoriating the Monarchy as the supine vassal of Berlin, the declaration affirmed, "We Bohemians no longer recognize the *raison d'etre* of Austria-Hungary. . . . We strive for an independent Bohemian-Slovak state. . . . We declare ourselves on the side of the Allies."

Out of the group in Paris emerged early in February, 1916, a Czechoslovak National Council for independence, and Czechophiles in other lands, the Bohemian Alliance in America, for instance, affiliated with this revolutionary body. Beneš, who was named secretary-general of the Council, rapidly consolidated his reputation for political astuteness; Masaryk undertook the chairmanship and a provincially-minded Czech Agrarian deputy in the Austrian parliament, Josef Dürich, was picked as vice-chairman. The outstanding Slovak on the Council was Štefánik, son of a Lutheran pastor, who, after a brilliant career at the University of Prague in mathematics and science pursued advanced studies in France. Joining the French air force in 1914, he presently renewed acquaintance with Beneš whom he had known in his student days; despite a dangerous heart condition, Štefánik developed into a tower of strength in the Czechoslovak émigré movement, introducing Beneš, for instance, to several top-ranking French statesmen, and supervising the organization of Czechoslovak armies in Entente countries. It is unclear as to just where he stood on the question of the governmental structure of the projected Czechoslovakia, though quite likely he wanted special administrative status for areas of Slovak speech.

Not only did the National Council station industrious agents in Entente capitals, it also organized world-wide revolutionary propaganda, carried on principally through the press, and it established ties with representatives of other émigré groups from the Dual Monarchy. At the beginning of February, 1916, Chairman Masaryk conferred with French Premier Aristide Briand, the Czech appraising the European political panorama, presenting the case for the break-up of the Hapsburg Monarchy, and an account of the work underway to restore Bohemia to the map. It was cheering to have the Frenchman express approval, however guarded, for the patriotic endeavors of the Czechs and the Slovaks, and other influential French statesmen assented to the principle of freedom, though not necessarily of independence, for Bohemia. In an interview with *Le Matin*, Masaryk explained, "If from the outset of the war the Entente had declared positively that the Austrian Slavs would be liberated and the Hapsburg Monarchy destroyed, Austria-Hungary instead of being a source of strength for Germany would have been a heavy burden. . . . The ruin of the Hapsburg Monarchy is the surest way to reduce Germany's dreams to naught. . . ." This gospel of *Austria delenda* which Masaryk iterated and reiterated, failed to strike a responsive chord in the breast of many Entente policymakers, not immediately in any case.

As well as in Britain and France, the burgeoning Czechoslovak movement was promoted in Russia, first by men who looked to the tsardom for national salvation. Not long after the fighting began, delegations of Czechs and Slovaks resident in Russia twice called upon Nicholas II and implored him to support the revival of an independent Bohemian kingdom. He was handed a map showing the future state, which covered not only regions of Czech and Slovak speech, but also Vienna and the province of Upper Austria! Without committing himself, the Tsar observed piously that he hoped God would help the Bohemians realize their aspirations; at the foreign office Sazonov, as has been indicated, preferred for a short while a Bohemian state as an autonomous partner in the Hapsburg realm.

Scarcely had the war started than Czechs and Slovaks, domiciled in Russia, made arrangements for a special corps known as *Česka Družina,* in the tsarist army. Members were Czech immigrants living in Russia, the officers being either Russians or Czechs, and they fought in campaigns against the Central Empires; it was intended to expand this force into a distinct Czechoslovak army by enrolling Czech and Slovak prisoners of war and deserters, but tsarist authorities responded frigidly to the plan, or they set as a prerequisite that prisoners must first take out Russian citizenship. It was plain enough to makers of policy in Petrograd that successful secessionist activity by a minority from the multinationality Hapsburg dominions might touch off untoward reverberations in the multinationality empire of the Romanovs. It is true, however, that a dramatic appeal in cadenced sentences to Czechoslovaks to rebel was prepared for issuance if and when tsarist troops penetrated to the provinces of the Slovaks and the Czechs. Little by little, the Czechoslovak Legion (as it came to be called) reached 3,000 men.[25]

The foremost representative of the Russophile faction among the Czechs, Karel Kramář, an individual of fixed and resolute purpose and of impeccable patriotic credentials, strongly favored a Romanov prince as viceroy of a Bohemia intimately aligned to the empire of the Tsar and member of a general Slav federation. Toward the middle

[25] Zeman, *op. cit.,* pp. 90–94; Arthur Hübscher, "Der Tschechische Verrat an Russland," *Süddeutsche Monatshefte,* XXII (1924–5), 73–74.

of 1916, the impulsive and overhasty Dürich, who saw eye to eye with Kramář, appeared in Russia in his new capacity of vice-chairman of the Czechoslovak National Council, and soliciting active help from influential Slavophiles, he proposed not only that a free Bohemia should be linked to the tsardom, but that his co-nationals should embrace the Orthodox faith! This Russophile orientation, so radically at variance with the program entertained by the Masaryk-Beneš element, provoked divisive controversy among Czechs in Russia, which persisted in a diluted version even after Dürich was unceremoniously dropped from the National Council. But the overthrow of the Romanov dynasty in March, 1917, converted the Russophile dream, as a practical proposition, into the deadest of dead mutton. No one can determine, however, whether the western orientation possessed deeper roots among politically articulate Czechs and Slovaks than affection for "brotherly and Slavic Moscow."

7.

To an instructive extent, the presentation of the political claims of Serbia and of the Southern Slavs generally, in the Entente countries paralleled the activity of Czech and Slovak émigrés. Two significant differences existed, however: no Yugoslav commanded the respect that Masaryk obtained, and fierce wranglings between Serbs and other South Slavs repeatedly filled the air with sulfur and threatened to frustrate fond national dreams completely. At bottom the issue was whether a Great Serbian state should be forged or a federal union of Serbs, Croats, and Slovenes—and no more than a superficial understanding on this basic issue had been attained when the war ended.

At the onset of the fighting, several partisans of Yugoslav unity from Dalmatia took refuge in Rome, where they commenced agitation. Outstanding among the Serb-Croat exiles was Frano Supilo, a gigantic individual of Croatian peasant stock, sometime a deputy in the parliament at Vienna, who had been editing a newspaper in Fiume (Rijeka). Genial and assertive, he could also be domineering and impatient with lesser men; through Alexander Iswolsky, tsarist ambassador to France, Supilo tried to convert Théophile Delcassé, French foreign minister, to the idea of a strong and united Serbo-Croat state which would include Istria and Dalmatia. Planting himself temporarily in London, Supilo won the good-will of several British ministers, notably Sir Edward Grey. Admirer though Supilo was of Italian culture and history, he stoutly opposed annexation of any part of Dalmatia by Italy, and he imagined that an accommodation could be devised, compatible with the interests of both Yugoslavs and Italians. Early in 1915, Supilo went to Petrograd to uphold South Slav interests, stopping in Serbia en route to quarrel dramatically with Pašić. The Premier resented Yugoslav idealism, and whatever he said, he thought inflexibly in terms of a Great Serbia. Supilo, on the other hand, wanted Serbs, Croats, and Slovenes—even though as a free-thinker he despised Roman Catholicism—to be equal partners in a Yugoslav federation.[26]

No more cordial were the relations of the stiffnecked Serbian prime minister with a second Dalmatian refugee and strenuous partisan of a federal Yugoslavia, Dr. Ante Trumbić. An able lawyer, far-seeing and courageous, sometime mayor of Spalato, and a deputy in the Dalmatian diet and in the Austrian parliament, Trumbić lacked however the impulsive dynamism of his friend Supilo; Italian national extremists tried to pin the tag *austriacante* upon Trumbić, though in fact his detestation of Austria blended pathology with patriotism. These men

[26] Carlo Sforza, "L'Idée Yugoslave: Supilo et Pašić," *Le Monde Slave*, XIV (3) (1937), 202–215.

and other exiles communicated with Steed, Seton-Watson, and like-minded Britons and Frenchmen; and South Slav colonies overseas, especially in the United States and Argentina, provided money for Yugoslav propaganda.

On September 21, 1914, Prime Minister Pašić outlined the territorial claims of Serbia as follows: first, the acquisition of all districts of the Dual Monarchy peopled by men and women of South Slav speech, including a wide belt of southern Hungary needed to protect Belgrade; second, Dalmatia and Istria, though the latter might be allocated to Italy, if that kingdom intervened promptly on the Entente side. After Serb troops recovered Belgrade in December, 1914, the Pašić ministry proclaimed as the supreme objective of the war "the liberation and unification of all our enslaved brothers, Serbs, Croats, and Slovenes."

It was evident that decisions on the South Slavs would be vitally affected by the thinking of the men on the Neva. While Foreign Minister Sazonov fondly alluded to the Serbs as "dear little brothers," one of his first diplomatic moves in the war era was an attempt to persuade Serbia to hand over land in Macedonia to Sofia in order to keep Bulgaria neutral. On the bigger problem of the Southern Slavs as a whole, Sazonov was curiously misinformed and prejudiced by allegiance to Orthodox Christian traditions. Distrustful of Yugoslavs affiliated with Roman Catholicism, he wished the Serbs to be the dominant factor in any South Slav state that might be created, and he disliked talk of a federal Yugoslavia; hence, his meetings with Supilo were distinctly less than friendly. The dynamic Dalmatian giant had gone to Petrograd specifically to stiffen resistance there to Italian territorial pretensions along the Adriatic; in an interview with *Novoe Vremya*, Supilo testily observed that the Italian appetite threatened to provoke a war with emerging Yugoslavia. His countrymen, he said, would probably prefer the Austrian yoke to lordship by Italy as the lesser of two evils. In spite of the manly endeavors of South Slav émigrés and their western friends, they were unable to prevent Entente pledges of Yugoslav-peopled lands on the Adriatic to Italy in the London Treaty.[27]

Meanwhile, South Slav exiles had organized a committee to advance the national interest, with headquarters first in Paris and after May, 1915, in London; fifteen men, all citizens of the Hapsburg Monarchy, eleven Croats, two Slovenes, and two Serbs, constituted the original members, and emissaries were dispatched to the leading Entente capitals and to Washington. Aside from spreading information about the union of Yugoslavs on the basis of equality for the three constituent groupings, the committee aimed to reach an understanding on the structure of the new state with the cabinet of Serbia and to fight the Treaty of London; it was only after the conquest of Serbia in the autumn of 1915 that Pašić and his colleagues manifested even the slightest interest in the committee. Trumbić, leader of the Croats of Dalmatia, presided over the committee and, with Supilo, was its guiding spirit; [28] also prominent was Hinko Hinković, a distinguished Croatian attorney and deputy, who, before the war ceased, moved to the United States, in search of backing for a republican Yugoslavia. The principal agent of the committee in Petrograd, Ante Mandić, a Croat, was a convinced Yugoslav federalist, who kept his London fellows informed on Russian interest in the Yugoslav dream (or rather the disinterest). Seton-Watson and Steed, advocates of South Slav federalism and strongly antipathetic to the Great Serbia doctrine, helped the committee immensely, but they were unable to convert Pašić to their way of thinking, and they were infuriated by the addic-

---

[27] May, "Seton-Watson and the Treaty of London," *op. cit.*
[28] Emil R. Gärtner, *Kroatien in Südslawien* (Vienna, 1944), pp. 21–22; Zeman, *op. cit.*, pp. 65–72.

tion of the Serbian London embassy to the plan of a Greater Serbia.

Lord Crewe received a committee delegation at the foreign office in July, 1915, spoke cheering phrases, but counselled against expecting lavish acquisitions of land. Yet on September 30, Sir Edward Grey promised Supilo British backing, as has been indicated, for South Slav unity after the war, with the proviso that Bosnia, southern Dalmatia, and Croatia should freely determine their status. While Supilo welcomed this statement, the Pašić ministry retorted that a plebiscite would be quite superfluous.[29]

In the autumn of 1915 a *South Slav Bulletin*, skillfully written and well printed, made its début in London and appeared regularly until the end of March, 1918. The initial issue carried letters of warm praise and encouragement from Seton-Watson and Ernest Denis, as well as contributions from leading Yugoslav writers. Throughout its life the *Bulletin* specialized in reports on the South Slav areas of Europe, but it also carried quite a little material on Yugoslavs in the United States, where it was claimed nearly a million brothers resided, probably more Croats than Slovenes and Serbs combined.

An official Serbian delegation visited London in the spring of 1916, Crown Prince Alexander identifying himself in a public address with the ideal of a common Yugoslav fatherland. This pronouncement was the first authoritative utterance from the Serb side, and Pašić, who held doggedly to his principle of "Serbia over all," was conspicuously absent when the speech was delivered. Tension between the committee and the premier increased when the latter told Russian journalists that Serbia, seeking only commercial frontage on the Adriatic, conceded hegemony in that sea to Italy, an extraordinary

---

[29] P. D. Ostović, *The Truth About Yugoslavia* (New York, 1952), pp. 79–80, 273 ff.

statement that thoroughly nettled many a Croatian exile who was wedded to Yugoslav unity. While Supilo never ceased to press for a precise understanding, putting Croatia and Serbia on the same footing in the projected Yugoslav state, Trumbić supported union without reservation, afraid lest controversy on the terms of unification might stultify liberation from the Monarchy; he even imagined that if Pašić were greatly antagonized, he might strike a bargain with Italy to partition Croatia! Since no acceptable compromise could be discovered, Supilo withdrew on June 5, 1916, from the South Slav committee and in a brusque letter of resignation hurled anathemas at politicians who differed with him. Rejecting the Great Serb notion, Supilo preferred a separate Croat state, to include as many Yugoslavs as cared to enter, and he spent himself attempting to win moderately-minded Italians to his views.[30]

British moral sympathy had been somewhat enlisted, meanwhile, on behalf of the Serbs, thanks substantially to the zealous activity of Seton-Watson. At the beginning of the war he had almost stood alone in combatting British ignorance about Serbia, in assailing the widespread conviction that the spunky Slav kingdom was beneath contempt, and in disseminating Serbophile propaganda. He largely founded and was the moving force in the Serbian Relief Fund, set up in September, 1914, which from first to last collected £1,000,000 to aid sick and wounded Serbs; heroic physicians and nurses from Britain and the United States were rushed to Serbia to fight the dread typhus, and scores of Serbian youths were taken to Britain,[31] France, or Switzerland to finish their

[30] *Ibid.*, 80–82; Charles Loiseau, "Frano Supilo à Rome," *Le Monde Slave*, V (1928), 161–178—based upon conversations of the author with the Croatian patriot. In 1917, Supilo died in exile and eleven years later his remains were interred in Dubrovnik (Ragusa).

[31] For a graphic, intimate account of relief activity, see Monica M. Stanley, *My Diary in Serbia* (London, 1916). See, also, Hanak, *op. cit.*, pp. 65–74.

education, subsidized partly by the British national treasury.

To counteract the general impression that the South Slavs were uncouth, irresponsible anarchists, devoid of civilized instincts, an exhibition of the sculptures of Ivan Meštrović was arranged (1915) in South Kensington Museum. The son of Croatian peasants of Dalmatia, Meštrović had studied with Auguste Rodin in Paris and then immortalized in stone the death of the Serbian nation and its resurrection. The international connections of Meštrović enabled him to acquaint men on the South Slav committee, of which he was a member, with leading lights in Entente countries and in Serbia. No less than Supilo, he wanted a federal Yugoslavia, and he lamented that the Russians were concerned only about the destiny of Orthodox South Slavs.

The Meštrović exhibition, which attracted throngs, was ceremonially opened by Lord Robert Cecil; later on, paintings of Serbian and Croatian artists were put on display in London, and the committee issued educational pamphlets, of which French translations were made, under the series title of the "South Slav Library." A very exceptional priest of the Serbian Orthodox Church, Nicholas Velimirović, who made a mark as a preacher in London and founded a hostel of St. Sava at Oxford, composed brochures—"Religion and Nationality in Serbia"—explaining how both Roman Catholic and Orthodox clergymen were kindling the sacred national flame among Yugoslavs, and he later carried on propaganda in the United States.[32] For the cause, Mrs. Fanny S. Copeland brought out an appreciative pamphlet on *The Women of Serbia*.

[32] During the Second World War, a Bishop now, Velimirović fell afoul of the Nazis and was thrown into the notorious concentration camp at Dachau; when released, he proceeded to England and finally made his home in the United States, dying there in 1956. Six years later, Meštrović, who had also settled in America, passed away at South Bend, Indiana.

Publicity activities in Britain on behalf of the South Slavs rose to a peak on Kossovo Day, June 28, 1916. Circulars announcing the commemoration were dispatched to twenty-three thousand churches, and schools were given a fulsome booklet, *Serbia, Yesterday, Today and Tomorrow*, written by Seton-Watson. On the holiday itself school buildings displayed the flag of Serbia, theaters resounded with the Serbian national anthem, thirty thousand copies of which were purchased, upwards of a thousand cinemas showed films about Serbia, newspapers lauded the unconquerable heroes of the Balkans in glowing phrases, and billboards were plastered with reproductions of "Heroic Serbia" from *Punch*. At St. Paul's the Archbishop of Canterbury "preached a real Yugoslav sermon" and youthful Serbian refugees sang; all in all, the response to the great national holiday of the Serbs far surpassed the expectations of the sponsors; [33] and in 1917 and 1918 the celebration was repeated, though on less grandiose dimensions.

Late in the summer of 1916, the "New Europe" coterie launched a Serbian Society of Britain—subsequently renamed the Yugoslav Society. It was dedicated to the proposition that the creation of a free Yugoslavia, which would frustrate the German dream of a realm reaching from Berlin to Bagdad, was a vital British interest comparable to an independent Belgium. The Society proposed to promote intimacy between Britain and all Yugoslav political groupings, working with like-minded societies, and to nullify if possible the Entente pledge granting northern Dalmatia to Italy. The greatly respected Lord Cromer of Egyptian fame, who subscribed wholeheartedly to the agenda of the Society, assumed the chairmanship. It was decidely an élite Society, enrolling only about three hundred members, and carrying on its activity through a set of committees and a council.

---

[33] R. W. Seton-Watson to Milenko R. Vesnić, July 17, 1916. Seton-Watson Papers. See, also, Hanak, *op. cit.*, pp. 75–79.

The Italian foreign office hotly resented the foundation of the Serbian Society, insisting that it was in fact an anti-Italian agency, even though a declared objective was to "work for a friendly agreement between the South Slavs and Italy." British lovers of Italy, assailed the Society furiously, and nothing Cromer and his fellows said could persuade them that the new organization was anything other than an instrument to thwart Italian territorial expectations on the eastern side of the Adriatic. When a Society manifesto of December, 1916, flatly proclaimed the liberation and unity of the South Slavs to be a British imperial interest, a running polemic opened up with anti-Serbs in Britain. Among them was M. Edith Durham, who had accumulated much first-hand knowledge of the Balkans and who had adopted the Albanians as her pet nationality. Miss Durham dwelt upon the fierce political controversies within the South Slav community, each branch of the nationality competing for supreme influence, and she insisted that Roman Catholics among the South Slavs were decidedly superior culturally to the Serbs; in her judgment many Catholic South Slavs would be quite content to remain with the Danube Monarchy, if autonomy were granted.[34] With Sir Arthur Evans bearing the main burden, British friends of Yugoslavia ridiculed the importance of pro-Hapsburg sentiment among the South Slavs and argued that liberation would prove a valuable military asset for Britain and her allies. The Entente, Evans appealed, should assert in a collective pronouncement that independence and union of all Yugoslavs constituted a definite article in the program for a new and brighter Europe.[35]

[34] Edith Durham to editor, *Manchester Guardian*, Dec. 6, 27, 1916, and Edward V. Arnold to editor, *ibid.*, Dec. 2, 22, 1916; Hanak, *op. cit.*, pp. 150–151, 192–197.

[35] Arthur Evans to editor, *Manchester Guardian*, Dec. 20, 27, 30, 1916; Arthur Evans to Seton-Watson, Dec. 28, 31, 1916. Seton-Watson Papers. A sharp, personal feud developed between Miss Durham and Seton-Watson.

8.

Rumors of a negotiated peace settlement with the empire of the Tsar often went the rounds in the Central Empires—and in western Entente capitals. Where so much smoke rose, there was fire. Within six weeks after fighting started, Count Sergius Witte, who had sought to stave off an armed conflict by means of a summit conference between the imperial cousins, Nicholas II and William II, was saying that Russia must "liquidate this stupid adventure as soon as possible." Called Russia's "unique statesman," with dubious accuracy, Witte predicted that if the Entente won the war, republicanism would be fostered in Russia, presaging the eclipse of the Romanov regime. Before 1914 was out, he was talking of peace on the basis of withdrawal of Central Power armies from Russian Poland, the cession to Russia of Galicia and of a portion of the Bukowina, then occupied by tsarist troops, and territorial rectifications along the Turkish border. The Count spoke the mind of Russian conservatism, which included court elements noted for gentle sentiments toward the Central Allies.

And ardor for the war sagged significantly among Russian military chiefs before 1914 had run to its close. Hungry for peace, tsarist soldiers surrendered en masse to the enemy, General Alexei N. Kuropatkin reported. On the other side of the battlefront, Count Tisza was in a mood as early as September, 1914 "to offer the Russians and the French a cheap peace"; the Magyar prime minister confessed total ignorance of German aims in the war. By year's end Conrad believed that the Monarchy would be well out of the war if it preserved its integrity and escaped payment of reparations; "We shall be happy if we get through with only a black eye," he wryly observed. Apprehensive of the economic and political repercussions of a prolonged war upon Russia, big business interests in Germany advocated putting out peace feelers, but Berlin policymakers pushed the suggestion aside.[36]

The climate of peace opinion in the tsardom sustained tentative gestures at negotiation with the Central Powers carried on through financiers, Scandinavian reigning families, and lesser channels. Now and again faint inklings that something was afoot trickled into the press of Russia; peace sentiments had their ups and downs, dropping when Witte died in March, 1915, rising in the autumn when the Grand Duke Nicholas was cashiered as commander-in-chief.[37] Earlier in 1915 Prince Gottfried von Hohenlohe, Hapsburg ambassador to Germany, who was well acquainted with Russia, proposed in a letter to Nicholas II that envoys of the two countries should consult in Switzerland on an honorable peace settlement, but the Russians interpreted the overture as a sign of Austrian weakness; they would do nothing until conditions were propitious enough to impose their own terms.[38]

Along in the spring of 1915 when the fantastic price that Italy set for neutrality leaked out, voices in Vienna recommended a quick compromise with Russia, even to the cession of Galicia, so that Austro-Hungarian military energies might be concentrated against the perfidious Latins to the south. Reports of a like character circulated in Italian diplomatic quarters, but no available evidence suggests that the Ballplatz ever seriously considered this gambit. During the spring and early summer of 1915 a highly-placed Russian court lady, Marie Vassilshikova, caught in the vicinity of Vienna when the war descended and there interned, addressed several passionate appeals

[36] Conrad, *op. cit.*, V, 910–911; Hohenlohe to Berchtold, Jan. 5, 1915, P.A., *Geheim*, XLVII/3–5.

[37] Rudolf Stadelmann, "Friedensversuche im Ersten Jahre des Weltkriegs," *Historische Zeitschrift*, CLVI (1937), 485–545; J. Lewin, "Erfolglose Friedensfühler im Weltkrieg," *Osteuropa*, II (1926–27), 507–517.

[38] Paléologue, I, 334–335.

for peace to Nicholas II and to Russian public men believed to have the ear of the Tsar. Whether prompted or not, she asserted that weight-carrying personalities of the Central Empires had besought her to act as intermediary with Petrograd. The arguments were advanced that Nicholas II could attain immortal fame by leading the way back to peace and, by sparing his empire further losses, he would preserve it as a bastion against possible irruptions by yellow marauders from Asia. It was also averred that slick Britain was exploiting Russia as a cat's-paw or that London, guilty of crude Machiavellianism, was seeking a separate understanding with Germany that would leave the Tsar in the lurch. These messages, however well-intentioned, infuriated Sazonov, and Nicholas II interpreted them as insulting, and no reply was made. When Vassilshikova ventured into her homeland for a *tête-à-tête* with the Tsar, she was, apparently, bundled off to an orphanage.[39]

While the armies of Nicholas II were retreating from the Polish provinces in 1915, Russian official and press quarters buzzed with talk of peace feelers from the Central Powers. To spike such stories, Sazonov authorized an American correspondent of the London *Times*, Stanley Washburn, to denounce the "fables" in an article captioned, *Will of Russia; no separate Peace*. Bethmann laid away dreams of a negotiated settlement for the time being, for it seemed to him that a formal overture, instead of encouraging a will to quit, would stiffen the Muscovite backbone.[40] Nicholas II told a delegation of Knights of St. George in February, 1916, "I will not conclude peace until we have chased the last enemy from our territory," and he bravely affirmed that no settlement would be entered upon except in full agreement with allies "to whom we are bound . . . by true friendship sealed with blood."

[39] Pierre Rain, "Nicholas II et Sa Diplomatie pendant la Guerre," *Revue des Sciences Politiques*, LII (1929), 105–127.

[40] Hohenlohe to Burián, Oct. 21, 1915, P.A., *Geheim*, XLVII/3–10.

However that may be, stories of impending discussions for peace with Russia, not entirely wishful thinking, recurrently turned up in the Monarchy.[41]

Rumors were quickened in July of 1916, when Sazonov, who had faithfully upheld the Entente alliance, gave way to Boris V. Stürmer, a notorious rogue, indifferent to any principle save expediency. Coming on the heels of informal peace talks in Stockholm by a vice-president of the Imperial Duma, Protopov, with Hugo Stinnes and other German financial magnates, the change in command at the Russian foreign office stimulated catchpenny hopes of a compromise settlement—and conversely depressed feelings in Britain and France.[42] Under these circumstances, civilian authorities in Germany preferred to proceed cautiously on promises of independence for the Poles, but they nevertheless yielded to the high command, anxious to obtain Polish military manpower. The Central Power declaration of November 5, 1916, on Poland reduced the chances of fruitful exchanges for peace with Petrograd, without wholly killing them; and unofficial conversations on peace continued in fact for several months more. Authoritative Russian denials of the persistent peace rumors grew so vehement that some western commentators felt sure that the stories had a substantial foundation, as in truth they had, and certain western newspapers even went as far as to sketch the contents of an alleged understanding between the Central Powers and Russia.[43]

The appearance of Miliukov in Switzerland nourished reports that he was striving to open the way for peace parleys through that neutral country; [44] yet a Duma resolution (December 15, 1916) expressed categorical refusal by the Entente to consider a compromise settlement at

[41] Redlich, *Tagebuch*, II, 117–118.
[42] Hohenlohe to Burián, Aug. 21, 1916, P.A., *Geheim*, XLVII/3–12; von Gagern to Burián, Sept. 30, 1916, P.A., Schweiz, *Berichte*, 1916.
[43] *Literary Digest*, LIII (1916), 1457, 1528.
[44] Von Gagern to Burián, Nov. 6, Dec. 29, 1916, P.A., Schweiz, *Berichte*, 1916.

all. Evidently, in the last months of Nicholas II's reign several vague suggestions for an immediate peace issued from Russian court circles, and Vienna was inclined to pursue them, but Berlin responded with a flat negative.[45]

[45] Cooke and Stickney, *op. cit.*, pp. 490–496; Edmund Glaise von Horstenau, *Die Katastrophe* (Vienna, 1929), p. 121.

8. Austria in Armageddon

AT THE OUTSET, THE WAR EVOKED POPULAR ENTHUSIASM in Austria unexampled since the struggle for liberation against Napoleon I. Gustav Cardinal Piffl of Vienna spoke the sentiments of many citizens in a sermon at St. Stephen's in which he declared, "It is the voice of God, which speaks through the roar of guns"; the Sudeten-born Cardinal felt the murder of Francis Ferdinand personally and poignantly, since the Archduke had been influential in securing him the highest ecclesiastical dignity in the Empire. For other Austrians, it seemed morally righteous to punish the trouble-making Serbs; as the British Ambassador Maurice de Bunsen informed his home office, a war by Austria-Hungary to destroy "the nest of assassins," was so "evidently just that it seemed to her people inconceivable that any country should place itself in her path." Aside from insolent Pan-Serbian pretensions, the conflict clearly possessed the elementary quality of self-defense against the despotic, profoundly dreaded empire of the Tsar. That consideration carried decisive weight for prominent Austrian Socialists, who, like their fellows in imperial Germany, solemnly condemned an appeal to arms early in the diplomatic crisis of July, 1914, and then, scornful of Marxist international doctrine, rallied patriotically under the Hapsburg war banner. The reasoning that prevailed was sharply etched by Viktor Adler, the most respected man in Austrian Socialism.

"Today," he said, "we are faced . . . with the question whether the Russian armies will march into Brünn, Budapest or Vienna. In such a situation I cannot investigate whether a Russian victory might be favorable for the fight to liberate Russian workers. If I feel the knife at my throat, I have first of all to push the knife away." [1] It was recalled that Karl Marx himself had written (1860): "The only reason which . . . justifies the existence of Austria as a state is her resistance against the onward march of Russia in the east of Europe. This resistance is helpless, inconsistent and cowardly, but tenacious." [2]

A Socialist newswriter, Karl Leuthner, brought forth the dubious doctrine that Russian imperialism, far from being the handiwork of the small governing classes, was deep-rooted in the masses of the country; the very character of the eastern colossus, he supposed, its limitless space, animated mooshik and grandduke alike with an irresistible urge to possess lands of other peoples.

On the day after Social Democrats in the German Reichstag, representing the most revered phalanx of Marxism in the world, approved war credits, *Arbeiter Zeitung*, Vienna organ of the Socialist party, carried an exciting editorial lauding "Deutschlands Tag"—a day "on which was displayed the dignity, grandeur, and sublimity

[1] Viktor Adler, *Aufsätze, Reden und Briefe* (5 vols., Vienna, 1922–1925), III, 106 ff.
[2] Quoted in Robert A. Kann, *The Multinational Empire* (2 vols., New York, 1950), II, 154.

of the German spirit . . ." Within a month the paper was
shouting to the Germany ally: "On to Paris." Massive,
enthusiastic throngs in Austrian cities and provincial
towns indulged in martial demonstrations, singing Hapsburg anthems, flaunting black-and-yellow flags, listening
to impassioned speeches. An eye-witness foreigner reported that Serbia was assailed as "a cunning, boastful,
malevolent dwarf" which had "slain the man on whom
Austria had built her hopes of a brighter future"; the empire of the Tsar was excoriated as "half bear, half man,
but wholly evil," and it had "encouraged and egged on
this arrogant pygmy." Austria must avenge the murder.
. . . If ever a nation went into a war as to a feast," he remarked, "as to a cleansing, strengthening bath, Austria-
Hungary surely did." Friend and foe of the Danube
Monarchy were alike astonished at the mighty surge of
martial emotions and the spirit of solidarity universally in
evidence.[3]

With understandable exaggeration, a Vienna publicist
observed "there is a single heart-beat throughout the
entire realm . . . a new Austrianness, a new Hungarianness
has been born and the varied peoples . . . gather . . . with
an enthusiasm that could not be greater if they were . . .
a single nationality . . ." The popular response lent credence to the theory that internal political troubles would
be submerged and mayhap the realm marvellously rejuvenated by the external challenge to its integrity.[4]

2.

The Austrian partner in the Dual Monarchy entered the
gigantic conflict under a more authoritarian regime than
prevailed even in tsarist Russia, for there the Duma was

[3] Wolf von Schierbrand, *Austria-Hungary, the Polyglot Empire* (New
York, 1917), pp. 186–189; Anon., "How the War Came to Vienna,"
Living Age, CCCXXII (1924), 443–447.
[4] Leopold von Chlumecky, *ÖR*, XL (1914), 247–50.

permitted to assemble. In Austria, however, the parliament, whose deliberations had been prorogued in March, 1914, was suspended, although not dissolved, and provincial assemblies, likewise, shut their doors. Until the spring of 1917, Austria was governed technically under a constitutional clause—Article 14—authorizing the issuance of decrees having automatically the full force of law. Yet no inconsiderable latitude was allowed local administrators in making revisions in decrees and strong-minded officials frequently winked at orders coming from the capital. "His Majesty and a very small cabinet of his own choosing," explained the American Ambassador, "augmented by two or three military experts, govern and administer absolutely this land of mixed races [sic], wherein public expression of opinion or discussion of state policy is impossible . . ." [5]

Becoming prime minister in November, 1911, Count Karl Stürgkh contrived to hold on until removed by an assassin's bullet nearly five years later. As a deputy for a full generation, this statuesque scion of an impoverished noble family of Styria, had built up a reputation as a specialist in education and as a clear methodical thinker, but he spoke ineffectively and wrote still worse; conservative, not to say reactionary in outlook, Stürgkh was by no means averse to rule by decree. His political advancement owed much to help rendered by Rudolf Sieghart, influential financier and newspaper magnate; not a strong personality, Stürgkh was inclined to defer to the wishes of more resolute spirits like Conrad and Tisza. His cabinet consisted overwhelmingly of Austrogermans; pleas from various quarters for the convocation of parliament, grow-

[5] Penfield to Lansing, July 29, 1916, U.S., *National Archives*, 863. 50/16. On this report, which filled thirty-five large-sized pages, Penfield observed, "You may think there is sufficient 'meat' in the document for a book." Dispatches from the Ambassador and his aides, which passed in a steady stream to the State Department, furnish much data on conditions and moods in the Monarchy until the spring of 1917 when the Embassy closed down.

ing in volume, went unheeded. For that stand, the argument was put that volcanic national feuds would burst out, as before the war, impair solidarity, and advertise to the enemy the internal weaknesses of the Empire. It is said that the prime minister remarked while passing the classic parliament house on the Vienna Ring during the war, "the greatest thing my ministry has done is to have turned that building into a [military] hospital." Authentic or apocryphal, the observation faithfully reflected the inner conviction of Stürgkh; yet the ministry kept in close touch with the presidents of the parliament or Reichsrat and with important politicians of varied national colorings.

Strictly speaking, Austria lived under a military dictatorship, operated through a war surveillance office, attached to the ministry of war, and containing delegates from half a dozen other ministries. Undisguised military administrations were set up in war zones, and an imperial decree (July 31, 1914) instructed field commanders in Galicia, the Bukowina, and in parts of Moravia and Silesia, "to issue decrees, give orders and enforce the same"; when Italy became a belligerent, army regimes were instituted in the Tyrol, Dalmatia, and adjacent areas.

Ordinary civil liberties were suspended before fighting actually commenced, and on November 4, 1914, trial by jury went by the boards. For a time, courts-martial administered criminal law, though later they were restricted to districts where civil courts had ceased to function. Courts often degenerated, for practical purposes, into instruments of the high command for use against dissident nationalists; many patriots were interned, imprisoned, or, after farcical trials, executed. Controversy between Austrian civilian authorities and the military grew into a running sore, the former feeling that army administration was harsh and politically harmful and the army chiefs retorting that the civilian officials were inclined to deal too leniently with subversive troublemakers. In the long run that domestic strife unquestionably impaired the machinery of state to a disastrous degree.

3.

Although parliamentary activity was proscribed, Austrian political parties did not fade away. The Socialists, strong in urban centers and commanding a sixth of the seats in parliament, split over matters of policy and principle into three fairly distinct factions—right, left, and center; Socialist publications, the daily *Arbeiter Zeitung*, the weekly *Die Volkstribüne*, and the more orthodox Marxist monthly *Der Kampf* catered to each of these party divisions. Spokesmen of the right, the largest group and much influenced by the majority or "patriotic" Socialists of Germany, included Dr. Viktor Adler, a founding-father of the party, Dr. Friedrich Austerlitz, talented publicist deeply versed in the law and the history of the Monarchy, and Engelbert Pernersdorf, Adler's life-long friend, but hardly more than a Socialist in name. In keeping with Adler's doctrine that "there is only one thing worse than war, defeat," this faction bent to the demands of the war without renouncing its right to criticize, and it cherished the dream that the war would advance the cause of social revolution by evolution; about eighty "patriotic" pamphlets were produced by Socialist right-wingers in the first half of the war. Deviations from the right group mounted as the warfare lengthened, a development well illustrated in the case of Alfons Petzhold, prized as the best poet of the Austrian industrial proletariat. His early verse "Krieg" (1914) and "Volk, mein Volk" (1915) might have been penned by a bourgeois lyricist, but "Stahlernen Schrei" (1916) voiced affection for all of humanity, and "Der Feurige Weg" (1918), reflecting the impact of the revolutionary upheavals in Russia, was downright anti-war in temper and consequently suppressed by the public authorities.

Dr. Karl Renner was the most striking figure in the Socialist middle group, a general favorite in the party, and one of the most remarkable Austrians of the twentieth century. Given to profound thinking on problems of nationality and economics, a parliamentary deputy since 1907, Renner, the statesman, presided over the Austrian Republic as chancellor after both world wars—in 1919 and again in 1945. To passions for scholarship and good living, he joined a passion for the betterment of his fellowmen, and he carried forward learned pre-war studies on means of preserving the multinationality Monarchy, a social and an European good in his eyes. If he had had his way the supranationality Hapsburg dynasty would have worked along with the industrial proletariat to transform the realm on the Danube into a federation of nations, based upon solid democratic foundations and upon cultural autonomy on personal, non-territorial terms for all nationality groups; a political community of that character, he contended, might form the prelude to a larger European federation. Regarding Renner as a visionary utopian, Leon Trotsky would one day ridicule him as "the bereaved theoretician of the Austro-Hungarian Monarchy." [6]

Renner diffused his political opinions in a stream of wartime essays—his pen was never dry, it was said—that later appeared in book form. As for the war itself, he interpreted it in Marxist terminology in *Marxismus, Krieg und Internationale,* published in 1917; the search for markets and the resultant clash of rival capitalisms provoked the war in the ultimate, he was sure. Scornful of idealistic explanations of Entente diplomacy, he insisted that England had seized upon the violation of Belgian neutrality merely as an excuse for unleashing a deadly imperialistic struggle.

[6] Kann, *op. cit.,* II, 157–165, 346–350.

Allied with Renner was Dr. Karl Seitz, raised in an orphanage, sometime a Viennese school teacher and among the first Socialists to win a seat in the Austrian parliament. A man of great natural dignity and rare charm, he heightened his stature after the war as mayor of Vienna.

On the left of the Socialist spectrum stood Dr. Friedrich Adler, son of Viktor, a devoted adherent of the international tenet of orthodox Marxism. He had been trained as a scientist and had taught in Zürich before turning into a Marxian publicist. His spirit was seared when the outbreak of war canceled a congress planned for August 23, 1914 to commemorate the fiftieth anniversary of the First International and the twenty-fifth birthday of the Second; he was thoroughly disgusted by the torrent of "hurrah patriotism" which gripped Socialists of warring lands. Friedrich and a small company of like-minded anti-war Marxists wished to throw down the Austrian military dictatorship and reinvigorate international Marxism; time and tide worked for this faction. Somewhere to the right of Adler must be placed Otto Bauer, an influential Marxist thinker, writer, and persuasive orator, who was captured in battle by the Russians late in 1914, and he spent his imprisonment in deepening his understanding of the Marxist creed.

To create a base for an international campaign for peace and to repudiate Marxists who had rallied to the war efforts of their respective countries, Swiss and Italian Socialists convened meetings of kindred minds at Zimmerwald (September 5–8, 1915) and at a second Swiss hamlet, Kienthal (April 24–30, 1916). These gatherings, which stand out as milestones on the road to the Third or Communist International, condemned "patriotic Socialists," summoned workers to hold aloof from the war effort, and appealed for a rebirth of international Socialism, but they made little impression upon Austrian disciples of Marx; no Austrian representative shared in the

Zimmerwald deliberations and only an obscure personality named Koritschaner appeared at the second meeting. Analyzing the Zimmerwald conference, Viktor Adler pointed out that with some inconsequential exceptions only minorities of the Socialist parties attended and he doubted whether the meeting represented a step toward the revival of Socialist internationalism, only mass hunger could accomplish that; misery induced by the war, he believed, was embittering the proletariat of all lands, to whom belonged the future.[7] Friedrich, however, and a handful of "Zimmerwaldists" dissented, holding that international Marxism had again become a living force and they strove to persuade "patriotic Socialists" to stop cooperating in the prosecution of the war.

Austrian Socialists of all tempers chose to stick with the party and to talk of the return of peace, but as articles in *Der Kampf* and Socialist party debates showed—elements of high drama were present when the Adlers, father and son, crossed verbal swords—viewpoints diverged radically on the surest road to peace. Jointly with Hungarian Socialists, the Austrians in April, 1915, approved a manifesto that amounted to peace without victory, and by the end of the year Viktor Adler was saying that military triumphs over Russia and Serbia assured the safety of the Monarchy and that peace should be quickly restored. Yet in March, 1916, the overwhelming majority of Socialists, assembled in Congress, applauded pro-war sentiments and were content with glittering generalities on Austro-Hungarian war aims; the leftists called stridently for the Hapsburg governing authorities to spell out in explicit language their terms for peace and to break off the fighting. It was standard practice at periodic meetings of the Socialists to demand the revival of parliament, relaxation of the censorship, amnesty for political prisoners,

[7] AZ, Nov. 14, 1915.

better care for wounded veterans, and heavier taxes on inheritances and on profits swollen by the war.

Representatives of Austrogerman bourgeois parties, as well as the Socialists, met from time to time and from that source issued interesting blueprints on ways to reconstruct the House of Hapsburg and infuse it with fresh energy.[8] Several schemes were designed to strengthen the political power of the Germans in Austria, by detaching Galicia, the Bukowina, and even Dalmatia, and by making German the official language of the state and obliging schools to teach it more extensively. As has been indicated earlier, the concept of Mitteleuropa in one or another of its variants attracted a good deal of speculation in Austrogerman quarters.

Speaking in October, 1915, Mayor Weiskirchner of Vienna expressed opinions widely shared in his Christian Socialist party.

A return to the old, dreary [political] conditions is out of the question. A new Austria must arise from the blood which flows on the battlefields, an Austria in which the Germans ought to take a position corresponding to their history and cultural importance . . . We desire that the battles which Germany and Austria have fought shoulder to shoulder should be followed by the deepening of the political alliance and an economic *rapprochement* which would secure predominance for the Central Powers in time of peace.

Since parliament was suspended, the viewpoints of the Christian Socialists and other Austrogerman parties on public issues were circulated in newspapers or by addresses subsequently printed. For Christian Socialism, the authoritative mouthpiece was the Vienna daily *Reichspost*, discussed farther along.

---

[8] Edeltrude Binder, "Doktor Albert Gessmann" (1950), p. 150, a doctoral dissertation in typescript at the University of Vienna.

4.

Not less than other belligerents, the mass of the subjects of Francis Joseph wanted to win the war and the whole machinery of society was set in motion to keep "chins up," to foster faith in eventual victory, and to prevent, if possible, the spread of despair and despondency. To buoy up popular morale, to strengthen the convictions that the Monarchy was engaged in a righteous cause, and that enemies cherished sinister war aims, all manner of Austrians enlisted in the service of war interpretation and propaganda. They endeavored to supply answers to the young Peterkin of Robert Southey's imagination.

> Now tell us all about the war
> And what they fought each other for.

Dignitaries of the Roman Catholic Church, among them Cardinal Skrbensky of Prague and Archbishop Joseph Stadler of Sarajevo, preached that the war was altogether necessary and just and summoned the faithful to work and pray for victory; no subject of Francis Joseph excelled Cardinal Piffl of Vienna in defending the management of foreign affairs and the prosecution of the fighting; true enough, the human agonies of the time were punishment for sin, he affirmed, but major benefits would assuredly accrue from the struggle.

The playwright Rudolf Hawel realistically depicted the influence of the Austrian clergy in *Einberufung*, a drama laid in a mountain village. In the early summer of 1914, peasants foregather in a tavern to exchange views on crops and on the likelihood of war upon hated Serbia. The local priest urges the countryfolk to support the war if fighting begins, in order to save their own properties, and when war actually comes, he calls upon every villager, not excluding a skeptical yokel named Bartl, to serve to the best of his ability for God, Emperor, and Fatherland "since this is a holy and righteous war." The hesitant villager yields to priestly persuasion. Socialist spokesmen ridiculed Catholic churchmen and the clerical press as grotesquely unable to decide whether the fighting was the work of "the Good God" or "the wicked Entente." "One priest is overpowered with shame and wrath," it was dryly explained, "that we should owe the misery of the war to a group of greedy millionaires, but another is happy that God through this world war, and its prolonged duration wills to attain His own particular purposes. . . ." [9] Since the majority Socialist leadership itself loyally cooperated in the war effort, strictures against the clergy smacked of the kettle calling the pot black; approaches differed, it is true, but the net result was identical.

University scholars and assorted men of learning, reputedly detached and impartial in their quest for truth-seeking, contributed their bit by enlightening ordinary "Peterkins" on the war and its issues; a Viennese society for precisely this purpose, indeed, came into being. At one point the internationally renowned Viennese expert on international law, Dr. Heinrich Lammasch, accused France of large responsibility for the coming of the war, since the Third Republic had allied with barbarous Russia and encouraged her to desperate adventure. The militantly anti-Slav historian of Vienna, Hans Uebersperger, expatiated on the Pan-slav menace, which reached a climax at Sarajevo; *Neue Freie Presse* frequently carried optimistic essays from his pen on the course of the grim struggle. When Turkey joined the Central Empires, for instance, and proclaimed a Moslem holy war against the Entente, Uebersperger gleefully anticipated Moslem uprisings in the colonial dominions of Russia, Britain, and France.[10]

[9] AZ, Sept. 26, 1915.
[10] NFP, Nov. 14, 1914.

His greatly respected colleague, Professor Oswald Red-lich in speeches and writings paid glowing tributes to the Emperor-King and other eminent Hapsburgers and dwelt upon the Muscovite peril, upon British "encirclement" diplomacy, and later, upon the perfidy of the Italian ally. Redlich expressed full confidence that the Monarchy would emerge rejuvenated from the ordeal of war and that nationality wrangles would somehow be surmounted. Another university historian, Ludo M. Hartmann, learned authority on medieval Italy and a Socialist by conviction, saluted the war as just and righteous, although previously he had been extremely critical of Ballplatz handling of relations with Serbia; he absolved the German ally of predatory expansionist ambitions. To sustain morale, the philosopher Heinrich Gomperz delivered popular lectures setting out the blessings of armed conflict, among other things, and then published them as *Philosophie des Krieges in Umrissen* (1915). A rector of the University of Vienna, Georg Reinhold assumed leadership in found-ing a newspaper for soldiers—*Die Landwacht,* which stressed that the war was being waged not only for sur-vival, but so as to ensure a brighter future for all and sundry. For the serious press of Vienna, savants of Ger-many wrote articles designed to reinforce the will to fight on to victory. Austrian authors of distinction glorified in verse and in newspaper stories the idealism for which the fighting was being conducted and extolled the heroism of the men at the battlefronts.

Widely diffused propaganda of confidence emphasized Austrian success in fending off the assaults of Turkish armies, centuries earlier, and, it was predicted that the hosts of Francis Joseph would, analogously, overwhelm Cossack barbarians; after that, as after the final thrust by the Turks upon Vienna, the realm on the Danube would enter upon a century of prosperity and progress. So also, popular memories were refreshed on the 1809 victory of the Archduke Charles over the seemingly invincible Napoleon at Aspern and on the manner in which Field-Marshal Joseph ("Father") Radetzky in 1848–49 had subdued Italian insurgents. Short, easy-to-read biographies of outstanding army commanders, such as lives of Conrad and Viktor Dankl by Ludwig Pastor, esteemed chronicler of the Papacy, were calculated to nourish mass confidence in the military chiefs, as were reassuring press reports on military prospects and the *esprit* of troops over the signatures of "big name" Austrian and German generals.

Österreichs Illustrierte Zeitung, featuring battle scenes and trench life, *Unsere Soldaten* (1915) containing vividly descriptive war pieces by Stefan Zweig and other literary celebrities, and *Patriotisches Bilderbuch*, adorned with a foreword by Prince Eduard von Liechtenstein carried the message of the war to city flat and peasant cottage. Whole series of propagandistic tracts for the times rolled off the press, and *Tiroler Soldaten Zeitung* and regimental field papers, contributed to by the finest Austrian writers, helped to keep popular morale up, to counteract dreariness and weariness. Among the authors of distinction who edited army newspapers was Robert Musil, who in time earned international renown by the novel *Der Mann Ohne Eigenschaften* (*The Man Without Qualities*, English translation, 1953); he turned to journalism after front-line duty and illness incapacitated him for active fighting. Naturally enough, Austrian attitude-molders harped upon the military prowess and the material strength of Germany and her Nibelungen fidelity to the common cause of victory.

Particular care was taken to capitalize upon and reinforce the profound mass respect for octogenarian Francis Joseph and to encourage a sense of duty to him as the embodiment of the Austrian homeland. Huge parades, fervent rendition of patriotic songs, religious devotions in Catholic and Protestant church and Jewish temple celebrated the birthday of the Emperor—August 18—and the day he acceded to the throne, December 2. At a birthday mass in 1914, in St. Stephen's, Cardinal Piffl served as celebrant and Counts Berchtold and Stürgkh mingled with a throng of worshippers, who closed the exercises singing Haydn's stirring anthem "Gott erhalte Franz den Kaiser." Press stories extolled the venerable ruler as the prince of peace, a superhuman pilot without whom the realm might suffer shipwreck, a man of sorrows and acquainted with grief whose long career of devoted labor for the common good deserved to be crowned with the laurel of military victory. To the same end, the deathday of beloved Empress—Queen Elizabeth was commemorated by tolling church bells, memorial rites at her coffin in Vienna's Capuziner tomb, and divine service at the imperial chapel in Schönbrunn palace.

Publicity to intensify mass loathing of the empire of the Tsar accented the Russian abuses visited upon Jews and the disabilities under which Russian Pole and Ukrainian suffered. The *Literarische Büro* at the Ballplatz managed this facet of propaganda, and it also dished out releases on the fighting to native and foreign journalists, and prepared pithy summaries of press information for the Emperor. News bureaus attached to other Austrian ministries and to military headquarters, likewise issued communiqués, but proposals to create a central agency to conduct psychological warfare never came to fruition and endless friction between officials handling war news and views and journalists hampered propaganda operations. Inspired by the notorious "Hassgesang gegen England" of the German Ernst Lissauer, a wealth of verse in a kindred vein appeared in Austria, but *Neue Freie Presse* protested energetically against the diffusion of this brand of war poetry, tagging it "unGerman through and through." [11]

[11] *NFP*, Sept. 21, 1915.

5.

Especial responsibility for acquainting the public with military developments, publishing stories of heroism and fortitude at the front, whether half the truth or more, spreading sentiments of optimism, combatting defeatism, and keeping citizens alert to their duties devolved upon the great press of Vienna, whose materials were freely copied by lesser papers across the realm. On the whole, newspapers faithfully upheld official policies, explained or conjured away privations on the home front and military reverses. Thus the evacuation of Lemberg (Lvov) (1914) appeared as "a regrouping of forces for strategic purposes," and next to nothing was printed about the humiliating defeats administered to Hapsburg arms by the Serbs; for a full week the ignominious Austrian expulsion from Belgrade in December, 1914, was wholly ignored by the press and even then bare dispatches simply recounted how Hapsburg troops had been pulled back in an orderly manner.

On one point, uniformity of opinion prevailed in the Austrian press: the iniquity of the censorship, a function of the war surveillance office. Copies of papers had to be submitted to censors for scrutiny well in advance of circulation and periodicals from neutral countries were subjected to searching inspection. Apologizing for blank spaces in its columns *Neue Freie Presse* remarked, "In the more important cases we have repeatedly closed up with white spaces in the paper in order not to disturb our readers by intrusions on the part of the censors." Hardly of less importance than government censorship was the newspapers' self-imposed suppression of information that might seriously disturb the public mind and emotions.

Attacks upon the censorship were delivered, also, in the name of Concordia, the Viennese club of secular journalists, and of the Puisverein, the Catholic counterpart. From late 1915 onward, papers complained, too, about the growing lack of newsprint (although the shortage was less acute than in Hungary) and rising costs of production. Many smaller papers fell by the wayside; taking the Monarchy as a whole, more than nine hundred sheets, almost all provincial, ceased publication before the war had reached its mid-point. To cut down on paper consumption, a government ban was laid in 1916 upon printing special issues of newspapers.

As the authoritative and sober voice of the Ballplatz, *Fremdenblatt* was carefully studied abroad, and a new journal *Viribus Unitis* (1915) carried semi-official interpretations of the origins of the war and the course of military affairs. Although blank spaces of the censor were frequent in the clerical *Reichspost,* and on occasion whole issues were banned, this daily doggedly supported the crown and governing authorities and espoused day in and day out the interests of the Catholic Church and the wishes of the Christian Socialist party. Richard von Kralik, a voluminous and prolific author, and Prince Alois Liechtenstein lent a certain intellectual distinction to writing on the war, as was true of editorial leaders by Dr. Friedrich Funder.[12] *Das Neue Österreich* (1916), likewise ultramontane in emphasis and tone and edited by Rudolf Hornik, enlisted talented Catholic writers to deal with a broad range of war-connected topics; Prince Ferdinand Z. Lobkowitz financed this journal.

If the historian had to choose only a single published source of information on Austria-Hungary for the war era, he would almost without hesitation prefer a file of the

---

[12] Friedrich Funder, *Vom Gestern ins Heute* (Vienna, 1952), pp. 521–588. Kralik wrote several chapters for a lavishly illustrated *Ruhmeshalle Deutscher Arbeit in der Österreichisch-ungarischen Monarchie* (Stuttgart, 1916), edited by Adam Müller-Guttenbrunn. Replete with fulsome glorification of the German-speaking population of Austria, it was intended to spread popular understanding of that element in imperial Germany.

Neue Freie Presse of Vienna. Boasting a circulation somewhat in excess of 110,000, less than half of which was distributed in Vienna, a third elsewhere in the Monarchy, and about a fifth abroad, this paper enjoyed an international standing not remotely approached by any Austrian competitor. Published twice daily, save on Monday, *Neue Freie Presse* was by no means free of patriotic distortion or dissimulation, and it was written from the comfortable assumption that government policy was invariably right, to speak broadly (scarcely the function that a "free press" traditionally existed to perform). It looked upon the war as a necessity and a potential benevolence.

"Why have Austrians been dying?" a typical editorial on war sacrifices inquired, and it answered, "for a free and happy Monarchy, for a country liberated from the fetters of the past. . . . They have died because they knew that their Fatherland could no longer exist under the goad of doubt and with hatred and disloyalty all around . . ." [13] The pages of the *Neue Freie Presse* chronicled an endless flow of report, intelligence, and rumor on happenings in every sector of wartime activity, recounted the work of the official class and the social doings of all ranks of men, sketched the tragic and the humorous, fighting and play, the exacting business of government and diplomacy, and everyday tangles of existence—insofar as censorship permitted.

Contributions by respected men and women in varied walks of life regularly appeared in the columns of *The Neue Freie Presse* and it presented authoritative communiqués from the headquarters of Central Power commanders, and maintained a corps of special war correspondents to which Alexander Roda-Roda, Alice Schalik and other well-known writers belonged. Highly colored reportage by Schalik, the only woman war correspondent accredited by the Austrian army in the Serbian and

[13] *NFP*, Oct. 31, 1915.

Italian campaigns of 1915, thoroughly nettled that satirical gadfly of Viennese journalism—and much else—Karl Kraus. For uncomplimentary strictures, the lady entered suit against Kraus and her infuriated brother even challenged the satirist to a duel, which never came off.

To no limited degree, the bourgeois *Neue Freie Presse* responded to the outlook, the tastes, and the intellectual passions of Moritz Benedikt, the proprietor and editor. An ebullient lion of a man, Benedikt in the war years might almost be compared to the British Lord Northcliffe; next to the master of the house in the Fichtegasse, someone slyly remarked, Francis Joseph was the most important personage in the Monarchy. Just a month after the fighting started, *Neue Freie Presse* commemorated its fiftieth anniversary with an immense special edition loaded with short pieces on a variety of subjects by scholars and statesmen, and for days on end, reams of congratulatory messages were reproduced, perhaps in part to distract readers from the alarming advances of Russian armies.[14]

On home affairs *Neue Freie Presse* spoke the mind of "liberal" and Austrogerman business interests, reproached national groupings for centrifugal tendencies, and pleaded for the perpetuation of the dualistic bonds with Hungary. Czernin, Koerber, Andrássy, and Wekerle, among Hapsburg public men, earned high marks, while Stürgkh and Tisza were targets of constant scolding. It gladly opened its columns to appeals for funds, extending from homes for blinded soldiers through the Red Cross, to help for Galician child refugees, and by 1917, seventeen different collections were receiving publicity. Aside from feature articles, short, sparkling, little essays called *feuilletons*, brightened hearts of readers or combatted Entente propaganda. In appreciation for his contribution to the war effort, Benedikt, to his unbounded delight, was named to

[14] *NFP*, Aug. 30, 1914. See, Adam Wandruszka, *Geschichte einer Zeitung* (Vienna, 1958), pp. 109–121, 136, especially.

the Austrian Herrenhaus in 1917, the first newspaperman ever so honored.

As was its habit, *Neue Freie Presse* ardently championed the alliance with Germany, so much so that the proprietor was accused of toiling "to make Austria an instrument in the German plan of world domination," and consequently Benedikt was charged with being more responsible than any other person for the ultimate dissolution of the Monarchy.[15] The traditionally friendly posture of this paper toward Great Britain and Italy disappeared after they became enemies in the war. It was freely and frequently asserted that the cabinet of London could have prevented an European war had it wished to do so. "It would have needed only a word," read a characteristic leader, "and the note with the time limit [i.e. the Austrian ultimatum of July 23, 1914] would have been accepted in Belgrade. However, Sir Edward Grey let Serbia be told that she must express regret for the Sarajevo murder, but otherwise need only act in her own interest"; and Britain could likewise have restrained the warmongers on the Neva, if the spirit in London had been willing.[16] Paradoxically, it was said, the British professed to be fighting for the freedom of small nations, while it still held Egypt and India in durance vile. The Entente accusation that Berlin aspired to world domination was dismissed as fantastic, legendary; Britain in fact dominated the globe, but if it persisted in fighting it would be toppled from its lofty pedestal.

Not only were Russian statesmen indicted as the chief architects of the war, but their country was held up to scorn as barbarous and uncivilized, as the maltreatment of minorities, Jews first and last, abundantly proved. After the revolutionary upheavals of 1917 had finally shorn the claws of the Russian bear, *Neue Freie Presse*

[15] London *Times*, Mar. 20, 1920—an obituary prepared possibly by H. Wickham Steed.
[16] *NFP*, Oct. 16, 19, 1915.

switched to seeking a quick end to the war, though not peace-at-any price, as captious critics averred.

Neues Wiener Tagblatt probably had a larger circulation in Vienna than *Neue Freie Presse,* and, though proud of a "liberal" heritage, it generally applauded the acts of the Stürgkh cabinet. Ownership of this daily passed to the Steyermühl, a syndicate effectively controlled by the adroit financier Dr. Rudolf Sieghart, who also dominated a second chain of papers, the Elbemühl. It was charged that Sieghart intended to dominate journalism in the Empire, but demands that he dispose of part of his press interests fell flat, though he did resign as governor of the powerful Bodenkreditanstalt banking house.

Edited by Heinrich Kanner, *Die Zeit* of Vienna enjoyed a reputation for political independence and for excellent, if often intemperate, writing by non-conformists. Copy by Kanner himself did much to establish the eminence of his paper, which frequently exposed viewpoints of the national minorities or of the Socialists, and included on its staff Baron Karl Werkmann, an intimate of Crown Prince Charles (his press attaché after he became Emperor). Once reproached for Serbophilism, interpretations in *Die Zeit* on home and foreign affairs oscillated considerably during the war, or at least until the end of 1917 when Kanner retired. Tisza in particular was often annoyed by censorious criticisms that appeared in this "liberal" sheet. But a more outspoken assailant of Austro-Hungarian public men and their policies was the *Arbeiter Zeitung,* whose emphases were picked up by smaller Socialist papers in the Empire, and it was scrupulously scanned in foreign countries. Editorial leaders consistently interpreted the coming of the war in harmony with Marxist doctrine. "Economic competition and commercial envy," a representative utterance read, "have entangled the peoples of Europe in this war, the most extreme expression of the inhumane qualities of mankind . . . Death is uniting that which life was incapable of doing." [17]

Time and again the *Arbeiter Zeitung* cried aloud against the crippling check-rein on information exercised by censors, its strictures outdoing in vehemence the more conformist bourgeois press. "What is publicly said has become a travesty of the innermost feelings of the people," it declared on June 11, 1916, "and stands in sharpest opposition to secret general opinion . . . The crying need of the hour is a thorough overhauling of the censorship . . . A small number of men insist on doing the thinking for millions . . . To allow the press to exist without permitting it to give even a carefully retouched image of public sentiment, can only cause mischief . . ." But this lament and plea, like others, fell upon stony ground.

Five months later, to illustrate, the censor's pencil cut five columns from an original eight column report on a Socialist conference of November 5, which blasted the autocratic power that industrial managers in collusion with military authority wielded over wageworkers; small wonder that the *Arbeiter Zeitung* adjured subscribers to read between the lines. Two left-wing Viennese papers of limited readership, *Morgen* and *Abend* often fell afoul of the censorship because of bold expositions of the harsh lot of "little men," and eventually they were completely suppressed.

Attached to the Austro-Hungarian war press service was a cinema division, headed by Sascha Kolowrat, a wealthy aristocrat, born in New York City, and a pioneer in Austrian film-making. Under his direction, movie houses were supplied with weekly documentaries on the war, including episodes from the fighting on various fronts. His agency also turned out films to promote the purchase of war bonds: pictures of battle scenes, sailors at Pola (Pula), conditions of life in the Polish occupation

[17] AZ, June 13, 1916.

zone and in Serbia, the majestic funeral of Francis Joseph, and the daily family round of the new sovereigns, Charles and Zita. A rather long film, "Wien im Krieg," possessed peculiar value, since it captured the realities of wartime living in the imperial capital; flashes of rollicking comedy brightened up the overall impression of gray drabness.

6.

Allegedly the Austrian satirist Karl Kraus coined the apothegm that in Berlin conditions are serious, but not hopeless, while in Vienna conditions are hopeless though not serious. If ever valid, which may be doubted, that snippet of arrant cynicism was not wholly accurate with the onset of war. As the nature of the hard ordeal was disclosed on fields of battle the silly myth that the imperial capital was nothing other than a community of elegant living, social splendor, and sophisticated refinement yielded to the watchword, *"Jetzt wird's ernst."* On the periphery of the city hastily thrown up breastworks, laced with barbed wire, were constant reminders that Cossacks might sweep in as once the legions of Napoleon had done; open spaces in the Prater and elsewhere were transformed into military drill-grounds. The downtown area of Vienna lost something of its normal verve as soldiers responded to mobilization, droves of hapless refugees flocked in from the war-torn eastern provinces, and public buildings became hospitals; early in the war, theaters, museums, and libraries were temporarily dark.

Yet newspaper advertisements in 1914 beckoning to choice Austrian summer resorts or extolling the merits of Waterman's Ideal Fountain Pen testified that a "business-as-usual mood" had not vanished. When winter brought a lull in the blaze and havoc of blood-letting, one had to listen to coffee house chatter or read newspapers to appreciate that a war was actually being fought, commented

Halstead, the consul of the United States, but his ambassador judged that "all classes seem heartily tired of the war, and wish it might immediately end, if peace could come with national honor." Viennese modistes and milliners exhibited their wares as usual for the Easter 1915 season and—again as usual—poked fun at the new Berlin styles, which resembled "the illustrations in a comic weekly." The longer the toll of death and of the imprisoned mounted, the harsher the hardships of living grew, the deeper the popular war weariness became. "Probably there is not one person in the Dual Monarchy who is not heartily sick of the war," the American Ambassador reported (April 15, 1916), "and wishes for an early peace." The intervention of Rumania "intensifies despondency," he later felt, and accentuated mass longing for the return of peace.

Throughout the war era, Mayor Richard Weiskirchner, protégée of the dynamic Christian Socialist Dr. Karl Lueger, presided over the Hapsburg metropolis. An experienced municipal servant, he had also been a Reichsrat deputy and Austrian minister of trade before election in 1912 as mayor. Forceful, instinctively socially-minded, and a capable organizer, Weiskirchner was virtually given a free hand by the city council to administer affairs, though he conferred frequently, to be sure, with leading councilmen, and when the council reassembled in February, 1916, it sanctioned some one thousand three hundred acts he had ordained. To spike falsehoods on human conditions in Vienna, which came from as far away as the United States, Weiskirchner issued periodical reports, which the Austrian press generously reproduced, and he often insinuated comparisons in his statements with conditions during the Napoleonic occupations of Vienna in 1805 and 1809.

Starting with the onset of the war immense perplexities faced the municipal government; for one thing, many business managers discharged employees, though presently the demand for workmen soared in response to military requirements. Profiteering was combatted by municipal purchase of food and fuel and resale at cost and by stentorian condemnation of "gouging" by the mayor. The sudden influx of refugees from the east raised acute sanitary worries; Asiatic cholera claimed a few lives, though it was rapidly brought under control, and to prevent smallpox, physicians vaccinated residents from house to house. Weiskirchner could report that in matters of public health Vienna yielded pride of achievement to no other continental city.

Refugee care taxed living facilities to the utmost, in an already congested community. By hundreds, then by thousands, fugitives trekked in until the imperial capital and its suburbs were sheltering upwards of 200,000. Jews among them brought ghetto traditions from the east and some of them engaged in questionable commercial transactions, which, given the habitual tendency of the untrained mind to leap from the particular to the general, fed the fires of anti-Judaism. Many refugees were settled in camps where small industries and a varied round of social and educational activities was set in motion; a proposal by Weiskirchner to transfer Jewish refugees to camps in Moravia elicited from Francis Joseph the remark, "If Vienna has no more room for refugees, I shall make Schönbrunn available for my Jewish subjects." Upon the reconquest of Galicia many fugitives returned to their ancestral homes, the rest preferring to linger in the west.

Sick and wounded Hapsburg soldiers had also to be provided for, and it was said exaggeratedly that Vienna resembled a vast hospital. Public edifices, school buildings, the mammoth Rotunda in the Prater, and aristocratic palaces housed ailing veterans, and in pleasant weather thousands of recuperating soldiers lined benches along the famous *Ringstrasse*. Civilians freely volunteered to reduce the heavy burden on the diminished medical personnel; by the end of 1917 over half the physicians of the realm were on duty with the fighting forces. From the United States a detachment of Red Cross workers went to Vienna (another group worked in Budapest), remaining thirteen months. The general public responded humanely to appeals for linen and woolen cloth, pieces of hospital equipment, or tobacco and old newspapers for patients; for the burial of military dead, regardless of creed or tongue, a section in the great Central Cemetery of Vienna was set aside. Scientists bent their talents to the urgencies of the war, Joseph Leitner, a specialist in surgical appliances devising artificial limbs (using American models), and surgeons Anton Eiselsberg and Klingenberg perfecting substitutes for hands.

Aside from emergency hospital service, Viennese civilians engaged in a wide range of relief undertakings to aid families whose men had been mobilized or were disabled or killed. Citizens who succored the poor and hungry proudly wore "black and yellow" emblems, and outstanding work was rewarded with a *Verdienst Kreuz*. To raise relief funds, gold ornaments and jewelry were converted into cash; women patriotically turned in golden wedding rings and wore iron bands in their stead. On a visit to the historic pilgrimage church at Mariazell in Styria, the American Ambassador was shown by the sacristan "several empty cases in the treasury of the Church;" it was explained that "their contents—pearls, diamonds, rubies and other gems—had been sold by orders from a high source and the money devoted to war purposes." On Schwarzenberg Square in central Vienna a large wooden *Wehrmann in Eisen* was erected, into which contributors to the widows and orphans fund were privileged to drive nails. Schoolmasters shepherded their pupils to take part in this ritual of patriotism, and even the Sultan of Turkey sent a gift to be translated into nails;

lesser Austrian communities boasted *Wehrmänner* of their own.

Working through established Catholic or Socialist societies or through improvised organizations, the Red Cross among them, Austrian women played an important role in relief activities for the wounded and refugees. Since manpower grew short, women also took jobs in factories and warehouses, on street railways, as letter carriers and helpers in building projects, and by the summer of 1915 women were performing half the labor on Austrian farms. "The entrance to the city palace of a princely family," observed the Ambassador from the United States, "is guarded by a sturdy provincial woman, who admirably regulates the going and coming of vehicles." Reminders of the sacrificial devotion of the great Empress Maria Theresa amidst wartime ordeals were invoked, and urban housewives, upon whom the brunt of privations fell, heeded admonitions to store up fruit and vegetables during the growing season.

Countess M. Stubenberg appealed "To Austrian Women":

> Frauen Österreichs—Hoch das Haupt,
> Werdet nicht erzittern
> Was Euch auch ein Schicksal raubt
> In den Schlacht gewittern.
> Steht in dieser grossen Zeit
> Schmetternd hellem Rufen
> Unbesiegbar, treubereit
> An des Thrones Stufen! [18]

"Scarcely a woman," wrote Ambassador Penfield (January 29, 1915), "from members of the Imperial family to wives of small functionaries, have failed to enroll as workers in the Red Cross or other helpful organizations.

[18] *ÖR*, XL (1914), 187.

All hospitals swarm with women voluntarily acting as nurses and their work is as earnest and patriotic as that of the peasant soldier on the firing line." And a year later he remarked, "When the history is written of Austria-Hungary's part in the world war, the chapter treating of the work of women should be one redounding to the credit of womankind for all time."

Hapsburg archducal families and lesser aristocrats actively engaged in war-connected tasks. Marie Valerie, youngest daughter of Francis Joseph, set the style by visiting the wounded in hospitals, and her husband, the Archduke Francis Salvator, headed a volunteer sanitary corps, promoted interest in the Turkish Red Crescent and in other projects. As Sister Stephanie, the Countess Elemer Lónyay, widow of former Crown Prince Rudolph, converted her castle into a hospital of two hundred beds and ministered to wounded soldiers under Red Cross auspices. Equally, the Archduchess Maria Theresa, grandmother of the heir-apparent Charles, set up an institution for the rehabilitation of men blinded in battle, and herself toiled as a Sister of Mercy. Impulsive, warm-hearted, and witty Princess Pauline Metternich, grand dame of Viennese society, cheered up hospitalized veterans and solicited funds to sustain artists whose means of livelihood had vanished.[19] The boon companion of Francis Joseph, Frau Katharina Schratt, a sweet, simple old lady now, turned her spacious villa in a Vienna suburb into a hospital, and worked in it alongside of aristocratic dowagers and personal friends.

Civilian moods reflected what was known of trends in the military campaigns, swaying this way and that with tides in the Polish and Serbian war areas, the intervention of Italy, and so forth. On the first anniversary of the tragedy at Sarajevo, it was generally prophesied in the great Vienna press that the outrage was by way of being

[19] Artur Gaspar, *Unsere Dynastie im Felde* (Vienna, 1915).

appropriately avenged. But the prodigious human toll of what was described as "the first universal disaster that has befallen Europe," was not overlooked. "Let only one command be heard," a commentator pleaded, "when peace is signed at last between governments, let everyone work with his whole heart and strength to reconcile the nations of Europe, and leave nothing in their hearts but the memory that the common horror and calamity has been borne by all alike." "We are waging this war," it was said, "at the expense of future generations," and the writer seriously questioned whether that was fair; censorship suppressed the remaining paragraphs of the article.[20]

After eighteen months of war, the American Consul Halstead could assert that "Vienna appears as a gay and seemingly carefree city . . . though gay, it is far from heartless. Rather it is charitable and sympathetic . . . Much of the gayety covers deep anxiety for relatives at the front . . . people of all classes have devoted themselves unsparingly to work to assist the wounded. . . . there is no public complaint," he went on. "It all seems to be taken philosophically and the discontent if more than usual is well-suppressed, habits of obedience and acquiescence in conditions and knowledge of the necessary result of any demonstration, each playing its part." But in the autumn of 1916, Ambassador Penfield was writing about a public mood "describable by no other words than utter and complete despair. The fact that Hindenburg, aided by Mackensen has been placed in supreme control of the armies of Austria-Hungary . . . has had a discouraging effect on every class of humanity . . . Even pulpit utterances seem charged with teachings preparing the people for an outcome of the war very different from what was expected.

At almost precisely the same time, the ambassador of Germany in Vienna, von Tschirschky, doubted whether

[20] AZ, Oct. 31, Dec. 12, 1915.

the Dual Monarchy could carry on much longer either militarily or economically. In a wide-ranging report to Berlin, he expatiated on the popular mood of depression in Austria, particularly because of faulty distribution of provisions, decline in crop yields, and Hungarian refusal to supply enough food; chaos reigned, he remarked, in public finance. Blaming both Austrian and Hungarian public leaders for the sorry situation, Tschirschky warned that the Dual Monarchy might well collapse from exhaustion in the spring of 1917. His superiors in Berlin felt that the ambassador painted the Hapsburg picture with too dark pigments.[21] Early in 1917, the American Ambassador reiterated that Austrian civilians were desperately war weary and eager for a quick peace, since they were going hungry and feared extreme privation, yet they seemed to be "unswerving in loyalty." Soldiers continued to fight "with pristine earnestness," but when men were conscripted for military duty they left home after nightfall without "pomp or circumstance." [22]

[21] Penfield to Lansing, Sept. 23, 1916, U.S., *National Archives*, 763.72/2932½; Zeman, *op. cit.*, pp. 95–98.
[22] Penfield to Lansing, Jan. 31, 1917, U.S., *National Archives*, 863.50/34.

9. Life Flows On

LIVING UNDER A MOUNTING SENSE OF PERIL AND DISTRESS, Austrian men of letters tended either to apply their talents to war interests or to trail off in a mood of sterile futility and defeatism. The foremost literary light, Hugo von Hofmannsthal—poet, librettist, playwright—while still in his teens had won general respect for the maturity, the poise, and sweep of his writings. Adoring the Monarchy (but despising Prussia), he composed patriotic little essays for the press, compiled diverting wartime reading lists, and edited propagandist tracts for the hour. But, as the fighting dragged along, Hofmannsthal switched to a pacifist credo, and in collaboration with fellow Austrian authors and the Frenchman Romain Rolland he issued a clarion declaration of independence, calling upon European man to release himself from the claims and chains of excessive nationalism.

His dear friend, Prague-born Rainer Maria Rilke, preeminently a European conscience with a style, spent half a year as a literary propagandist, attached to the ministry

317

of war, a frightfully irksome assignment for a sensitive thoroughly unmilitary person, however much his superiors endeavored to make his environment congenial. Rilke in *Five Songs* lauded the spirit of combat and the grim god of war, tried to persuade readers that he was all athirst for victory, but his cosmopolitan past soon gained the upper hand, and he turned to acrid denunciation of the loathesome facets of human nature brought to the surface by the war—by the "rhythmic convulsion of the universe" (in his own phrase)—profiteering, exploitation, and a holiday for truth.

A second genius of Prague antecedents, Franz Werfel, for the vigor and directness of his verse pointed to as Walt Whitman reborn, had a chequered wartime career. Before the war, as a conscript he had fallen under the frown of his officers because of political unorthodoxy, and as punishment for writing anti-military, warmly humanitarian, poems (*Einander*, 1915), Werfel was forced to serve over two years with the army on the Russian front. His keen understanding of the secular currents abroad in the realm on the Danube and of central European humanity in general was displayed in short stories, assembled in *Twilight of a World* (1937); his gifts as a novelist, therein revealed, were to be amply confirmed between world wars —*Forty Days of Musa Dagh,* and *Song of Bernadette.*

The veteran author of the Styrian countryside, Peter Rosegger, earnestly applied himself to psychological warfare (*Heim zur Scholle*), or to delivering lectures on Austrian lyrics of war from ancient of days, or collaborating with Father Ottokar Kernstock in glorifying the goodness and hardihood of the Styrian folk—*Steirischer Waffensegen* (1916); unimpressed critics dismissed the work as portraying Austrians as heroes and angels and the enemy as crude barbarians, devoid of conscience. Characteristic of Rosegger's wartime writing in verse was "Greeting to our troops in the field."

Bin ein alter, müder Mann,
Der nicht schlagen, schiessen, kann,
Doch bring' ich in deutscher Sprach'
Euch die liebe Heimat nach. . . .

✿   ✿   ✿

Und auf diesem Ruhmesritt
Bringt ihr uns den Frieden mit,
Frieden für ein langes Leben
Alles weitere wird sich geben.[1]

A poet of stature, though more noted for prose and
semi-fictional autobiographies, the humanist Stefan Zweig,
brilliant, compassionate, independent in mind, passed
through an evolution in the war years similar to Werfel
and Rilke. Exempted from active military service on physical grounds, Zweig was assigned to the war department
and set to work collecting proclamations issued by the
Russians during their occupancy of Galicia, drafting cita-
tions for Austrian deeds of heroism and distinction, and
editing a propagandist journal, *Donauland.* In the midst
of the conflict, Zweig composed a lofty drama on peace,
Jeremiah, which, he wrote, "expressed my pacifistic ideas
on war and its problems. I merely uttered what others did
not dare to say openly: hatred of war, distrust of victory." [2]

In book form the play had a large sale, and though the
views expressed did not automatically command respect,
they happened to be symptomatic of growing weariness
with war. Forbidden on the Austrian stage, the tragedy
was presented in Zürich, whither Zweig betook himself
to await the outcome of hostilities and to unite with Rolland and other like-minded writers in declamations
against war. "Polyphon" (1917), tinged with pacifism,
touched the heart of many a youth of Europe.

[1] *Neues Wiener Tagblatt,* Sept. 1, 1915.
[2] Stefan Zweig, *The World of Yesterday* (New York, 1945), p. 256.

Somewhat apart from these writers was Hermann Bahr, engaging, prolific, and remarkably versatile man of letters, whose allegiance to the House of Hapsburg persisted until the fall thereof. Whatever his thoughts became in the darkness of night, he stood forth during the war as a "mystical" (his own term) and staunch defender of the Austrian mission and tradition. As shown in *Schwarzgelb* (1917), a monument to his literary skill, Bahr firmly believed that the war would infuse renewed energy into the tired Hapsburg body, or, in his language, "I mistook the dying afterglow for the first flush of dawn and the smiling death of Austria for a holy springtime." Having re-entered the Catholic communion, he passionately saluted Mother Church (*Himmelfahrt*, 1916), as the indispensable instrument for keeping multilinguistic Austria-Hungary intact and as a spiritual force rendered the more helpful by the anxieties and gruelling torments of the war. Bahr teamed up with lesser Vienna literary luminaries in a wartime committee to foster wider interest in literature, painting, and music by means of pamphlets, exhibitions, and concerts.

Authors of fiction of second rank who illuminated the moods and ways of wartime Austria included Raoul Auernheimer (*Die verbündeten Mächte*, 1915), who came to the conclusion that the men at the Ballplatz bore major responsibility for the outbreak of war, the priest Sebastian Rieger (or Reinmichel), who produced an epic tale, (*Auf Unseren Ewigen Bergen*, 1916), exhibiting fine comprehension of the embattled Tyrolese, and a jolly portrayal of Viennese citizens at war (*Wien in Kriege*, 1916) by Heinrich Rienössl. Though he tossed off a few brief comedies, the once popular Arthur Schnitzler, eschewed challenges raised by the war, and so sacrificed much of the esteem he had built up before 1914.[3]

[3] Other wartime writers worthy of passing mention were Anton Wildgans, naturalistic poet and playwright (*Armut*, 1915): Richard

Bohemian Germans joined in noisy loyalist demonstrations before the consulate of imperial Germany in Prague, and mobilization of Czech reservists proceeded without much trouble. It is true that when a Czech regiment—the 28th—drawn from Prague and its environs, moved off in September, soldiers were heard singing, "We are marching against the Russians, but nobody knows why," and civilian onlookers shouted, "Don't shoot your Slav brothers," but the regiment fought eight months before turning openly disloyal. The consul of the United States in Prague, Charles L. Hoover, reported (September 26, 1914), "When the soldiers departed from Prague . . . there seemed to be some discontent among a few . . . but knowing the penalty for disobedience I doubt that they will openly express it. . . ." British soldiers on the Serbian front noticed crude Czech scrawlings on Austrian railway cars, "Export of Bohemian meat to Serbia." [1]

Yet a Czech newspaper, *Glas Naroda,* speculating on a Russian declaration that the war was being waged to liberate Slavs, asked:

From what are the Slavs to be liberated? From the freedom and self-government which they enjoy under Austria-Hungary? They will hardly be tempted to exchange these benefits for the despotic rule of a corrupt [tsarist] bureaucracy. As for the Czechs, they often oppose the ministry, but are always warmly attached to the State. . . . Austria gives equal rights to all the nationalities in the Empire. . . . Russia does not tolerate any other nationalities in her dominions. . . . [2]

Thomas G. Masaryk in conversation with Prince Francis Thun, Governor of Bohemia, stressed Czech affection for the Russians and the Serbs and detestation of Prussians, and complained that German-speaking residents of

---

[1] Eduard Beneš, *Bohemia's Case for Independence* (London, 1917), pp. 53–70, cites evidences of disaffection among Czech troops.
[2] Quoted in *Annual Register,* 1914, p. 347.

Prague were too ostentatiously "black-and-yellow" loyalist; since some of them were of the Jewish tradition he warned that a pogrom might break loose unless authority imposed restraints upon their exuberance. The Czech professor complained, too, over the inadequate medical care provided for wounded Czech soldiers and over falsely optimistic military communiqués that poured from Hapsburg army headquarters. In the first phase of the war Austrian authorities seem to have been more concerned over pacifist aversion to war among Czechs, especially among Socialists, than over anti-Hapsburg sentiments. The only prominent Czech civilian arrested in the autumn of 1914 for political reasons was Reichsrat deputy Václav Klofáč, chairman of the small National Socialist party; he was accused of interfering with mobilization and of being a Russophile, as in fact he was.

More than once, important Czech politicians like Mayor Groš of Prague declared that the Czechs wished the Central Empires to achieve speedy victory, and Czech-oriented Cardinal Skrbensky displayed no resentment when he was greeted with "Die Wacht am Rhein" at a birthday celebration for Francis Joseph in 1915. Czech parliamentary deputies, save for a few disciples of Masaryk and the Bohemian large landlord faction, set up in November, 1916, a Czech political front to promote national ends. Galicia had just been promised broader home-rule and the organizers of the Czech committee hoped autonomy might be secured for Bohemia; they wanted, also, to be ready to protect and promote Czech interests, if and when the Austrian parliament resumed operations. The committee, chaired by the esteemed Dr. Mattuš of the Old Czech party, avowed fidelity to the Monarchy and its "great historical mission," but called for the reorganization of the empire on federal lines with equality of treatment for all the national communities; presently, Czech political party chiefs despatched a loyalist, laudatory telegram to General Svetozar Boroević, a devoutly Hapsburgophile Croat.[3] Quite obviously, it is impossible to determine the intensity of feeling or the sincerity that underlay these manifestations of faithfulness to the Hapsburg crown, though plainly many a Czech politician at home had not been converted to the philosophy of dismemberment of the Monarchy preached by Masaryk and other émigrés.

3.

Progress of the Russian military machine westward in 1914 emboldened Czech partisans of independence. In the ears of Czech secessionists hummed the touching, gentle sentiments of the opening verse of the Czech national anthem.

> Where is my home? Where is my home?
> Brooks are running through the meadows,
> Pines are whispering on the hills,
> Orchards dressed in spring's array
> An earthly paradise portray,
> And this land of wondrous beauty
> Is the Czech land, home of mine.[4]

School children gaily sang, "Maria Theresa lost Silesia, Francis Joseph will lose everything." Pamphlets and poems saluted the impending triumph of the tsarist armies, whose victories in Galicia were celebrated at champagne parties, and Czech enthusiasts flaunted blue, white, and red emblems of Slav solidarity. Ardor for the empire of the Tsar cooled down among Russophiles, however, after the tide of battle turned against the eastern colossus.

[3] Willy Lorenz, *Die Tschechischen Parteien im Alten Österreich* (Vienna, 1941)—a useful, though thin, doctoral dissertation, prepared in the Nazi intellectual atmosphere. On Klofáč and lesser Czech politicians, see Zeman, *op. cit.*, pp. 17–22.

[4] R. H. Bruce Lockhart, *Jan Masaryk* (London, 1951), p. 5.

Communication between Czech national patriots at home and the "emigration" in the West, best personified by Masaryk and Beneš, was maintained principally by means of a remarkable secret society called the "Maffia," whose full history, replete with dramatic adventures, still awaits telling. Czech politicians of varying outlook and temperament, but united in desiring national freedom, were drawn into the Maffia; among them was Antonin Švehla, spokesman of small landed proprietors and a prudent and effective worker with the emigration. Identity of Maffia members was concealed in pseudonyms, Masaryk being disguised as Hradecký and Beneš as Spolný; before going abroad the elderly Prague professor had devised a long-range program for the Maffia.[5] Men of the Maffia indulged in sabotage and espionage, fostered defeatism among Czech civilians and soldiers, and engaged in other treasonable, revolutionary activities. Almost incredible ingenuity was displayed in eluding Austrian police vigilance; until nearly the end of the war, the Maffia escaped detection and regularly communicated with the emigration by messages smuggled in suitcases with secret pockets, fountain pens, and the like. For wartime endeavors, many a member of the society was rewarded with a post of distinction in the Republic of Czechoslovakia.

As the war moved along, Hapsburg military authorities struck hard at real or suspected Czech dissidents, and it was felt in the military command that Governor Thun dealt too leniently with disloyal Czechs. A large-boned cavalier of old Bohemian landlord stock, Thun had served a brief term as Austrian prime minister, and he was known to favor appeasing concessions to Czech nationalism. Many a German-Bohemian politician detested him because he had permitted Czechs to gain the upper hand in civil offices and because of his intimacy with the Czech

[5] Franz Arens, "Die Tschechen und der Weltkrieg," *Preussische Jahrbücher*, CXCVIII (1924), 292–298; Zeman, *op. cit.*, pp. 82–83.

nationalist firebrand, Karel Kramář.[6] Demands that this Czechophile governor should be forced to resign were repulsed for a time in Vienna on the score that his resignation would touch off disturbing repercussions at home and abroad. But in March 1915, Thun, to his own great surprise, was replaced by Count Max Coudenhove, formerly a top bureaucrat in Austrian Silesia. Straightaway, changes were effected in key governmental positions in Bohemia; Dr. Gottfried Kunz, an impeccably reliable Austrogerman, for instance, was appointed chief of the Prague police.

Substantial tightening of press regulations symbolized the sterner administration of Coudenhove. Already *Národní Listy* (National Journal), Prague mouthpiece of Kramář's Young Czechs, had experienced rough going.[7] At the outset of the war, in a Serbophile mood, the paper likened the struggle to the Biblical duel between David and Goliath, yet before long it was writing gaily of the brotherhood of Czechs and Germans; then, in December, 1914, for sharp criticisms of governmental policy, censors prohibited publication for eight days. Only prudential caution on the part of Dr. Adolf Stránský, a fiery Czech deputy and editor of *Lidove Noviny* (Peoples' Newspaper), saved that paper from suspension. Thun threatened to ban *Čas* (Time), Masaryk's personal organ, but decided that suppression would produce more harm than good; after the change in the governorship, Czech newspapermen were obliged to keep their pens out of the darker hues of patriotic ink.

The most notorious instance of Czech military defection occurred in April, 1915, when nearly all of the 28th Regiment deserted to the Russians; smaller contingents of Czechs or individual soldiers had also gone over to the enemy, singing "Slavs come along." An ecstatically Pan-

[6] Gebsattel (consul of Germany in Prague) to Bethmann-Hollweg, Mar. 28, 1915. FO. 533/299, no. 2468.

[7] Karel Hoch, "L'Evolution de la Presse Tchèque," *Le Monde Slave*, XI (4), 263–282, especially, 269–273.

Slav, Czech poet, Rudolf Medek, recorded his emotions on escaping to tsarist lines this way, "That night when I left the Austrian trenches and went over to 'them,' my heart missed a beat, and my soul shone with joy when I heard the first shout of the Russian sentry . . . 'Who's that talking?' I remember that I wanted to fling myself upon that soldier's breast, and so fling myself upon Mother Slavia." Yet a note of reservation intruded, "But perhaps in flinging myself upon the breast of Mother Slavia I would fling myself upon the breast of a Jew or a Baltic German. . . ." Inside the empire of the Tsar, harsh realities disillusioned the Czech deserter, for he wrote, "Good God, how different the country of which our Slavophile hearts once dreamed of. . . . In the soul of these people we saw heaven and hell. Love without measure and bounds—and the hatred and savagery of an animal devouring its own young." Subsequently, Medek fought against the Bolsheviks in Siberia, returning home by way of the United States.

Long since, the surrender of the 28th Regiment had been followed by a frontal campaign of Austrian military officialdom upon Czechs suspected of sedition. In May, 1915, Kramář, Dr. Alois Rašin, a Maffia organizer, and Dr. Joseph Schreiner, headman of the sokols, were seized on the charge that they had been undermining troop morale; their homes in Prague were searched, and they were hauled off to Vienna for trial. It was even rumored that ex-Governor Thun had been imprisoned for intriguing to become king of Bohemia!

The arrests created a great stir in Prague and troops from Hungary were hurried in to ensure the preservation of order. Kramář above all the rest excited official Austrian suspicion for he had an established reputation as a clever and devout Russophile; a rough-and-ready polemicist, he was a sterling specimen of Czech nationalism, and he possessed dogged tenacity, a piece of psychological equipment essential for the crusader or the fanatic. Coming from a wealthy industrial family, Kramář had been well educated, had married a Russian, and maintained a residence in the tsardom. Many a time and oft he had publicly demanded the reconstruction of the Monarchy on federal principles and he had vituperatively denounced the alliance with imperial Germany. As well as a Russian wife, Kramář had a Russian heart, it was not inaccurately said—and therewith sublime faith in the tsarist "steamroller." When the war broke out he eagerly anticipated a parade of Cossacks down the spacious Wenceslaus Square of Prague and he would enthusiastically have welcomed a Romanov grand duke as viceroy of Bohemia and Moravia. When arrested, admiring Czechs extolled him as a "living martyr" to the patriot cause.

After a protracted and politically tendentious trial, whose proceedings filled eighteen tightly-packed volumes, an Austrian court on June 3, 1916, declared Kramář and three colleagues guilty and ordered death by hanging. On the basis of daily summaries of the trial, Austrian Professors Josef Redlich and A. F. Pribram, both rather impartial and detached observers, reached diametrically opposite conclusions on the guilt of the accused men. In any case, the verdict of the court represented a major victory for the Austrian military administration, for as Dr. Karl Grabmayr, presiding judge, remarked, no legal proof of traitorous behavior had been adduced. Ex-Governor Thun caused a sensation by proving that an incriminating letter written to him by Kramář before the war had been materially altered by the prosecution in order to convict the Czech politician of treason. Czechophile Auguste Gauvain declared in the Parisian *Journal des Débats,* "If Austria allows such sentences to be executed, there will later on be other gibbets erected in the Hofburg."

Attorneys for the defense had tried to save Kramář by pointing out that he had been an intimate acquaintance of Prime Minister Stürgkh, which infuriated *Habsburg-treue* Austrogermans; one militant, Friedrich Wichtl, a Reichsrat deputy, stridently summoned Stürgkh to resign and then proceeded to compose a blistering, venomous indictment of Kramář for anti-Hapsburg machinations, old and new, even charging that the Russophile Czech was responsible for the general European war! [8] Although the Supreme Landwehr Tribunal of Vienna reaffirmed sentences of death for Kramář and his co-defendants, Emperor Charles commuted punishment to penal servitude and early in 1917 they were set free, and returned triumphantly to Prague.

During the incarceration and trial of Kramář, other well-known Czechs felt the heavy hand of Austrian authority. Imprisoned were Socialist newspaperman, František Soukop, several Reichsrat deputies, and managers of banks, who allegedly had discouraged the purchase of Austrian war bonds, and had traitorously trafficked with the emigration abroad. Masaryk's home in Prague was ransacked, his property declared forfeit as a traitor, and his wife, a cultivated American-born lady in delicate health, was subjected to exasperating pettinesses. Their thirty-six-year-old daughter, Alice, was imprisoned for the better part of a year, and Madam Eduard Beneš was likewise arrested. The jail sojourn of Miss Masaryk seems not to have been too unpleasant, certainly nothing faintly resembling the treatment meted out to political prisoners by the Gestapo and Stalinist secret police of a later generation; she was allowed to have books and permitted to correspond freely with her mother.[9] Reports that she was about to be executed inspired feminist circles in the United States to appeal to President Wilson to intercede

---

[8] Friedrich Wichtl, *Dr. Karl Kramarsch, der Anstifter des Weltkrieges* (Munich, 1918). On Czech subversive activity, see Zeman, *op. cit.*, pp. 72–88.

[9] Alice G. Masaryk, "From an Austrian Prison," *Atlantic Monthly*, CXXVI (1920), 577–587, 770–779.

on her behalf, but that effort had little or no bearing on the decision to release her. It was rumored that the younger Masaryk son, the ill-fated Jan, was to be hanged as a way of punishing his traitorous father, but in fact he served as an officer with Hungarian troops in Russian theaters of war; and the son of the imprisoned Klofáč lost his life fighting the Italians on the Isonzo front.

As part of the drive against Czech disaffection, the sokols, ostensibly gymnastic clubs, but in reality the very wellsprings of patriotic nationalism, were dissolved (or, more accurately, forced underground); at the time over a thousand branches enrolled more than 130,000 adult members, disciplined, and ready for sacrifices in response to instructions from Masaryk, their most eminent "brother." Czech newspaper suspensions became more frequent, pamphlets and books of an anti-Hapsburg character were confiscated, and attempts were made by officials to shackle patriotically minded Czech men of letters.

4.

Outstanding among the Czech authors was Victor Dyk, lyric poet and dramatist, whose youthful, quixotic nihilism had given way to resounding Czech nationalism. Keenly satirical, he interpreted the war as a providential instrument to bring about Czech national freedom; that theme and ardent love of country Dyk set out in "Lehke a Těžké Kroky" ("Light and Heavy Steps," 1915) and in "Anebo" ("Or," 1918), which is remembered as his finest poem of of the war years. In part, the latter verse embodied his meditations in jail, for he was locked up for writing *The Mysterious Adventures of A. I. Kozulinova,* a devastating attack upon wartime conditions in general, especially the malevolence of Austrian courts-martial, thinly disguised as a satire on tsarist Russia. The Czechs, Dyk proclaimed, could either languish under Hapsburg rule or strike for freedom in a manner that would echo down the corridors of time.[10]

Thrown into jail, too, was Josef S. Machar, warmly admired for his poetry, and by vocation a Vienna bank clerk. He was arrested for a seditious poem printed in the United States without his knowledge, it appears, and while in prison he composed a revealing account of his experiences and of "the military persecution" of the Czechs "and of mischief-makers within," which was published as *The Jail: Experiences of 1916* (English translation, 1921). Passionately hating the Hapsburg dynasty and the Roman Catholic Church, Machar lashed out violently against both institutions and lavished praise upon Masaryk, imaginative, bold, inventive, the anointed savior of the Czech nationality. "Honor is due only to those who went forth in darkness and staked everything upon their labors," Machar thought, and yet personally he had no yearning for the sort of immortality reserved for the martyr. Wrote he, "The age of romantic martyrdom is over," and that sober judgment was not forgotten. As another service to the patriotic cause, Machar transmitted to Masaryk, the "Pastor" as he called him, valuable information supplied by one Kovanda, a servant in the employ of Baron Karl von Heinold, at the time Austrian minister of the interior; on the sly, Kovanda copied private papers of the minister and handed them on to Machar.

Pętr Bezruć, pen name of Vladimir Vašek, also drew a prison sentence for fierce excoriation of Austrian officialdom; he had previously made a name for himself with poetry describing the harsh lot of Czech miners in his native province of Silesia. Poets of lesser stature who managed to avoid arrest were Petr Křička, who wrote about the Galician war theater, and Frana Šramék, whose charming lyrics of army existence possessed an autobiographical flavor.

[10] H. Jelínek, "La Mort d' un Grand Poète Tchèque, Victor Dyk," *L'Europe Centrale*, VI (1931), 353–354.

A revealing and diverting epic on the First World War, with little pretension to literary art, was written after the armistice by the Czech Jaroslav Hašek and published in an abridged English version as *The Good Soldier Schweik* (1930). It is a tableaux of crude, farcical escapades in which Hašek was personally involved, displaying Czech cleverness—and obtuseness—in resisting Austrian authority in wartime; on these interesting pages much is disclosed about the shortcomings of the Austrian official class and barbed thrusts are hurled at army chaplains. For alleged insult of Emperor Francis Joseph, Schweik, a disreputable scavenger of Prague, was ordered into the army and shipped to the Russian front; short on courage, spineless, with a congenital distaste for work and indifferent to the fame that heroism might earn, Schweik led a wayward course, talking incessantly, and coining coarse jests. Eventually, he was captured, precisely the personal fate of the eccentric Hašek, who joined the Bolsheviks and blossomed out as an organizer of a Czech army contingent in Soviet Russia. A Czechoslovak military order of 1925 prohibited soldiers from reading this distinctly anti-army tale.

For the tercentenary of the death of Shakespeare, Jaroslav Kvapil, Czech dramatist and poet and a Maffia man, organized an elaborate celebration, intending thus to demonstrate affection for the Entente. Historian Kamil Krofta published reading lists for Czech schools, directing attention to distortions in history texts designed to foster loyalty to the House of Hapsburg, and the musician Jaroslav Jeremiáš composed a moving oratorio on Jan Hus, the supreme Czech national hero. National hope and faith were nourished, too, in the well-attended Prague theater by cryptic allusions to "the promised land" and related themes in Biblical, mythological, and historical plays. Frequently Austrian authority banned the presentation of dramatic productions with a patriotic Czech flavor and even sought to curb the singing of popular folk melodies deemed seditious. Yet repression, instead of stifling the

Czech national flame, seems in fact to have fanned it.

It is easy, however, to develop an exaggerated impression of the harshness of Austrian wartime administration in the areas of Czech speech or of the intensity and popularity of separatist sentiments. From first to last probably 5,000 Czech civilians were condemned by Hapsburg courts-martial and about four times as many were interned; compared with Nazi ruthlessness in the Second World War, for instance, Austrian treatment of Czech dissidents seems mild and tame. The veteran consul of the United States in Prague, Charles L. Hoover, reported (January 17, 1916) that the Bohemian capital was quieter than at any time since the fighting began; by then, of course, the armies of Nicholas II had been rolled eastward, stalemate prevailed on the Italian and French battlefronts, and Serbia had been overrun. The American estimated that as many as a thousand Czechs might have been arrested to that time for political crimes. Hoover wrote:

With the exception that fewer horses and automobiles are seen on the streets and that numbers of wounded soldiers go about the streets, I am compelled to say that life here seems absolutely normal. The streets are crowded with well-dressed people and coffee houses, cinematographs, theaters and cabarets are going full blast. Of course, I am not speaking of underlying conditions but of the general appearance of things.

The Bohemian national spirit which was so rampant before the war has absolutely evaporated. To judge from what the Germans say, no Czech was to be considered as anything but anti-German before the war, but superficially, at least, that is certainly not the case now, for one constantly hears Czech officers proclaiming loudly in broken German the superiority of everything German. At every victory the Czech houses are beflagged and the Czech newspapers are more Germanophile than the Germans themselves. Germans volunteer the information that this is all the result of official orders and that the Czechs say nothing, but whatever the cause may be there is no questioning the fact that on the surface at least there is loyalty to the Government. It is safe to say that practically all political arrests made are made on information volunteered by Bohemians [Czechs?].

The principal leaders of the national movement, that is, the Czech members of parliament from Prague . . . are all under arrest or are in hiding in foreign countries. One scarcely ever hears their names. One of the Czech newspapers recently published an editorial advocating a 'neuorientierung' for all Czech political parties on the basis, briefly, of the recognition of Bohemia's status as an integral part of the Empire. All the other papers hastened to protest that this was not necessary as they had always been loyal Austrians.

It is not safe to say whether this attitude of the Czechs is due to official pressure, but the Czechs are certainly showing no spirit in defending what I had been led by the Germans to believe was the political creed of all of them, that is, the separation of Bohemia from Austria. Evidences appear that the looseness which was tolerated before the war is to cease and that the cultivation of Bohemian national aspirations . . . is to receive a check. . . .

Regarding the reports of wholesale executions of Bohemian [Czech] soldiers, I may say that the only person who has been executed in this region since the outbreak of the war was one Czech soldier who was guilty of mutiny and striking an officer.

. . . I forgot to mention the most important step taken by the Government with respect to the Czechish national movement, that is, the suppression of all Czech societies, including the Sokol society which . . . was regarded as the very center of the Pan-Slavistic movement.

This morning three more of the Bohemian [Czech] members of parliament have been arrested for high treason . . . they are to be tried in Vienna.[11]

---

[11] Charles L. Hoover to Penfield, Jan. 17, 19, 1916, *American Embassy Papers*, Vienna, vol. XLIII (1916–17); cf. Zeman, *op. cit.*, pp. 115–117.

5.

Just before the war, the Polish-speaking element of Austria, dwelling in the crownlands of Galicia and of Silesia, where they were intermingled with Czechs and Austrogermans, numbered nearly 5,000,000, compared with about 12,000,000 Poles in Russia, 3,000,000 in Prussia, and perhaps as many as 3,000,000 overseas. It was a cruel fate that obliged young Poles fighting under three alien flags to make war upon their national brothers. "Look at my family," cried Count Joseph Potocki, "I am a Russian subject; my brother Roman is an Austrian subject; one of my brothers-in-law is a German subject; all of my cousins and nephews, because of circumstances of inheritance, are likewise divided among the three nations. In the bosom of the same race [sic] we are condemned to kill each other." All told, better than fifteen per cent of the soldiers in the Hapsburg armies were drawn from Polish homes, approximately 200,000 died in the war and over 300,000 sustained serious injuries.

Many an articulate Pole under the rule of Russia or of Prussia envied his compatriots in Austria, for they possessed a considerable measure of local self-government and practically dominated the Galician political panorama, lording over the Ukrainian or Ruthenian minority there; far more Russian Poles deserted to the Central Empires than Slavs of the Hapsburg Monarchy voluntarily surrendered to the Russians. Austrian Poles elected a large delegation of deputies to the Vienna parliament where their solidarity enabled them to gain ministerial berths and important posts in public administration, and in close parliamentary divisions, the Polish Club frequently exercised the balance of power. The outstanding Polish political personality of Austria, Léon R. Biliński, a whole-souled Hapsburg loyalist, filled the office of joint Austro-

Hungarian minister of finance from 1912 to 1915; few public men were as familiar with the complicated constitutional mechanism of the Monarchy as Biliński.

Rival armies surging forward and backward ravaged Galicia and Russian Poland almost literally from end to end, compelling multitudes to flee for safety and condemning many more to beggary and destitution; only Belgium, if indeed it, suffered more terribly. Relief committees were organized in Cracow (Kraków) by Archbishop Adam Sapieha and at Vevy, Switzerland, but humanitarian attempts by American agencies to succor distraught Polish civilians fell flat.[12] Why should shipments of food and other supplies be allowed to enter Belgium, but not the Polish areas, Stefan Zweig querulously inquired in an Easter (1915) contribution to the *Neue Freie Presse.*

Among politically active Poles of Austria, a small but influential group identified itself with the Polish National Democratic party in the empire of the Tsar. Led by Duma deputy Roman Dmowski, this party held that a national destiny must be sought in reconciliation and cooperation with Petrograd and, by indirection, with Paris and London. Some Austrian Poles as well as their relatives in Russia reacted enthusiastically to the delphic Russian manifesto of 1914 promising autonomy for a re-united Poland under the scepter of Nicholas II. Representative of the element which adopted a Russophile orientation was Professor Stanislaw Grabski, economist at the University of Lemberg (Lvov). When the Central Powers reconquered Galicia in 1915 he and other like-minded Poles took up residence in the tsardom where they worked hand-in-glove with the Polish National Democrats.

But Hapsburg loyalism was pronounced among Aus-

---

[12] Ernest P. Bicknell, "The Battlefield of Poland," *Survey*, XXXVII (1916–17), 231–236; *ibid.*, "Begging Bread for Poland," *ibid.*, 398–402.

trian Poles interested in public affairs, especially among conservative landlords and the Roman Catholic clergy; the mass of the unpolitical peasants tended to follow these traditional leaders, and one wing of the Galician Peasants party called "Piast," mostly richer peasants, lined up firmly in the Austrophile camp.[13] Besides, a significant minority of Polish moderate Socialists, called "social patriots," collaborated with the Hapsburg authorities, not out of any particular affection for the Monarchy, to be sure, but because of detestation of Russia and in the conviction that an Austrophile posture promised more in the direction of national resurrection, in vindicating a line in the national anthem, "Poland is not lost forever." The leader of this faction, Josef Pilsudski, in fact disliked linking the interests of Polish freedom to the House of Hapsburg, which could only be a junior partner of Germany, he felt, yet he was perfectly willing to make use of the Monarchy "as a sword against Russia and a shield against Germany." In explanation of his refusal to strike a definite political understanding with Vienna, he remarked (March, 1917), ". . . I do not wish to associate myself with the dead, and I do not see any reason to fortify or revive the Hapsburg Monarchy through injections of Polish blood . . . Austrian schemes can only bring about a new partition of Poland." [14]

Born under the flag of the Tsar, Pilsudski, who was destined to become the supreme hero of Poland reborn, attained an almost magical sway over ordinary Poles and had the distinction of becoming a legend while he still lived. Although Pilsudski admired Napoleon and the Polish troops, who under the command of the Corsican had fought for the freedom of their Motherland, he was not himself a military man by training. He appreciated, however, that a Polish military force would eloquently

---

[13] Josef Buzek, "Die Polen und der Krieg," ÖR, XL (1914), 346–347.
[14] Quoted in Komarnicki, op. cit., p. 115.

speak a language peculiar to itself. Years before the war, he had organized small fighting contingents and cells of youthful Polish intellectuals in schools and universities of Polish Austria; in 1913 and 1914, his band of "sharp-shooters," many of them students and craftsmen who were fugitives from Russia, had grown appreciably. Allied with Pilsudski was a second founding-father of the Polish Socialist party of Galicia, Ignaz Daszýnski, editor and eloquent deputy in the Austrian Reichsrat since 1897, a determined antagonist of social inequities and of tsarist Russia, in his eyes the supreme obstacle to Polish nationhood.

On August 16, 1914, Polish factions in Galicia founded a central committee, Die Obersten Polnischen National-kommittee (OKNP), which approved the formation of a Polish fighting force, envisaged by many a Pole as the nucleus of a national army.[15] At almost the same time Polish politicians, Austrophile conservatives leading, organized a Supreme National Council (NKN) to oversee Polish troops enrolled in Hapsburg armies and to seek ways and means of attracting Poles everywhere to the banners of the Central Empires. Briefly, the headquarters of the Council were situated in Vienna, where a weekly journal in the Polish interest was printed in the German language—*Polen*—but in 1915, the seat of operations was returned to Cracow, ancient and charming capital of the Polish nation. Austrophile Professor Ladislaus L. Jaworski served as president of the Council, while one Cienski, at best tepid in his Austrophilism, supervised activities in Lemberg (Lvov). This faction wished Galicia and Russian Poland to be merged under the Hapsburg crown, and loudly protested when German, not Austrian troops occupied Warsaw; resentment flamed higher, when tsarist Poland, as has been previously explained, was divided

[15] Tschirschky to Bethmann-Hollweg, Feb. 25, 1915, no. 1370, and May 30, 1915, *F.O.* 553/334.

into a German and an Austrian zone of occupation. Polish political affairs took a novel turn with the November, 1916, manifesto of Berlin and Vienna promising freedom to Russian Poland alone; after transferring responsibilities to a newly-founded State Council, the original National Council dissolved itself (January 14, 1917).

Austro-Polish politicians of a conservative disposition looked sympathetically upon various schemes to attach a Polish state in some fashion to the realm of the Hapsburgs—the so-called Austrian-Polish solution. But the Polish national shield had another side, displeasing to Vienna and to Berlin alike, for in September, 1916, Pilsudski came to the parting of the ways with his erstwhile ally. At the start of the war a small, but spirited band of his "legionaries," had staged a daring raid into the Poland of the Tsar and thereafter his rather raw guerrilla contingent, 4,000 strong, had given a good account of itself in fighting the Russians; on imperial order, Polish soldiers had taken an oath of allegiance to Emperor Francis Joseph and technically, at least, they belonged to the military services of the Dual Monarchy. In point of fact, three Polish brigades were constituted, Pilsudski commanding one, Colonel Joseph Haller and a second Austrian-born Pole, the other two, but enrollment of Austrian Poles in the legion ceased in 1915; at the peak the organization contained around 14,000 soldiers. Polish served as the language of command and the Polish flag of the white eagle was carried, but equipment was wholly supplied by the Austrian military; a small number of Polish women enlisted for Austrian propaganda and intelligence work.

What Pilsudski wanted was essential autonomy for the legions, but that claim met with invincible resistance from the Austrian high command, and it was over the basic issue of the political status of his troops that Pilsudski resigned his command. Many of his lieutenants quit with him though by no means all; for instance, Wladyslaw

Sikorski, destined to become prime minister of Poland in the dread autumn of 1939, choose to remain with Austria. As a gesture of appeasement authorities in Vienna agreed to regard the legions as an auxiliary force within the Hapsburg army, under the name of the Polnische Hilf-corps, a concession that amounted to something, but far less than a Polish army, Polish-administered, that Pilsud-ski desired.

Simultaneously with the joint Austrian and German pronouncement of November, 1916, on Russian Poland, the cabinet of Vienna announced that a fuller measure of home-rule would be conferred upon Galicia—clear indi-cation that this key province would not be allowed to enter any Polish political structure outside of the realm of the Hapsburgs. Indeed, Biliński fashioned a framework of government for Galicia, providing for a bicameral legislature with the lower house to be elected on a broad franchise basis, and with safeguards for the political and educational interests of the Ukrainian minority. The proj-ect failed, however, to enlist much backing in weight-carrying quarters of Vienna and was soon forgotten.

6.

While some Austrian Poles, a minority within the Polish minority, rejoiced over the prospect of greater autonomy for Galicia, spokesmen of the Ukrainian nationality in the province protested belligerently, for they had set their affections upon an autonomous crownland in the eastern portion of Galicia where their kith and kin clearly pre-dominated. Tempers cooled somewhat, after Prime Min-ister Koerber gave assurances that he would insist that the Poles must deal decently with the Ukrainians; some Ukrainian leaders harbored the belief that the Berlin government would oblige Austria to satisfy national ex-pectations, at least in part.

Like the Poles, the Ukrainians, or the Ruthenians as the Austro-Hungarian branches of this nationality were known, lived under varied flags. Far and away the largest bloc, maybe 30,000,000, was subject to the Tsar, over 3,500,000 dwelt in Galicia, more than 300,000 in the Austrian province of Bukowina, nearly half a million in Hungary, and as many as two millions more in the Americas. How far sentiments of nationalism had penetrated the mind and emotions of the Ukrainian masses remains a matter of inconclusive debate, though national feelings were doubtless more widespread and more intense among Hapsburg Ukrainians than among their Russian cousins. Ukrainian politicians and the intelligentsia cherished divergent political goals: an Austrophile faction (or better Ukrainophile) was minded to cooperate with Vienna, believing that way was best to realize the long-range goal of a united and independent Ukrainian state, while a pro-Russian element looked to the tsardom for national salvation.

Upon the outbreak of the war, Ukrainian members of the Austrian parliament organized a Ukrainian National Council, which declared that the Ukrainians would prosper most under the aegis of the House of Hapsburg and summoned co-nationals everywhere to smite Russia, hip and thigh.[16] At Lemberg (Lvov), émigrés from the Russian Ukraine, a good few of them Social Revolutionaries who had fled after the abortive 1905 Revolution, founded a "Union for the Liberation of the Ukraine," dedicated to revolutionary action in the empire of the Tsar; and an

---

[16] Austriacus, "Die Österreichischen Ukrainer und der Krieg," ÖR, XLII (1915), 92–93. At the Ballplatz a glowing appeal to the Ukrainians of Russia was composed over the name of Francis Joseph. It recalled the disabilities laid upon the Ukrainians in the tsardom, blamed the men on the Neva for the war, and proclaimed that Hapsburg armies came as brothers, collaborators in the revival of Ukrainian culture and sponsors of a reign of justice. "Fight for freedom and a happy life," urged the manifesto, which appears never to have been published. P.A., XLVII, *Krieg*, Türkei, 8, b–11.

Ukrainian Legion similar to Pilsudski's volunteers was likewise created.

Upon the Russian invasion of Galicia in 1914, the Union switched its base of operations to Vienna where a newspaper, *Dilo* (*Work*) was printed and a periodical *Ukrainische Rundschau,* was edited by Dr. Vladimir Kuschnir. Propagandist books and pamphlets in several tongues were distributed and emissaries of the Union carried on diversified and fruitful activity on behalf of a free Ukraine with war prisoners from the Russian Ukraine, largely segregated at Freistatt in the province of Upper Austria; similar propaganda was diffused among Ukrainian soldiers held captive in Germany and in areas of Ukrainian speech overrun by the Central Empires. Representatives of the Union worked busily in Bulgaria, Turkey, Italy, and the United States, maintained contact with a modest Ukrainian revolutionary underground movement in Kiev, arranged for Ukrainian prisoners released by the Central Powers to go back to their homes to promote Ukrainian patriotic interests, and sought to rally assistance for the Ukrainophile national cause in influential circles of Vienna and Berlin. Funds to finance these varied undertakings were generously supplied by the cabinets of Berlin and Vienna and by Ukrainian settlers in the United States.[17]

Certain Ukrainian extremists dreamed of a wide-ranging national kingdom presided over possibly by the Hapsburg Archduke Wilhelm (Vasili Vishevaniy). For the purpose of inciting Ukrainians of Russia to rebel a "Pontus Expedition" was talked of—Austrian and German warships, that is, would make raids along the Russian Black Sea coast and then set agents ashore to foment insurrec-

---

[17] Hohenlohe to Berchtold, Oct. 22, 31, 1914, P.A., Preussen, *Berichte,* 1914; Helga Grebing, "Österreich-Ungarn und die 'Ukrainische Aktion,' 1914–18," *Jahrbücher für Geschichte Osteuropas,* VII (1959), 270–296; Fritz Fischer, "Deutsche Kriegsziele . . . im Osten," *Historische Zeitschrift,* CLXXXVIII (1959), 290–293; Roman Smal-Stocki, "Actions of 'Union for the Liberation of Ukraine' during World War I," *The Ukrainian Quarterly,* XV (1959), 169–174.

tion. How seriously that bizarre project was considered, it is impossible to determine, and in any event, Austrian military and naval chiefs eventually vetoed it.[18]

7.

When the armies of Nicholas II swept into Galicia in the first weeks of war, some Ukrainian clergymen and local civil servants welcomed the invaders and willingly toiled with and for them, but many Ukrainian political figures took refuge in Vienna. On the eve of the invasion, the Grand Duke Nicholas issued a proclamation, paralleling his utterance on the Poles, reminding the Ukrainians of the Monarchy of their historic ties with Russia, summoning them to cast off the Hapsburg yoke, "hoist the banner of a great, undivided Russia," and to fight the Central Empires. Eastern Galicia is "an old Russian land," explained Count Vladimir A. Bobriński upon installation as military governor of the conquered province. Retreating Austrian forces seized hundreds of Ukrainians whose loyalty was suspect and they were clapped into vile concentration camps at Thalerhof near Vienna, Kufstein, and other points; malicious stories about Ukrainian untrustworthiness were circulated by Galician civil servants apparently of Polish stock.

Tsarist political and religious officials inaugurated a ruthless Russification campaign in the occupied districts. The saintly and greatly beloved Archbishop of the Uniate Church,[19] Andreas Szeptycki, and hundreds of parish priests were banished to Russia, and until the March,

---

[18] Conrad, op. cit., IV, 197 ff.

[19] This Church, a blend of Roman Catholicism and Orthodox Eastern Christianity, was devised in 1596, largely by Jesuit fathers. Uniates acknowledged papal supremacy, but retained the Orthodox ritual, the traditional liturgical language, and required parish priests to marry. The faith had been virtually extinguished in the empire of the Tsar. Consult Stanislas Smolka, Les Ruthènes et les Problèmes Religieux du Monde Russe (Berne, 1917).

1917, revolution the Archbishop languished in Suzdal monastery, ordinarily a place of detention for recalcitrant Orthodox clergymen; the imprisonment of this religious and national leader embittered Roman Catholic Slavs everywhere.[20] Foreign Minister Sazonov, a deeply religious man, speaking the mind of official Russia on the Uniate deviationists, remarked, "I respect the Roman Catholics, though I deplore their religious error, but I hate the Uniates, and despise them because they are renegades."

Along with the fierce crusade against the Uniate clergy, Russian agents sought to coerce ordinary Ukrainian citizens into the Orthodox communion; the official paper of the tsarist occupation in Lemberg (Lvov) commented, "the authorities will encourage forcible conversions to Orthodoxy . . . new Uniate priests are not to be admitted without special permission of the governor-general in each particular case. . . . All Uniates who wish to be converted to the Orthodox rite will be received with open arms." [21] Archbishop Eulogius, who was put in charge of Orthodox interests in Galicia by the Russian Holy Synod, pressed propaganda so vigorously that even Governor Bobriński recoiled in disgust, and tsarist commanders angrily complained, "We ask for guns and you send us priests."

As other facets of headlong Russification in eastern Galicia, Ukrainian schools and bookshops, newspapers, and societies were suppressed. On a triumphal tour of the province, Nicholas II referred to the "indivisible Russia," extending to the Carpathians. Russian tactics in Galicia aroused a storm of protest in secular as well as in religious circles of Europe; and in the tsarist Duma, liberally-minded Cadet deputy Pavel Miliukov hotly denounced

[20] Kurt I. Lewin, "Andreas Count Sheptysky . . . ," *Annals of the Ukrainian Academy*, VII (1959), 1656–1667.

[21] D. Doroshenko, "The Uniat Church in Galicia, 1914–17," *Slavonic Review*, XII (1933–34), 623.

what had been done, saying, "The government sent to Galicia the scum of the bureaucracy and the methods pursued there by the Russian authorities became a European scandal." [22]

After Austrian arms recovered eastern Galicia, Russophiles in the thousands, old and new, escaped to the tsardom or were imprisoned, and during the temporary Brusilov reoccupation of 1916, Russification was not revived. Austrophile sentiments, meantime, had unmistakably moved upward. It was a shrewd move to appoint an Austrogerman, General Hermann von Colard, as governor of Galicia in June, 1916, in place of the Pole, Witold Korytowski, once finance minister of Austria; astute, that is, from the standpoint of the Ukrainian population, though the appointment angered impulsive Polish politicans. Familiar with both the Ukranian and the Polish tongues, Colard treated Ukrainian sensibilities tenderly during his short administration; by way of balance a strong Polonophile was named chief of police in Lemberg (Lvov).

Historically, many an articulate Ukrainian had looked to the government in Vienna for protection of national rights and interests against the dominant Polish element, and now Ukrainian politicians pushed for the division of Galicia into two distinct provinces, the eastern one to be managed by Ukrainians. If an arrangement of that character had come to pass, eastern Galicia might possibly have developed into an Ukrainian Piedmont, a political nucleus around which the entire nationality might have coalesced, but Polish politicians viewed that prospect with hardly less alarm than Russians. Whether Prime Minister Stürgkh actually promised to set eastern Galicia off as a separate crownland, as Ukrainian publicists asserted, is unclear, but, in any event, no positive step to that end was taken. At just this point, exiled Russian Ukrainians in

[22] Quoted in Komarnicki, *op. cit.*, p. 68.

Switzerland were worried over rumors that the cabinet in Vienna was toying with the idea of ceding the Austrian Ukrainian districts to Russia as part of a separate peace settlement.[23]

8.

Mutual animosities within the three sections of the Yugoslav nationality—Slovenes, Croats, and Serbs—and nearly universal distrust of Italy gave the South Slav question in Austria a rather different complexion from the Czech or Polish problems. Almost twice as numerous as Austrian Croats and Serbs put together, the Slovenes manifested relatively little consciousness of political affinity with their linguistic cousins; in fact, Slovenes, without any tradition of independence and lacking a historical foundation for political alignment with Croats and Serbs, were, on the whole, profoundly devoted to the Hapsburg dynasty and to their Roman Catholic faith.[24]

Scarcely had the war started than the Slovene Peoples' party, headed by Dr. Ivan Šušteršić, an old-line advocate of a Yugoslav state inside the Hapsburg realm, published a warmly Hapsburgophile declaration of appreciation and loyalty. Even the militant priest Dr. Anton Korošec, who as an editor had been preaching Slovene autonomy, observed that if Slovenes were allowed to control their schools, he would not oppose making German the official language of the region. Member of the Austrian parliament from 1906 until the break-up of the Monarchy, Korošec presided over the Slovene Club there; later in the war, he turned into the foremost Slovene apostle of secession and an independent Yugoslavia.

Much earlier an earnest band of South Slavs in Austria

[23] Von Gagern to Burián, Dec. 12, 1916, P.A., Schweiz, *Berichte*, 1916.
[24] S. W. Gould, "The Slovenes," *Social Studies*, XXXVI (1945), 310–315—a dispassionate survey, such as is rarely found.

began to work for a united and free Yugoslav state, founded on federal principles. Among them was Professor Janez E. Krek, relentless opponent of Šušteršić, and perhaps the most respected Slovene political personality; upon his death in 1917, his mantle passed to Korošec. The beloved Slovene poet, Oton Zupančić, lined up on the side of national freedom, and a small clique of Slovene secessionists operated a secret intelligence network in Vienna to promote the cause of South Slavdom.

By and large, Austrian officials dealt with known advocates of Yugoslav unity without kid gloves. More than a score of Slovenian priests were rounded up on charges of betraying military secrets to the enemy, though all were eventually acquitted. Assorted politicians and intellectuals of Dalmatia and Istria, known to desire the political consolidation of the South Slavs, were herded into concentration camps or imprisoned elsewhere. The dramatist, Ivo Vojnović, for instance, was interned at Spalato (Split) until his health broke and then he was moved to a hospital in Agram (Zagreb) and kept under police surveillance; fervent Yugoslav patriotism distinguished his finest plays, focused upon his native Ragusa (Dubrovnik) and the decline of its remarkable patrician class. As an author and as parliamentary representative of the Dalmatian islands, the Croat Ante Tresić-Pavičić had enthusiastically acclaimed independence for the South Slavs; he, too, was placed under arrest and detained until an amnesty decree of Emperor Charles in 1917. By way of compensation for wartime hardships, Tresić-Pavičić was appointed Yugoslav ambassador to the United States. A versatile man of letters, Niko Bartulović, noted for writings on peasants and fisherfolk, and a passionate exponent of Yugoslav nationhood, appears to have escaped internment by Austria, but in the Second World War he fell afoul of Tito's Partisans and was put to death.

As has been explained, certain Dalmatian public leaders,

such as Ante Trumbić and Frano Supilo, fled to the West and participated actively in the South Slav Committee which propagated the idea of a unified Yugoslavia in Entente countries and in the United States. Prominent anti-Hapsburg citizens of Bosnia were arrested or kept under close surveillance; Ivo Andrić, for example, a promising young man of letters and member of a Bosnian revolutionary society, was imprisoned for three years. His post-war novels, vividly describing the colorful past of Bosnia, earned him the sobriquet of "the Yugoslav Tolstoy," and, in 1961, he was awarded a Nobel Prize. Aleksa Šantić, the leading poet of Bosnia whose verse had passionately arraigned Hapsburg rule, escaped detention. When Serbian troops thrust into Bosnia in 1914, many a local patriot joyously avowed allegiance to the goal of South Slav independence, and when the invaders were driven out, not a few Bosnians accompanied the retreating forces.[25]

Scores of Bosnian youths were imprisoned in 1914 on charges of treason and at a decidedly macabre trial in Banjaluka over a hundred and fifty Serbophile Bosnians —deputies of the provincial assembly, Orthodox priests, and schoolmasters among them—were tried for conspiring to overthrow the government or to hamper the prosecution of the war. As in the parallel Kramář case, evidence partly genuine, partly fabricated was taken at Banjaluka for almost six months, starting in November of 1915. Almost a hundred of the accused were declared guilty, sixteen ringleaders being sentenced to death; the rest were fined or imprisoned. The severity of the penalties was undoubtedly intended to intimidate other Bosnians who disliked the prevailing Hapsburg regime; thanks to the intervention of the king of Spain, the condemned men

[25] Ferdinand Hauptmann, "Ein Reisebericht Dr. Ludwig Thallóczy's aus Bosnien," *Mitteilungen des Österreichischen Staatsarchivs*, XIII (1960), 404–449.

were reprieved. However much repressive measures may
have restrained activities in Bosnia harmful to the conduct
of the war, they by no means suffocated the dream of
Yugoslavia. Yet among South Slavs of Austria—as of Hungary—pro-Hapsburg sentiments increased after it was
learned that Italy had been promised parcels of Yugoslav-
inhabited territory to enter the war on the Entente side.

9.

Austrian citizens of Italian speech exceeded 750,000,
residing principally in the southern section of the Tyrol,
and in Trieste, which was badly crippled economically by
the war.[26] Anti-Hapsburg resentment in the stricken port
mounted when Austrian authorities obtusely removed a
statue of the composer Giuseppe Verdi for "aesthetic reasons." Agitation for the removal of the governor, Prince
Conrad Hohenlohe, for alleged favoritism to a testy
Slovene minority in the city, was repulsed in Vienna,
where it was reasoned that his dismissal would be construed by the cabinet of Rome as Austrian weakness.
When Austro-Italian diplomatic relations neared the
breaking point, police arrested Triestinos, who might
cause trouble, if war came; Trieste reeled with excitement
when war was actually declared by Italy. Pro-Hapsburg
elements staged street parades, singing and in other ways
manifesting loyalty—then they turned to anarchy plunder-
ing Italian cafés and shops, and in many cases putting
their contents to the torch; fire destroyed a handsome new
building of the Italian newspaper *Piccolo*. To protect the
community from further mob violence a local militia force
of 1,500 men was hurriedly whipped into shape.

Emotions of articulate Italians in the south Tyrol were
churned up when the foremost Socialist of the area, Dr.

[26] Hans Kramer, *Die Italiener unter der Österreichisch-Ungarischen
Monarchie* (Vienna, 1954), sympathetic to Austrogerman interests.

Cesare Battisti fled to Italy in August, 1914, and pleaded for war upon Austria-Hungary. An impassioned irredentist, Battisti told audiences in Italy, "Today my whole province shudders with impatience, as it waits for liberation. . . . The eagles of Austria and Germany must have their beaks and claws cut"; until shortly before his death, he wished Italy to acquire only the southern extremity of the Tyrol, not the whole area subsequently called Alto Adige. Author of distinguished works on geography and editor of the Socialist paper *Il Popolo,* Battisti had sat in the Tyrol assembly at Innsbruck and in the Vienna parliament, which for a time afforded him a shield of immunity.[27] Although an Austrian reserve officer, Battisti entered the Italian army after belligerency was proclaimed. Wounded and captured he was tried by an Austrian court-martial as a traitor and hanged in July, 1916, in the square of his native Trent (Trento); after 1918 a stately monument to his memory was erected there. It was said that "the scaffold which killed Battisti compelled the world's consent to the aspirations of Italy"; undoubtedly his heroic martyrdom heightened sympathy in Entente countries for the sweeping ambitions of Italian irredentists. Austrian authorities expelled Italian irredentist Bishop Gudisci from Trent, tried to get his successor Cölestin Endrici to cooperate and then temporarily banished him; but Austrian commanders who demanded sterner punishment of subversion were unable to prevail against the civil officials in the district.

In an interesting disquisition on the peculiar problems of the multinationality Hapsburg realm, the Socialist daily of Vienna made the important point that "the ordinary civilized European has not the faintest idea of the difficulty of making it possible for eight very strong-willed nationalities to live together." The Hapsburg union, read-

[27] Kramer, *op. cit.,* pp. 117–120; Ezio Mosna (ed.), *Cesare Battisti* (Trento, 1956), eulogistic paens to a scientist, prophet, and martyr.

ers were reminded, antedated the merger of England and Scotland, of Burgundy (in a sense) with France, of Odessa and Petrograd with Russia. If the nationalities should separate from the Monarchy, all alike would bleed to death; no acceptable solution of nationality aspirations, to be sure, had yet been discovered, though the paper wishfully imagined that "the ground was solidly prepared for a possible settlement." With justifiable pride it was pointed out that "in no state have the various nationalities, even the smallest, advanced so steadily as in Austria, and this can be counted as the great merit" of the reign of Emperor Francis Joseph.[28]

[28] *AZ*, Nov. 24, 1916.

11. Embattled Hungary

THE KINGDOM OF THE CROWN OF ST. STEPHEN DIFFERED FROM its Austrian partner in several important respects. Smaller in population by about forty per cent, even including the semi-autonomous kingdom of Croatia (more exactly, Croatia-Slavonia), it was likewise smaller in area, though geographically more compact.

Although industry had grown impressively from a low level in the two decades before the war, thanks partly to subsidies from the public treasury, two out of three Hungarians depended on the soil for their daily bread. Unlike Austria, too, the parliament of Hungary, a national institution existing before the country had chairs, it used to be said, met regularly throughout the war era. Political power was vested, as had historically been true, in the Magyar gentry and the hereditary aristocratic classes, and the large non-Magyar national communities — Rumanians, Slovaks, South Slavs—had precious little representation in royal governing bodies; yet no minority in Hungary provoked concern comparable to the Czech dissidents in

Austria. It was the proud claim of the patriotic Magyar that his country which had valorously defended western civilization against the Moslem, constituted the authentic bridge between West and East.

2.

Management of Hungarian public affairs revolved more around personalities than principles or party purposes, and for the Magyar ruling caste—or many of its members—state business had customarily been a sort of pleasant diversion. The pre-eminent wartime personality was Count Stephan Tisza, a man born to rule, a formidable tooth-to-nail fighter, harsh, remarkably insensitive to criticism, courageous, fiercely patriotic to the marrow of his bones, and an unwavering champion of the integrity of historic Hungary. He possessed to the full that imperturbable self-confidence which is the foundation of effective political leadership, and since his family lived in the eastern reaches of the kingdom, its fortunes had been intimately bound up with Transylvania. Grimly and fatalistically Calvinist in his religious philosophy, Tisza believed that government must be conducted with an iron hand concealed in a not-too-velvety glove; his brusque, not to say his contemptuous manner of speaking, frequently aroused the maximum resentment of political adversaries. It is not impossible that Tisza imagined "That the breath of worldly men cannot depose the deputy elected by the Lord." Becoming premier in June, 1913, he held on nearly four years.[1]

The Czechoslovak "emigration" flayed Tisza as the incarnation of "the sullen hatreds and exasperated pride of his clan. . . . In him there is united the fatalism of the

[1] May, *Hapsburg Monarchy*, 353–356. Biographers of the masterful Magyar tend to trip themselves up with hero worship, and picture him in less than "warts and all" coloring. Instructive on the war era is Gustav Gratz, "Graf Stefan Tisza," *BM*, XIV (1936), 92–116.

old school Calvinist, the reckless audacity of the wandering cavalier. . . . and the stubbornness of the lawyer. . . . who is aware that no cause is lost in the hands of a cunning advocate." [2]

On the foundation of his personal correspondence and political memoranda a rounded profile of the wartime Tisza can be constructed.[3] Only with profound misgivings had he acquiesced in the Ballplatz policy toward Serbia after the Sarajevo tragedy, but once the tocsin of war had sounded he experienced a temporary sense of exhilaration, inspiring him to write (August 27, 1914) that "for twenty bitter years I was oppressed by the idea that the Austrian monarchy, and with it the Magyar nation, were doomed to destruction . . . In the last few years [however] things began to take a better turn . . . in the momentous days of this great time the decision [on survival of the realm] will be reached." Many another pubic man in Hungary shared essentially that confident point of view.[4]

Antagonists to the left in politics not only upbraided Tisza with the erroneous charge that he was the chief author of the war, but held him responsible for the prolongation of the agonizing struggle; time and again the Premier expounded the doctrines that the Monarchy was fighting a war of defense, free of ambition to annex substantial tracts of territory, and eager for the restoration of peace on the principle of a just equilibrium of power. After Britain unsheathed the sword, Tisza questioned whether the Central Allies could overcome their pack of enemies; the war, he asserted, "is due to England's envy of Germany's industrial advance. England's war is the war of despots of the sea against the freedom of the sea. The Central Powers are fighting today against England for

[2] *La Nation Tchèque*, Oct. 15, 1916.
[3] Ladislas Lanyi, *Le Comte Étienne Tisza et la Guerre de 1914–18* (Paris, 1946); Gustav Erényi, *Graf Stefan Tisza* (Vienna, 1935).
[4] Oskar von Wertheimer (ed.), *Graf Stefan Tisza, Briefe* (Berlin, 1928), p. 63.

what England once fought for herself." [5] Salvation must be sought, he fondly reasoned, in diplomatic negotiations for peace, and his faith sank to a low ebb when tsarist forces stormed into the city of Lemberg (Lvov).

As prime minister, wholly dedicated to the welfare of his country, Tisza handled exacting duties in parliament, meddled in the larger problems of Hapsburg military strategy, kept abreast of currents in foreign policy, the details of armament production, sanitary facilities for the troops, and, on occasion, he even performed funeral rites for fellow-Calvinists who had fallen in battle. Letters which he penned to anxious wives of men serving with the colors were models of courtesy and kindliness—another Tisza this than the two-fisted politician. Arch-loyalist, that he was, he retained the confidence of Francis Joseph, who placed very high value on the Magyar's political sagacity. Nonetheless, Tisza pushed hard and steadily to make Hungary the predominant partner in the realm, and, as a stubborn adherent of the Austro-Hungarian dualistic pattern devised in 1867, he set his face like flint against any and all schemes for constitutional reordering of the Monarchy. Scarcely had the guns started booming than he recited his creed on this fundamental matter with force and clarity. "The Hungarian nation, cannot . . . allow itself to be put in a position where it might be outvoted . . . It cannot surrender the constitutional rights which it has acquired at the cost of centuries filled with bloody struggles, and it cannot permit itself to sink to the status of a province in an enlarged empire . . ." [6] For the military might and prowess of imperial Germany Tisza had the utmost respect, and the authorities in Berlin on their part, esteemed him as no other public man in the Danubian realm. He seems not to have been disturbed by a modest propa-

[5] *NFP*, Nov. 3, 1915.
[6] Tisza to Burián, Aug. 11, 1914, Wertheimer, *op. cit.*, p. 53.

ganda, emanating from Germany, to install Prince Eitel Friedrich of Prussia, as king of Hungary.

The well-known American servant of humanity, Jane Addams, on a peace-seeking errand to Budapest in the spring of 1915, sketched this portrait of the austere first minister: He "looks curiously like General [Ulysses S.] Grant, only that he is very tall and broad-shouldered . . . he is a Presbyterian. He impresses one as a rather sombre, stern man with great resolution, but not as the fire-eater, the fierce war lord, that the Austrians had described to us: certainly to us he said nothing of the glories or gains of war, only of its senseless horrors." [7]

Before 1914, Count Julius Andrássy the younger, the principal spokesman of the "liberal" dissidents in Hungarian public life, had been a relentless political opponent of Tisza, just as in the previous generation, their fathers had been contentious rivals. But, Andrássy's patriotism was ardent, and when war came he declared a kind of parliamentary truce saying that "political disagreements have existed in Hungary . . . but no differences of opinion existed that we must win this war . . ." His recommendations for a coalition ministry Tisza turned aside with scorn, and Andrássy was more than once cut to the quick because the Prime Minister vetoed his appointment to the embassy in Rome and to other important diplomatic posts. Grand seigneur that he was, a patron of the arts whose Budapest palace was stocked with masterpieces of the Italian Renaissance, Andrássy dwelt in the aristocratic climate of the eighteenth century, aloof from ordinary folk; but his devotion to the Hapsburg crown assumed heroic proportions.

Well-educated, erudite, versed in the diplomatic art,

[7] Jane Addams, *et. al., Women at the Hague* (New York, 1915), pp. 43–44. Miss Addams was permitted to hold a peace rally in Budapest. She went away feeling that the Hungarians had lost interest in the war and might be ready for a compromise settlement with Russia. Cf. *NFP*, Jan. 17, 1915, Ap. 26, 27, 1915.

Andrássy contributed generously to the press in the war era and spoke often in parliament on international prospects and problems, war aims, and related themes. British commercial jealousy, he devoutly believed, had much to do with the oncoming of war, and so did the French yearning for *revanche* upon Germany. Frequently he observed, though not consistently, that the House of Hapsburg coveted no territory of a foreign power and wished only to preserve the integrity of the realm against Muscovite savagery. "Imperative military considerations," he thought at one time, "may make it necessary . . . to retain possession of strategic points. Geography is the loftiest principle of statecraft—above considerations of nationality." [8]

As has already been indicated, Andrássy liked to be consulted by the Ballplatz when important diplomatic transactions were in train, and, profoundly convinced that Russia and Pan-Slavism were mortal perils to the Dual Monarchy, he was a staunch Germanophile, like his father who, in 1879 as foreign minister, had concluded the original Austro-Hungarian treaty of alliance with Berlin. "Our sympathies for Germany have grown keener," he remarked. The demonstrated strength of the Central Power Alliance, he asserted, "is founded on permanent interests common to both states . . . and must be drawn still closer." Taking an active and sustained interest in the Polish question, Andrássy strongly advocated the resurrection of Poland and its incorporation as a third state in the Hapsburg complex. For services to the realm, he was rewarded with the Golden Fleece of the Hapsburgs, an honor seldom conferred, but his burning ambition to take charge at the Ballplatz was not realized until the Monarchy was in the very throes of death. [9]

[8] *NFP*, Ap. 23, 1916.
[9] Viktor Naumann, *Profile* (Munich, 1925), pp. 253–266; Julius Andrássy, *Diplomacy and the War* (Eng. trans., London, 1921), a praiseworthy effort to deal dispassionately with extremely controversial matters.

If anything, the personal antagonism toward Tisza of Count Albert Apponyi, high priest of the Hungarian Independence party, exceeded that of Andrássy. Yet when the call to war sounded, Apponyi greeted the crucial decision with a laconic "at last"—he had particularly a settlement with Serbia in mind; he, too, proclaimed a parliamentary armistice and abandoned his pre-war crusade for the separation of Hungary from Austria. Wishfully, Apponyi fancied that the monarch, out of gratitude for full cooperation in the war, would grant appeasing concessions to Hungarian national pride, and, in any case, his allegiance to Hungarian independence hardly extended to the reigning dynasty; even after the passing of the Monarchy, he stood forth as an ardent apostle of Hapsburg legitimism.

Long saluted as "the grand old man" of the Hungarian kingdom, Apponyi had regaled the Budapest parliament with matchless eloquence for over forty years; he not only commanded unusual moral prestige among Magyars, but boasted valued associations with distinguished foreigners, among them the Americans, Theodore Roosevelt and Nicholas M. Butler, president of Columbia University. Several times Apponyi was pointed to as the ideal representative to undertake a mission to the New World for the purpose of propagating the Austro-Hungarian interpretation of the war or to fill the ambassador's chair in Washington. Tisza, however, prevented him from being named, for he was too useful in restraining the parliamentary opposition in Budapest.[10]

Count Michael Károlyi was a vastly more militant figure in the Hungarian Independence camp. Scion of a patrician family, he had been brought up in keeping with the customs of the opulent magnate. Tall, gangling, handicapped by a cleft palate and hardly helped by a dark El Greco

[10] Harold Steinacker, "Graf Albert Apponyi," *Jahrbücher für die Geschichte Osteuropas,* II (1937), 272–280; Oscar Jászi, "Count Albert Apponyi," *Nation,* CXVII (1923), 376–377; *NFP,* Nov. 8, 1914.

cast of countenance, Károlyi had some odd quirks in his make-up and in his ambitions; in intellectual orientation, as well as in politics, he leaned strongly toward unorthodoxy. Impulsive and impressionable, his undisciplined outlook on life had been colored by the writings of Charles Darwin and Herbert Spencer, of Voltaire and Ernest Renan; bit by bit, he edged into a personal and rather sentimental version of Marxism. His loyalty to the Hapsburg dynasty fluctuated violently, and he liked to be thought of as a disciple of Louis Kossuth, revolutionary and republican chieftain of 1848–49. Just before the war, as a passionate exponent of Hungarian national freedom, he had visited Magyar colonies in the United States to raise funds for independence propaganda and to foster separatist emotions. Only after the fighting began did he manage to get back home, and he promptly belabored Apponyi for pledging the Independence party to support the war effort unconditionally.

Considered a wrong-headed intellectual dwelling in a cloud-cuckoo-land by the rest of the opposition to Tisza (Károlyi's attractive little wife was the step-daughter of Andrássy), the eccentric Count chafed under the truce in parliament and threatened to revive the scandalously disorderly scenes that had tormented the Budapest legislative chamber before 1914. Genuine reforming zeal inspired him to stand forth as the aristocratic tribune of ordinary fellows, to advocate universal manhood suffrage and the distribution of large landed proprietorships among the soil workers; small wonder that Károlyi was reviled as a traitor by the Magyar ruling class. For unwearying condemnation of the German alliance, for frankly avowed affection for France and Britain, both of which he knew at first-hand, for relentless criticism of the way the war was managed, for insistent demands that the objectives of the fighting should be officially spelled out, this *enfant terrible* was repudiated by conservative Hungarian patriots as the dread enemy of the Fatherland.

It was Károlyi's conviction that if the Central Empires emerged victorious from the armed struggle, a German yoke would be tightly snaffled upon Austria-Hungary, while if they lost the war the Monarchy would be dissolved; hence, his advocacy of a compromise settlement while there was still time. But that posture did not mean that Károlyi wanted peace at any price; he flatly told parliament in August, 1916, that the country must "fight unswervingly for the integrity of Hungary and the defense of Transylvania." As a soldier, Károlyi served in the cavalry, returning to Budapest whenever parliament was sitting; when other deputies patriotically applauded Central Power successes in battle, Károlyi was prone to sit ostentatiously with folded hands.[11]

3.

On an overall view, the popular response in Hungary to the coming of war in 1914 duplicated that in Austria, and the anti-Hapsburg clamor of a few months before swiftly disappeared. "Revenge, pride, power, glory, manhood," remarked one observer, "love of country, the intoxication of the hour, the flame of national instinct, the magic of an inspiration; in this tremendous whirl of spontaneous feeling Hungary took the field." Streets in the heart of Budapest resounded with martial airs and an immense mass procession, bearing transparencies of Emperor-King Francis Joseph and William II of Germany, paraded to the palace of popular Archduke Joseph, who responded to a lusty serenade with ". . . To-morrow, I go to the battlefield, prepared to die for the Fatherland if necessary. I place my trust in God, who has never left Hungary in the lurch. He is with us now!" Christian bishops issued pastoral letters summoning the faithful to war duties, Cardinal Csernoch explaining that the Monarchy was fighting

[11] Oscar Jászi, "Count Károlyi—Hungary's Exiled Statesman," *Current History*, XX (1924), 618–623.

in self-defense and that material and cultural benefits would assuredly flow from the war. The new heir-apparent and his wife, Charles and Zita, were wildly acclaimed on August 2, 1914, in Budapest.[12] Rural reservists were decorated with victory wreaths. Music and flags bore witness to martial enthusiasm in Croatia, except for communities of Serbs, scarcely less than in Hungary proper.[13] Some part of the war fervor in Hungary was due, it is true, to the labors of professional agitators and of police in organizing mass demonstrations.

Spirits were enheartened by the expectation that troublesome Serbia would quickly be humbled and that peace would return by Christmas; disaffection in areas of Rumanian and Serbian speech occasioned little trouble. A cacophonous note, however, was sounded by Dr. Oscar Jászi in the journal *Világ* (*World*), which catered to noncomformist bourgeoisie and for a wing of the small Hungarian Socialist party. "Outside the feudal class and *haute finance* the whole public opinion of the country," he wrote, "is for peace and feels that it would be a crime to raise hecatombs for the South Slav ghost, which cannot be frightened away with the bloody instruments of war." But that small voice was drowned in a torrent of patriotic exuberance.

By many an ordinary Hungarian the struggle was looked upon as a war of defense against the tsarist colossus and that conviction increased in the autumn of 1914 when spearheads of Russian armies penetrated across the Carpathians and onto the Hungarian plains. Great Britain was hardly thought of as an enemy at all; for the aristocratic class happy, legendary memories of England were deeprooted, and British citizens residing in Hungary were treated considerately. The Hungarian Society of Britain,

[12] *NFP*, Aug. 2, 3, 1914.
[13] Prince Ludwig Windischgrätz, *My Memoirs* (London, 1921), pp. 57–58; Joseph Szterényi, "Die Monarchie wie Sie ist und Sein Soll," ÖR, XL (1914), 285-290.

parenthetically, adopted resolutions condemning imperial Germany and her rulers.

Hungarian attitudes toward the German ally varied considerably. Admiration for the military power and presumed invincibility of Germany, and admiration for its efficiency and talent for organization were heightened by the feeling that Germany was the victim of a dastardly, Machiavellian plot on the part of the Entente, jealous of German industrial and commercial progress and bent upon its destruction. Tisza believed that Hungary faced the greatest challenge to national existence since the reign of Maria Theresa, and he later contended that the war was proving fully the value of the dualistic partnership and that Hungary was the stouter pillar of the Hapsburg realm.[14]

Morale in Hungary, as in other belligerent countries, reflected what was publicly known about the current military situation, the diplomatic prospects, and, in cities and towns, the conditions of living. Loud complaints were heard because Hungarian regiments were dispatched to Galicia—foreign soil—to oppose onrushing tsarist armies, leaving Hungary itself virtually defenseless. On September 27, 1914, the American consul in Budapest, William Coffin, reported that widespread despair already prevailed because of Russian penetration onto Hungary soil and the simultaneous appearance of cholera; government and people alike, he supposed, were "heartily sick of the war and are beginning to be apprehensive that whichever side may win Austria-Hungary and especially Hungary are bound to be heavy losers." Corruption and administrative incompetence, not least in furnishing assistance to families of mobilized men, provoked a great deal of popular criticism.

As in Austria many palaces of the aristocracy of Hun-

[14] Tisza to a Friend, Sept. 7, 1915, *Összes Munkái* (6 vols., Budapest, 1924–1937), IV, 81–95. This work herafter is cited as *ÖM*.

gary were converted into hospitals, and titled ladies busied themselves as nurses, or with care of children, maternal welfare, and aid to refugees, of which about 200,000, half Magyars, half from other nationalities, sought sanctuary in Budapest.[15] No man outmatched Tisza in looking after the interests and well-being of the troops. He peppered correspondence to the Hapsburg supreme command with stiff demands that regiments from Hungary should be permitted to display the national flag, and insisted, too, that the wounded should be cared for in hospitals in which attendants understood and spoke the several languages of the Hungarian kingdom, that prayer-books should be made available to the troops, and that orthodox Jews should be allowed to observe their religious customs without restraint.

4.

Meeting for short sessions throughout the war the parliament of Hungary served as a forum of discussion and as a political sounding board; until the reopening of the Austrian legislature in the spring of 1917, the serious press of Vienna carried extensive accounts of parliamentary proceedings in Budapest. It was far from being a representative assembly, since only about 6 per cent of the population were privileged to vote; in the lower chamber neither the industrial wageworkers nor the landless peasantry had an elected spokesman, and in a body of 453 a mere 50 deputies were not Magyars—of that 50, 40 came from Croatia. Many deputies attended parliament in colorful military uniforms and the first session of the war era passed off with order and tranquillity unexampled for years.

But as hostilities dragged on, the surface calm drooped

[15] Josef Szterényi, "Ungarische Kriegsfürsorge," ÖR, XLI (1914), 202–205.

and traditional political disharmonies reasserted themselves.[16] Either in the chamber or privately, deputies raised questions on a broad range of public subjects—management of foreign policy, supplies of food and military equipment, the high cost of living, or the economic treaty (Ausgleich) with the Austrian Empire. In 1915, Stephan Rakovsky, in the name of the Catholic Peoples' party, brought up the issue of broadening the franchise right, a subject that had been hotly discussed for years; it was argued that extension of the suffrage would ensure full cooperation of the troops in winning the war. Just as previously, Tisza adamantly resisted tampering with the electoral law; for in his thinking, if politically illiterate citizens were given the vote, they might easily fall prey to trouble-making agitators to the irreparable damage of the Hungarian state, and in any case the ordinary fellow, he argued, was not interested in the right to vote. As he put it, ". . . the Hungarian soldier in the trenches does not care about the suffrage; he is only longing for a leave of two weeks in order to till his lot; he doesn't think of the suffrage but only of his folks and the Fatherland . . ."[17]

While Andrássy saw nearly eye to eye with Tisza on electoral reform, Károlyi adopted a manhood suffrage position, and he and a handful of like-minded deputies spoke up for dissolution of large landed estates, urging that wounded veterans at least should be awarded acreages of their own. With uncommon vigor Andrássy retorted that a catastrophic decline in crop yields might follow land parcellation—and that was that. Reiterated demands for a coalition ministry were rejected by Tisza, unless he should retain the prime ministership, and to that his parliamentary opponents would not agree; Tisza made no bones about stating that it was absolutely vital

[16] Fürstenberg to Berlin, Nov. 26, Dec. 12, 1914, F.O. 553/288.
[17] Quoted in Oscar Jászi, *The Dissolution of the Habsburg Monarchy* (Chicago, 1929), p. 363.

for Hungary and for Austria-Hungary that he stay on as Premier.

The favorable swing of the military fortunes of the Central Empires in 1915 strengthened the faith of Tisza and he was soon telling the great German ship-master, Albert Ballin, that the military objectives of the Monarchy were on the verge of accomplishment: Serbia had been crushed, Galicia had been liberated, Russian ascendancy in the Balkans had been ended—only Italy remained. But in the summer of 1916, dark clouds accumulated in the Hungarian political sky. Shocked by the astonishing Brusilov offensive, Andrássy renewed the demand that the anti-Tisza deputies should be allowed a weightier voice in the conduct of state business. And Károlyi and a clique of twenty-odd deputies, which included Count Theodor Batthyány, Martin Lovászy, and Julius Justh, veteran war horses of separatism, cut loose from the Independence party and organized the Independence and 1848 party. Before long, this highly contentious faction clamored for franchise extension, for a searching investigation into the conduct of military affairs, for an independent Hungarian army, for a precise statement on war aims, and even for a compromise peace settlement without annexations and prescribing compulsory arbitration of quarrels between nations in the future. Károlyi told parliament that Hungary must secure compensation for the tremendous sacrifices of blood and money, not in territory, but in the form of independence, and, he added, "I believe that the time for peace is no longer distant."

The wide-ranging agenda of Károlyi and Company naturally infuriated Tisza and men in the loyal parliamentary opposition, but it elicited hearty applause from representatives of the hard-pressed Hungarian urban proletariat, notably of Sigismund Kunfi, an erstwhile village schoolmaster, who had emerged as the leading Socialist journalist and orator of Budapest. Foes of Tisza in parlia-

ment chose to harass the ministry by offering interpella-
tions—as many as twenty at a single sitting—accompanied
by lengthy speeches. Apponyi in a powerful address
revived the claim for an independent Hungarian army
and railed against a long-term economic treaty with Austria or with the German Empire; he also let it be known
that he thought the management of the Ballplatz ought to
be entrusted to a statesman more imaginative and more
competent than Burián—a point of view shared by Andrássy, who seems to have been intriguing to obtain the
foreign secretaryship for himself.[18]

Turbulence reigned in parliament after Rumania declared war in August, 1916, and its armies advanced headlong onto the fertile plains and pleasant cities of Transylvania, forcing refugees to crowd into Budapest bearing
tales of enemy bestialities. Taunting Tisza with responsibility for the disasters, Károlyi and Company shouted
for his head on a charger; more sedate critics blamed the
executive authorities of the Monarchy for "inexcusable
neglect," and once more raised the cry for a coalition
cabinet headed by someone other than Tisza. Confidence,
declared Andrássy, had been completely shattered, "We
must secure for ourselves a new leadership"; blank spaces
of the censorship appeared in anti-ministerial Hungarian
newspapers in place of editorials censuring the handling
of diplomatic relations with Rumania. Unabashed by opposition attacks, the solid phalanx of Tisza deputies rallied to the support of the Prime Minister with lusty cheers.
While Tisza tagged speeches by critics as scandalous,
Vienna's *Arbeiter Zeitung* countered that they "are all
that remains of freedom of criticism in Austria-Hungary."
"Rumania will not escape her fate," Tisza cried prophet-
ically, "Our holy duty is . . . to maintain scrupulously
the unity of the nation in its struggle for existence." He

[18] Fürstenberg to Berlin, Aug. 25, Sept. 9, 1916, F.O. 553/288. *ÖM*,
IV, 271–272.

loyally defended Ambassador Ottokar Czernin against accusations of negligence or stupidity in transactions with the cabinet of Bucharest, but he felt that Burián had outlived his usefulness at the Ballplatz and sought backing for Count John Forgách as his successor; the moderate Hungarian opposition, however, indicated a decided preference for the polished and ambitious Andrássy as foreign minister.

Summing up matters, the experienced American consul in Budapest concluded that the anti-Tisza crowd had profited from the Rumanian belligerency, and that Tisza, for all his power and prestige, must soon retire as premier.[19] While Tisza managed to quell the furious storm in parliament, he seemed to have lost something of his legendary élan; recriminations slacked off, however, when Central Power armies briskly hurled the Rumanian invaders out of Transylvania. The popularity of Germany mounted to unexampled heights and Hindenburg attained the dignity of Hungarian sainthood.

5.

Wartime economic perplexities in Hungary closely paralleled those of Austria. Since about three-quarters of all the external trade of the kingdom were carried on with Austria, the Entente blockade had only limited direct significance, yet sales of goods to the United States in 1915 amounted to only ten per cent of the previous year. Ever alert to the interests of Hungarian agriculture, Tisza was perfectly willing to have grain purchased in foreign countries to meet food requirements of the Monarchy, provided the grain paid normal import duties.

By and large, town dwellers in Hungary fared better in food supply (though less well in clothing and shoes) than

---

[19] Coffin to Penfield, Sept. 5, 1916, *American Embassy Papers,* Vienna, vol. XLIII (1916–17); cf. AZ, Sept. 6, 1916.

their counterparts in Austria. But Hungary also felt the pinch; prices of many kinds of foodstuffs rose sharply in Budapest in the first year of the fighting, fish and meat (never, to be sure, important in the diet of the ordinary family), costing anywhere from twice to nearly four times as much as before the war, and the price of potatoes nearly doubled, though the cost of other vegetables increased only slightly. The middle classes, in general, were able to satisfy their basic wants, but working class families were hit hard; their food was coarse and expensive; increasing quantities of rice were consumed, and urban mass protests against living costs were not uncommon. Under war conditions of life and labor, wheat and rye harvests in 1914 and again in 1916 approached three-quarters of the pre-war average and in 1915 stood even higher, but the yield of barley that year was far below normal, furnishing little surplus for Austria even if the Hungarian authorities had had the best will in the world to help their partner.[20]

Maximum prices, as in Austria, were set by the government, controls over consumption were steadily tightened, and the use of grain in beer-making was reduced by forty per cent. Symptomatic of the decline in public morality, profiteering in foodstuffs pursued a merry course. In the port community of Fiume housewives frequently found it impossible to procure meat for a week or more; even fish were in short supply, and leather, coal, and hospital necessities became ever more difficult to obtain. With the onset of war, many factories in Fiume virtually ceased operations, except for tobacco processors turning out cigarettes and "Virginia" cigars, very strong and with mouthpieces of straw-reed.

Surveying the economic scene in January 1916, Consul Coffin commented upon "the great vitality" shown by Hungarians, a very serious depreciation of the currency,

[20] Tisza to Sylvester, Oct. 16, 1915, ÖM, IV, 194.

and a fictitious prosperity. Agricultural interests were pocketing enormous profits, industry was operating at maximum capacity, and luxury trades were booming; since the shooting started, Coffin remarked, textile factories had earned enough "to almost write off their capital investment and still have large cash balances." Cards for rationing bread had recently been issued, but he did not think that Hungary had been much harmed by exports of foodstuffs to Austria and to Germany. "There is as yet no material exhaustion noticeable," he concluded, after eighteen months of fighting; "the country is now buoyed up by military successes," though "apprehension is already observable and the discussion of a *Zollverein* [with Germany] has caused considerable anxiety." A list of food prices attached to the consular report revealed that costs of meat and of dairy products had advanced in Budapest over the preceding six months, although not very much. On a visit to the Hungarian capital, Mrs. James W. Gerard, wife of the ambassador of the United States in Berlin, found the inhabitants well-supplied with food, gay, and confident after dazzling military triumphs over Serbia and Russia.

As 1916 moved along, however, it became evident that straitened living conditions were sapping morale on the home front and in the armed forces. Food and secondhand clothing commanded exhorbitant prices; the workweek in certain plants shot up to eighty-five hours, and consumption of alcohol by workmen increased significantly. To satisfy labor requirements, women workers in factories greatly increased and many children as young as eight years were employed. As in Austria, military authorities supervised industry, and unruly workmen were subject to court martial.

A rule of two meatless days a week and no fats on one day was imposed, and to piece out the grim war diet, consumption of the flesh of horses and of dogs moved up substantially. "Our women go to market early in the morning, some of them at five o'clock," observed *Az Est,* "in quest of necessaries and they return at ten without anything . . . their eyes full of tears." According to another Budapest paper, *Pesti Napló* (*Pest Daily*), Germany possessed nearly a monopoly on the export of food from Bulgaria and Turkey with the result that citizens of Munich were living better and more cheaply than Budapesters in peacetime.

During a debate on food in parliament on September 29, 1916, the stormy petrel Károlyi complained that Hungary suffered more from shortages than Germany and offered statistics to prove that costs of food had gone up more than twice as fast in Hungary as in Germany; and he claimed that Hungary was making greater sacrifices in general than the northern ally. Soldiers of the kingdom, he said, had protected Germany from invasion, and along with Austrians had borne the brunt of the fighting on the eastern fronts. While Károlyi believed the German alliance should be observed as long as the war lasted, he stridently demanded equality in sacrifices. Germans residing in Budapest founded a society to combat criticism of the Fatherland and to widen sympathies between the two countries.

At the end of 1916 trained observers from the United States appraised in detail Hungarian standards of living. Although the quality of food available in Budapest had deteriorated, enough was on hand to satisfy minimum requirements until the next harvest, but milk, sugar, and lard were at times not to be had and the capital had just been afflicted by a potato famine. The poorer classes were suffering terribly. In Croatia stocks of provisions had dwindled rapidly in the preceding six months, and the diet of the poor was restricted to potatoes, cornmeal, cabbage, and bread. Taking the kingdom as a whole, the harvest of 1916 yielded only about half the normal supplies, leaving nothing or next to nothing for shipment abroad, and visions of quick grain reinforcement from conquered Rumania had failed of realization. Country folk, adept at hoarding and concealment, were getting along reasonably well. Grave as were the food perplexities, the insufficiency of fuel, lubricating oil, and railway rolling stock presented even more formidable problems, it was reported.[21] By then it appeared that the war had reduced the Hungarian population by about five per cent. Soldier losses, not reckoning cripples, approached 700,000 and the birth rate had dropped to under half the pre-war level; in 1916 deaths in the civilian population exceeded births by something like 94,000.

6.

Relations between Hungary and Austria, far from harmonious before 1914, worsened in wartime, and animosities multiplied the darker the military prospects looked. Food supplies for Austria constituted an endless source of acrimonious bickering, and Austrian commanders were often accused of throwing Hungarian lads into the most dangerous sectors of the battlefronts. Károlyi assailed the Tisza ministry for supinely tolerating Austrian arrogance in handling Hungarian troops—"persecution" he called it. "The greater our successes on the battlefield, the more the Hungarians are persecuted," he protested; the Prime Minister begged the deputies not to inflate a few unsavory incidents into a brash generalization, and he read out a fulsome letter from Field Marshal Archduke Friedrich extolling Hungarian martial prowess and heroic sacrifices.

Extremely touchy himself on any issue affecting Hungarian rights or interests, Tisza had constantly to be on guard lest the partisans of independence should be able

---

[21] Penfield to Lansing, Jan. 10, 1917, U.S., *National Archives,* 853. 50/25.

to build capital out of a real or alleged national slight or discrimination committed in Vienna. When a few hundred geese seized in Russian Poland passed exclusively to the hungry Austrian capital, the press of Budapest growled harshly and Tisza felt obliged to remonstrate with Austrian officialdom. He raised a rumpus whenever he believed that Hungarian troops were not getting a fair share of credit in publicity on the fighting or if he felt that Hungarian industries were not awarded a decent proportion of the contracts for military goods.[22]

Shipments of foodstuffs to Austria were limited, Tisza pleading that stocks at home were low or that provisions had to be sent to Croatia and Bosnia. He urged that the possibilities of cutting down on army food consumption should be fully explored and that Austrian grain purchases should be increased in neutral Rumania, regardless of cost. Throughout 1915 and 1916, discussions on the food problem with Austrian officials absorbed much of the time and energy of the Magyar Premier, but shipments never reached pre-war quantities and dropped lower as the

Responsible Austrians, Mayor Weiskirchner among them, cried out angrily about Magyar food hoarding and selfishness, but to all entreaties and protests Tisza retorted that Hungary was in fact doing her utmost, stinting herself, or was handicapped by the inability of the railways to move crops. Andrássy, on the other hand, believed that Hungary both could and should ship more food to Austria, and, at the same time, he urged that methods of grain collection in Bohemia and Moravia should be tightened.

On other sectors of the economic front, Hungary chose to pursue a more or less independent path; agencies regulating the consumption of metals, for instance, were

---

[22] Tisza to Stürgkh, Aug. 17, 1915, and Tisza to Archduke Friederich, Jan. 21, 1916, *ÖM*, IV, 115–116, 380–386.

[23] David F. Strong, *Austria: Transition from Empire to Republic* (New York, 1939), pp. 47–50.

not coordinated with those of Austria, which accentuated problems of military and civilian provisioning. With time, a complete prohibition was laid upon the sale of leather and timber to Austria, though the latter commodity was exported to Germany which was able to pay with goods desired in Hungary. Traditions of economic collaboration between the two partners in the Monarchy underwent severe strain—and deterioration.

Nonetheless, Tisza, on occasion, achieved ecstatic heights of eloquence in lauding the dualistic system. It was gratifying "to see the Hungarian national tricolor fluttering with the black and yellow flag on the houses of Budapest and Vienna. This proves," he remarked, "that the war has brought the souls of Austria and Hungary nearer to each other." Professedly, he desired to draw firmer the cohesive bonds of the two countries,[24] but Tisza had a low opinion of Austrian officialdom, and he frequently quarreled with senior personalities in the supreme command—whom he regarded as Magyarophobes and favorable to federalization of the Monarchy. It was his conviction that after the war Hungary would speak more decisively than ever on issues of concern to the whole Danubian realm. In Magyar circles the desirability of having the Hungarian prime minister serve as Hapsburg chancellor and even of having Magyar as the official language of the realm was occasionally canvassed.

To celebrate the birthday of Francis Joseph in 1915, Tisza headed a colorful pilgrimage of Hungarians to Schönbrunn and delivered a moving panegyric on the solidarity of the Double Monarchy and the certainty of eventual victory; in a kindred spirit, eminent Hungarians contributed pieces to *Neue Freie Presse* dwelling upon the common bonds between the two countries. Much pleased, the Viennese paper ventured (October 2, 1915) to suggest that forthcoming conversations to renew the

[24] Anonymous, "Tisza's Neujahrsrede," *ÖR*, XLVI (1916), 97–103.

decennial Austro-Hungarian economic treaty would see "brother dealing with brother," even though in the past renewals had been tough, exacting ordeals. Suggestions from the Austrian side that the existing treaty might be prolonged until the war was over found no favor with Tisza; talks for a new economic pact, he announced in January, 1916, would presently start and only after that task had been completed would Hungary be in a position to consider closer economic ties with imperial Germany.

Austrian spokesmen wished the new economic arrangements to run for twenty or thirty years, instead of the customary ten, and they argued that Hungary was able to shoulder a larger proportion of the joint expenses of the realm than hitherto; in contrast, Tisza contended that the Hungarian financial obligation should be pared down and that tariffs on soil products and cattle should be raised. Unless these changes were accepted by Austria, the Prime Minister would feel obliged to resign, he confided to Francis Joseph. Financiers and industrialists of Hungary wanted clauses in the treaty that would stimulate the growth of machinofacture at home, while extremist politicians were quite prepared to dissolve the economic alignment with Austria completely and have Hungary go it alone.[25]

Austrian and Hungarian experts conferred on a new economic treaty, with a good deal of debate revolving—literally that—around duties to be levied on imports. Each side eventually consented to certain concessions desired by the other and a draft treaty was actually written. But before the finishing touches could be put on the pact,

[25] Just before the war Hungary had concluded a copyright convention with the United States, independently of Austria. Elmar Damborsky, "Die Verlängerung des Ausgleiches Österreich-Ungarn, 1867" (Vienna, 1948), pp. 75 ff.—a doctoral dissertation in typescript at the University of Vienna; Tisza to Francis Joseph, Feb. 9, Ap. 16, 1916, ÖM, V, 30–39, 143–145.

Stürgkh had been murdered and, Koerber, the new Austrian premier, insisted upon substantial alterations in the original text. Little love was lost between the two prime ministers, for Koerber had not forgotten that when he had headed the Austrian cabinet early in the century, Tisza had tagged him, reproachfully, as "a distinguished foreigner." When Koerber visited Budapest to discuss the economic *Ausgleich*, the press of the capital urged Tisza to give the Austrian detailed information on the privations Hungary was undergoing; since the Hungarians would not accept revisions in the tentative treaty which Koerber considered indispensable, he washed his hands of the knotty problem, thus advertising anew and strikingly the difficulty of holding together two countries with disparate economies and divergent state ambitions.[26] Hungarian politicians and editors then and later were greatly divided on schemes for broader economic intimacy—some sort of a customs union—between the Hapsburg Monarchy and imperial Germany. Certain economic specialists argued the advantage of securing easier access to the German market for Hungarian agricultural wares, but other voices—and they were the weightier—warned that the more efficient factories of Germany would strangle the budding industries of the kingdom, and Socialist theoreticians concurred.[27]

7.

If the press of Hungary was less afflicted by the gag of censorship than the papers of Austria—few foreigners of course were familiar with Magyar, the language of all

[26] Tisza to Francis Joseph, Nov. 7, 1916, *ÖM*, V, 417–420; Gustav Grátz and Richard Schüller, The *Economic Policy of Austria-Hungary During the War* (New Haven, 1929), pp. 13–25.
[27] Heinrich Herkner, "Die Stellung der Sozial-demokratie zur Wirtschaftlichen Annäherung Deutschlands und Österreich-Ungarns," *ÖR*, XLVII (1916), 121–124.

the politically significant newspapers with one exception
—it suffered severely from a chronic shortage of newsprint, and the deficiency was charged up against Austria,
the traditional supplier. In 1916 the government strictly
regulated the amount of space in papers to be allocated
to advertising and, indeed, the number of pages each
paper might print in a week. Information on the course of
the fighting was published in greater detail than was permitted in Austria and criticism on the management of
public affairs was in general more outspoken. The press
of wartime Hungary enjoyed in fact broader freedom
than it would know again for many a long year.

All the major political factions of the kingdom had their
journals, and *Pester Lloyd*, perhaps the best of them and
printed in the German language, was reputedly the
mouthpiece of the Ballplatz; representing financial and
business interests, *Pester Lloyd* consistently extolled the
virtues of alignment with Austria. In the Magyar language, *Budapesti Hirlap* (*Budapest News*) most fully con-
formed to western conceptions of serious journalism, and
its editors were imbued with the unquenchable conviction
that the safety and welfare of the kingdom of St. Stephen
depended upon the powerful German ally. ". . . the
Magyars are unswervingly loyal to the alliance with Germany," proclaimed a typical editorial leader (July 11,
1916), "the German Empire will always be able to count
upon the swords of those legendary heroes, who, together
with the Germans, are just now beating the Russians, the
French, and the English, and settling at the same time,
by themselves, the treacherous ally of yore [i.e. Italy]."

While *Az Ujság* (*The News*) customarily spoke the
mind of Tisza, the opinions of his more restrained adversaries were disseminated in *Az Est* (*The Evening*) and
Pesti Hirlap (*Pest News*), both of which were noted for
intensely Magyar chauvinism. Károlyi used the *Magyarország* (*Hungary*) of which he was the principal share-

holder, to spread his views, and *Világ*, edited by Jászi, served as a forum for democratic "radicals"; *Népszava* (*The Peoples' Voice*) was allowed rather surprising latitude in setting out the interpretations of Socialism, but the circulation was small.

Under the duress of war, the things of the mind and spirit in Hungary—never so active nor so fruitful as in Austria, experienced acute hardships. Among the novelists, Sigismund Móricz realistically painted the rigors and meanness of Hungarian village existence, the land-hungry peasantry, and mercenary landlords in *A Fáklya* (1917), translated into English as *The Torch* (1931), and Cécile Tormay, prized for her polished literary style and national enthusiasms, brought out *The Old House* (1915; English translation, 1921). Facets of wartime living (though published later) were appreciately portrayed by Francis Móra in *The Song of the Wheatfields* (English translation, 1930), betraying the impact of the war and post-war upon rural Hungary, and in *Siberian Garrison* (English translation, 1936), by Rodion Markovits, the autobiography of a Russian captive.

More faithfully, doubtless, than other Hungarian men of letters, the poets captured the alternating moods of national exhilaration and defeatism. Traditionalists Geza Gyoni and Alexander Endrödi, sincere and patriotic men, saluted the coming of war with rapturous fervor, but shortly employed their verse to describe the pathos of combat and its horrors. A second school, the lyricist Andrew Ady standing foremost, assailed the prevailing Hungarian social regime and the political status quo; a son of Transylvania gentry, Ady brought down on his head the charge of un-Hungarianism, to coin a term. Proudly cosmopolitan in his personal philosophy, he interpreted the war as an unmitigated catastrophe, not alone for his homeland, but for mankind everywhere; someone dubbed him the poet laureate of the Károlyist political interest. Responsibility for the involvement of Hungary in the conflict Ady attributed solely to the alignment with Austria and he flatly asserted ("In the Van of the Dead") that Hungarian troops were ordered to the most hazardous sectors of the battle lines by the Hapsburg high command.[28]

Two kindred spirits, Michael Babits and Frederick Karinthy, conceived of the fighting, bleeding, and dying as a national disaster, and the latter satirically approached problems of society in a version of *Gulliver* (1916). The best known Hungarian playwright, Francis Molnár, devoted his literary skills partly to military journalism, writing descriptive, reverently patriotic copy from army camp and battlefront; his dramatic productions of the war era (*Fashions for Men* and *Carnival*) were light, frothy, diverting, inconsequential. The prolific playwright and novelist, Francis Herczeg (of German stock) likewise toiled away as a warrior with words, editing a monthly review, *Hungarian Observer*, which expounded the interpretations of Tisza, particularly. As in Austria and Bohemia, the tercentenary of the death of Shakespeare was appropriately celebrated in Hungary under the direction of the Kisfaludy Society, which had taken as its special province the promotion of interest in the greatest of English men of letters; a learned commission set to work revising the Magyar translation of Shakespeare's writings, which had been made half a century before. Throughout the war the dramas of Shakespeare were regularly produced in the Hungarian National Theater—on one occasion, a presentation of *Hamlet* lasted more than six hours! [29]

The foremost Magyar composers, Béla Bartók and Zoltán Kodály, who had achieved world-wide renown for

[28] Watson Kirkconnell, "The Poetry of Ady," *Hungarian Review,* III (1936–37), 501–514.

[29] Charles Sebestyén, "The Cult of Shakespeare in Hungary," *Hungarian Review,* III (1936–37), 154–163.

collections of the folk-tunes of the Hungarian nationalities, added modestly to their reputations between 1914 and 1918. Bartók completed *The Wooden Prince*, a ballet, and an opera, *Prince Bluebeard's Castle*, and, for a concert to benefit war widows and orphans, Kodály prepared *Old Hungarian Soldiers' Songs* for orchestra. Their compatriot, Erno Dohnányi, conductor and pianist as well as composer, distinctly an internationalist in outlook, seems not to have produced any new music of significance.

8.

Compared with Austria, the government of Hungary had written a long record of blatant unenlightenment in dealing with national minorities—principally Rumanians, Slovaks, South Slavs. Among their intelligentsia, rigorous Magyarization combined with growing nationalist cults had encouraged active disaffection and fostered separatist sentiments; and yet with relatively little resistance soldiers of the several nationalities responded obediently to the call to arms.[30]

Mixing patriotic exhortations with little gestures to appease national susceptibilities, Tisza strove to ensure loyal cooperation in winning the war, and he proudly boasted that the pre-war bitterness among the minorities had been submerged in a sacred union to defend and preserve the common homeland. Under the life-or-death ordeal of war, the Prime Minister wrote, Hungary had shown herself to be the stout bulwark of the Dual Monarchy with all elements of the population cooperating; Ukrainians and Serbs of Hungary had proved more reliable than their relatives in Austria, and Slovaks were far more trustworthy than the Czechs. No revolutionary conspiracy comparable to that which emerged in Bohemia disturbed the internal peace of Hungary. An entry in the diary of a Hungarian

[30] Fürstenberg to Berlin, Dec. 12, 1914, no. 59, F.O. 553/288.

officer, captured while fighting the Italians, vividly illustrates the psychological confusion concerning patriotic allegiance that must have existed for many a thinking man. "They abuse me for not being a patriot," he jotted down. "I was born a Slovak. I passed my infancy in Vienna, my early youth in Bohemia, two years at Budapest, three years in Switzerland and then Paris—and after that a poor devil is expected to know what he really is and actually to be an Austrian patriot." [31]

The Rumanian-speaking minority of nearly three million in Transylvania and in the Banat of Temesvár (Timișoara) possessed peculiar importance due to the interest of the Bucharest government in the welfare and destiny of this folk. Irredentist feelings had grown acutely sensitive among the small, educated class of Hungarian Rumanians. Sporadic talk of revolt against Magyar lordship was heard with the coming of the war, and yet, as one Rumanian intellectual recorded, "Like slaves, we responded to the summons of our masters . . . " [32]

Some leaders of the Rumanians in Hungary appealed to their compatriots to support the war effort wholeheartedly in return for the benefits which citizenship in the Monarchy had afforded. Rumanian peasants in Hungary were undoubtedly, family for family, materially somewhat better off than their counterparts in the kingdom of Rumania—the Regat. Declared the Transylvanian politician, Alexander Vaida-Voevod, sturdy champion of the Rumanians of Hungary and in 1919 Prime Minister of Greater Rumania:

In our people and in our intellectuals there is a deep conviction that we owe our culture and our progress to the House of Hapsburg. It is deeply realized that the political

[31] James R. Rodd, *Social and Diplomatic Memories* (third series, London, 1925), pp. 277–8.
[32] Octavian C. Táslăuana, *With the Austrian Army in Galicia* (London, n.d. [1918]), pp. 5–25.

struggle between Magyars and Roumanians can only be considered as a dissension among brothers, all the more so since in view of the common danger of annihilation by Russia both peoples are welded into one by the unbreakable ties of common vital interests, now and evermore.[33]

No one had surpassed the Hungarian sociologist and publicist, Oscar Jászi, in condemnation of the iniquities of Magyarization and in advocacy of humane policies toward the nationalities, and yet he warmly praised the Rumanian minority for its response to the demands of the war. Tisza understood that it was hopeless to try to appease passionate partisans of the union of the Rumanian-peopled regions with the Regat, but time and again he protested energetically to the military authorities because of the arbitrary arrest of Hungarian Rumanians on suspicion of traitorous activity; on the other hand, he recurrently complained against the appointment of Rumanian-speaking officers to key posts on army staffs.

Urgently pressed by the Berlin government and by King Carol I of Rumania, Tisza consented to make concessions to the Rumanian element, which might strengthen the pro-Central Power forces in the Regat, but he had to proceed cautiously lest other national communities in Hungary should set up a clamor for comparable rights.[34] After private consultations in the autumn of 1914 with John Metianu, metropolitan of the Rumanian Orthodox Church, Tisza promised broader rights to the Rumanian minority in matters of schools, of the language of officials, of voting, and also amnesty for political exiles. While moderately-minded Hungarian Rumanians expressed satisfaction over these pledges, staunch irredentists both in Hungary and in the Regat felt that not enough had been promised and they doubted whether the concessions

[33] Quoted in Paul Teleki, *The Evolution of Hungary* (New York, 1923), pp. 153–154.
[34] Tschirschky to Ballplatz, Sept. 21, 1914, no. 418. F.O. 553/328.

would in fact be carried out; even ex-Prime Minister Alexander Marghiloman of Rumania, an exponent of neutralism, was disappointed. Recommendations by meddlesome officials of Germany that Transylvania should be accorded home-rule infuriated Tisza, for autonomy might well stimulate secessionist currents, and no more acceptable was a program of reforms for Transylvania drawn up by the Hapsburgophile Dr. Aurel Popovici, prescribing greater freedom for Rumanian schools and churches and changes in local and central administration.[35]

A roving trouble-shooter of imperial Germany, Matthias Erzeberger, after conferring with Christian Socialist and Transylvanian personalities in Vienna, besought Tisza in June, 1915, to placate the cabinet of Bucharest by varied concessions to the Rumanians. He proposed, for instance, that small parcels of land along the frontier should be ceded to Rumania, and that promises to improve the lot of Hungarian Rumanians should be extended; specifically, the Rumanian language should be used more extensively in administration, more Rumanian schools should be authorized, and the electoral law should be revised so as to ensure the return of some thirty Rumanian-speaking deputies to the Budapest parliament. But Tisza thought that too much had already been promised to the Rumanian minority, and he felt that no matter what was done—or left undone—the Bucharest government would not abandon the posture of neutrality.[36]

From the German Embassy in Bucharest, dispatches to Berlin warned and warned again that press muzzling in Transylvania and imprisonment of clergy and other natural leaders there were harming the cause of the Central Empires in Rumania, furnishing grist to the mills of the Entente interventionists. By means of public meetings

[35] Tschirschky to Ballplatz, Oct. 5, 1914, no. 1089, and Tisza to Tschirschky, Oct. 6, 1914, F.O. 553/330. On Popovici, see May, *Haps burg Monarchy*, pp. 481–482.
[36] Epstein, *Erzberger*, pp. 140–141; Funder, *op. cit.*, pp. 533–534.

and the press, refugees from Transylvania who fled to the Regat, notably the poet Octavian Goga and Father Vasil Lucaciu, once jailed in Hungary for sedition, nourished sentiments favorable to war upon the Hapsburg Monarchy.

Tisza obstinately refused to read the signs of the times. True enough, Rumanians guilty of espionage had been arrested, but the overwhelming mass of this folk was faithfully upholding the interests of the crown of St. Stephen, and he hotly repudiated assertions that youths from the Rumanian minority were called up for military duty in higher proportion than men of other national communities and were stationed at the most perilous positions on the fighting fronts; in his judgment, Rumanians were inferior as soldiers and their death toll correspondingly lower than that of Magyars, Slovaks, and others.[37]

After Rumania declared war in August, 1916, and her armies advanced into Transylvania, the Rumanian National party of Hungary issued a manifesto denouncing the invaders and proclaiming that "several millions of Rumanians [in Hungary] live loyally and in satisfactory conditions . . . they well know how to defend the Fatherland and the throne of the King against every enemy . . . " The response in Transylvania to the invasion of soldiers from the Regat was as divided and as confusing as the intermingling of tongues and of political sympathies in the province; only the dogmatist can say confidently whether the politically articulate inclined more heavily to union with the kingdom of Rumania or against it.

An interesting and not uninstructive controversy involving the Rumanians of Hungary broke out between Jászi and Károlyi and Company. In a magazine article Jászi rebuked the Károlyi set for abusive remarks about the Rumanian minority and once more he assailed the government in Budapest for the unenlightened treatment

[37] Tisza to Czermin, Jan. 10, 1916, ÖM, IV, 362–364.

meted out to that people. Whereupon the Károlyi mouthpiece *Magyaroszág* thundered that " . . . constant charges
made by a Magyar of the inhuman oppression of non-
Magyars can be used to incite the Rumanians to hatred
against the Magyar nation . . . " and were detrimental to
the Magyar reputation in foreign lands. "It is a sad fact,"
the paper commented, "that among . . . our foreign
slanderers the Magyar Oszkar Jászi has taken the place
of the English Scotus Viator [R. W. Seton-Watson]," In
spite of this vituperative exchange, before many months
had rolled away Károlyi and Jászi were working in
double harness.[38]

"What is really needed," Jászi thought, "is that in those
states in which races [sic] speaking different languages
are living side by side, a more democratic and humane
policy should in the future be adopted towards these
various nationalities," and he ridiculed "the crazy belief
that the present war can solve all the complicated questions of nationality." His blueprint for reasonable tranquillity in a multinationality state called for democratiza-
tion of political and social affairs, security for the fundamental interests of national groupings, schools and law
courts included, and freedom for each national community
to cultivate its own language and culture.[39]

9.

South Slavs, Croats, and Serbs in Hungary, as in Aus-
tria, were found in more than one administrative area.
From the constitutional point of view, the kingdom of
Croatia, though part of the lands of the crown of St.
Stephen, possessed a unique status, and possessed a
limited measure of self-government. Croatia boasted an

[38] *Everyman* (London), Nov. 10, 1916.
[39] G. Lowes Dickinson, *et. al., Problems of the International Settlement* (London, 1918), pp. 10–11.

assembly (Sabor) of its own which exercised limited authority over certain regional affairs and sent representatives to both houses of the Budapest parliament; the royal governor (or ban) was appointed by the crown on recommendation of the Hungarian ministry. Approximately ninety per cent of the inhabitants of Croatia spoke Serbo-Croat, the census of 1910 showing 1,630,354 Croats and 644,955 Serbs; upwards of 400,000 more Serbs and half as many Croats, almost all of them peasants, dwelt in the southern and western sections of Hungary proper. Politically active Serbs, adherents of the Orthodox Church, tended to sympathize with the Yugoslav ideal. Unsure of the trustworthiness of Serb-speaking soldiers when war came, Hapsburg military authorities posted many to labor battalions and imprisoned others, which incensed Tisza who thought persuasive evidence of disloyalty had not been produced.

Certitude concerning Croat attitudes on the war is quite out of the question, though at the beginning of the struggle a good deal of martial enthusiasm prevailed. Streets of Agram (Zagreb), the Croatian capital city, resounded with Austrophile demonstrations and raucous denunciations of Serbia and the Serbs; in the local assembly, deputies belonging to the small, pro-Hapsburg Frank party shouted, "Honor the memory of the [late] Heir-Apparent!" "Down with the Serbs!" The outstanding personality of the Croat Peasant party, Stjepan Radić, warmly applauded the Austrian declaration of war upon Serbia.

On the other side, Croatian enemies of the Monarchy or of the attachment to Hungary manifested pro-Entente sympathies, which led local authorities to suspend certain newspapers and to order many arrests and some executions. Presently, however, Russian military reverses and knowledge of the pledges of Dalmatian territory under which Italy had entered the war tended to switch the pendulum of sentiment against the Entente. Since stocks of food were better in Croatia than in adjoining South Slav areas, smuggling flourished until Hungarian officials jacked up border controls; after that, thousands of South Slav children in famine districts were brought into Croatia and cared for until the end of hostilities.[40]

Croatian literary men offer little help on the state of feeling about the war. Political views were absent from the lyrical verse of Vladimir Nazor and from the writings of Milan Begović, dramatist; in 1922, a shrill, satirical exposé of the Hapsburg military machine and its wartime impact upon ordinary civilians came from the pen of Miroslav Krleža (*Hrvatsk; Bog Mars*). Historically, soldiers recruited in Croatia had distinguished themselves for fidelity to the House of Hapsburg, and for many a Croat aversion to the Serbs was quickened by the conviction that youths of Serbian stock had assassinated the Archduke Francis Ferdinand precisely because he was believed to desire the creation of a Great Croat state, including Dalmatia and Bosnia-Herzegovina, as a third partner in the Hapsburg Monarchy.[41]

From start to finish, Croatian soldiers, especially men from the harsh Lika district, lying between the Sava River and the Adriatic, fought well against the kingdom of Serbia; they were keenly humiliated by the lickings administered to Hapsburg arms by the forces of Serbia and thirsted for revenge, which in 1915 they helped to achieve. Croatian troops likewise wrote a notable record

---

[40] Von einem Kroatischen Politiker, "Die Kroaten und der Krieg," *ÖR*, XLI (1914), 9–12; Jerome Jareb (ed.), "Leroy King's Reports from Croatia," *Journal of Croatian Studies* I (1960), 93–101, 106–108. Cf. Rudolf Kiszling, *Die Kroaten* (Graz, 1956), pp. 97–103. An American who had resided in Croatia for more than a year reported little zest for the war. New York *Times*, Dec. 23, 1914.

[41] Stanko Guldescu, "The Background of the Croatian Independence Movement," *South Atlantic Quarterly*, LVI (1957), 316–317. It seemed to some Croats that the murder of King Alexander of Yugoslavia at Marseilles in 1934 was merited punishment for the death of the Hapsburg heir-presumptive in 1914. *ibid*. See, Zeman, *op. cit.*, pp. 54–62.

in fighting Italians and Rumanians, and from Croatia came two of the ablest Hapsburg commanders, General (later Field Marshal) Svetozar Boroević and Stephan Sarkotić, level-headed Austrian commandant in Bosnia.

In June of 1915 the Croatian assembly at Agram (Zagreb) convened for the first time in the war era. Several deputies suspected of disloyalty, who in spite of parliamentary immunity had been interned, were now set free. Vice-President Dr. Pero Magdić declared that the Croats were ready for heavy sacrifices to defend areas inhabited by Croats and Slovenes against treacherous and covetous Italy, and he was sure that after the war all Croats would be politically unified; the assembly dispatched a telegram to Francis Joseph in fact requesting a promise to that effect. These gestures kicked up a lively controversy in the Hungarian parliament where J. Rakovsky of the Independence party indignantly protested against the very conception of a free Croatia, which would incorporate, presumably, Bosnia, Dalmatia, Istria, and part of Carinthia. Tisza endeavored to pour oil on the troubled waters by reminding the deputies that Croatia belonged in indissoluble union to Hungary.

The Croatian assembly as a body neglected to adopt a specific declaration of loyalty to the Hapsburg crown or even to pass a general resolution pledging cooperation in the prosecution of the war, and individual deputies made no effort to conceal their Yugoslav convictions. Articles in newspapers of Dalmatia, an Austrian province, recommending the formation of a united South Slav state under the Hapsburg scepter profoundly angered Tisza, who demanded that the censorship should clamp down on stories of that character.[42]

Following the conquest of Serbia and Montenegro in

[42] Tisza to Stügkh, Sept. 18, 1915, *ÖM*, IV, 163–164; consult, Josef Brauner, "Bosnien und Herzegovina," *BM*, VII (1929), 313–344, esp. 330.

1915, discussion flared up anew in Hapsburg political circles on ways and means of solving the South Slav problem constructively. Not a little support emerged in Vienna for a Yugoslav state as a third member of the Hapsburg complex, but Hungarian sentiment, personified by Tisza, once more repulsed trialism as an old and illusory quackery. Only fragments of the Serbian frontier having strategic importance, the Prime Minister contended, should be annexed, though the remainder of the country, not awarded to Bulgaria or to Albania, might be loosely attached to the Dual Monarchy economically.[43] Before long he was protesting, as was his habit, that Hungarian interests were being disregarded by the Hapsburg military government of Serbia and Montenegro and that policies were being pursued there on the hypothesis that one day these conquered lands would be integrated with the Monarchy in some fashion; on his insistence no inconsiderable revisions in military administration were effected. Recurrent gossip of backing in Vienna for a Croatian state to embrace South Slavs generally, provoked fierce condemnation by the Magyar statesman.[44]

10.

On the unwavering loyalty of one linguistic minority, the Germans, the government in Budapest could rely without reservation, in spite of a good deal of friction before the war. Numbering over 1,000,000 and dispersed widely, the German-speaking element resided chiefly in Transylvania (Saxons), in the Banat of Temesvár (Swabians), and in the extreme west—the Burgenland. Descended from German immigrants of six centuries and more earlier, the Saxons had contrived to preserve their

[43] Tisza to Burián, Dec. 30, 1915, ÖM, IV, 336–345.
[44] Tisza to Archduke Friedrich, May 25, July 14, 1916, ÖM, V, 8–19, 22–24.

German heritage amazingly well—in the purity of the language, attachment to the creed of Luther, and in inherited folkways. Ties with imperial Germany were varied and extensive; a visitor to Brassó (Kronstadt) in Transylvania might readily have imagined that he had landed in a community of southern Germany itself. Given the traditions, it was not unusual that this German element rested its faith for ultimate victory in the war squarely upon the empire of William II. Men of German speech had made their way into important positions in the armed forces of the Monarchy, where their familiarity with the German language was an invaluable asset; someone has remarked that the affluent Saxon "looked down his social nose on the lower orders from an angle at least as near the vertical as the impoverished great-grandson of a historic noble family." [45] That pride was reflected in the military record of the Germans in Hungary, second to none among the peoples of the multinationality realm, and they devised admirable welfare programs to meet the special social needs thrown up by the war. Upon the Rumanian invasion of Transylvania, the staff of the principal German-language newspaper the *Siebenbürgisch Deutscher Tagblatt,* moved to the quarters of *Pester Lloyd* in Budapest and continued operations. [46]

In the northern counties of Hungary lived just about two million Slovaks whose cultural peculiarities had suffered greatly from relentless Magyarizing agencies. Except for a limited coterie of intelligentsia, active Slovak participation in public affairs was small, and it is easy to develop an exaggerated image of the popularity of the movement for the merger of the Slovaks with their Czech neighbors; that ideal, seemingly, kindled far more enthusiasm among Slovak civilians and soldiers abroad, whether

[45] Carlile A. Macartney, *A History of Hungary, 1929–1945* (2 parts, New York, 1956), Part one, p. 17. The identification of the Germans with the interests of Hungary found poetic expression in a volume, *Hände Weg,* edited by Richard Huss (Debreczen, 1917).

[46] Adolf Höhr, *Siebenbürger Sachsen im Weltkrieg* (Vienna, 1916).

in Europe or emigrants in the United States, than among the unpolitical townsfolk and peasantry inside Hungary. It may be recalled that the French educated Slovak scientist, Milan Štefánik, an officer in the army of the Third Republic, belonged to the policymaking circle of the Czechoslovak exiles. Until the last stage of the war the most respected Czechophile at home, Dr. Milan Hodža, a deputy in the Hungarian parliament after 1905, one day to become prime minister of Czechoslovakia, preferred to work for Slovak autonomy within Hungary rather than to seek unity with the Czechs. Early in the war his newspaper, *Slovenský Dennik* was suspended, and Hodža was called up for military service and assigned to a desk job in Vienna which, necessarily, restricted his political activity. Certain anti-Magyar Slovak intellectuals were arrested, as was the fate of a lawyer, Janko Jesenský, who passed from prison into the army, and was captured on the Russian front; when it was learned that he had translated works of the Russian poet, Alexander Pushkin into the Slovak language, Jesenský was allowed virtual freedom and he became vice-president of the Czechoslovak patriot committee that was set up in Russia.[47]

Even less politically conscious than the Slovaks was the fragment of the Ukrainian national community, about five hundred thousand, who were Hungarian citizens. Illiterate and backward, for the most part, this folk had been subjected to effective Magyarization and manifested little evidence of political discontent. Equally, the small colony of Italians in Hungary, principally in and about the port of Fiume (Rijeka), presented no special problem; as Tisza observed, if the Italians were intelligently handled, even in such small things as street names in Fiume, they would match the most patriotic Magyars in allegiance to the crown of St. Stephen.

[47] The life and labor of Slovak villagers under Magyar administration during the war have been related with color and insight by the Slovak novelist, Milan Urban, *Živý Bič* (1927, translated as *Living Whip*).

12. Two Monarchs

ON THE LAST AFTERNOON OF NOVEMBER, 1916, THE MASSIVE portal of Vienna's Gothic Cathedral of St. Stephen swung wide so that the corpse of venerable Emperor-King Francis Joseph might pass through on the way to its final resting place in the nearby Church of the Capuchins—in the crowded crypt of the most eminent Austrian Hapsburgs. Emerging from the Cathedral, three close relatives of the deceased ruler took their designated places behind the casket, the new monarch Charles on one side, in the uniform of a Field Marshal, his consort Zita, clothed in conventional black on the other, and between them the four-year-old Crown Prince Otto, who presumably would one day reign over the strangest and most picturesque realm on the face of Europe. A mourning throng followed —a hundred or so royalties, among them Tsar Ferdinand of Bulgaria and the Crown Prince of Prussia; Emperor William II, though in Vienna, was prevented by illness from participating in the last rites for the late sovereign. Then came members of the Hapsburg archducal clan, the

422

children of Archduke Francis Ferdinand in the company, diplomatic representatives, and leading nobles of the realm.[1]

Funeral obsequies to the smallest detail on the cortége, requiem mass, and burial honored the impressive, conventional pageantry of Hapsburg tradition; the wrinkled old stickler for form, Prince Alfred Montenuovo, grand master of the court, saw to the arrangements. For six days, the body of the Emperor, dressed in a marshal's parade uniform and resting in a black coffin, gold embroidered, had lain in state at Schönbrunn palace; round the casket, lighted candles were set, a receptacle of holy water, and at the foot, a crucifix. By turns priests, court servants, political celebrities, such as the American ambassador and his wife, had offered prayers at the imperial bier, but the general public was debarred.

In the evening of November 27, the casket was hauled away to the parish chapel in the ancient Hofburg in the heart of Vienna. Eight coal-black horses, their hoofs muffled with rubber shoes, pulled a heavy, creaking hearse, preceded, flanked, and followed by swarms of mounted torchbearers, and marching in the cavalcade of death were warriors with medieval weapons and costumes, modern soldiers and their equipment, ministers of state and imposing dignitaries in exotic carriages. Curious Viennese in the thousands silently watched along the four-mile journey from Schönbrunn to the Hofburg or knelt on wet pavements, as if oblivious of the pneumonia weather. At appointed periods over the next three days, anyone might pass by the coffin; each morning solemn masses proceeded without halt, and twice daily church bells of Vienna rang out in melancholy lament for hours. On Thursday, the 30th, the funeral cortége moved down

---

[1] George Schreiner, "Tragic Life and Death of Franz Josef," *Current History*, XXI (1924), 214–219—an eye-witness account by an American reporter.

Kärntnerstrasse, Fifth Avenue of the Hapsburg capital, to the crowded Cathedral, where a stately, though abbreviated service of consecration was conducted, and at last to the Capuchin sanctuary. Again great throngs of onlookers, civilians and men in uniform, reverently observed the procession; the steep toll of war casualties, intensifying physical hardships, and the haunting specter of the unknown future chilled the emotions of spectators.

For the ordinary onlooker, Francis Joseph may well have seemed hardly more than a legend, a lonely old gentleman, with gray whiskers parted in the middle, handsome in presence, who sat in Schönbrunn, as a folk melody expressed it, weighed down by the staggering burdens of the imperial and royal crowns. Portraits of the patriarchal sovereign, hanging in homes and in every schoolroom hard by a crucifix, had, to be sure, stamped an indelible image upon memories. For three solid generations and more the birthday of Francis Joseph had annually been celebrated with feasting and avowals of affection, and an anthem in his honor was learned by heart and sung on every suitable occasion. Tradition had created a vision of Francis Joseph as the "Emperor of Peace," enshrined in the verse of Friedrich Moser:

> Wer kennt den Friedenskaiser nicht?
> Der Österreich regiert,
> Der vierundachtzig Jahre zählt,
> Das Szepter heut noch führt.
> Franz Josef ist's, der greise Mann,
> Der Ruh' den Völkern bot.
> Man hat ihn sechs Jahrzehnte schon
> Bedacht mit Mord und Tod.[2]

At the Church of the Capuchins, Montenuovo, obedient to ancient ritual, advanced to the door and, after banging

[2] Cf. "Fritz Kreisler's Tribute to his Emperor," New York *Times*, Dec. 13, 1916.

on it with a staff, demanded admission. From within the Guardian Father, as though taken unawares, inquired in deep, sepulchral tones:

"Who is there?"
"His Majesty, the most sovereign Emperor,
Francis Joseph."
"I know him not."
"The Emperor of Austria and the Apostolic King of
Hungary."
"I know him not."

After a third knock on the church door, the Guardian Father asked,

"Who demands to enter?"
"A man of sin, our brother Francis Joseph."

Thereupon the door was gently opened and the coffin was carried to the subterranean crypt. After the lid of the coffin had been lifted, the Father Guardian, asked whether he recognized the body, answered affirmatively. The lid dropped and was locked with two keys to be guarded forever by the Capuchin brothers.

2.

If it be true, as the seventeenth-century English jurist John Selden put it, that "a king is a thing men have made for their own sakes, for quietness' sake," then Emperor-King Francis Joseph stood well in his calling, for in his last decades his very being somewhat attenuated the asperities and animosities of peoples in the multinationality realm. The old monarch seemed indeed to be, like Dr. Watson, "the one fixed point in a changing world." Not only was his person the focal objective of political loyalties, for Austrogerman and Magyar, for Slav and

Latin, but he embodied the common concern for law and order. Symbol of unity and dynastic patriotism, Francis Joseph had lent a special inspiration to the realm of many tongues, and to speak critically of him in the open was akin to sacrilege. Well into the war period he remained very much alive, notwithstanding a crude Viennese *bon mot* to the effect that he had died, but did not know it.

Throughout the ordeal of war the Emperor resided at cherished Schönbrunn, surrounded by his immediate family and an entourage of aristocratic courtiers. There he had been born; there he had played at the feet of Emperor Francis I, father-in-law of the first Napoleon; there he had carried on a good deal of official business and weathered personal vicissitudes in an unending stream; there at last he had found peace. Too old to indulge in his favorite relaxation of hunting, he chose not even to go on holiday to beloved Ischl and its encircling mountains of which he was so fond. The new heir-apparent Charles and his flourishing household were established part of the time in a wing of Schönbrunn, and the Emperor often called to play with the children or to chat. He had not relished his own son Rudolph, nor the Archduke Francis Ferdinand, but he developed a real liking, it appears, for the youthful Charles. "I think very well of Charles," he was heard to remark shortly before his death; "He tells me his opinion frankly, but he knows how to obey when I have made up my mind." And yet the new Crown Prince, like his predecessors, was denied any direct share in large public decisions; he was forbidden to create a personal secretariat as Francis Ferdinand had done, though senior state servants were instructed to acquaint him with the work of their departments.

Ever welcome at the imperial chateau was Frau Katharina Schratt, living in a villa just beyond the palace grounds, whom the Emperor had first come to admire when she was the reigning beauty of Vienna theatrical society. A genial and vivacious matron, younger by a generation than the monarch, though in her sixties now, she maintained an intimately discreet companionship with him to the end. While his body lay on the simple iron bed of a soldier, Emperor Charles ushered her in and she placed two roses in the hands of her dead friend; afterwards, she kept her lips tightly sealed.

Throughout the war years, as had long been his custom, Francis Joseph methodically plowed his way daily through a mass of routine business, now and then interrupting his isolation by visiting veterans in hospitals and chatting with wounded soldiers. From time to time he was waited upon by an official celebrity or a delegation of his subjects; in September, 1915, for instance, a contingent of Magyars and Croats filling two-hundred and fifty equipages called to pay respects to their sovereign, who listened to a rose-colored portrayal of the future of the realm by Count Tisza. His spirit was cheered by a visit of William II of Germany, soon after Serbia had been militarily thrashed, and he grew quite fond of the ever-victorious German commander August von Mackensen. Shortly before he died and despite grave illness, he received Burián and Conrad in lengthy audiences, and on his very last day he heard a three-quarter hour survey of military successes and prospects from the lips of the commander-in-chief, the Archduke Friedrich.

The Emperor followed the course of the fighting with avid interest and in detail, though he took no part in strategic decisions or otherwise meddled with the conduct of the war. The early disasters at the hands of Russia and of redoubtable Serbia, alike rained cruel blows upon him, and the Brusilov offensive of 1916, coming simultaneously with the failure of the Austrian thrust out of the Tyrol, cast the old gentleman into deep pessimism; then came the disturbing word that faithless Rumania had marched triumphantly into Transylvania, but Francis

Joseph went to his rest in the knowledge that the invasion had been repulsed and that the conquest of Rumania had fairly begun. Regarding Conrad as "clever but not wise," the Emperor more than once considered demoting him from the post of chief of staff but never did so, though he consented to unity of command with Germany, which somewhat diminished the prestige of Conrad. That decision Francis Joseph came to reluctantly, for his aversion to Prussia, springing partly from military defeat in 1866, had not been wholly effaced and he disliked certain nasty practices resorted to by the German ally in waging war. Proud of his Hapsburg lineage, almost unbelievably so, he never ceased to think of himself as the first of German princes and of the Hohenzollerns as parvenus by comparison.

It seems evident that after the first month or so of the fighting, the Emperor harbored no illusions concerning the eventual outcome of the contest. "The struggle is beyond our strength," he mourned in the second year of the war; and again in July of 1916, he remarked, "Things are going badly with us; perhaps worse than we suspect; the starving people can't stand much more. It remains to be seen whether and how we shall get through next winter. I mean to end the war next spring, whatever happens. I can't let my realm go to hopeless ruin." Whatever his innermost convictions, publicly this human symbol of imperial unity never ceased to strum the victory chord; on the 1916 anniversary of the outbreak of war, he lauded "our glorious allies, heroically resisting the constantly renewed attacks of superior forces," and he praised the civilian populations of the Monarchy for their unflagging contribution to an eventual and enduring peace. Victory, he proclaimed reassuringly, would soon come to rest on the banners of the Central Empires.

Profoundly hurt by the assassination of Prime Minister Stürgkh, the last major political act of the Emperor was to appoint Koerber as first minister of Austria. At an interview with him, the monarch grew excited over reports of renewed friction between the Hapsburg and German general staffs and of squabbling over the destiny of the Russian Poles. When Koerber disclosed information on political disaffection, gathering mass privations and the like, such as Stürgkh had deliberately tried to conceal, Francis Joseph is said to have observed, "If that is the case we must seek peace without taking my ally into consideration at all."

Throughout his long reign, Francis Joseph was extremely conservative, displayed a high sense of public duty, and an incredible command of the minutiae of state business. To the last, he shouldered his heavy tasks conscientiously and with diligence, never deviating from his code of courtesy and dignity.[3] Respectable and respected he certainly was, with a fair share of lovable qualities, though endowed with an unimaginative and rather narrow intellect. Feeling himself a father responsible for the well-being of his large and quarrelsome family, accepting as unchallengeable dogma the archaic conception of the divine right of monarchs to rule, he considered himself accountable to the Almighty alone. "The state of monarchy is the supremest thing upon earth; for kings are not only God's lieutenants upon earth and sit upon God's throne, but even by God himself they are called gods." So James I of England had explained matters in 1610; so devoutly Francis Joseph believed to the hour of his death.

Confronting him at every turn were awesome dilemmas that crop up in any and every multinationality political structure: How could diverse peoples be ruled by means of a common administration and laws? How could con-

[3] Eduard Steinitz (ed.), *Erinnerungen an Franz Joseph I* (Berlin, 1931), revealing vignettes by functionaries around the throne; Heinrich von Srbik, *Aus Österreichs Vergangenheit* (Salzburg, 1949), pp. 221–241.

flicting aspirations of the nationalities be reconciled without utterly destroying the imperial fabric? How, in a word, could the motto of the ruler, *"Viribus Unitis,"* be translated into political effectiveness? Seldom fully candid with his principal counsellors, whom he selected and dismissed to the end, the Emperor eschewed schematic theories on the management of state affairs. The tradition of *fortwursteln,* of jogging along, of piecemeal concessions, of muddling through somehow had taken firmer root in the Hapsburg Monarchy than in some other states, though too much can be read into the interpretation that when the hand of Francis Joseph was removed the machinery of government "ran down and was utterly destroyed."

3.

On November 18, 1916, it became apparent that death would not long be postponed. The Emperor ate sparingly, drank a little wine, smoked his customary cigar, and toiled away on public papers at his desk in an old blue uniform. On the 21st, he rose early as a matter of habit and set about his daily chores, but growing fatigued in a few hours and gasping for breath, he was placed in bed. "Wake me at 4:30 as usual," he called to his valet. "I am not finished with my work." Falling into a coma, he passed away about nine in the evening.[4] His last will and testament bequeathed the bulk of his private fortune to agencies to assist invalid soldiers, to charity, and the remainder to two daughters and their families. Mayor Weiskirchner of Vienna laid plans for a worthy memorial to the Emperor in the form of a statue to be placed before either the Votivkirche or the City Hall, but the project never materialized.

It is an intriguing exercise, susceptible to wide and

[4] Egon C. Corti and Hans Sokol, *Der Alte Kaiser* (Graz, 1955), pp. 463–469.

diverting ramifications, to speculate on the trend the stream of history would have taken if Francis Joseph had passed away upon reaching the scriptural three score years and ten, instead of lingering beyond his eighty-sixth birthday—four years longer than Queen-Empress Victoria. Did he obtain the crown too early and wear it too long? If he had been so inclined, he might have persuaded workaday policymakers that the perdurance of the realm necessitated drastic constitutional changes, though he understood that a program of that order would invite the stubborn, if not the invincible, resistance of the Magyar ruling caste. As a second glaring sin of omission, he neglected to use his exalted station and his immense personal prestige to enlarge the scope and responsibilities of the parliaments in Vienna and Budapest.

How, in fact, did contemporaries appraise the ruler and his reign? An editorial leader in the Socialist daily of Vienna observed,

He was not one of those great men that lead humanity along new ways or "fashion fate" according to their own desire . . . In such a conglomerate state as ours, monarchical power is a thing of great weight. A long reign has something cohesive about it, independent of the sovereign's personality and based on habit only. The long duration of the Emperor's reign created a feeling of stability in the State and his death is thus a wrench, a fall, a sudden awakening . . .

Estimating Francis Joseph soberly and disinterestedly, we may say that if he followed historic necessities at a considerable distance and certainly never anticipated them, he did not exert himself to resist them especially. A historian might tax him with laxity and hesitation, but not with obstinacy. True, the democratic idea that tends to lessen the power of monarchs is so modest and timid in Austria that there was no question of serious encroachments for the crown to resist.[5]

[5] AZ, Nov. 22, 1916.

For the London *Times,* H. Wickham Steed, composed a long, somewhat bilious estimate of the Emperor, which was published only in an abridged version. Conceding that he had been "a great figure on the stage of the world," and no "shadow-king," Steed denied Francis Joseph the title of a great statesman, or even of a great man, simply "a great personality." He had shown "unflinching constancy" in time of peril and disaster, and "asserted his prerogatives with inflexible firmness"; naturally kind-hearted and a lover of little children, he had nonetheless dealt mercilessly with erring or unfortunate ministers. His "simplicity and humor, unaffected *bonhomie,* love of gossip and cards" proved that he was "a true Hapsburg and a true child of Vienna." "Beyond his devotion to the dynasty and his desire to transmit its possessions undiminished to his successor," Steed supposed, "he seems to have had no positive purpose." [6]

Francis Joseph's "greatest sin was that he was a Hapsburg," commented the Milan *Corriere della Sera* delphically. From a more remote coign of vantage, an American editor thought that the Emperor was "perhaps more concerned for the dignity, position, and future of his house than for the welfare of his subjects." The writer envisaged the change in monarchs as having important possibilities "at no distant time," though without immediate bearing upon the war.[7] As might be expected, the Czech Masaryk painted a harsh, distinctly propagandistic portrait of the ruler to whom he had renounced allegiance. He wrote:

Ever since his accession, Francis Joseph has been blinded, by the inveterate imperialism of the House of Hapsburg, and this infatuation makes him responsible for the present war. Defeated twice by the Russians and even by the despised Serbians, the army of Francis Joseph surrendered to the

[6] London *Times,* Nov. 23, 1916; see, Hanak, *op. cit.,* pp. 212–213.
[7] New York *Times,* Nov. 22, 1916.

Prussian generals and he himself became the merest vassal of Berlin . . . He was neither kind nor generous, nor was he ever noble, reliable or true, however the paid eulogist may insist upon such qualities . . . Not even the pungent phrases of a Tacitus could do justice the theme of Hapsburg degeneration . . .

Over in Prague, by way of contrast, the eminent Czech historian, Josef Pekař, praised the late sovereign for "the loving care" with which he had followed the progress of the Czech nation. A not unsuitable epitaph for Francis Joseph was penned by Lady Walburga Paget, who learned to know the lonely monarch while her husband was British ambassador at the court in Vienna. "He was a great gentleman, kind, generous and sincere as far as a very weak man can be so. His life was one of continued and conscientious labor for what he conceived to be the good of his Empire, and he was most beloved by his subjects. His patience was without end and his resignation to the will of God entire. R. I. P." [8]

4.

For many a younger, progressively minded citizen of the Hapsburg realm, the accession of Emperor-King Charles resembled the coming of spring after a long winter, the sunrise after the dark of night. "With our young king," remarked Károlyi's *Magyarország*, "the younger generation succeeds to the throne, and where should hope rest if not with it?" An aspiring poet welcomed him with:

> Wir grüssen dich, junger Habsburgersohn,
> Wir neigen uns tief vor deinen Thron!

[8] *The New Europe*, I (1916), 201; Zeman, *op. cit.*, p. 99; Lady Walburga Paget, "The Lonely Emperor," *Nineteenth Century*, LXXXII (1917), 1171–1179, esp. 1179.

Das Glück ist dir wohlgesinnt,
Das nur Stolze und Junge nimmt,
Es hat dich der Sturm in den Arm
    genommen,
Du hast den Thron im Krieg übernommen,
Du warst in dem Sattel mit einen
    Sprung,
Denn du bist jung!
Die Glocken, sie hatten zum
    Sturme geklungen,
Da hast dir schon einmal den
    Erbfeind bezwungen,
So führ uns auch weiter in
    diesem Krieg
Den Weg zum Sieg! [9]

Immediately upon becoming monarch, Charles I issued a proclamation extolling the virtues and achievements of his august predecessor and promising the war-weary population to do everything he could "to put an end to the horrors and sacrifices of the war at the earliest possible moment, and to restore the sadly missed blessings of peace to my peoples." The assumption that the new sovereign wished hostilities to terminate quickly gained globe-wide currency—and so did rumors that he was transferring family jewels and securities to neutral countries.

In the opinion of Professor Louis Eisenmann, one of the most knowledgeable French experts on the Monarchy, Austria-Hungary consisted only of the dynasty and the aristocracy. Of the new rulers he wrote, "a young couple, without great intelligence, without merit, . . . who are overwhelmed by a heavy inheritance of crime and error," while "the nobility, amounting at most to a hundred families, professed no nationality, no fatherland, and was genuinely cosmopolitan." More than two years before Charles' accession, the American ambassador in Vienna

[9] *NFP*, Dec. 24, 1916.

had sympathetically appraised him as having "certain talents that are requisite for rulership," and capable of taking up "the responsibilities of continuing the work of his great-uncle . . . The criticism that one hears most often is that he is immature and unskilled in dealing with affairs of great importance."

True enough, Francis Joseph had come to the throne when he was only eighteen, but, as Count Berchtold pointed out, "It was then a different Austria . . ." and he might have observed also, "a very different Europe and world!" The American ambassador reported that Charles had been "thoroughly schooled as a soldier and for years performed his duty as an officer expecting and receiving no favor." Concerning the Crown Princess Zita, he commented that she was "a superior person in many ways. Her mentality and charm of manner are recognized by all who know her. Her command of languages is equal to that of her husband. Both speak perfect German, French, and English, while Italian is the Archduchess' mother tongue. Their home life is simple and domestic in an unusual degree. . . ."[10]

Shortly before he became sovereign, Charles let it be known that he would spend only the bare minimum of time and energy on paper work, and would concentrate on familiarizing himself more thoroughly with the Monarchy and its peoples—"all sorts of men." In fact he did precisely that, conferring with leaders of the nationalities, with Socialists, and other spokesmen of industrial workers as well as with intellectuals, public personalities, ministers of state, and men who belonged to the advisory circle of the late Francis Ferdinand. He was desperately eager to behave and think along lines that would win friends and influence people, and he had no hankering to duplicate the unenviable role of Romulus Augustulus, though

[10] Penfield to Bryan, July 13, 1914, U.S. *Foreign Relations*, 1914, *Supplement*, 22–23.

that was exactly what came to pass. At the time that Charles acceded to power it appeared to Ambassador Penfield that he was popular with his subjects and that he gave promise "of wise and beneficent rule . . . It seems reasonable to believe," he went on, "that he may regard the German Kaiser as a ruler whose example is worthy of emulation. This is but conjecture—what his political views may be none outside his confidence can know . . ." [11]

5.

Charles Francis Joseph was born in 1887, the son of Archduke Otto, brother of Francis Ferdinand, who died in 1906 after gaining renown as a horseman and as a boorish, high-living bohemian. His mother, the robust Archduchess Maria Josepha, was cast in quite a different mold; a Saxon princess, she doted dearly on her Roman Catholic faith and preferred a spartan manner of living, and it was this quiet, pious lady, to whom Prussians were anathema, who supervised the upbringing of Charles. After tutoring at home, he studied at the famous gymnasium in Vienna conducted by the Scottish Brethren, and frequented by middle-class youths; he acquired considerable acquaintance with history and reputedly could converse in seven languages, though he spoke Magyar with a strong German accent. Specialized training of a mature character he received from masters drawn from both the German and the Czech divisions of Prague University, and his formal education was supplemented by extensive travels in western Europe; he visited England in 1911, for instance, to attend the coronation of King George V, and somehow he picked up a working knowledge of the United States. Wherever he went, he delighted in travelling rapidly, whether by rail, motor car, or air-

[11] Penfield to Lansing, Dec. 3, 1916, *American Embassy Papers*, Vienna, Vol. XLIII, 1916–1917.

plane. His devotion to Catholicism was deep-rooted and comprehensive.[12]

From boyhood, Charles had been preoccupied with military affairs in the garrisons where his father was stationed, and later while serving with the army himself. During the war he commanded troops in the Russian, Italian, and Rumanian theaters, earning high marks from his superiors. The Crown Prince prided himself on a host of acquaintances and friends, including officers of his own generation, who wished to persuade him that he was profoundly wise; flattery and adulation beclouded his vision and distorted his judgment. He learned to dislike officers from Germany and he indulged in the fashionable Austrian pastime of circulating barbed witticisms about the arrogance and idiosyncrasies of Reich Germans.

Good-natured, attractively modest, industrious, warmhearted and personally charming, Charles won the favorable regard of civilians, as Penfield noted. His standards of personal behavior were exemplary in strong contrast to many of his archducal relatives; rumor-mongers to the contrary, no debauchery, no scandal besmirched his reputation. As Emperor, when the cupboards of so many of his subjects stood bare, Charles ordered that no luxuries, not even white bread should appear on the imperial table; guests turned up their noses at the fare set before them.[13]

No more than average in native intelligence, Charles, due to some quirk in his personality, frequently recoiled from making a decision which a sound assessment of alternatives dictated. His was a nature more suited to follow than to initiate and press energetically, though doubtless he would have come off splendidly as a constitutional sovereign of the British type. Too gentle, too human, Pro-

[12] Reinhold Lorenz, *Kaiser Karl und der Untergang der Donau Monarchie* (Graz, 1959), pp. 1–65, 81–86.

[13] Lorenz, *op. cit., passim;* Ludwig A. Windischgrätz, *Ein Kaiser Kämpft für die Freiheit* (Vienna, 1957), pp. 50–51, 77–79—a subjective work of piety and affection.

fessor Heinrich Lammasch, who knew the young ruler well, aptly described him. "Charles never had a fair chance; but his feet were on the right path and his heart was in the right place," thought Socialist leader Viktor Adler, while his colleague Karl Seitz remarked, "We could wish for no better president of a Republic . . ." Another politician, a critical Magyar this time, remarked, "In his manner and speech, Charles was direct and spontaneous, and he encouraged plain speaking. He was one of those to whom everyone soon laid bare their hearts," but, "although anxious to be attentive, he was a bad listener and had difficulty in concentrating," and "he always agreed with the person with whom he was speaking. On one occasion three Hungarian politicians had audiences with the King and each was convinced that Charles had appointed him Premier. He also had an unfortunate habit of telling what he thought of the man who had just left the room." [14]

A eulogistic Englishman falsely pictured Charles as nearly a superman, "a great captain, worthy of his namesake at Aspern, a peacemaker who sought to spare the world a year of war, a statesman with remedies for all the ills of his complicated realms, a patriotic monarch, . . . so true a saint that miracles are already recorded at his tomb." [15]

6.

Charles shouldered his gigantic responsibilities in a mood of dedication and with powerful urges, emphatically declared, to hasten the restoration of peace and to preserve the Hapsburg realm intact. No question but that he

[14] See, General Landwehr, *Hunger* (Vienna, 1931), pp. 306–315, a thoughtful, judiciously balanced estimate of the Emperor by the food administrator, who conferred with him almost daily; Michael Károlyi, *Memoirs* (Eng. trans., London, 1956), pp. 79–82. For an evaluation of Charles by Masaryk, see, Hanak, *op. cit.*, pp. 222–223.

[15] Herbert Vivian, *The Life of Emperor Charles* (London, 1932), p. 101.

hated the war, for which he held all the belligerents responsible in varying degree, with the heaviest onus resting upon Serbia and Russia, who had "lit the torch of war by the organized murder of Francis Ferdinand and the Russian mobilization"; Britain had converted the conflict into a global struggle.[16]

Although Charles fully appreciated the dependence of the Dual Monarchy upon imperial Germany, he resented, not less than Francis Joseph, the domineering or patronizing posture so often adopted by Berlin, and he dreaded the possibility that Austria-Hungary might be reduced to the merest satellite of the German sun. He showed no cordiality for Mitteleuropa in any version, and he spoke out against the German resumption of unrestricted U-boat warfare, without, however, carrying his opposition to the breaking point; his "Sixtus" peace gesture, to be examined in another context, nearly disrupted the bonds with the great northern ally. Many a sober judge has argued that the widely-advertised longing of the Emperor for the cessation of hostilities encouraged defeatism among the disparate peoples in his dominions, and grievously impaired the will to keep the war going. Momentarily, the smashing Caporetto victory over the Italians in the autumn of 1917 tempered Charles's pessimism on the eventual outcome of the war, but that mood soon yielded to the desirability of making a compromise peace in response equally to his humanitarian instincts and to military and economic realities.

The new monarchical broom swept away a good deal of the top personnel of the realm, though no distinct policy innovations were introduced. Instead of distant Teschen, Charles selected Baden near Vienna as the headquarters of the supreme command, and he took up residence not far away at Laxenburg castle.[17] Count Heinrich

[16] Polzer-Hoditz, *op. cit.*, p. 160.
[17] Lorenz, *op. cit.*, pp. 250–262; Paul Molisch, "Zür Kritik Kaiser Karls von Österreich," *Preussische Jahrbücher*, CCXXXI (1933), 4–23.

Clam-Martinic was installed as Austrian premier, urbane Prince Conrad Hohenlohe, who had been anointed with a drop of democratic oil, supplanted the doddering Montenuovo as court manager, and Count Ottokar Czernin took over at the Ballplatz. These imposing aristocrats were once attached to the private staff of Archduke Francis Ferdinand, his cronies, indeed, and thought of themselves as his political legatees. Released from the foreign office, Burián resumed the more agreeable berth of joint minister of finance, and his predecessor, Berchtold, bobbed up as director of the Court Chancery.

To head his civil cabinet, Charles picked his boyhood companion, Count Arthur C. Polzer-Hoditz, clever, cultivated, and ambitious, albeit a loyal *serviteur* of his master and subsequently one of his biographers. Baron Karl Werkmann, in the office of press attaché, undertook to build up the personal popularity of the Emperor in ways (or with exuberance) sometimes disapproved by the crown. Before long Tisza was obliged to relinquish the helm in Hungary.

In the department of military affairs, Charles personally assumed the dignity of commander-in-chief of the Austro-Hungarian armies and General Artur Arz von Straussenburg, commander in the victorious campaign against Rumania, supplanted Conrad as chief of staff. General Rudolf von Stöger-Steiner, more the courtier than the hard-fisted soldier, became Austrian war minister in place of the veteran, Baron Alexander von Krobatin. All in all the new imperial broom swept widely.

7.

Charles and Empress-Queen Zita enjoyed an idyllic homelife, and, however different in natures, they formed an ideal partnership. Daughter of Duke Robert of Parma, who lost his throne while a boy, Zita had been educated in Bavaria and at the Convent of St. Cecilia on the Isle of Wight, where one of her sisters served as Mother Superior; amidst the harassments of the war, the extremely pious Zita spent much time in religious devotions. Physically appealing and gentle in voice and manners, the "Cinderella princess," met Charles in 1909 and two years later they were married in a brilliant wedding at Villa Wartholz in Schwarzau, the Parma family estate in Austria, south of Vienna. By the time Charles became Emperor, the union had been blessed with four children, another was born during the rulership, and three more subsequently—before Zita was thirty. Intelligent, strong in character, serene in moments of crisis, and tenacious to a degree, the Empress-Queen cherished high ambitions for her husband and her children, recalling in this respect and in others, Alexandra, last Tsarina of Russia; when, under the bludgeonings of fate, Zita and her family took refuge in the United States, she persisted in retaining the title of Empress. Her war relief activities, which had been skillfully publicized by official propaganda agencies, assured her a friendly welcome when she came to the throne. Acrimonious debate has raged on the measure of influence Zita exerted upon her amiable husband in the area of public affairs; the truth would seem to be that her opinions carried a lot of weight, though less than mistrustful, hostile antagonists, in Germany especially, fancied. For Prussia she had no affection, for France no hatred.[18]

Distrusted as once had been true of the unfortunate Marie Antoinette, Zita was tagged "the Italian" by ene-

[18] Wedel to Bethmann-Hollweg, undated, probably Mar. 1917, and Ap. 26, 1917, F.O. 553/330; Count Wedel, "Zur Wiener Hofpolitik"; *Preussische Jahrbücher*, CLXXXI (1920), 289–296. Prince Bernhard von Bülow contended that the Court of Vienna was dominated by three ladies, the mother, the wife, and the mother-in-law of Charles, of whom the former German Chancellor wrote: "Maria Josepha is an idiot; Zita a little intriguer, and her mother is simply a malicious cow." *Memoirs*, III, 298.

mies who believed she had communicated valuable military secrets to Italy, though how any daughter of the House of Parma could be really sympathetic to the kingdom of Italy which had dispossessed her family, no malicious scandalmonger bothered to investigate or to clarify; besides, she was scarcely an Italian at all, coming rather from the cosmopolitan Bourbon family. That tie, together with the knowledge that two of her brothers were Belgian officers, fostered the suspicion that the sympathies of the Empress-Queen lay with the Entente, but accusations of treachery must be dismissed as groundless legends, figments of fevered imaginations. Zita was firmly convinced that the dualistic alignment with Hungary must be perpetuated and that fighting should stop as soon as an honorable peace could be arranged. At a luncheon in May of 1917 her attitude on the war came out clearly in conversation with Admiral Henning von Holtzendorff of Germany. To Emperor Charles, the German said: "I am aware that you are an opponent of submarine warfare. You are against the war altogether."

Zita retorted, "I am against the war like every woman who would rather see people happy than suffering."

"Suffering?" Holtzendorff inquired, "what does that matter? I work best on an empty stomach; you just have to tighten your belt and stick it out."

"I dislike to hear talk of sticking it out," Zita cut in, "at a well-laden table." [19]

8.

On the very first day of his reign, Emperor Charles made a fateful decision by consenting to be crowned king of Hungary promptly, disregarding advice that the issue should be deferred as long as possible—Hungarian law pemitted six months, though the king could not legally

[19] Polzer-Hoditz, op. cit., pp. 193–194.

sanction any legislation until he had been formally crowned. The pledge on coronation had been exacted with indecent haste by the imperious Tisza who intended to make absolutely sure that Charles would not put off the ceremony until at least an attempt had been made to alter the constitutional framework of the realm by decree. By taking the coronation oath, in which he promised to maintain the integrity of the royal constitution and of the lands of the crown of St. Stephen, Charles made it extremely difficult, if not impossible, to reform the structure of the Double Monarchy as a whole. In correspondence on plans for the ceremony the prideful Magyar jealously ensured that procedure would conform with ancient Hungarian ritual and that every iota of Hungarian political prerogative would be meticulously safeguarded.

Principally from ultramontane sources in Rome, gossip reached London that the Emperor would proclaim at the time of the coronation a Yugoslav state inside the Monarchy. This creation, which would be under the direct control of Hungary, would consist of Croatia, Dalmatia, Bosnia-Herzegovina, Montenegro, and the western half of Serbia; this novelty in the south, so rumor affirmed, would form the counterpart to the recent commitment to the Poles of Russia in the north,[20] though, of course, nothing in fact came of the story. Indeed, when the Ban of Croatia requested in the assembly at Agram (Zagreb) that a delegation should attend the coronation festivities, a hostile deputy named Pavelić protested; "We reject this invitation. Hungary oppresses her South Slav subjects. The Hungarian government is corrupt and brutal. The coronation of the King thus represents for us the enthronement of that tyranny." Such plain speaking finished, the opposition deputies ostentatiously paraded out of the chamber.

[20] Seton-Watson to Sir Edward Carson, Dec. 21, 1916. Seton-Watson Papers.

Not less rancorous was a memorandum drawn up by the South Slav Committee in London on the occasion of the coronation. After accusing the cabinet of Vienna of provoking the war in order to destroy Serbia, the Committee declared that the Yugoslavs were "released from allegiance to the dynasty and all further ties with the Monarchy"; and it called for the merger of all South Slavs under "the glorious dynasty of the Karageorgević."

Quaint medieval pageantry and lush ceremonialism attended the induction of Charles as king of Hungary.[21] During a brief spell of uninhibited emotionalism Budapest put the privations and agonies of the war out of mind and indulged in festive carnival. Arriving in the city on December 27, 1916, Charles and Zita discovered carpets of flowers and pine needles strewn on the streets and triumphal arches stretching across them; gay streamers, Hungarian national flags, and old brocades fluttered from buildings, and bells pealed joyously in honor alike of the royal pair and of the recent seizure of Bucharest by the armies of the Central Empires.

Two days before the coronation the Hungarian royal insignia was fetched to the Royal Palace and circumspectly unpacked in the presence of both houses of parliament. Once the crown had been fitted to the small head of Charles, the insignia was replaced in its box and the coat of St. Stephen placed on top to be hauled by a six-horse coach to the Loretto chapel, adjoining the coronation church of St. Matthias, and there put under heavy guard. The king-designate dutifully autographed a royal diploma handed up by a parliamentary deputation.

For the coronation festival of December 30, Charles arrayed himself in a blood red uniform of a Hungarian cavalry officer, and on every hand he was surrounded by captains of the royal bodyguard. From the palace, Charles

---

[21] Lorenz, *op. cit.*, pp. 263–273.

set forth on a white charger, Zita and Otto, their eldest
son, travelling in a gold-encrusted carriage of state. The
accompanying procession, made up of hussars, municipal
functionaries, state servants, parliamentary deputies,
garbed in picturesque national costumes, moved into the
coronation church, whilst a second delegation went to
the chapel to fetch the mystic royal regalia. Popular
enthusiasm flamed high with hearty *"eljens,"* outbursts
of elation and loyalty, streaming from thousands of
throats, animated by a mystical sense of kinship with the
royal family; windows along the route of the royal procession commanded fantastic prices. At the crowded
church, members of the Hapsburg family, magnates from
Austria and Hungary, and representatives of the diplomatic corps witnessed a dedicatory service lasting three
hours. The primate of Hungary, Cardinal Csernoch, was
assisted by the towering Tisza, in the stead of a palatinate,
an office then vacant. It seemed sacrilegious to many devout Hungarian Catholics—and to political opponents of
the Premier—that a follower of John Calvin should be
permitted to perform semi-religious functions, but Tisza
insisted that the dignity should be his and the lower
branch of parliament, which had jurisdiction in the question, consented by a majority in excess of a hundred.[22]

Charles stepped to the high altar, fondled a Bible with
both hands, and, then, having recited the royal oath, he
was anointed by the Primate with holy oil on the right
wrist, the right arm, and between the shoulders. After
that, the oil was ceremoniously removed and the king
was invested with the coat of St. Stephen, assumed to
have come down from the eleventh century. Part of a
coronation mass was sung and a petition was addressed to
the Almighty asking victory over the enemies—which
Budapest jokesters irreverently supplemented by "with the

[22] Fürstenberg to Bethmann-Hollweg, Dec. 21, 1916, no. 48, F.O.
553/330.

help of Hindenburg and Mackensen." Thereupon, Tisza laid the holy crown of St. Stephen on the royal brow and an aide placed a scepter and an orb in the king's hand; as if to seal the elaborate performance, the audience applauded lustily and bells on the churches of the capital sounded hosannas. "The elaborate ceremony," observed the American Ambassador, "was gone through without hitch or regrettable incident, and the young King and Queen were acclaimed in a manner leaving no doubt of their popularity . . ." [23]

When the religious pageantry had ended, King Charles rode up Coronation Hill to a traditional mound containing earth fetched from each Hungarian county and brandished a naked sword to the four points of the compass in testimony of his determination to guard and to preserve the kingdom intact against all adversaries. Back at the palace a coronation dinner was eaten; substituting for the palatinate, Tisza offered the King water in a golden basin and an archbishop handed up a towel. Whenever the King raised a wine glass to his lips the entire company rose and remained standing until he handed the glass to the official cupbearer. On a golden platter a huge fish was brought to the banquet only to be whisked away immediately as a benefaction for the poor, in keeping with hoary custom; and similar patterns were followed with other delectable foods. A swarm of Hungarian dignitaries each had special rites to execute: the lord equerry carrying the sword of state, the lord chamberlain assisting the monarch in changing his clothes, the lord high steward bearing the sacred sword of St. Stephen, the lord treasurer the cross of peace, the cupbearer the "oath cross," and the royal herald and royal doorkeeper holding venerable banners aloft.

Small wonder that the whole colorful episode reminded

[23] Penfield to Lansing, Jan. 6, 1917, *American Embassy Papers,* Vienna, vol. XLIII (1916–17).

one guest of a magnificent performance of *Parsifal,* or that a second observer likened the coronation to "a page from Froissart's *Chronicles,* with a few field-gray modern touches." It was on this festive occasion that the King conferred the coveted Order of the Golden Fleece on Count Andrássy, an honor never awarded Tisza; knowing ones interpreted the discrimination as evidence of royal displeasure with the Prime Minister. As gestures of good will to partisans of Hungarian independence, the wife of Károlyi was remembered with a minor distinction, and King Charles promised to live half of each year in Hungary and that little Otto would be schooled in the language and culture of the Magyars.

Never again would Budapest witness a public spectacle of these glittering proportions. War or no war, the rhythm of life rolled irresistibly onward. "The king is dead! Long live the king," had resounded, however, for the last time.[24]

[24] Promises by Charles to be formally crowned in Austria and in Bohemia were never fulfilled. Under Austrian law coronation was not required, simply a declaration by the emperor to uphold the constitution.

13. War and Diplomacy

THE CRITICAL YEAR 1917 WITNESSED TWO EPOCHAL CLI-maxes: revolutions in Russia and the entry of the United States as a combatant. At the beginning, Conrad summed up the military outlook for the Monarchy. "If the decision in the spring is not in our favor, we can scarcely reckon on any favorable change in the situation with the forces which would then remain available. . . . The Central Powers would have played their last card." Prompt, massive offensives of joint Austrian and German armies, he recommended, should be mounted against Italy from the Trentino and in the Isonzo theater, but the German impresarios, Hindenburg and Ludendorff, refused to countenance the proposals and they were laid on the shelf. Simultaneously, Hindenburg told Archduke Joseph of Hungary that if the Central Empires should go down to defeat the Monarchy would be destroyed; "The hungry wolves fighting for gain will rend her asunder, and in the end they will devour each other. . . ."

So often in conflict with the German high command,

Conrad quarreled too with the new Emperor Charles. Conrad thought him not only immature but too lenient in dealing with traitors and defeatists. The Austrian official war history tells us that "the rift between the twenty-nine year old ruler and his sixty-five year old military adviser had grown wider from day to day.... The young Emperor was ambitious to hold the reins himself, and was strengthened in this endeavor by his immediate circle. Again and again Conrad found that decisions were made against him, both in small and large matters." On March 2, 1917, Conrad was demoted to commander on the Italian front, General Artur Arz taking over as chief of the general staff, a post he filled until the end of the war. A great admirer of his German opposite numbers and well-attuned personally to the Emperor, Arz remained aloof from the sphere of politics.[1]

No little criticism of the management of the war cropped up in Austro-Hungarian civilian quarters. In December, 1917, the military committee of the Austrian delegation, in a full-dress debate on conditions in the services, accused officers of arrogance and peculation, of sending unfit soldiers into battle, and of intolerable interference in the administration of civilian affairs. To fill up ranks, lads of eighteen years were called to the colors in January, 1918. Sustained efforts were put forth to make the daily round of the troops a little jollier, as for instance, "soldiers' homes" sponsored by the crown, in which diversions were available; field newspapers written by and for soldiers were printed in eight languages, and also illustrated journals, such as *Donauland*.[2]

---

[1] General Artur Arz von Straussenburg, *Zur Geschichte des Grossen Krieges* (Vienna, 1924); Rudolf Kiszling, "Baron General Artur von Straussenburg," Neue Österreichische Biographie, X, 117–122.

[2] H. R. Fleischmann, "Das Soldatenheim an der Front," *ÖR*, LIII (1917), 137–138; *ibid.*, "Von Kriegs—und Feldzeitungen," *ibid.*, LV (1918), 84–87.

2.

The March, 1917 upheaval in Russia, the gathering chaos and military disintegration there, exerted varied repercussions upon the Monarchy and drastically altered the military situation in the eastern theater. As well as they could, Austrian and German "verbal warriors" accelerated the disintegration of the martial spirit in the Russian forces.[3] It was assumed in Vienna that serious fighting in the East was over, but in July, Russian troops, poorly weaponed and low in morale though they were, mounted a surprise attack across the blood-stained fields east of Lemberg (Lvov). Called the "Kerensky offensive," in honor of its instigator, the eloquent minister of war in the Provisional Government, the Russian drive caught the Hapsburg armies unawares and initially hammered them back; again the eastern stretch of Galicia fell to the enemy and the oil fields were endangered. At long last, cried the London *Spectator,* the eastern giant had awakened to his new world, and prospects revived of forcing the Danube Monarchy to throw in the sponge.

In point of fact, this last large Russian military contribution to the eventual Entente victory stopped abruptly. On July 19, German divisions hurriedly switched from the West, joined the Austrians in unleashing a powerful counterstroke, and Kerensky's forces, with Bolshevik emissaries nefariously at work in every unit, simply folded up. Regiments mutinied, butchered the officers, and deserters in the tens of thousands crossed over to the enemy side, or trekked back to their native villages. For more than a month Austro-German armies pushed eastward and by then the territory of the Monarchy had been virtually

[3] F. Novotny, "La Propagande Austro-allemande sur le Front Russe en 1917," *Revue d'Histoire de la Guerre Mondiale,* III (1925), 49–77.

cleansed of the foe; only token security forces had to be maintained along the Russian borders, while to the north, the Germans plunged into the city of Riga, within easy range of Petrograd itself. Annoyed because the Germans claimed exclusive credit for the great gains, Charles decorated Hapsburg commanders serving in the East with a lavish hand. As for Russia, it slithered into the momentous Bolshevik coup of November, the prelude to a separate peace treaty with the Central Empires.

3.

On the Italian battlefronts, the ebb and flow of fighting inclined a little to one side in 1917 and a bit to the other, until Central Power resources were mobilized in one of the most spectacular campaigns of the entire war—a full-scale drive toward Venice which was checked only a short day's walk from the objective. Fighting started in May, Hapsburg forces retreating somewhat between the upper Isonzo sector and the Adriatic—in a region studded with seemingly impregnable rock fortresses, crags and cliffs, and honey-combed with caves concealing guns. When the peril to Trieste became acute, the Austro-Hungarian armies counterattacked, recovering almost all that had just been given up and coralling a larger bag of Italian prisoners and deserters than they had themselves sacrificed.

Again in mid-August, Cadorna launched a fresh offensive on the Isonzo—the eleventh in the region and the heaviest of all. Pushed by an enemy superior in men and metal, the Austrians recoiled in orderly fashion, and journalists in the West envisaged a major Italian triumph, the London *Times* describing the Isonzo area as the brightest spot in the military panorama. Prime Minister Lloyd George, who regarded an all-out assault upon the weakened Monarchy as the quickest way of ending hostilities, urged that Italy should be substantially reenforced so that the Hapsburg withdrawal could be converted into rout. ". . . Austria is anxious for peace," he knowingly explained, "a great military defeat would supply her with the necessary excuse."

At that juncture, British arms were immersed in the murderous Passchendaele battle, which has evoked more loathing than any other conflict in modern British history, and French troop esprit had cracked ominously; so a hearty blow by the Italians against the Austrians would have pierced the gloom encircling the West. Actually, the offensive strength of Italy had passed high meridian and, as witnessed by a growing volume of voluntary surrenders, soldier morale was out of harmony with the purposes of Cadorna and his colleagues. Battle lines swayed to and fro, but in September, 1917 the violence of the red, white, and green thrust petered out. Again the staying qualities of the multinationality and war-wearied forces of Emperor Charles astonished military pundits, though, to be sure, natural environment was a potent ally of the defense. Stopping the campaign, Cadorna decided to hold off until the spring of 1918 for a really decisive effort.

Arz, meanwhile, had reverted to Conrad's strategy designed to knock Italy out of commission in the manner of Serbia and Rumania. Appealed to for reinforcements, the German high command answered negatively at first, Ludendorff, who had little faith in the fighting value of Hapsburg armies, preferring instead to stamp out lingering embers of resistance in Rumania. Yet in time he yielded to the logic of the Conrad-Arz plan and switched seven veteran German divisions and artillery units to the Isonzo front; with characteristic arrogance, Ludendorff later claimed that he was the real architect of the campaign. Five times previously German forces had cooperated effectively with the Austro-Hungarians: in the encounters of

1914–15 in and about Galicia, in the subjugations of Serbia and of Rumania; in the arrest of the menacing Brusilov drive of 1916, and in the final expulsion of the Russians from Hapsburg soil after the Kerensky offensive. In some respects the sixth and last joint enterprise of consequence surpassed its predecessors; hardened soldiers of Germany again infused fresh vigor and confidence in Hapsburg ranks. The German General Otto von Below commanding, the armies of the Central Empires were massed along a weak and relatively quiet zone of the Isonzo battle line, hard by the small Alpine market hamlet of Caporetto (Karfreit)—whence the usual name attached to the campaign. Deserters conveyed knowledge of what was underway to the Italian command, but not in time to be of much help.

Preliminary to the Central Powers' attack, enemy lines were drenched with propaganda leaflets telling the Italians that they were only pulling chestnuts out of the blazing fire for "perfidious Albion," or spreading the subversive doctrines of Bolshevism. Softening up the foe with "verbal bullets," formed in Byron's nice phrase, "the murmuring prelude to the ruder gale." Amidst beastly weather, in the early morning of October 25, the Central Allies unloosed a terrific bombardment, then ground forces, with skill and determination, swiftly penetrated the Italian front. By evening prospects for success by the attackers were bright; General Alfred Krauss in *Die Ursachen Unserer Niederlage* (1921) persuasively contended that Hapsburg divisions cleared the way for their German allies—whose commanders tried to take all credit for the breakthrough for themselves.

By invoking gas, an entire Italian army was thrown into panic; surrender of a few troops set loose an avalanche; discipline melted, and half the fighting front caved in. Cadorna ordered withdrawal, the retreat being disastrously impeded by Italian civilian throngs crowding the highways. An Austrian officer on the spot vividly recounted what actually happened.

We glided through the Italian positions without meeting a soul; lines which had bristled with troops a couple of days earlier were now desolate and the batteries which harassed us so cruelly were standing forlorn. We could not use the roads, as every thoroughfare was strewn with the most incredible jumble of discarded possessions. . . . We passed through Italian divisional headquarters where the steaming macaroni was still in the pot—we raced past columns of tired hungry Dagos on the run and we hurried through the villages where the bewildered inhabitants did not know if they ought to laugh or cry.[4]

Three days after the massive drive commenced, the Central Empires crashed into Udine, the erstwhile Italian headquarters, and by November 3, they crossed the Tagliamento River, forty miles from the jumping off area; the enemy was pressed back to the stouter rampart of the Piave River. Themselves amazed at the swift progress, the Austrian and German commanders fell to disputing on strategic priorities, which, together with inadequate transport, interfered with pursuit of the demoralized foe —and maximum exploitation of the breakthrough. Hungry Hapsburg soldiers casually stopped to gobble down Italian food which fell into their possession.

Half a mile wide, many-branched and subject to destructive floods, the Piave raised an impassable obstacle for the invaders; many bridges had been destroyed and the highways lay in deplorable shape. If as Below later remembered, his personal objective was the French city of Lyons, that dream was frustrated. Fully expecting to enter Venice in triumph, Emperor Charles hastened to

<hr />

[4] Francis Weiss, *Waltzing Volcano* (London, 1944), p. 212; Hugh Dalton, *With British Guns in Italy* (London, 1919); one of the great novels on the war relates Italian conditions unforgettably: Ernest Hemingway, *A Farewell to Arms* (New York, 1929).

the scene of the fighting, but that sweetmeat was denied him. Tardily, Anglo-French soldiers were rushed in to stiffen Italian resistance, and, as the official Austrian history of the war acknowledges, they rendered a good account of themselves. As sometimes happened, London *Punch* faithfully portrayed the trend of history; just before Caporetto "Avanti Savoia" pictured sturdy sons of Italy straining forward across rugged mountain terrain, bayonets at the ready, and uniformed King Victor Emmanuel brandishing the bright sword of victory. After the humiliating reverses, Italy "At Bay" was personified in *Punch* by a grenadier who kept the fight going in rocky fastnesses, while British and French soldiers riding up, their swords unsheathed, exhorted their ally to "Stick to it." [5] Across the Atlantic, the slashing success of the Central Powers helped to tilt the scales to an American declaration of war upon Austria-Hungary.

Upwards of 265,000 Italians had fallen captive and estimates of desertion soared almost 100,000 higher, though the wounded and killed probably did not exceed 30,000; immense quantities of supplies, armaments, and horses enriched the invaders. Crowning the sensational débâcle, Cadorna was replaced as chief of staff by General Armando Diaz, saluted as the finest brain in the Italian military hierarchy, who had deported himself admirably during the Caporetto retreat. There is much validity in Cadorna's apologia that poor troop *esprit de corps*, enfeebled by defeatism diffused by the enemy and by Socialist and by Church agencies, explained the staggering chaos more than the valor or technical skill of the Central Empires. Also, the wide social gulf between Italian officers and men facilitated enemy propaganda biting away at morale. On the Italian home front, too, intense popular discontent prevailed, since the ordeal of war, with

[5] London *Punch*, Sept. 12, Nov. 7, 1917.

heavy casualties and severe privations, had lasted far longer than statesmen had predicted.

In a measure, Cadorna paid the penalty of circumstances which not even a Napoleon could have controlled; in his memoirs he caustically indicted both his own government and the Entente for failing to fulfill promises of men and material given him. It must be said, too, that not long after the seemingly irretrievable Caporetto disaster, the fighting spirit of the Italian forces, enheartened by the presence of British and French reinforcements, recovered with unexpected rapidity. Ordering Field Marshal Sir Henry Wilson to Italy, Lloyd George remarked, "The whole future of the war rests on your shoulders. You must get us out of the awful rut we are in." The hard-boiled British commander felt himself that the strategy of the Central Powers was superior, for he said, "We take Bellecourt, they take Rumania; we take Messines, they take Russia; we take Paschendale [sic] they take Italy." Belatedly, on November 7, 1917, the Entente governments set up a Supreme War Council.[6]

Coming almost concurrently with the Bolshevik *coup d'état* in Russia, the sweeping advance against Italy revived popular hopes in the besieged Danubian fortress for a victorious end to the conflict. Press reports on the brilliant strategic gains against Italy excited for a time visions of a new "Sedan"; the Emperor momentarily laid aside his private passion for peace through diplomacy. That the detested Italians would quickly recuperate from their deep wounds appeared improbable.

Before the echoes of Caporetto had receded, Conrad initiated an offensive out of the Trentino, but heavy snows and stubborn Italian resistance soon brought the drive to a standstill. Sober Austrian commanders appreciated that, despite the collapse of Russia and the advance in Italy,

[6] C. E. Callwell, *Field Marshal Sir Henry Wilson* (2 vols., New York, 1927), II, 19–21.

time was working inexorably against the Central Empires; the German U-boat arm had failed to produce predicted results, the limitless resources of the trans-Atlantic colossus were being more fully applied in the struggle, and inside the Hapsburg Monarchy the economic strain grew progressively more intolerable.

4.

While the contest on land proceeded, the Austro-Hungarian navy faithfully performed its task of preventing Entente seapower from working along with the Entente armies. Upon the death of Admiral Haus in February, 1917, headship of the fleet passed to Admiral Njegovan, a Croat, who epitomized his philosophy with the statement, "We shall come out only when the Italian fleet lies before Pola." Holding the dreadnaughts to a strictly defensive posture, smaller Austrian seahawks roamed the Adriatic and staged raids upon Italian communities and coastal shipping. Daring seamen of Italy, on their part, repeatedly penetrated Austrian harbors, sinking the antiquated battleship *Wien* at Trieste in December, 1917, and damaging a sister ship, the *Monarch*. In what was hailed as "a true and proper adventure of Ulysses," Italian planes bombed the Cattaro (Kotor) naval stronghold, without, however, inflicting much injury.

Upon the resumption of intensified submarine action in February, 1917, Hapsburg U-boats operated in general collusion with German corsairs to destroy Entente cargo carriers in the Mediterranean. Altogether, in the war era the Monarchy possessed twenty-seven submarines, small in size compared with the German type and capable of cruising only relatively short distances; seven were sunk and another irreparably damaged. Entente defenses stretching across the Strait of Otranto formed a standing obstacle to passage to and from the Mediterranean. On

May 14 and 15, 1917, after reconnaissance sorties, a formidable Hapsburg assault upon the barrier was delivered under the immediate direction of Captain Nicholas Horthy, a professional sailor of Transylvanian gentry stock. Commanding the cruiser *Novara* and accompanied by four warships, destroyers, and U-boats and with modest air support, Horthy struck straight at the Otranto drifter line, wrecking in all about twenty-five enemy vessels; several others ran up the white flag. During a short cruiser engagement, the *Novara* was badly damaged (Horthy himself was hit), but the vessel and its companions managed to limp back to Cattaro; on balance, the Monarchy had scored a modest victory. In 1918, the British navy took charge of the Otranto rampart, tightened it with the help of American and Japanese units, and rendered transit to the Mediterranean more hazardous. A mass Austrian attack in April, 1918, availed nothing, save injury to two British cruisers.

Idleness on the big Hapsburg war vessels and indifferent "chow," fostered indiscipline and unrest among crews, recruited almost exclusively from South Slavs. In January, 1918, sailors at Pola (Pula) joined with striking arsenal workmen in protest over food conditions, and menacing mutinies occurred in February on ships anchored in the Bay of Cattaro. News of recent proletarian disturbances in Austrian cities touched off open rebellion. Starting on the flagship *St. Georg,* disorders spread to the *Kaiser Karl VI,* and then to smaller craft; on about forty ships at Cattaro with some 6,000 sailors, veritable bedlam prevailed and ominous red flags were hoisted. Ringleaders drafted a petition of grievances asking for more and better food and tobacco, longer shore leaves, and, more importantly, for peace without delay. Austro-Hungarian naval authorities contrived to placate moderate elements, but extremists led by a Slovene petty officer, Antun Sesan and Czechs would not hear of compromise; and on the *St. Georg* an embryonic "soviet" was organized. Officers were placed under guard by the mutineers, who appealed for support to left-wing politicians in Vienna and Budapest. Yet, when challenged by troops on the shore and by reliable sailors from Pola, and when awed by the arrival of German submarines, the resolution of the insurgents faltered; after three days of turmoil they surrendered. Courts-martial tried about 800, and many were condemned to death, but Viennese Socialists intervened, and only four were actually shot.[7] As a sequel to the disorders, Horthy, whose daring exploits had won him the respect of the naval rank and file, was raised to the supreme command of the Austro-Hungarian fleet.

5.

While the quest for peace by arms dragged along, a search for peace by diplomacy likewise proceeded. Soon after the accession of Charles, Count Ottokar Czernin was given charge of the Ballplatz, and he remained until April, 1918. The faithful Burián had incurred the enmity of Berlin by his unyielding opposition to the revival of unlimited submarine warfare. For him the sudden request for his resignation resembled a bolt from the blue and betokened a decline in prestige for Tisza, his patron and friend; the change in command at the Ballplatz plainly embarrassed Budapest papers friendly to the Prime Minister. "Only ten days before his removal from the Foreign Affairs Ministry," commented the American Ambassador, "Burián had been the man of the hour in the Dual Monarchy, as it was known that he had been the creator of the peace note of the Central Powers."

Concerning the new foreign minister, the State Depart-

[7] Bruno Frei, *Die Roten Matrosen von Cattaro* (Vienna, 1927) containing extensive excerpts from official documents; Julius Braunthal, *In Search of the Millenium* (London, 1945), pp. 203–207; Lieutenant Braunthal was on duty with the fleet at Cattaro; Zeman, *op. cit.*, pp. 140–141; Richard G. Plaschka, *Cattaro-Prag* (Graz, 1963), best work on the Cattaro mutiny.

ment learned, "Czernin . . . only forty-five . . . is regarded as a modern diplomatist who will bring the freshness of energy to the office. . . . His work in Bucharest is highly spoken of. . . . He is as much of an aristocrat as Count Berchtold." [8] The *Neue Freie Presse* extolled Czernin as an experienced diplomatist, thoroughly aware of the horrors of war, who "must long for the day when his name will enter history as the signer of an honorable and lasting peace." "Let him remember," adjured the *Arbeiter Zeitung*, "that he is expected to produce peace and nothing but peace." Rather an enigma, still awaiting a full-length biography, Czernin has attracted the slings and arrows of staunchly Hapsburg writers, who hold him to have been disloyal to the crown, and of Germanophiles, who detest him as the wily accomplice of Emperor Charles in faithlessness to the German ally. [9]

By birth a high Bohemian blueblood, Czernin had fortified his social eminence and pride of caste by marriage to a daughter of the affluent Kinsky family. As a young man, he acquired a smattering of university learning and then entered the diplomatic service from which he withdrew because of illness and because he wished to manage his estate; already he had represented the patrician landed interests in the Bohemian assembly, and in 1912 he was named to the Austrian upper house. A ready and dynamic speaker and an effective penman, Czernin made a mark in public affairs; he worked in vain to reconcile the Czechs and Germans of Bohemia and was known as a partisan of fundamental change in the constitution of the realm, revisions contrived to satisfy the principal national communities of the entire Monarchy. For six years, more-

[8] Penfield to Lansing, Dec. 26, 1916, *American Embassy Papers*, Vienna, vol. XLIII, (1916–17).

[9] Ottokar Czernin, *Im Weltkriege* (Berlin, 1919). (English version, *In the World War*, New York, 1920); for a severely critical appraisal of this apologia, consult Karl Wortmann, "Ottokar Czernin und die Westmächte im Weltkriege," *Historische Vierteljahrschrift*, XXIV (1929), 199–252; see also Polzer-Hoditz, *op. cit.*, pp. 128–145.

over, Czernin belonged to the intimate Belvedere clique that surrounded Francis Ferdinand; if the relations between the two men had turned lukewarm after 1911, the Archduke still reposed great trust in the spirited Bohemian grandee and sponsored his appointment to the Bucharest Embassy in 1913.[10] His handling of the delicate Rumanian situation had enhanced his reputation, even though he had not succeeded in persuading the cabinet of Bucharest to hold to neutrality.

Cultured, intelligent, charming in manners, schooled and skilled in the techniques of diplomacy, though hardly an orthodox practitioner of the craft, Czernin tended to act upon impulses; his temper was easily ruffled, and he found it difficult to hold steadily to a diplomatic tack. Supranational in his political creed, he believed profoundly in the mission of the House of Hapsburg, and very much the aristocrat, he thought that government by the best was best for the governed. He understood fully the value of the German alliance, but if viewpoints conflicted, as, for instance, on the revival of the U-boat weapon, he naturally was more concerned to uphold the interests of his homeland. If understanding of the times be taken as the hallmark of a statesman, Czernin qualified, for he accurately judged the desperate plight of the Monarchy and the impossibility of imposing conditions of peace upon the enemy; any lingering faith in victory appears to have vanished from his mind when the United States was drawn into the maelstrom. After that, the most that could be expected, he reasoned, was a compromise settlement.

The summons to the Ballplatz came unexpectedly to Czernin, who had no special bonds with Charles. While he thought the Emperor meant well, he felt he was too immature and too limited in native ability for

[10] Robert A. Kann, "Count Ottokar Czernin and Archduke Francis Ferdinand," *Journal of Central European Affairs*, XVI (1956), 117–145.

the ponderous burdens placed upon his narrow shoulders. The Foreign Secretary conceived of himself as a tutor who must instruct a mediocre pupil; sharp and mutually painful controversies frequently erupted. And Czernin distrusted the ladies at the imperial court and vented his spleen upon senior officials who disagreed with him on diplomatic strategy. Whereas once Czernin had spoken out loudly against the oppressive Magyar governing oligarchy, as foreign minister he courted Tisza and listened attentively to his recommendations.[11] Upon taking up his duties, Czernin dismissed the two top permanent officials at the Ballplatz, Baron Karl von Macchio and Count Johann Forgách, the latter being succeeded by Baron Ludwig von Flotow, a veteran diplomatist, too. Czernin set great store on the judgment of Baron Friedrich von Wiesner, head of the foreign office press bureau, and of Count Ferdinand Colloredo, chief of the ministerial cabinet; Czernin's brother, Otto, was dispatched to the legation in Bulgaria. In November, 1916, Count Botho Wedel, arrived in Vienna as German ambassador, remaining until the downfall of the Monarchy, and he was an easier man to get along with than his volatile and deceased predecessor, Tschirschky.[12]

6.

Shortly before Czernin became foreign secretary, the Central Empires issued an appeal to the Entente for talks on peace by negotiation.[13] This move had been considered as early as July by Burián, who reasoned that neither set of belligerents could achieve a decisive victory,

[11] Gustav Gratz, "Die Letzten Briefe des Grafen Stefan Tisza," *BM*, XVI (1938), 1098–1110.

[12] Werner O. von Hentig, "Botschafter Graf Wedel," *BM*, XXI (1943), 122–124.

[13] François Charles-Roux, *La Paix des Empires Centraux* (Paris, 1947), pp. 91–123.

and that the Central Empires were likely to become exhausted before their opponents. It is very questionable
whether the Ballplatz really imagined that a settlement
by diplomacy could be brought off, but a gesture for
peace would at least counteract war-weariness at home
and might nourish pacifist sentiments in enemy countries.

Supporting that interpretation was an interesting appraisal of the prospects for peace composed in June,
1916, at the American Embassy in Vienna. The survey
followed closely on the heels of addresses by President
Wilson in which he hinted that his administration might
be willing to act as mediator to restore peace and that
the United States might participate in a general association of nations to reduce the likelihood of another struggle. As a fundamental ingredient of enduring peace, Wilson prescribed self-determination for nationalities. Welcomed by the *Arbeiter Zeitung,* the utterances of the
President provoked audible resentment from other serious
Austrian papers, and even the normally judicious *Zeit*
reproached the professor in the White House as nothing
other than an Entente partisan.

It seemed to the American Embassy that Hapsburg
makers of policy, for several specific reasons, had no desire that fighting should cease "before some of the issues
of the struggle have been settled in a way making a re-
currence of strife next to impossible." The recent success
in floating a war loan had encouraged the hypothesis that
additional funds for military purposes could readily be
obtained as required, and the trend of the war upon
Italy nourished the hope that this enemy would presently
be humbled, while the historic Anglo-German naval encounter off Jutland on the last day of May, 1916 generated
feelings that the Central Empires might be able to dictate peace terms in the near future. Finally, it was believed that Wilson, however exalted his concern for the
restoration of peace, would not be acceptable in the role

of mediator, since he had identified himself with the principle of national self-determination, whose implementation might doom the multinationality Hapsburg realm.

Yet Burián understood that the transcendant objective of war is peace and he knew that large blocs of public sentiment in the Monarchy craved the end of hostilities. When a caller asked Premier Stürgkh whether advocacy of peace was a mark of madness, the Prime Minister rejoined, "Mad? . . . Every hour of the day and far into the night men come through that door and say to me, 'We want more men for the trenches—we want more guns—more ammunition—more money. Mad indeed? You are the only sensible person that has passed through that door for a long time." [14] Viktor Adler stated at a conference of Socialists, "We demand peace negotiations. . . . We stand for peace without annexations . . . a free Poland, free Balkan states, and if possible a voluntary union of these free states with Austria, which must develop into a democratic, federal state, if she is to survive." He urged the Central Power policymakers to reveal the terms on which they would lay down their arms; the censorship cut away part of the address. [15]

In August, Francis Joseph authorized Burián to consult with the other Central Powers on a peace offer, but the entry of Rumania into the war and negotiations with Berlin on the text of the peace bid held up action. Bethmann, who had already urged seeking peace promptly, with Wilson serving as mediator, responded with alacrity to Burián's proposal; unless a negotiated settlement were brought off, the sequence of events, the German chancellor believed, would be: resumption of U-boat operations without restraint, the intervention of the United States

[14] David Lloyd George, *War Memoirs* (6 vols., London, 1933–36), IV, 2039–40.
[15] AZ, Nov. 16, 1916. The speech was made on November 4.

and the certain defeat of the Central Empires. For nearly a month, starting on October 17, 1916, conversations on a peace note proceeded between Vienna and Berlin, and the cabinets of Sofia and Constantinople were admitted to the exchanges.

The Ballplatz wanted war objectives spelled out concretely as a basis for discussions with the Entente, without necessarily considering the terms as absolutes. Specific points on the Hapsburg agenda were the territorial integrity of the Central Empires and of France, the restoration of Belgium with guarantees to protect German interests in that country, the creation of a Polish kingdom, the cession of Courland and Lithuania to Germany by Russia and minor alterations of Russian frontiers desired by Vienna, rectifications of the Austro-Italian boundary, an Austrian protectorate over Albania, acceptance of the principle of "freedom of the seas" with Russia allowed unrestricted transit through the Turkish Strait, no indemnities, though the Central Empires might be given commercial advantages by enemy powers, and German recovery of her overseas holdings and her annexation of the Belgian Congo.

Bethmann generally acceded to this set of conditions, though he insisted that Germany must acquire small parcels of pre-war Belgian and French territory and that France should pay an indemnity. The Chancellor opposed the publication of concrete peace terms, on the logic that any conditions which the Entente would be likely to accept would not satisfy popular expectations in the Central Empires. The German supreme command, which considered the Chancellor a weakling, demanded that as terms of peace the German position in the Belgium of the future must be extended, and that Britain, Russia, and France must agree to make financial reparation but the military hierarchs dropped the latter particular on the urgings of the Chancellor. Without any feasible alternative available, Burián accepted the German agenda, not excluding the point that no definite statement of reasons for keeping the war going should be divulged, a stand that ruined in advance any chance of an overture for peace accomplishing anything. The veriest tyro in diplomacy must have realized that the Entente would reject the bid as a purely propagandist maneuver. The cabinets of Turkey and Bulgaria endorsed the peace move, which would be unveiled as soon as Bucharest capitulated. That came to pass on December 6.[16]

Vienna fretted over the procrastination of Berlin in issuing the peace message, but on December 11, Burián told Penfield positively that next day the Central Powers would invite the Entente to consider a conference to terminate hostilities. It was stated in the Austrian note that the Monarchy had "frustrated the intentions of the enemy" and was in occupancy of extensive tracts of enemy territory. It was futile for the Entente to go on fighting; therefore, Austria-Hungary desired a "candid and loyal endeavor to come to a discussion" paving the way to peace. The Central Powers, it was asserted, by this proposal for discussions demonstrated afresh their "love of peace"; the Entente cabinets should disclose their terms of settlement.[17]

On the very day that the Vienna peace note was dispatched Count Julius Andrássy, possibly prompted by the Ballplatz, made public his reflections on the aims of the war. Asserting that the Entente was bent upon the partition of the Dual Monarchy and the dismemberment of her

[16] Pro domo, no. 5384, Nov. 2, 1916, Pro domo, no. 5491, Nov. 9, 1916, P.A., *Geheim*, XLVII/13; *Aufzeichnung über die Verhandlungen in Berlin am 15. und 16. Nov. 1916* (dated Nov. 18, 1916), P.A., *Geheim*, XLVII/3–16. See Wolfgang Steglich, *Bündissicherung oder Verständigungsfrieden* (Göttingen, 1958), based upon considerable examination of the diplomatic literature.

[17] James B. Scott (ed.), *Official Statements of War Aims and Peace Proposals* (Washington, 1921), pp. 5–6.

allies, he warned that a settlement of that radical character would surely invite a war of revenge; Entente advocacy of the principle of self-determination of nations, he dismissed as "only a cloak under which our enemies aim at power. . . . We are only waging a defensive war," he reiterated. While Andrássy thought that lasting peace would not be served by a complete victory of either group of combatants, he said, "Today when our military successes have assured our position it is to our interest to make peace on the basis of our success." And he supposed that settlements could be worked out that would preserve "the honor and vital interests of all the great powers now fighting us." [18] A minor poet, Louis K. Anspacher, derided the Austrian peace overture as "The Last Weapon":

> Let us beware the snare,
> Fight to the end!
> Let us not cease to fight!
> There is no peace in sight!
> Until they bend
> Into the dust!

Couched in equally imprecise language, the German note on peace discussions defiantly called attention to the "indestructible strength" of the Central Power bloc; only vaguely was it hinted that concessions might be offered to the Entente to achieve a compromise settlement. Without a murmur of dissent, Viennese newspapers of varied shades of political opinion applauded the peace balloon, though Count Heinrich Lützow, a retired diplomatist, tempered his praise with a cautious admonition that the gesture would be unavailing.[19] In the Hungarian parliament, Tisza and Apponyi applauded the action, but Károlyi spoke of it in pessimistic tones, and he begged the

[18] *NFP*, Dec. 12, 1916.
[19] *NFP*, Dec. 16, 1916.

authorities in Vienna to repudiate all thought of annexation of occupied territory. Privately, it was remarked that
the bid for peace possessed merely propaganda potential,
though it might animate President Wilson to take positive steps toward mediation.

The peace appeal of the Central Powers encountered
heavy seas in Entente chancelleries. Some top-ranking
Frenchmen, Premier Aristide Briand among them, imagined at the time that Austria-Hungary could be detached
from Germany, though precisely how that objective
could be brought about they were at a loss to explain.
So far as the Monarchy was concerned, Briand on the
quiet listed French aims as limited transfers of territory
to Serbia and to Rumania (on Italy he was silent), and
the incorporation of Galicia in an autonomous Poland.
After considerable confidential discussion the Entente
cabinets curtly brushed the Central Powers' bid aside as
"empty and insincere." The new British Prime Minister
David Lloyd-George, who shortly before had declared
that the Central Empires must be knocked out, said that
unless the Germans were willing to put forward solid
and acceptable guarantees for the future, no overture to
end hostilities by diplomacy could be entertained; under
no consideration would the Entente stick its collective
head in a noose. Unofficial British circles, interested in
the nature of the peace for which the war agonies were
being endured, protested that the cabinet had not sufficiently discussed conditions of settlement in public.

Responding to the Entente rejection, Emperor Charles
issued a manifesto to the armed forces asserting that the
enemy had refused "the hand that has been held out to
them without even waiting to hear our conditions. . . .
Our sacrifices have not sufficed; fresh ones are demanded
of us. The blame falls entirely upon our enemies. . . .
Yours now to continue the iron reckoning. . . . Forward
in the name of God." Czernin professed to believe that

the peace gesture had greatly impressed civilians in
Entente lands and he felt that a favorable opportunity to
renew the overture would present itself before long; for
the Monarchy peace was imperative, he said—and kept
on saying. Reviewing the Entente reply, *Arbeiter Zeitung*
argued that rejection was expected, since the Central
Powers implied that the enemy was responsible for the
war and had already been whipped; further and more realistic efforts to stop the fighting were strongly recommended. Berlin, however, would not even consider a
second overture on the reasoning that it would be con-
trued to mean that the Central Powers were losing faith
in their ability to win the war. Tisza pressed upon
Czernin the urgency of convincing the Entente publics
that the Monarchy sincerely longed for peace." [20]

7.

On December 18, President Wilson requested all the
belligerents to disclose the terms on which they would
cease fighting and to propose ways of preventing a second outbreak of international violence; answers would
serve, he said, as a prelude to talks to reconcile divergencies and so open the door to the restoration of peace.
Acting thus, the President wished to ensure that the
United States would not be involved in the war, to enhearten pacific elements in the warring countries, and
to gain for himself a hand in peacemaking. Both officially
and in the press, the response in the Danube Monarchy
to the Wilsonian peace bid was decidedly sympathetic
—though, if mediation was to be undertaken by the head
of a neutral state, Czernin much preferred the king of
Spain. The Hungarian publicist, Oscar Jászi had hopefully written in *Vilag*, "this winter the children will be
told tales not about imaginary heroes, but about an

[20] Tisza to Czernin, Jan. 3, 16, 1917, ÖM, VI, 59–63.

American professor who . . . will one day embark for Europe. His voyage will mean the happiness of mankind. White bread and white milk and other good things will be theirs once more. . . . At a given moment, Wilson may become the greatest man in history, the bearer of peace and happiness to millions of men."

In its answer of December 26 to Wilson, the Ballplatz stated that direct conversations for peace between the belligerents would be the best approach and suggested that representatives should meet on neutral ground; the Monarchy was entirely prepared to cooperate with Washington in seeking means of avoiding future conflicts. The Berlin reply was set forth in parallel phraseology.[21] Dumba, former representative of Francis Joseph in Washington, analyzed at length and with learning the idea of a league to keep the peace, and he heartily applauded the President's initiative and Czernin's reply.[22]

The authorities in Berlin were displeased by Wilson's request for precise terms of peace, and they were opposed to his personal participation in any negotiations, since he was regarded as strongly sympathetic to the Entente. The error in that appraisal was shown by the anger which the tone of Wilson's appeal aroused in Entente countries, above all in Great Britain; during the recent presidential election campaign, serious Entente newspapers had expressed a decided preference for Charles E. Hughes, the opponent of Wilson.

It was not until January 10, after consultations between foreign offices, that the Entente published its answer to Wilson. For the first time, these governments laid down as an object of the war radical territorial alterations in the Danube Monarchy, citing as a basic condition of settlement the liberation from foreign domination of the Italians, Rumanians, Slavs, and Czechoslovaks. No little ambiguity attached, however, to the word liberation; did

[21] Scott, *op. cit.*, p. 23.
[22] *NFP*, Dec. 27, 1916, Jan. 13, 14, 27, 1917.

the Entente cabinets mean political independence or in some areas simply home rule? Czechoslovaks were Slavs of course, and the specific reference to them was inserted in the reply on the insistence of France, coached by Beneš; the hearts of the Czech emigration leaders were wonderfully lifted.[23] But the omission of the term Yugoslavs, as demanded by Italy, embittered South Slavs at home and abroad; as for the Poles, the western Entente cabinets were content to allow their destiny to be determined by the men on the Neva. Serbia, Montenegro, and Rumania, the Entente note affirmed, would have to be evacuated and paid indemnities, and the Central Powers would have to pull their troops off the soil of the Tsar. Although the terms in the Entente reply bearing upon Austria-Hungary have been called a landmark on the road to the destruction of the Monarchy, western policymakers in no sense considered themselves absolutely committed, as subsequent diplomatic transactions amply demonstrated.

Inside Austria-Hungary the Entente answer was interpreted as positive proof that the enemy was waging a war of annihilation and dismemberment. That theme Czernin publicly expounded, and a company of Vienna university savants angrily reiterated the view and ridiculed the theory that the national communities were oppressed and yearned for liberation; Slavic peoples in the Monarchy, it was contended, had attained levels in material well-being, culture, and political rights unexampled among Slavs in the rest of Europe. Essentially the same position was adopted by representative spokesmen of the nationalities, to the discomfiture of émigré Czech and South Slavs patriots, who glibly explained that declarations of fealty were extracted by coercion and consequently were meaningless.[24]

The response to the Wilson peace bid disclosed in fact

[23] Jaksch, op. cit., pp. 156–157.
[24] Fremdenblatt, Feb. 21, 1917; Zeman, op. cit., pp. 117–118.

that the belligerents had not reached the point where they were willing to sacrifice real or fancied national interests in order to stop the bloodshed. Rebuffed though the President had been, he proceeded on January 22, 1917, to deliver his famous "peace without victory" message, framed in general and flexible language, but endorsing the principle of self-determination (an independent Poland was cited by way of illustration) and insisting upon armament limitation and an international organization to preserve the peace. The address excited lively repercussions in Austria-Hungary. The *Neue Freie Presse* had often badgered Wilson as pro-Entente, shown by his allowing the sale of American munitions to the enemy and the flotation of loans; application of self-determination, it declared, would fly in the face of a good deal of the history of the United States, as, for instance, the annexation of Texas and the Civil War which had been fought to keep the South in the Union against its will. Except for the meritorious idea of a league of nations, the speech of the President, instead of being the bread which Europe wanted and expected, resembled a stone. Professor Josef Redlich gruffly dismissed the message as the twaddle of an unctuous Puritan. The Women's Peace League of Vienna, on the other hand, passed resolutions lauding Wilson, and the *Politische Gesellschaft* of Vienna listened to an address by Julius Meinl, wealthy merchant and civic leader, pleading for frank discussions on peace terms, but insisting that the Monarchy must be preserved intact. The Meinl speech touched off a vigorous debate on war aims among outstanding Hapsburg public personalities.

In Hungary, leading journals of opinion and the official world responded very favorably to the President's speech, *Pester Lloyd* remarking that the advocacy of a league to keep peace put the man in the White House on a pedestal alongside of Immanuel Kant; it liked, too, Wilson's proposal for a free and united Poland. Károlyi and his set clamorously called for a peace settlement based upon Wilsonian foundations. Greatly depressed at the time by the toil and sorrows of the war, Tisza warned that the Entente wished to disrupt both Austria and Hungary; and he devoutly believed that if the United States took up arms the doom of the Monarchy would be irreparably sealed.[25] After conferring with Czernin on the line he should take, Tisza told the Hungarian Parliament that the Monarchy intended to pursue the search for an agreement to end the war, but the Entente conditions of peace, he emphasized, were remote from Wilson's, and since the enemy was bent upon tearing the Hapsburg realm to pieces, the war must be pressed with the utmost vigor; yet the Monarchy stood "ready to do everything that might guarantee to the peoples of Europe the blessings of lasting peace." Minority peoples in the Monarchy, Tisza would have the world believe, enjoyed a considerable measure of freedom, though, to be sure, the Magyars as the largest and most important national grouping tended to predominate and to impress their character on the others. So anxious was the Calvinist chief of Hungary to have his precise attitude placed before the Calvinist chief of the United States that he dispatched a summary of his address (written in faulty English) to Penfield for transmission to Washington.[26] Bellicose chauvinists in Germany shrilly denounced the Magyar Premier as a "peace without victory" turncoat, to which admirers retorted that he was "a tried and true statesman." [27]

All prospect of peace by compromise was shattered by the decision of the German military chiefs to revive un-

[25] Sidney B. Fay, "Papers of Count Tisza, 1914–1918," *American Historical Review*, XXIX (1923–24), 303 ff.

[26] Tisza to Penfield, Jan. 25, 1917, *ÖM*, VI, 115–116.

[27] Hohenlohe to Tisza, Feb. 23, 1917, P.A. Preussen, *Berichte*, 1917; *Neues Pester Journal*, Feb. 24, 1917.

restricted submarine operations, regardless of the reaction in Washington. On February 3, four days after receiving the Berlin U-boat decision, Wilson broke off diplomatic relations with Germany; reluctantly, the cabinet of Vienna identified itself with Berlin on the submarine question, though Washington chose not to sever relations.

8.

Previously, in August, the Ballplatz had learned that the German Admiralty was making ready to resume unrestricted application of the submarine weapon, whose use since April of 1916 had been severely limited by virtue of a commitment to the United States. Then and later, Conrad endorsed intensified U-boat warfare without qualification.[28] In response to an inquiry from Vienna, the Wilhelmstrasse indicated that the civilian authorities, cognizant of the risk of drawing the United States into the conflict, had not altered their opposition to U-boat warfare, and assurances were vouchsafed that no revision in German policy would be made without consultation with the Danubian ally.[29] From the embassy in Switzerland, the veteran diplomatist, Baron Alexander Musulin, dispatched an extremely acute analysis of the implications of indiscriminate submarine warfare; that document, together with a speech of September 29 by Bethmann in which he seemed to be yielding to narrow military considerations, led Vienna to implore the civilian officials in Berlin to hold firmly against wholesale U-boat warfare. The point was reiterated that unrestricted sinkings would invite Washington to belligerency, and other

[28] Conrad to Burián, Aug. 30, 1916, P.A., *Geheim*, LXVII/3–14; see Kurt Naudé, *Der Kampf um den Uneingeschränkten U-boot-Krieg, 1914–1917* (Hamburg, 1941), a detailed exposition, useful for understanding the German viewpoint.
[29] Hohenlohe to Burián, Sept. 4, 1916, P.A., *Geheim*, XLVII/3–14.

neutrals might well follow the American example; at the very least, no decision should be taken until after the presidential election in the United States. Ballplatz apprehensions were somewhat soothed by reassurances that the Berlin ministry had not changed its viewpoint on the use of the U-boat.

At about the same time officials in the Vienna Foreign Office laid under study an elaborate exposé and argument on the submarine written by Bertrand Molden, a perspicacious Viennese watcher of diplomatic affairs. This document dwelt upon the prevailing public mood in America which might sweep the country into war swiftly, and it directed attention to articles by the former Hapsburg minister to Washington, Baron von Hengelmüller, in the *Deutsche Review* revealing how popular passions had precipitated war with Spain in 1898, and another in a British publication emphasizing that Americans distinguished sharply between the loss of property due to Entente sea warfare and the loss of lives, especially of women and children, by reason of submarine action.[30] Given the patriotic temper of America and its aspiration to leadership in the English-speaking community, resumption of the U-boat war would raise the very real danger of American intervention, which if it happened, would mean, inescapably, the defeat of the Central Empires. If the United States came in, Molden reasoned, any possibility of inveigling Russia into a separate peace would go a-glimmering; but if resumption of full U-boat operations were withheld, a new tenant might move into the White House and demand, as a minimum, that the Entente blackade on Central Europe be sufficiently loosened to permit passage of food for non-combatants.[31]

On January 9, 1917, the fateful decision was taken in

[30] James D. Whelpley, "Neutrals' Efforts for Peace," *Fortnightly Review*, CVI (1916), 506–515.
[31] Molden Memorandum, Oct. 4, 1916, P.A., *Geheim*, XLVII/3–15.

Berlin to resume uninhibited submarine action, starting on February 1. Obsequiously the German civilian authorities bowed to the imperious will of the top military and naval chiefs. Hindenburg bluntly declared that whatever the diplomatic consequences might be, shipments of goods to the Entente from the United States must be interrupted immediately, else he could not accept responsibility for the outcome of the conflict; personally the Field Marshal heavily discounted the value of American intervention to the enemy. Secretary of State Karl Helfferich, hitherto a sturdy foe of an unrestricted U-boat campaign, executed a complete somersault, and shouted jubilantly, "By the fall the Island Kingdom will sprawl like a fish in the reeds and beg for peace"—doubting Thomases a few months later would cast this language in his teeth. In the name of the Social Democrats, Dr. Edward David declared, "We express ourselves quite openly . . . that submarine warfare will, we think, bring great misfortune upon Germany," to which Foreign Secretary Arthur Zimmerman rejoined, "From a military point of view America is as nothing." He claimed that even if the United States should raise a substantial army, which he doubted, it could not transport troops to Europe and supply them. On a courtesy call to Germany when the epochal U-boat decision was being taken, Czernin protested vigorously that the calculations of the Admiralty were dead wrong, and presently he dispatched the able von Flotow to Berlin to set out the position of Vienna in full detail.[32]

At the invitation of Emperor Charles, who was, if anything, more strongly opposed to the German submarine policy than the Foreign Minister, the head of the German Admiralty, Henning von Holtzendorff, journeyed to Vienna, to defend the German case; accompany-

[32] Czernin to Hohenlohe, Jan. 12, 1917, P.A., *Geheim*, XLVII/3–5; Czernin, *op. cit.*, pp. 153–168.

ing him was Zimmerman. At a meeting on January 20, 1917, attended by the highest political personages of the Monarchy, save for Burián, the most uncompromising opponent of submarine warfare, Holtzendorff, recited the litany of German policy; unless the Entente were whipped before the end of 1917, Germany from sheer exhaustion would collapse; an enlarging fleet of U-boats guaranteed that Britain could be beaten to her knees in anywhere from three to six months. Only Conrad and Admiral Haus assented to the German reasoning wholeheartedly; Czernin and Tisza poked holes in the logic and dwelt upon the catastrophic consequences that would follow the certain intervention of the United States. The Emperor saw eye-to-eye with the Foreign Secretary, but, as Czernin laments in his reminiscences, "We knew that Germany had definitely made up her mind to start the unrestricted campaign and that therefore all our arguments could have no practical value"; in point of fact, on the day before the Vienna conference, Germany had sent a note to Washington announcing the early resumption of unrestricted submarine action. Incensed alike by the German decision itself and the cavalier treatment of an ally, Czernin toyed with the notion of breaking with Berlin; yet "with a heavy heart," he acquiesced in the German verdict. Angry beyond words when informed that U-boats had already been posted to battle stations, Emperor Charles bitterly protested, and then gave in, wiring William II piously that they must trust in the help of the Almighty.[33]

By way of readying the public mind for a breach between Germany and the United States, the press of

[33] Karl to Wilhelm II, Jan. 22, 1917, P.A., *Geheim*, XLVII/3–15. The German Admiralty favored the Ballplatz with three memoranda, running to beyond one hundred and thirty pages, arguing anew the necessity of full submarine activity, assessing the diplomatic implications, and demonstrating statistically how Britain would speedily be starved into surrender. Freyberg to Czernin, Jan. 25, 1917, *ibid.*

Vienna published articles on the iniquities of the British starvation blockade (*Aushungerungspolitik*), on the flotation of a British loan by the House of Morgan, on the deep popular longing in the United States to stay out of the war, proved by the re-election of Wilson to the presidency, and on the rising tide of antipathy in America toward Great Britain. Against the day when submarine destructiveness would be resumed, Czernin instructed Hapsburg diplomatic officers in neutral capitals to clarify for the governments and the press where they were stationed the motives that prompted the U-boat decision; they were to stress the defensive nature of what the Central Powers intended to do and that the Entente had not only spurned the bid for peace by diplomacy, but had vowed to destroy the realm of the Hapsburgs. For the enlightenment of mankind everyhere, Czernin expatiated on the necessity of appealing to the submarine in order to counteract the horrible consequences of the British blockade. "Our people are half starved all the time. Babies perish by the thousands. . . . Unless this war comes to an end soon, the effects of this chronic food shortage will impair the health of the entire nation. . . . We must shorten the war. We believe that it will be shortened by the use of the submarine." [34]

Through diplomatic channels, Czernin apprized Washington that there was virtually no likelihood that an Austro-Hungarian submarine would torpedo a vessel flying the Stars and Stripes because commanders had been explicitly instructed not to attack them. No official in Austria-Hungary doubted the magnitude of the U-boat decision or that it would add America to the formidable array of enemies; Tisza during parliamentary debate defended U-boat warfare mainly as reprisal for Entente mining of wide areas of the high seas and hoped that the terrible struggle would be over before the

[34] George A. Schreiner, *Iron Ration* (New York, 1918), pp. 238–241.

United States, if it intervened, could effectively apply its resources to the fighting. For the conservative opposition, Andrássy expressed regret over the verdict on the submarine, nonetheless he approved what had been done, and so did Apponyi. The determination of the enemy to rend the lands of the crown of St. Stephen asunder sufficiently justified, the latter argued, recourse to the U-boat; every Hungarian would fight to the last drop of his blood to prevent national ruin. On the other hand, "the determined pacifist" Károlyi exclaimed, "I cannot greet with joy the sharpening of the war. . . . I regret it from a humane point of view; I regret it from a Hungarian point of view." His spirited crony, Ludwig Holló, in a daring parliamentary speech (listened to only by Károlyi's Gideon band), violently blasted submarine warfare, upbraided Germany as the author of the war, and demanded parliamentary debate on terms of peace.

Newspapers spread assurances that the Central Powers possessed enough submarines to carry the momentous decision to a triumphant conclusion and so hasten the end of the fighting; if Wilson, in defiance of his devotion to peace, led the United States into war, the Central Empires were prepared for that eventuality. After sounding popular sentiment in Vienna, the journalist, Emil Ludwig, one day to win international notoriety as the writer of romantic biographies, summed up the mood as one of confidence, a feeling that the United States would probably not come in, if for no other reason, than because of fear of attack by Japan. However, if the United States should take up arms, it would not affect the outcome of the war, since, as had been proved during the recent imbroglio with Mexico, the American army was inconsequential and could not rapidly be expanded into a major fighting force; kindred interpretations were put about by less well-known Austrian newswriters. The prospect that Britain would soon be confronted by the

specter of hunger was greeted with undisguised satisfaction. In an address to the *Politische Gesellschaft* and
in a contribution to *Pester Lloyd,* Dr. Béla Székely, Hun-
garian-born correspondent for the Wheeler press syndicate of the United States, presented remarkably well-
informed and shrewd appraisals of the diverse forces in
America working for and against intervention. Baron
Julius Wlassics argued learnedly in *Pester Lloyd* that
nothing in "international law" prohibited unrestrained
application of the U-boat. Rumanian oil fields, damaged
in the recent fighting, were again in operation, according
to the *Westungarischer Grenzbote,* and were capable of
satisfying the fuel requirements for submarine campaigns. Shipping and commercial interests of Japan, jubilantly declared the *Fremdenblatt,* were taking over business which Britain could no longer handle because of
the shortage of cargo vessels.

9.

Despite all that had transpired, news that Washington
had formally broken off diplomatic relations with Berlin
struck many a citizen of the Hapsburg Monarchy with
the impact of a thunderbolt. The Emperor dreaded lest
Spain would emulate the trans-Atlantic giant, and thus
the return of peace would be further delayed. "Berlin,"
he cried, "has been struck with blindness and will plunge
us into ruin. We shall lose the war, we are bound to lose
it, if America comes in. It is a crime against our people,
to keep them hoping for victory. I have given orders that
the press is not always to be trumpeting about victory,
but it's no use. The press listens to the German Embassy
rather than to us. . . ." And a little later, Charles observed, "if people are always being told how splendid
things are, they will have no preparation for a peace of

surrender. It is not enough that I alone should desire peace. I must have the whole country and the ministers firmly on my side." [35]

So depressed was Professor Redlich by the march of events that he longed to escape the ordeal of civilization by withdrawing to a Tibetan monastery, there to ponder upon the Vedas! But Austrian and Hungarian newspapers generally preferred the interpretation that the American President had acted in harmony with his Anglophile prejudices; he who had hitherto been an undercover foe of the Central Powers had now come out into the open, and Secretary of State Lansing was likened to the vile and treacherous Sonnino. As seen by the *Arbeiter Zeitung*, "the submarines are called the appropriate instruments to combat hunger with hunger. . . . For two years the Central Powers have been threatened with starvation . . . one device for starvation has now provoked another." [36] Still believing—or professing so to do—that the United States would not fight, Andrássy discovered a parallel between Wilson and Palmerston, both intent on keeping Europe in turmoil for the selfish advantage of their own country. Leading Hungarian papers, which had lately been praising Wilson's labors to restore peace, now alluded to the real possibility of an Austro-Hungarian conflict with America. If the United States became a belligerent she would be doomed, it was said, for immigrants from the Central Empires would provoke ruinous trouble. *Az Est* contended that if supplies had not passed from America to the Entente, the war would have been shortened by two years, and the peace moves of the White House were dismissed as hypocritical and pharisaical. [37]

[35] Polzer-Hoditz, *op. cit.*, pp. 188–189, 222.
[36] *AZ*, Feb. 6, 1917.
[37] London *Morning Post*, Feb. 16, 1917.

Impressed by a book, A *Conclusive Peace*, fresh from America, Professor Lammasch questioned whether the United States would actually fight; in any case he could discover no tangible reasons for an armed clash between America and the Danube Monarchy—a point of view shared by von Hengelmüller.[38] It seemed to the *Reichspost* of Vienna that Wilson should in fact rejoice over the invocation of the U-boat weapon, since peace would thereby more speedily be resorted. At the outset of the new campaign, exciting reports, not grossly distorted, told of the immense losses of Entente merchant tonnage; cold statistics, it was supposed, would give pause to the war party in the United Staates. To steady morale, *Fremdenblatt*, after fastidious calculations, showed that the Central Empires held enemy territory seventeen times more extensive than the section of the Hapsburg Monarchy and of Germany in the possession of the Entente.

Worry over what Washington might do was momentarily eclipsed in the press by news and views on the explosive March upheaval in the empire of the Tsar. But when the notorious Zimmerman note, in which Berlin sought to incite Mexico to attack the United States if the latter went to war with Germany, became public property, a wave of anti-German passion swept the Monarchy. The Ballplatz petulantly complained that this gambit and lesser ones injurious to Hapsburg interests had been entered upon without consultation; lamely, the Germans promised to reform, without, however, convincing Vienna that this would in fact be done.[39]

[38] Charles F. Taylor, *A Conclusive Peace Presenting the Historically Logical, and a Feasible Plan of Action for the Coming Peace Conference, Which Will Co-ordinate and Harmonize Europe and the World* (Philadelphia, 1916)—an ambitious agenda, to speak moderately.

[39] Czernin to Hohenlohe, Mar. 5, 1917, Hohenlohe to Czernin, Mar. 8, 1917, P.A., Preussen, *Berichte*, 1917.

10.

As has been indicated, Washington held open the line to Vienna, which might prove serviceable in getting restraints imposed upon German undersea warfare or might facilitate further maneuvers in the name of peace. In the light of various reports on war-weariness in the Danube Monarchy and of widespread longing for the cessation of hostilities, Wilson decided to investigate the chances of detaching Vienna from Berlin; he was ignorant of the undercover "Sixtus" conversations initiated by Emperor Charles, presently to be examined.

In talks with Ambassador Penfield, Czernin strove to drive home the point that the Monarchy sided with her ally on the submarine issue because the Entente desired to tear down the House of Hapsburg, which wanted nothing more than a peace resting upon Wilsonian principles. If the President were minded to apply pressure in the Entente capitals, the Austrian argued, hostilities would soon stop and the name of Wilson would "shine with everlasting letters in the history of mankind." Encouraged by this statement, the President fancied that Vienna might break lose from Germany if assured of territorial integrity, and to that end, Wilson solicited British approval for conditions of peace which would not entail the dismemberment of the Monarchy. At first, Prime Minister Lloyd George repulsed the request, though after tardy consultations with certain of his trusted advisers, including Foreign Minister A. J. Balfour, the mercurial Welshman assented to the proposal in the sense that the British ministry would consider any genuine peace offer that the United States might submit on behalf of Vienna. The Briton indicated that Bohemia (despite the "liberation" of the Czechoslovaks' affirmation in the Entente reply to Wilson of January 10) and Hungary could remain with Austria, though wartime commitments on Hapsburg territory to allies would have to be fulfilled, and the whole transaction would have to be conducted in total secrecy, it was stipulated.

Instructions were dispatched from Washington to Penfield, in a confidential note which the Ambassador was to decipher personally, to tell Czernin that he possessed information to the effect that the Entente had no intention of disrupting the Dual Monarchy, unless prolongation of the war produced a shift in thinking. Penfield was authorized to entertain "any comments, suggestions, or proposals," the Vienna cabinet might care to offer on an early settlement. But the Ballplatz firmly declined to consider exchanges on peace unless Germany and the smaller allies took part, and from that position Czernin could not be budged; then and later, betrayal of allies was morally repugnant to him, and on severely practical grounds, he appreciated that an independent peace would invite German invasion of the Monarchy and would incite admirers of Germany in Austria and Hungary to open resistance. Czernin was, however, "disposed to enter upon conversations for a general peace" and for that purpose he was ready to send an agent to a neutral country to confer with Entente representatives. Secretary Lansing liked the idea of a secret parley broached by Czernin. "They may gradually drift into a discussion of a separate peace," he observed. If the United States could smooth the path to talks, something of value might yet emerge, and in any case, nothing would be lost. For more than a year longer Washington dreamed of driving a wedge between Vienna and Berlin.[40]

At just this point, foreign policy thinking at the Ball-

[40] Victor S. Mamatey, *The United States and East Central Europe, 1914–1918* (Princeton, 1957), pp. 54–62.

platz was embodied in instructions for Count Albert Mensdorff when he set off as ambassador to Denmark. The alliance with Germany was indissoluble, the docment affirmed, and the Monarchy would cooperate in the U-boat campaign to the limit. Justice being on the side of the Central Empires, they would fight on, if necessary, to ultimate victory, though they were amenable to a peace settlement without annexations; but the restoration of the territorial status quo of 1914 was impossible in the case of Russian Poland and certain frontier rectifications elsewhere would be necessary. Since the Entente had scorned the olive branch extended by the Central Powers, responsibility for the continuance of the war rested squarely on the enemy.[41]

11.

Visions of a settlement with Vienna partly account for Wilson's omission of a request for war upon the Danubian Power when on April 2, 1917, he summoned the United States to fight Germany; publicly it was explained that Austria, unlike her ally, had "not made war upon us or challenged us to defend our right and our honor." Upon the outbreak of German hostilities with the United States, the cabinet of Vienna faithfully manifested solidarity with Berlin by sundering diplomatic ties with Washington. During a farewell call Emperor Charles confided to Ambassador Penfield, "Please tell President Wilson that I want peace, peace, peace and will do anything possible to secure peace." [42]

The Vienna press endeavored to quiet popular alarms by repeated reminders that the participation of America

[41] Czernin to Hohenlohe, Feb. 14, 1917. P.A., Preussen, *Weisungen,* 1917.
[42] New York *Times,* Oct. 21, 1918.

in the struggle entailed little change, since, for years, war materials had been flowing to the Entente powers from the New World and that the United States could neither raise significant armies nor land them in Europe if it did.[43] In the view of the *Reichspost,* wicked Free Masons had exerted a potent influence upon the American verdict for war, while Socialist Karl Renner interpreted the diplomacy of the United States as bourgeois lust for world economic mastery. The *Grazer Post,* however, welcomed the belligerency of the United States as "a gift of Providence . . . since after the war the United States will be the sole power capable of paying a big indemnity to the Central Empires. . . ."—precisely how the cat would be belled, the writer refrained from telling.

On the day of the diplomatic break with Washington, papers in Budapest appeared with eloquent blank spaces and laconic comments that "our leading article today was disallowed." In the next issue, *Az Est,* which escaped the rigorous censorship applied to the opposition press, captiously upbraided the Ballplatz, saying, "This nation had no wish to receive such a strange gift at Easter, and we think our loyalty to Germany did not demand this step on our part." [44]

12.

Looked at in isolation, from the lofty observatory of history, the "Sixtus affair" of 1917 stands out as a bizarre chapter in wartime Hapsburg diplomacy—and not the least instructive and entertaining one. It was a striking illustration of the pitfalls of personal diplomacy and of the truism that the shortest distance between two points in international politics is frequently a tortuous journey. Yet the Emperor Charles in pursuing this adventure,

43 *NFP,* Ap. 3, 4, 6, 1917.
44 London *Morning Post,* Ap. 24, 1917.

this gamble in uncertainties, responded to the fundamental urge of monarchical preservation.[45]

Eager to see the fighting cease, spurred on by the
court entourage, and generally supported by Czernin,
the Emperor decided to sound out the French cabinet
on peacemaking, in what was no doubt the most important of the many efforts to restore peace by diplomatic
action. As the principal emissary the crown employed
Prince Sixtus of Bourbon, brother of the Empress Zita,
who had fought in the Belgian army, and who as a
French national had an entreé to senior statesmen in
Paris. A novice in diplomacy, though intelligent and
tactful, the Prince himself longed for the return of peace;
Count Thomas Erdödy, a boyhood chum of the Emperor,
acted as liaison man with Sixtus—the "missus dominicus."
Months before, hints of willingness to consider peace
by diplomacy had emanated from a French clique centering upon Aristide Briand, premier and foreign minister. As instructed, Sixtus conferred in mid-February,
1917, with President Poincaré who acquainted Briand
with what was afoot. The Frenchmen indicated that they
were not unreceptive to the general proposition of peace-
seeking, though they wished to know what terms of settlement the court of Vienna had in mind; for the
French, the essentials of peace included the acquisition

[45] Reinhold Lorenz, *Kaiser Karl*, pp. 325 ff.; Georges de Manteyer
(ed.), *L'Offre de Paix Séparee de l'Autriche* (Paris, 1920); Tomás von
Erdödy, *Habsburgs Weg* (Vienna, 1931); Prince Sixte de Bourbon,
"Austria's Peace Offer: Afterthoughts," *Dublin Review*, CLXX (1922),
274–284; Philip Amiguet, *La Vie du Prince Sixte de Bourbon* (Paris,
1934); Polzer-Hoditz, *op. cit.*, pp. 225–261; A. Demblin, *Czernin und
die Sixtus Affaire* (Munich, 1920), by an intimate of the foreign
minister; Antoine Redier, "L'Impératrice Zita et l'Offre de Paix Séparée,"
Revue de Deux Mondes, LX (1930), 174–202; Alexandre Ribot, *Journal
. . . et Correspondences Inédites, 1914–1922*, (Paris, 1926), contains informative documents; Charles Appuhn, "Les Négociations Austro-Al-
lemandes du Printemps de 1917 et la Mission du Prince Sixte," *Revue
d'Histoire de la Guerre Mondiale*, XIII (1935), 209–223; Geneviève
Tabouis, *The Life of Jules Cambon* (Eng. trans., London, 1936), pp.
297–300; Lloyd George, *War Memoirs*, IV, 1983–2034; *History of the*
[London] *Times*, IV, 327.

of Alsace-Lorraine and the Saar Valley, the restoration of Belgium and Serbia, and the annexation of Constantinople by tsarist Russia.

Charles replied that he was not thinking at all in terms of a separate peace; as one point in any compromise settlement, Vienna would require solid assurances that Serbia would behave as a good neighbor. He disclaimed any intention of destroying Rumania or of territorial aggrandizement, but would insist upon firm guarantees for the security of the Hapsburg realm. Belgium ought to be restored, the Emperor agreed, but only Berlin could decide the future of Alsace-Lorraine; Charles was inclined, however, to urge Germany to hand over a portion of the "lost provinces" to France.

Meanwhile, the March revolution had occurred in Russia, bringing the downfall of the House of Romanov and heightening confidence of ultimate victory in the Central Empires, and Briand had been replaced by the elderly Alexandre Ribot, who was willing to continue peace talks, though with hardly the vigor of his predecessor. Secret exchanges culminated in a notorious letter of March 24, 1917 addressed by the Emperor to Sixtus, but intended for Poincaré to whom it was presented a week later. After praising the valor and vitality of both his own country and of France, Charles promised to do all in his power to obtain from Germany "a settlement of her just claims in Alsace-Lorraine," which meant simply that he would speak up to Berlin on French aspirations insofar as they were "just"—the crucial word. Beyond that, the Emperor approved the French point of view on Belgium and on Serbia, which should have "a natural approach to the Adriatic"; because of the revolutionary commotions in Russia he chose to withhold his thinking on the writhing Slav colossus.

Not a word suggested that Charles was minded to make peace independently of his allies; not a syllable implied that he had taken to heart the counsel of Bismarck that "no nation is obliged to sacrifice its existence on the altar of treaty fidelity." What he coveted was a draft understanding with the Entente, as the preliminary to consultations with the other Central Empires, all with the objective of putting "an end to the sufferings of Europe." [46] Czernin possessed no exact knowledge of the content of the Sixtus letter, though at precisely this point he was exploring conditions of peace by negotiation with Berlin, which emphatically declined to go along with Ballplatz thinking.

Suspicions that the "Sixtus Letter" represented a wily stratagem hatched in Berlin, yet disturbed by mutinies in the army, the French chief of state passed the communication along to Lloyd George, who reacted enthusiastically. Talk of peace with Vienna hardly sounded queer to the ears of the Welshman, for he had already communicated with Washington on that subject, and in January he had sent a special agent to Scandinavia to explore reports circulating there of Austrian soundings for peace—the stories appear to have had no foundation. The only British statesman informed of the Sixtus transaction, the Prime Minister imagined it contained realistic possibilities of opening the door to a negotiated settlement. He and the Frenchmen inferred that Charles was prepared to make peace unilaterally, though that hypothesis rested on the word of Sixtus, not on the language of the Emperor. Supposing, too, that Vienna favored the cession of Alsace-Lorraine and the Saar to France, they decided to inform the Italian ministry of what was afoot and to ask it to forego certain territorial clauses in the Treaty of London relating to the Danube Monarchy in exchange for acquisitions at the expense of Turkey.

---

[46] Manteyer, *op. cit.*, pp. 96–98. Hartmut Lehmann, Österreich-Ungarns Belgien-politik im Ersten Weltkrieg," *Historische Zeitschrift*, CXCII (1961), 83.

When Sixtus learned of this decision he was terrified lest the Italians should publicly reveal the negotiations, and he was certain that any settlement acceptable to the Consulta would be rejected in Vienna.

The cabinet of Rome was admitted to the Sixtus secret, even though the Frenchmen dreaded that if a truce with the Monarchy were concluded, Italy could not be trusted to go on fighting. In a conference *à trois* on April 19, 1917, at St. Jean de Maurienne, Lloyd George broached the question of seeking an accommodation with Vienna, stressing the military advantages that would flow from a settlement. Sonnino "turned scarlet with indignation" when it was hinted that terms of a deal would require drastic revision in the territorial clauses of the Treaty of London; by way of compensation Turkish territory in the Smyrna area was suggested. In the end, the London pact of 1915, which hung around the neck of the western policy-makers like an albatross, was confirmed, in effect, and Italy was assured Turkish lands to boot!

Apprized of the Italian stand, Sixtus was also informed that further consultations were pointless unless Vienna were willing to make concessions to Italy; without the acquiescence of the men in Rome, arrangements for peace were out of the question, Lloyd George observed. While Charles wished the talks to go on, the maximum he would offer Italy was the Trentino, and even for that concession compensation would be required in the form of a slice of the Italian empire in Africa.

The British Prime Minister learned that at mid-April, Italian military headquarters had put out peace feelers to the Monarchy through Swiss diplomatic channels, proposing to break off the fighting if the Trentino were handed over; the Consulta, curiously, was ignorant of this subterranean stroke. The Welshman wished Poincaré to meet with the British and Italian kings to ascertain whether Victor Emmanuel assented to the peace maneuver of his military hierarchs, but the King rebuffed the request, though quite probably he had sanctioned the bid to Vienna; in any case, the Ballplatz listened with deaf ears.[47] Yet Lloyd George was reluctant to relinquish all hope of contracting a bargain with Austria, and he brought forth the idea that he, Czernin, and the new French Premier should hold a téte-à-téte, but Ribot dissented and Sixtus dismissed the gambit as impracticable. Following a final chat on June 5, 1917, between Prime Minister and Prince, the Sixtus transaction came to its close.

Whatever prospects of a successful outcome the soundings of Vienna may have had—and they were slim at best—were blasted by Italian intransigeance and by the unwillingness of western statesmen to break with Rome. Reflecting in the mellowness of old age on the Sixtus affair, Lloyd George felt the episode illustrated the homely truth that "when you are working with allies, it is just as difficult to negotiate an honourable peace as to wage a successful war."[48] From Czernin, Berlin policymakers learned that conversations of sorts were underway between Vienna and Paris; ascribing them to the malign influence of Zita and her family, the Germans seem not to have been notably disturbed, nor were they influenced in the direction of peace.[49]

Even though the Sixtus parleys produced no tangible results, Charles countenanced a second gesture similar in pattern. This time Captain William de Hevesy of the Austro-Hungarian army served as emissary; he had lived in France and was personally eager for a peace deal. On July 28, 1917, the Emperor said, "Well, you want at any price to make peace for me?" and added, "I am of

[47] Czernin to Storck, Ap. 2, 1917, and Czernin to Hohenlohe, Mar. 31, 1917, P.A., *Geheim*, XLVII/13.
[48] Lloyd George, *War Memoirs*, IV, 1983.
[49] Grünau to Czernin, June 1, 4, 1917, Lersner to Czernin, June 4, 1917, F.O., 553/330.

course faithful to the alliance with Germany. But that must not go so far that for it we should suffer destruction!" With the imperial blessing, but without Czernin's knowledge, de Hevesy conferred with French and British agents in Switzerland, but this move achieved no more that did the Sixtus exchanges.[50]

13.

Although Czernin had a hand in the Sixtus business, he imagined that feelers put out from France through Poles in Switzerland offered brighter potentialities for peace. At a mid-March meeting, when German statesmen were in Vienna, Czernin disclosed his intention of exploring this chance. Hesitantly, the Germans approved, though they preferred that the spokesman from Vienna should be an individual of no particular distinction; yet the Foreign Secretary had already picked as his representative Count Albert Mensdorff, former ambassador to Great Britain and an outspoken Anglophile. He set off for Switzerland on what the press described as a mission to investigate hospital facilities, but talks which he held with the French got nowhere since they demanded, as a first step, that the Monarchy promise to cede territory to Italy. At that particular point, the intervention of the United States in the war somewhat lessened French sentiments for peace.

If Czernin's post-war utterances are taken at face value, after the United States became a belligerent, he doubted that the Central Empires could win through. His supreme aim, in consequence, was to seek, in collaboration with Berlin, a peace of understanding with the West, and in pursuit of that purpose he had the consistent backing of Emperor Charles. However, German

[50] William de Hevesy, "Postscript to the Sixtus Affair," *Foreign Affairs*, XXI (1942–43), 566–570.

intransigeance, which from the spring of 1917 onward meant practically the demi-gods Ludendorff and Hindenburg, frustrated all hopes. Indispensable prerequisites for a settlement by diplomacy, as Vienna appreciated, were German concessions in Alsace and the restoration of Belgium, and for any such deal, if it could be brought off at all, Germany would expect compensations in eastern Europe, involving the abandonment of the Austrian formula on Poland.

Upon taking the helm at the Ballplatz, Czernin, like his predecessor Burián, favored for a time the inclusion of a Polish state in the Hapsburg realm, despite the November 1916, promise of independence for Russian Poland. At a Hapsburg crown council of January 12, 1917, war aims came under review, and it was generally agreed that the Monarchy should work to realize the Austro-Polish solution, Tisza alone dissenting. It was agreed, too, that boundary rectifications in the Balkans must be sought, and the dismemberment of Rumania, recommended by Conrad, was debated, though no decision was made.

During the mid-March visit of senior German officials to Vienna, Czernin argued that the Monarchy must have peace quickly because of internal conditions and prospects which he sketched in bleak colors—as he did repeatedly in ensuing weeks. The Germans, on their part, outlined minimum and maximum conditions for a peace of reconciliation with France. Concerning eastern Europe, Czernin played a waiting game, but let it be known that Austria-Hungary would have to share equally with Germany in any territorial aggrandizement; to a crown council of March 22, 1917, Czernin remarked that if Germany were allowed to absorb Polish territory, she might then meet French claims on Alsace-Lorraine, and for the loss of Galicia in such a transaction, the House of Hapsburg might appropriate a portion of Rumania. This program was repulsed by Premier Clam of Austria, by Burián, warm exponent of the Austro-Polish formula; and Tisza hardly deserved encomiums for stating that any land that might be taken from Rumania would have to be incorporated into Hungary. Against the background of this inconclusive discussion, Czernin on March 26–27 conferred with the Germans at Berlin, and during the conversations, the Austrian expressed doubt as to whether the Monarchy could fight on beyond the autumn, certainly a fourth winter of war would be impossible to sustain.[51] Delphically, the Germans implied that their country might seek to appease France in the west, if assured of wide territorial gains in the east, and the Monarchy in turn might take over a section of Rumania. Nothing actually came of this very tentative understanding (if indeed it can be called an understanding) on spheres, for at a meeting at Schloss Homburg in Hesse, participated in by the two Emperors and their principal political and military counsellors, the Germans absolutely rejected concessions to France, and Charles reaffirmed his predilection for the Austro-Polish solution.[52]

For public consumption, Czernin frequently declared that the Monarchy wished peace restored quickly, had no intention of destroying any enemy power, while the Entente, in contrast was bent upon dismembering Austria-Hungary—a Utopian fancy, he remarked, since the armies of the united Central Powers were pushing the "frightful drama" to its close and an honorable settlement impended.[53] Yet in his heart of hearts the foreign secretary was haunted by the dread that the Monarchy might shortly collapse from within. In an illuminating, highly confidential memorandum of April 12, 1917, composed

[51] Rudolf Neck, "Das 'Wiener Dokument' von 27. März 1917," *Mitteilungen des Österreichischen Staatsarchivs*, VII (1954), 294–309.
[52] Polzer-Hoditz, *op. cit.*, pp. 240–243.
[53] *Die Zeit*, Mar. 30, 1917; *Fremdenblatt*, Mar. 31, Ap. 1, 1917; *NFP*, Mar. 31, Ap. 14, 1917 (letter Czernin to Weiskirchner).

for the enlightenment of the Berlin policymakers, statesmen and military chiefs alike, Czernin painted in somber hues the economic and military situation of the Monarchy; the Germans were warned that their ally stood on the brink of exhaustion and that it was folly to overestimate the potency of the submarine weapon. The Czernin analysis read in part: "It is quite obvious that our military strength is coming to an end. . . . Any further endurance of the sufferings of the war is impossible . . . in the late summer or in the autumn an end must be put to the war at all costs"—this point was italicized. "If Germany were . . . to embark on another winter campaign there would be an upheaval in the interior of that country." He emphasized that the Slav-peopled provinces of the Monarchy had been profoundly affected by the March Revolution in Russia and that the multinationality Hapsburg state in waging war had to contend with perplexities unmatched in Germany. Consequently, Czernin pleaded for the enunciation of comprehensive and detailed peace terms, even involving "great and heavy sacrifices." [54] It appears that Czech secret agents got hold of a copy of the Czernin memorandum and transmitted it to Entente governments; whether true or not, the cabinets of London and Paris—as well as some private citizens—soon learned of the document, which naturally encouraged Entente faith in peace by victory.

The Germans dissented sharply from Czernin's exposition, contending that the military prospects were distinctly favorable for the Central Empires, that the U-boat would swiftly force Britain to cry for peace, that Russia would soon pull out of the contest and that America could render little effective military help to the drooping Entente. Enough munitions and food were available to

[54] This document was first published on December 12, 1918, in the *Reichspost* of Vienna.

satisfy Central Power requirements, it was reassuringly said, and the Central Powers should seek to make a separate peace with Russia. Nonetheless, Czernin's piteous plea for an understanding on the objectives for which the fighting was being conducted elicited an affirmative response in Berlin.[55]

[55] Klaus Epstein, "The Development of German-Austrian War Aims in the Spring of 1917," *Journal of Central European Affairs,* XVII (1957), 24–47; Fischer, *op. cit.,* pp. 453–456.